Creative People at Work

Creative work demands a relationship between self and world. Courtesy of the Vincent van Gogh Foundation/National Museum Vincent van Gogh, Amsterdam.

CREATIVE PEOPLE AT WORK

Twelve Cognitive Case Studies

Edited by

DORIS B. WALLACE

Bank Street College of Education

HOWARD E. GRUBER

University of Geneva
and Teachers College, Columbia University

New York   Oxford
OXFORD UNIVERSITY PRESS
1989

Oxford University Press

Oxford   New York   Toronto
Delhi   Bombay   Calcutta   Madras   Karachi
Petaling Jaya   Singapore   Hong Kong   Tokyo
Nairobi   Dar es Salaam   Cape Town
Melbourne   Auckland

and associated companies in
Berlin   Ibadan

Copyright © 1989 by Oxford University Press, Inc.

Published by Oxford University Press, Inc.,
200 Madison Avenue, New York, New York   10016

Oxford is a registered trademark of Oxford University Press

Library of Congress Cataloging-in-Publication Data
Creative people at work: twelve cognitive case studies/
edited by Doris B. Wallace and Howard E. Gruber.
p.   cm.   Bibliography: p.   Includes index   ISBN 0–19–505604–3
1. Creative ability.   2. Creative ability—Case studies.
I. Wallace, Doris B.   II. Gruber, Howard E.
BF408.C747   1989   153.3′5—dc 19   88–25558   CIP

2 4 6 8 9 7 5 3 1

Printed in the United States of America
on acid-free paper

Preface

> To run true to type is the extinction of a man, his condemnation to death. If he cannot be assigned to a category, if he is not a model of something, half of what is needed is there. He is still free from himself, he has acquired an atom of immortality.
>
> BORIS PASTERNAK, *Doctor Zhivago*

Our book is about how creative people do what they do. It has three main aspects: we present a unifying theoretical approach to creative work, one that welcomes and takes account of the natural diversity of creators and their products; we grapple with the problem of simultaneously insisting on the uniqueness of each creative person and remaining true to the goal of contributing to the scientific understanding of creativity; and we provide a set of case studies of creative people at work, illustrating both the unity of our approach and the diversity of creative people.

By the same token, our aim has *not* been to search for the origins of creativity or to provide one general model of the creative personality. To do so is to reduce the creative process to formula and to pigeonhole creative people into specific slots and types. In short, it is not possible to generalize about creativity and the creative personality, as contradictions and gaps in the previous literature on the subject demonstrate. For example, some writers have drawn an image of the creative scientist as a tough-minded, ultra-sane son of the Protestant Revolution. Others have depicted a dreamy, intuitive, somewhat crazy, often Jewish intellectual. For ecumenical reasons we add that Gregor Mendel was a devout Catholic monk and that his belief in a well-ordered immortality may have been helpful in the early stages of genetics.

The same conclusion, that each creative person is unique, applies to the arts. In their book, *Born Under Saturn: The Character and Conduct of Artists,* the Wittkowers (1963) searched the annals of the history of art, looking for common features among artists. They concluded, quite happily, that "cultural trends have a determining impact on the formation and development of character," and consequently there is no "timeless constitutional type of artist" (p. 293).*

* R. Wittkower and A. Wittkower. *Born Under Saturn: The Character and Conduct of Artists. A Documented History From Antiquity to the French Revolution* (New York: Norton, 1963).

We go further and emphasize the uniqueness of each creative artist *within* periods of cultural history. Even such intimates as Picasso and Braque, or Auguste Rodin and his apprentice, mistress, model, and fellow sculptor, Camille Claudel, were far more different than they were alike.

The unique beings of whom we write are by no means isolated social atoms. Indeed, a central question for our times is how people who differ greatly can nevertheless come together in fruitful, cooperative syntheses. Although it is not a primary theme of this book, an *arrière-pensée* always with us is the conception that a creative person is unique and yet a social being. He or she makes a difference to the world because of this uniqueness, but only on the condition of having an effective relationship with that world.

The opening chapters explain our theoretical and methodological positions: the "evolving systems approach" and our use of the case study method. The two points are linked. The creative person is a unique configuration, organizing purpose, knowledge, and affect, each evolving under the influence of the work itself and of the external milieu. Precisely because of this complexity and changefulness, the case study method is indispensable.

Case studies of 12 individuals make up the main part of the book. Presented more or less in chronological order, they are written by colleagues who have been associated with us for many years in various ways—as co-members of a monthly discussion group, as participants at national and international symposia, and in some cases, as former dissertation students. The point of view that informs this book is a result of that very process of collaborative thought. Moreover, the editorial process entailed a rather strenuous exchange between authors and editors, as we worked toward developing as coherent a treatment as our subject would permit.

At the same time, the individual case studies were not written by following one common recipe. That would have violated the whole spirit of our approach. On the contrary, each author *explores* his or her subject to illuminate some aspects of the creative process that are particularly salient in that person. Coherence is provided by our common approach, which (1) is developmental, describing and analyzing the evolution of aspects of the creative work; (2) uses historical reconstruction by examining not only the creative products themselves but also notebooks, journals, letters, drafts, sketches, and interview statements and recollections of the subject; and (3) is sensitive to the multiple contexts in which the individual operates, including work tasks and enterprises, family and private worlds, professional milieux, and the social-historical period.

Of the 12 case studies in this book, eight are of scientists and four of artists. Some identify and examine particular *processes* found in creative work. Linda Jeffrey's study of the process of revision in early versions of William Wordworth's *The Prelude,* Jeffrey Osowski's analysis of families of metaphor in William James's thinking in psychology, and Robert Keegan's identification and examination of a "thought-form"—gradualism—in the diverse enterprises of Charles Darwin are all investigations of distinct processes in creative work.

Frederic L. Holmes, in his studies of individual scientists, had, like Howard Gruber, found that painstaking, long-term struggle characterizes creativity in science. In his essay in this book, Holmes compares and contrasts styles of scientific discovery in the biochemical work of Antoine Lavoisier and Hans Krebs. Similarly concerned with scientific creativity, Ryan Tweney traces Michael Faraday's efforts in the discovery of the relation between electricity and magnetism.

In a somewhat different vein, Fernando Vidal gives us a study of the little-known young Jean Piaget. He examines Piaget's early prose poem *La Mission de l'Idée* in the historical context of World War I and its aftermath in Europe. Vera John-Steiner, in her study of the development of the writings of Anaïs Nin, similarly emphasizes the importance of the social-historical milieu, in this case the milieu of artists living in Paris between the world wars.

The chapters by Margery Franklin and Doris Wallace are each concerned with the development of one complex enterprise in the artistic manifold. Franklin's essay about the New Mexico sculptor Melissa Zink examines the dramatic emergence and development of a new medium in this artist's work. Wallace focuses on the long-evolving structure of Dorothy Richardson's auto-biographical *Pilgrimage*—the pioneering stream-of-consciousness novel.

Finally, two authors in this book pay special attention to the often-neglected aesthetic component of creative effort in science. Crystal Woodward, herself an artist, writes about her father, Robert Burns Woodward, and the aesthetic qualities of his work in organic chemistry (for which he earned one and almost two Nobel Prizes) and their meaning for him. And Arthur Miller describes and analyzes the place of intuition in the work of Albert Einstein and in the development of physics at the beginning of the century.

In Chapter 14 —"Creativity and Human Survival"—we dwell on the moral side of creative work and on the role of the creative person in society and history.

Finally, a word about the term *subject*. In our introductory chapters, we often refer to the individual in a case study or biography as the "subject." This term is not to be confused with the subject in traditional psychological research, known most often as *S*. The *S* is a mere object, part of the apparatus of the study, whose main identifying characteristics are determined by the experimental design. The *S* is an *unperson*. Our *subject,* on the other hand, is a person to be reckoned with, a full-blooded force in the real world and a long-term resident in the investigator's mind.

New York, New York D.B.W.
August 1988 H.E.G.

Acknowledgments

In a book with 12 authors, a complete list of acknowledgments would be very long. As the editors, we thank our co-authors as well as those individuals who helped us in various ways—by giving us suggestions or criticisms and by encouraging us in our use of the evolving systems approach and the case study method: Rudolf Arnheim, Howard Austin, Jeanne Bamberger, John Broughton, Colin Beer, John Ceraso, Sara Davis, Dorothy Dinnerstein, David Feldman, Matthias Finger, Gloria Fromm, Howard Gardner, Christiane Gillièron, Adrienne Harris, Helen Haste, Robert Lawler, Lonnie Sherrod, Robert Rieber, Edna Shapiro, Ben Snyder, Jacques Vonèche, and Marta Zahaykevich.

Among the authors of this book, we owe special thanks to Margery Franklin and Robert Keegan for their help in the editorial process.

We thank also the various institutions that have helped us, with grants and fellowships and day-to-day support, during the years that went into making this book: the Institute for Advanced Study, the National Institute of Mental Health, the Social Science Research Council, Bank Street College of Education, Rutgers University at Newark, and the University of Geneva. In addition, we thank Jeffrey House, Joan Bossert, and Marion Osmun, our editors at Oxford University Press, for their good humor and good judgment.

Contents

Contributors

MARGERY B. FRANKLIN
Department of Psychology
Sarah Lawrence College
Bronxville, New York

HOWARD E. GRUBER
Faculté de psychologie et des sciences de l'éducation
University of Geneva, Geneva, Switzerland;
and Department of Developmental and Educational Psychology
Teachers College, Columbia University
New York, New York

FREDERIC L. HOLMES
Section of the History of Medicine
Yale University School of Medicine
New Haven, Connecticut

LINDA R. JEFFREY
Department of Psychology
Glassboro College
Glassboro, New Jersey

VERA JOHN-STEINER
Department of Linguistics
University of New Mexico
Albuquerque, New Mexico

ROBERT T. KEEGAN
Department of Psychology
Pace University
Pleasantville, New York

ARTHUR I. MILLER
Department of Philosophy
University of Lowell
Lowell, Massachusetts;
and Department of Physics
Harvard University
Cambridge, Massachusetts

JEFFREY V. OSOWSKI
New Jersey State Department of Education
Trenton, New Jersey

RYAN D. TWENEY
Department of Psychology
Bowling Green State University
Bowling Green, Ohio

FERNANDO VIDAL
Faculté de psychologie et des sciences de l'éducation
University of Geneva
Geneva, Switzerland

DORIS B. WALLACE
Division of Research, Demonstration, and Policy
Bank Street College of Education
New York, New York

CRYSTAL E. WOODWARD
Village des Arts en France
Cleveland Institute of Art
Lacoste, France

Creative People at Work

1

The Evolving Systems Approach
to Creative Work

HOWARD E. GRUBER

What might we ask of a theory of creative work?

Surely not that it give an account of inscrutable processes that lead to miraculous products. If it is to be a scientific undertaking, such a theory must explain how knowable and sometimes well-known processes, organized in new ways, bring about the great marvels of human thought and invention. On the other hand, if it is to be about creativity, it must deal not with the predictable and repeatable—the stuff of normal science—but with the unique and unrepeatable.

Given this dilemma, there are several alternative paths from which to choose. One path—the path of Holy Cow!—is to search for some special trait or ability, itself unexplained, which explains creativity. A second path—the path of Nothing But—is to reduce the creative to the ordinary, to deny altogether its specialness. A third path, the one we take in this book, is to focus attention on the way the creative person is organized as a unique system for recognizing, embracing, and doing the new job at hand. To see and understand this system requires neither fragmentary measurement nor ineffectual mystification, but patient attention to each unique creative person at work.

This book, then, is a collective effort to elucidate the idea that each person is a complex, organized system and must be understood in her or his uniqueness. What is sauce for the goose is *not* sauce for the gander. Or as William Blake put it, "One Law for the Lion and Ox is Oppression."

This chapter and the next examine the relations among three issues: our interest in extraordinary individuals, our choice of the case study method, and our point of view—the evolving systems approach to creative work.

We take for granted that some human acts and products are creative, and others are not; some people lead creative lives, others do not. But we are not looking for a philosopher's stone, or ground rhinoceros horn, or other magic that makes creativity happen. Rather, we ask how creative work works. What do people do when they are being creative? How does the creative person organize and deploy his or her resources to do what no other person has done? How do the special organization and special set of tasks come about?

Our emphasis on the uniqueness of each creative person has an important consequence for the kind of theory we seek. On the one hand, we reject the idea that one grand theory can account for all creative work. On the other hand, we insist that each creative person is a coherent knowing system whose functioning we must understand. In other words, for each case we seek a "theory of the individual" (the phrase was coined by Newell & Simon, 1972)—a grasp of how each creative person creates.

Creative work involves the functioning of the whole mind. Any given discussion will emphasize those aspects of this enormously complex set of processes that are particularly salient in a case or group of cases, at that point in the discussion, at that moment in history, etc. For the purposes of this chapter we say that a work is creative if it is (1) original, (2) purposeful on the part of the creative person, and (3) harmonious or compatible with other human purposes, needs, and values. Let us refer to this last property as *felicity*. As we shall see, there are intimate connections among originality, felicity, purpose, and difficulty.

The Evolving Systems Approach

In this chapter I dwell on the interplay of purpose, chance, and insight. But my aim is more general: to explore and cultivate the set of attitudes we call the evolving systems approach.

The approach is *developmental* and *systemic:* Creative work evolves over long periods of time. It is purposeful work and there is a constant interplay among purpose, play, and chance.

The approach is *pluralistic:* The creative person enjoys and exploits not one but many insights, metaphors, social relationships, projects, heuristics, and so on.

The approach is *interactive:* The creative person works within some historical, societal, and institutional framework. The work is always conducted in relation to the work of others. At the same time, the creator works alone, even when intimately bound up with others. This interaction produces varying patterns of conflict, influence, and collaboration.

The approach is *constructionist:* The creator participates in choosing and shaping the surroundings within which the work proceeds, the skills needed for the work, and the definition of the ensemble of tasks. Little is given and nothing that is taken is accepted as is. The creator must reconstruct and take possession of whatever he or she needs for the work.

The approach is *experientially sensitive* (or phenomenologically aware): The creator is not considered simply as the doer of the work, but also as a person in the world. Such a person has emotions and aesthetic feelings as well as social awareness of the relation of his or her work to the world's work, its needs, and feelings.

Can Creativity Be Measured?

Perhaps the question—Can creativity be measured?—is inappropriate. We might better ask, *Should* creativity be measured? What good will measurement do? Some of the perplexities entailed in deciding whether to measure it can be seen by examining trait theories of creativity, for they are the major expression of the ethos of measurement.

I believe that trait theories, or attempts to list the psychological characteristics that favor creativity, will never get very far. What is pertinent, important, and rare at one place, in one domain, at one moment in history will be irrelevant or commonplace elsewhere. On the island of Tonga almost everyone can juggle well, and many beautifully. Even worse for trait theories, they must promise an exactitude they can never deliver, for they require measurement of the creative person on a number of variables, using tests that apply also to less creative subjects. Only such a procedure can provide the necessary basis for saying, with psychometric precision, that a particular individual has more or less of such and such a trait or combination of them. But if the creative person is unique, he or she is not *politely* unique on just those variables the psychometrician has chosen for the perfection of his measuring instruments. Rather, our subject has become extraordinary in ways that will not even be in the books until his or her achievement is accomplished and recorded. This is one of the fundamental connections between our interest in extraordinary individuals and our choice of the case study method, a subject that is examined more fully in the next chapter.

A recent book (Jackson & Rushton, 1987) on "scientific excellence" demonstrates the dilemma facing those who would "measure" creativity on one or a few dimensions. The authors of the 16 chapters of the book pay close attention to problems of measurement of "excellence" and to statistical analysis of the impact of scientific work. The result is that, except for one or two chapters, the individual disappears. In particular, the most excellent individuals—names like Galileo, Newton, Darwin, Freud, and Einstein—are missing. More pointedly, since the book is about contemporary science, only three Nobel Prize winners are mentioned, and those briefly in connection with their opinions about the conditions of creativity rather than for any discussion of their work. One typical study, cited at some length in the book, deals with 4070 faculty members of "the top 100 departments of psychology in the United States, Canada, and the United Kingdom" (Rushton, Murray, & Paunonen, 1987, p. 129). There are really two points at issue here. First, the quantitative approach to creativity necessarily forces the criterion level downward; second, the quantitative approach prevents and perhaps even prohibits serious scrutiny of the individual. In this book, we are certainly not criticizing efforts that focus on the creativity of those below the summit of Mount Olympus. Indeed, the cases represented here are not all at the same level. But we do insist that the serious study of creative work requires careful and prolonged attention to the individual and must pay special attention to the very great.

David Rapaport relates the story of the Hungarian count who is an expectant father in a hospital waiting room. The nurse comes out of the delivery room bearing an armful of babies and announces that he is the father of triplets. The count adjusts his monocle, studies the babies, and declares, pointing, "I choose that one." Similarly, Simonton, when confronted with the complexities and perplexities of a full view of the creative process mentions what he considers to be four fundamental aspects of creativity: process, product, person, and persuasion. He concludes,

> If we cannot assume that all four aspects cohesively hang together, then it may be best to select one single definition and subordinate the others to that orientation. As a social psychologist . . . I naturally opt for creativity as persuasion. (Simonton, 1988, p. 387)

Over and over, the investigator who avoids the study of the case in favor of readily measurable variables confronts the Hungarian count's choice.

Turning from psychometry and historiometry to typology, Gardner's (1983) proposal of multiple intelligences, while not claiming to be the last word on the varieties of creative mind, is valuable for indicating that we need not seek a single pathway in our pursuit of the Grail. Similarly, Feldman's (1980) emphasis on the specificity of each domain of creative endeavor, and on its historical development, suggests that characteristics appropriate in one domain at one point in its history may not be the characteristics of promise under other circumstances.

Uniqueness

In one sense it is a truism to say that the creative person is unique, since that is true of every human being. But the key point is that the student of creative work makes the understanding of that uniqueness the central goal of the investigation. If there is to be a scientific understanding of creative work, it cannot be limited to those few things we may find that some creative people have in common. Instead we must search for a general approach to the description and understanding of unique, creative people.

If a single departure from existing norms were enough to produce a creative outcome, the event in question would be much more common, that is, less original, and then we would not deem it so creative. It is a good guess that the creative individual departs from existing norms in a number of ways. This multiple deviance has as a first consequence the extreme rarity of any particular combination. (The probability of any particular combination of rare events is the product of their individual probabilities, and therefore very small.) It has the further consequence that a novel organization of the person's resources must emerge. Moreover, at any given moment in history, not one but many environments are available, and the creative person both chooses and constructs a milieu that suits the needs of the enterprises in question. The creator's external environment is not a given and resources are not "gifts"—they are the ever-changing results of constant work (Gruber, 1982; Wallace, 1985).

The fact that the creative person produces a unique impact on his or her external milieu has the effect of partially concealing the very uniqueness of which we speak. Others come along who emulate and elaborate. Even in the loneliest creative effort there is some communication with others, and often creative work is not so lonely. Because the creative process is protracted, there is opportunity for others to take the same direction long before the work is finished. As the distance of history obscures detail such nuances in sequence can be easily confused, and thus the creative person is seen as produced by a trend, rather than producing it. Shifting the direction of influence in this way devalues the individual and does nothing to advance a correct view of creative work as deeply social in nature. To capture the social aspects of the creative process we must deal with the complex interactions among unique individuals.

Three Loosely Coupled Subsystems

The task of understanding creative work requires a conception of the creative person as an evolving system in an evolving milieu. Each such system is comprised of three subsystems—organizations of knowledge, purpose, and affect. Each of these subsystems has a dual aspect: in one sense it has a life of its own, in another it contributes to the internal milieu of the others.

Although the subsystems constitute one another's internal milieus, they are only loosely coupled. A change in one subsystem does not precisely and unequivocally determine events in the others. The joy attendant on achieving a long-sought goal has little direct effect on the person's total state of knowledge and no readily predictable effect on his set of purposes. Without depriving the person of the soul-filling joy of the moment, if we take a slightly longer time perspective, we may even say that the joy can coexist with a sense of frustration about other projects not doing so well. To be sure, the completion of one project often opens the way to just such a change in the focus of attention from the newly achieved pinnacle to the next morass. But which morass? It is common among creators to have a number of projects in progress and in mind. We can make the relatively weak prediction that an important achievement will lead to a redeployment of resources. But only a thorough and sensitive case study can even suggest how the next choice will be made. Our subject is a moving target.

Thus, precisely because these internal subsystems are only loosely coupled and the system as a whole is only loosely coupled with its external milieu, the creative person is, as Isaac Newton put it, "never at rest" (Westfall, 1980).

Deviation-Amplifying Processes

Granted, people who lead creative lives have much in common with people who do not. But there is a fundamental way in which they differ: creative people commit themselves to creative tasks. In other words, they hope to make some change in the sum of human knowledge and experience. This is a commitment of some moment, and it is a choice, for it is entirely possible to make the opposite commitment: to live in the hopes of not causing a ripple. Indeed, most life processes are homeostatic in the sense that deviations from existing norms are corrected, eliminated. This is a widespread characteristic of physiological systems, such as temperature control mechanisms, and it is emulated in mechanical systems, such as thermostatically controlled heating systems. Social systems, too, have many mechanims for minimizing deviance.

But under some conditions deviation-amplifying systems (Maruyama, 1963) are viable, and they are always necessary for creative work. To take a very simple example, the repetitive performance of a skilled act can be assimilated to a homeostatic deviation-correcting system or to a deviation-amplifying system. In the former case, when deviations from a norm are detected, the goal is to eliminate them. In the latter case, when deviations occur, they are welcomed and the goal is to explore and elaborate them: they are made a part of the creative person's hope for something new under the sun. Because deviations always occur, the choice is always there to be made.

Piaget (1936/1952) described the constructive function of repetition in babies, and I extended this line of thought to creative work (Gruber, 1976), but it is a relatively unexplored area. Even the humble example of repetition is directly pertinent to our present discussion, for if one looks closely at almost any creative process, one sees a great deal of repetitive work. There are other sorts of deviation-amplifying processes, and it will be the task of our future research to discover and clarify them.

Novelty and Progress

> If I have seen further it is by standing on ye sholders of giants. (Isaac Newton, February 5, 1676)

A thought similar to the idea expressed in Newton's remark had appeared earlier: "In comparison with the ancients, we stand like dwarfs on the shoulders of giants" (Bernard of Chartres, about A.D. 1100, cited in Merton, 1965/1985). This version reflects a belief in degeneration since the Creation ("There were giants in the earth in those days." *Genesis* 6:4). But by the time Newton gave the phrase its better known form, it seemed clear that human knowledge is in some sense progressive, which is the manifest sense of Newton's remark. Two more centuries elapsed before the ideas of progressive organic evolution and evolution of the human mind were clearly enunciated and firmly established. Newton may conceivably have intended humility (*only* by standing on the shoulders of giants); or he may have been vaunting himself as a giant among giants; or he may simply have been making a suggestion to his colleagues about a useful strategy; or, as Manuel (1968/1979) suggested, the remark may have had a concealed meaning, a sneer Newton directed at his rival, the hunchback Robert Hooke. This much, however, is clear: he presupposed that human knowledge advances.

Later discussion of Newton's famous phrase has often turned on the image of the person standing there: pygmy, ordinary man, or giant too? Although Newton may have tactfully left a little ambiguity for us to mutter over, it is certain that he did not think of himself as an intellectual pygmy, and more than that, he needed a strong self-image to do the wonderful work he did.

Let us explore Newton's phrase a little further. We suppose that creative work is always progressive in the sense that it is new, that it builds on the work of its predecessors, in some way or other going beyond them. Newton's image is one of just that kind of growth.

Now if we think of building as a mere incremental process, brick on brick, it does not sound very romantic or exciting—this is hardly creative struggle or epiphany. Well, sometimes, we are sure, creative work is just that patient kind of building. Newton's phrase allows for that, and he himself was certainly a patient builder, sometimes.

But Newton's phrase allows for something else as well, the way a climber reaching one summit discovers unseen valleys and new and higher ranges never seen before.

Progress need not mean only "higher and higher" but can also mean "further and further" from some starting point. Imagine first a figure in a plane which can expand at different rates in every possible direction, so that one or more lines of development might be discerned. Then imagine that at any point along any line some new line of development might begin, not necessarily in the original plane. We would eventually have an expanding multidimensional web of great complexity, always moving outward but with no stable center discernible.

Because "outward" is defined only with regard to some particular starting point, some developmental lines might seem to be moving back toward previously developed areas. Thus the web of human knowledge and experience would grow without limit both larger and denser. In such a web would the exploring person be lost? Not subjectively, or at least not always, for although there is no real center, she would often feel herself to be at the center.

We say that creative work must produce novelty, but whatever we might hope to mean by novelty changes as human history moves on in time, always unfolding new possibilities. This idea of creative work as producing progressive change in human experience raises a second problem for trait theories: it makes it impossible and undesirable to compose a stable list of traits that describe the novel works or their creators.

Chance and Purpose

The Darwinian theory of evolution through natural selection ascribes a crucial role to chance. Many anecdotes about creative work suggest that chance plays a large role in it; for example, consider Archimedes or Becquerel. Some theoreticians proposed an "evolutionary epistemology" in which chance plays the central role in the creation of new knowledge (see especially Campbell, 1960). I agree that chance sometimes plays a prominent role—and that *some* role for chance may be in principle required in all creative accomplishment. Still the main thrust here is that creativity is *purposeful* work. Can we reconcile these two ideas? We argue that some such reconciliation is a necessary part of any account of the creative process.

Indeed, almost everything written about the role of chance in creative work brings out the role of purpose. Rather than pitting them against each other in our theory, a more promising path may be to see how they work together. Imagine a perfectly orderly, harmonious, and unchanging world. There would be no need for purpose. To be sure, simple tropisms, like the moth flying toward the light, would exhibit themselves. But think of the kind of high human purpose that begins with a vision of things as they are not, that anticipates difficulties—surmounting some and avoiding others—that responds to surprises without losing sight of its goals. A system exhibiting purposes such as these can come into being only in response to the imperfections of adaptation, the uncertainties of the world, and the inadequacies of our knowledge and skills. When someone is "purposeful," we mean that he or she cannot easily be deflected from the pursuit of a chosen course. Together, the deflections and the responses to them illuminate the purposes, not only for onlookers like us, but for the striving creative subjects themselves.

Probably the chief contemporary exponent of the role of chance in creative work is Donald Campbell. But it should be noted that his Darwinian model combines "blind variation and selective retention" (Campbell, 1960), thereby leaving room for my insistence that creative work is purposeful.

It is also notable that Simonton, who acknowledges his intellectual debt to Campbell, uses the idea of chance in a highly qualified way that in good measure resembles the position I take here (Simonton, 1984, 1988). If it is agreed that chance and purpose both play a role, saying that the choice of which pole to emphasize is a mere matter of taste would trivialize the discussion. Rather, the key point is that the evolution of human purpose transforms the operation of chance. Purposeful work that does not take cognizance of the chanciness of the world, including the inner world, will not lead to creative outcomes.

The concept "purpose" got a bad name in earlier times when it seemed to imply a teleological view of the universe as a whole. In psychology, the behaviorist movement wished to expunge the term "purpose" along with all other "mentalistic" terms. But the idea that humans and other organisms have purposes that can be understood in scientifically legitimate ways has been undergoing rehabilitation ever since Darwin's *The Descent of Man* (1871). Indeed, even during the heyday of behaviorism, an early cognitive behaviorist, Edward Tolman, published *Purposive Behavior in Animals and Men* (1932). A modern turning point came just after World War II with the appearance of Norbert Wiener's *Cybernetics, or Control and Communication in the Animal and the Machine* (1948). Maybe the crazier the world the more purposeful our images of self must become.

Networks of Enterprise

When we speak of creative work as purposeful, we have in mind a conception of work as complex human activity organized to achieve specified ends (Gruber, 1988; Gruber & Davis, 1988). To describe the pattern of work in the life of a creative individual we have adopted the organizing concept of a "network of enterprise." We use the term *enterprise* to stand for a group of related projects and activities broadly enough defined so that (1) the enterprise may continue when the creative person finds one path blocked but another open toward the same goal and (2) when success is achieved the enterprise does not come to an end but generates new tasks and projects that continue it.

Enterprises rarely come singly. The creative person often differentiates a number of main lines of activity. This has the advantage that when one enterprise grinds to a halt, productive work does not cease. The person has an agenda, some measure of control over the rhythm and sequence with which different enterprises are activated. This control can be used to deal with needs for variety, with obstacles encountered, and with the need to manage relationships among creator, community, and audience.

A second outstanding characteristic of enterprises is their longevity and durability. To take only one example, Milton began the work that led to *Paradise Lost* in 1640 but did not complete it until 1667. It was the major project within the enterprise of writing epic poems; that enterprise was one among several—politics, prose pamphlets, and the shorter poems.

Both the objective and subjective conditions of all work, commonplace and creative, are constantly changing, although often slowly. This gives rise to impulses toward innovation. Ordinarily, such impulses must be resisted or treated cautiously, for the main function of ordinary work is reliable production, whereas innovation is always potentially disruptive. When the work is concerned with producing the necessities of life, even relatively small obstacles and delays can turn into disasters.

Another important characteristic of work is that the time between its inception and its completion is often long enough that interruptions form a natural part of the process—to rest, to deal with incursions from outside the work process, to cope wtih unforeseen difficulties, and so on. A powerful strategy for minimizing the disruptive potential of interruption is to organize the job as a whole into subunits that can each be smoothly completed before an interruption occurs; these must be stable enough to endure until the work is taken up again (see Simon's essay, "The Architecture of complexity," 1969).

Creative work is peculiar in its relation to these two issues. It puts a premium on innovation and must consequently be organized so as to accept the risks of disruption, delay, and failure. But it can reduce some of these risks by developing a specialized organization into subtasks. This organization is not given to the creative person, but it is something he or she must construct in the course of living and working.

In constructing the network of enterprise the individual faces a tradeoff between density and breadth. Piaget, for example, had a very broad network, including projects pertinent to epistemology and logic, history of science, psychology, sociology, and biology—all fields in which he did substantial work. One choice this pattern forced on him was his decision to study the abstract and universal "epistemic subject." In contrast, his lifetime collaborator, Bärbel Inhelder, was gifted in relating to and understanding the individual child and the rich diversity of each real "psychological" subject. The close collaborative relationship of these two scientists shows that such choices do not necessarily provoke irreconcilable conflict. People with different networks of enterprise can and must collaborate (Gruber, 1988).

The fact that different kinds of activity entail different sorts of risk adds to the usefulness of a diversified network of enterprise, allowing the creator to be by turns daring and secure, as emotional needs wax and wane. Darwin the taxonomist constructed for himself an eight-year haven from the slings and arrows of a hostile world, classifying his worldwide collection of barnacles and writing his four-volume treatise on fossil and extant members of the order Cirripedes. Darwin the theoretician was engaged in a more risky enterprise. He had no way of knowing in advance whether he would succeed. "Mine is a bold theory!" he wrote in his private notebooks (see Gruber, 1981a).

Self-Concept and Network of Enterprise

The network of enterprise impinges on the creative person's self-concept in a number of ways. First, and most important, by constituting the person's organization of purpose, it defines the working self. Each creative person has certain conceptions of his or her life tasks. Although we think of the creative person as highly task-oriented rather than ego-oriented (see Amabile, 1983), it is also true that the set of tasks taken as a whole constitutes a large part of the ego: to be oneself one must do these things; to do these things one must be oneself.

Second, the network of enterprise provides a structure that organizes a complex life. In the course of a single day or week, the activities of the person may appear, from the outside, as a bewildering miscellany. But the person is not disoriented or dazzled. He or she can readily map each activity onto one or another enterprise.

Third, as already indicated in the discussion of Darwin, by providing different levels of risk and other kinds of emotional coloration, the network of enterprise allows the person to choose tasks that fit different moods and needs. Similarly, the network provides an organization of goals within which the person can set different levels of aspiration. There is no reason to suppose that this level is a constant over the whole life and the whole network. Darwin was a pigeon fancier, but he had no need to strive to be a great breeder. For him, consorting with pigeon breeders was a way of steeping himself in the art and lore of breeding, knowledge that he could turn to good account in other enterprises, in the zone of his greatness.

Finally, the network of enterprise helps the creative person to define his or her own uniqueness. The creator may or may not be obsessed with this issue of uniqueness, but it is my conviction that people who lead creative lives generally *intend* to do so, and define themselves accordingly. "I am a mathematician," proclaims Norbert Wiener in the title of his autobiography. That modest man Albert Einstein, when he was 26 years old, wrote to a friend, "I promise you four papers . . . the first . . . deals with radiation and the energy characteristics of light and is very revolutionary" (Miller, 1981).

In his autobiographical poem *The Prelude,* William Wordsworth wrote of himself:

> . . . But I believe
> That Nature, oftentimes, when she would frame
> A favored being, from his earliest dawn
> Of infancy doth open out the clouds
> As at the touch of lightning, seeking him
> With gentlest visitation; not the less,
> Though haply aiming at the self-same end,
> Does it delight her sometimes to employ
> Severer interventions, ministry
> More palpable—and so she dealt with me.
> (J. Wordsworth, Abrams, & Gill, 1979, p. 48)

Whatever the correct etiology of his poetic power may have been, it is clear that from a young age Wordsworth thought himself a poet and "a favored being." But the gods' "touch of lightning" does not mean that Wordsworth, like Plato's Ion, could be persuaded that he worked "not through knowledge but by inspiration" (Plato, 1910). On the contrary, Wordsworth's image of the poet was of a growing, thinking, willing person:

> What is a poet? . . . He is a man speaking to men: a man, it is true, en-dued with more lively sensibility, more enthusiasm and tenderness, who has a greater knowledge of human nature, and a more comprehensive soul, than are supposed to be common among mankind; a man pleased with his own passions and volitions, and who rejoices more than other men in the spirit of life that is in him; delighting to contemplate similar volitions and passions as manifested in the goings-on of the universe, and habitually im-pelled to create them where he does not find them. (W. Wordsworth, 1801, 1909, p. 937, written about 1801)

Difficulty, Duration, and Purpose

If a million long-lived monkeys typed for a million years, they would never purely by chance type *Hamlet*. But suppose one miraculous day they did? It would not be a creative act. There would be no one capable of sorting out all the nonsense and finding the masterpiece. And if someone did find it? He or she would label it an accident, not a creative act. Or look around for Shakespeare.

Never in a million years, true enough. But serious creative work does take a long time. Compared to the few milliseconds of a lightning bolt, with which the creative act is sometimes compared, the actual process is very long in-deed, to be reckoned in months, years, and often decades. Fortunately, the network of enterprise and the vision that sustains it are capacious and durable enough to sustain the individual work through periods of dormancy and recalcitrance. To understand the temporal shape of the creative process we must consider the intricate relations among difficulty, duration, and purpose.

If a work was both felicitous and easy, many would be doing it and we would not see it as especially creative. If it was original but incompatible with human purposes, we might see it as crazy or merely odd. When DiMaggio makes that great catch or Nijinsky that leap, we say they make it "look easy"—knowing all the while that this is a hard-won easiness. Huxley saw that Darwin's theory was, once enunciated, simple. "How stupid not to have thought of that!," he cried, but he never suggested that Darwin's road had been easy, nor would anyone who gave the *Origin of Species* a serious reading.

If there were no constraints, nothing would be crazy, and novelty might not be so difficult to produce. Part of the difficulty of achieving a creative out-come arises from the need to make it compatible with human purposes. The creative person may very well start with a wild idea. Soon enough it becomes familiar and, within a private universe, no longer seems so wild. But to be effective the creator must be in good enough touch with the norms and feel-ings of some others so that the product will be one that they can assimilate and enjoy. Even the person who is far ahead of the times must have some community, however limited or special, with whom to interact. When the gap between the creator and others grows too great, there are basically two main strategies available: modify the work to make it more acceptable, or educate the potential audience so that they will be prepared for the great surprise. The two approaches are not so different, since this education entails showing others the way from the present to the future.

"Not Enough to Have a Certain Dexterity"

The difficulty of creative work leads in turn to the characteristic duration of the task. It is *long,* hard work. Sometimes the last steps of the creative process look easy; confusing this phase with the process as a whole can lead to exaggerated ideas of its spontaneity and ease. We consider that purposeful growth—making oneself the kind of person who can do the creative task in view—is a part of the process.

To be sure, there are seemingly sudden appearances of great works. But if we look more closely, say, at the adolescent Picasso, we will see an adolescent shaping himself, beginning to form a style of work, thinking about the very issues with which he will later grapple effectively. By failing to take adolescence seriously as part of the creative life we create for ourselves this appearance of suddenness. Picasso *was* precocious. But his productions at age 14 were not yet great art. He was, it is true, only 12 or 13 by the time he was ready to paint works that looked like an artist's work and not a precocious child's. But he had then been drawing and painting for at least five years. It is safe to say that *no case* of early achievement occurs without a long apprenticeship (see Bloom, 1985; Feldman, 1986).

Let us look at a difficult case. Van Gogh's life might seem to support an almost opposite thesis. He began late and his whole career as an artist lasted only 11 years. He could work at a furious pace, often turning out a canvas a day. The individual canvases might be produced extremely fast. But is that the right time perspective in which to see Van Gogh? His creative achievement was to give us another way of seeing the world. If we see sunflowers or landscapes differently now, his way, it is not because of one painting, but an oeuvre. The evolving systems approach permits us to accommodate sudden moments of insight, furious bursts of work, and slower processes of growth—all linked together by the common thread of purpose.

Van Gogh's letters to his brother Theo (I use the version edited by the poet W. H. Auden; Van Gogh, 1963) teem with his sense of time and purpose. We see him thinking into the past and into the future:

> Now by continuing this furious work during Next February and March, I shall hope to have finished the quietly composed repetitions of a number of studies I made last year. And these together with some canvases you have already had from me, such as the "Harvest" and the "White Orchard," will form a tolerably firm foundation [for a hoped-for exhibition]. (From Arles, January 28, 1889)

We see him envisaging a change in his style:

. . . staying here means making progress. And to make a picture that will really be of the South, it's not enough to have a certain dexterity. It's looking at things for a long time that ripens you and gives you deeper understanding. When I left Paris I did not think that I should once think Monticelli and Delacroix so *true*. It is only now, after months and months, that I begin to realize that they did not imagine it all. And I think that next year you are going to see the same subjects all over again, orchards, and harvest, but with a difference coloring, and above all a change in the workmanship. (From Arles, September 26, 1888)

We see him persisting through illness:

This new attack, my boy, came on me in the fields, on a windy day, when I was busy painting. I will send you the canvas. I finished it in spite of it. (From St. Remy, August 18, 1889)

On Eureka! Experiences: A Clarification of Illumination

Theoreticians of creativity often lay great stress on the role of sudden insight, sometimes virtually identifying creativity with the occurrence of such Eureka! experiences (also known as "aha experiences"). In some treatments of insight it is coupled with the idea of chance recombinations: the very absence of intention permits the sudden new arrangement. One very full and rich treatment of the topic from this point of view is Arthur Koestler's *The Act of Creation* (1964). If such an account were correct, it would undermine the whole argument of this book that creative achievement is accomplished chiefly through purposeful work. We do not query the occurrence of Eureka! experiences in the course of some—perhaps even all—creative lives, but we do question the validity of telescoping the essence of the creative process into a moment, an "act."

In truth, our knowledge of insight is limited. The most celebrated instances—those of Archimedes, Kekulé, Darwin, Poincaré—are known chiefly through accounts given many years after the event. Coleridge's account of his composition of "Kubla Khan" in a dream has been reexamined by Perkins (1981), among others. It is yet another case of a 20-year-old memory presented as a white-hot experience. More important, at least two drafts are known, and examination of them suggests a typical process of protracted constructive work. Finally, both the poem and the story Coleridge told of its composition fitted in well with his larger purpose of exploring, through poetry and opium, strange states of being.

So-called flashbulb memories are a similar phenomenon. Neisser (1982) showed that they are probably all post hoc constructions in which the memory for the event is unconsciously tailored to the person's conceptions.

We would like to know some simple things about insight. Do they occur at all, or are they really post hoc reconstructions? Let us for the present assume that even though memories of them may be fallible, they really do occur. How frequent are they? Are they a mixture of small and great? What proportion of them are fruitful and what proportion misbegotten? Are there some creative individuals who do not report them? Are they really millisecond flashes, or do they have an inner structure, somewhat spread out in time? Are they entirely involuntary, or does the person have some measure of control over their occurrence and course of development? Are they examples of primitive thinking and primary processes, or do they take more rational forms? Since we cannot address all these questions here (see Gruber, 1981a, 1981b), we consider those that seem most central to the exposition of our own approach.

Frequency and Magnitude.   Probably our best single source of information is an unpublished document by an experimental psychologist, Herbert Crovitz. He kept a detailed notebook of his scientific activities over a 10-year period, starring every entry that represented an "illumination." The frequency of such entries varied between two and three per week. From my reading of the Darwin notebooks, which sometimes give direct textual evidence of sudden insights, my guess is that Darwin's rate was somewhat higher, perhaps as many as two or three per day.

Not all sudden insights are correct, important, and enduring. Let us assume that someone like Darwin has about one good idea per week, surely a conservative estimate. This means about 50 per year, or 500 per decade. Seen in that light, the individual moment of insight does not represent such a sudden break with the past; instead, the steady occurrence of such moments expresses the proper functioning of the system that constitutes the creative person at work.

Duration of the "Moment of Insight."   For the present it is impossible to give any direct measure of the duration of an insight. But let us suppose that some insights resemble the process of making sense out of a fragmented picture. If so, this suggests that they would take between 5 and 10 seconds, or possibly much longer. A moderately complex dream may take between 5 and 60 seconds. I have made notes on some of my insights as they occurred. Often a sort of aura—a sense that something is happening—precedes the full and explicit awareness of just what happy thought is "happening." This description is similar to the feeling one gets, while listening to a joke, of a build-up to laughter. Similarly in sexual experience, the orgasm announces itself before it arrives.

The issue of duration is important to our conception of the place of insight in the scheme of things. If it were an involuntary millisecond flash, faster even than a sneeze, we might see it as happening *to* the person, unpurposefully. But if the duration is long enough, there is time for the person to monitor the insight—to protect the moment from disturbance if it is a welcome thought, change direction if unwelcome, and so on. A few seconds may make all the difference.

Insight as Part of a Protracted Process.   It seems safe to say that *all* examples of creative insights occur within protracted creative processes. Consider the celebrated moment in which Darwin, while reading Malthus's *Essay on Population,* finally saw the pertinence of natural selection to the problem of evolution. This case gives us a good opportunity to compare the original event with the remembered insight, because we have a record of the former, in a very full context, in his notebooks, and of the latter in his autobiography. The later recall is much telescoped, and makes it appear as if Darwin's great moment on reading Malthus came out of the blue and thereupon transformed his thinking. Neither point is correct. In the notebooks, we can see the insight developing, with almost the same idea reached a number of times over a period of months. It is closer to the mark to describe Darwin on reading Malthus as finally *recognizing* an idea he has had, almost within his grasp, for some time. In spite of the recollected transforming power of the moment, in the event, as the notebooks show, it took Darwin perhaps a week or two to change direction, to seize hold of his own insight and follow it up—there was no instantaneous transformation of his point of view.

Although Poincaré's account of one of his mathematical discoveries is often cited as a classic case of sudden insight, (As he put his foot on the step of the bus . . .) his own account, written 30 years after the event, describes the discovery as consisting of seven episodes, taking place in different places over a period of months. This is a case of the reader's telescoping and distorting the event, for Poincaré's version is readily available (1952).

Similarly, Wertheimer's (1945) reconstruction of Einstein's train of thought in which he developed the theory of special relativity depicts 10 "acts" considerably spread out in time. Wertheimer's work was based primarily on retrospective interviews with Einstein in Berlin in 1916 and later (i.e., at least 10 years after the event). Further work by Holton (1973) and Miller (1981) corrected Wertheimer's picture, showing the process to have been more complex and more open to interaction with the world of other physicists, but no less protracted. As Einstein recounted the process, it began when he was 16 years old and reached a first terminus 10 years later with the publication of his paper on special relativity. Again we see that precocity does not mean instant achievement.

The Role of Insight in Creative Thinking. All of the reservations thus far expressed should not be taken to mean that I am skeptical of either the occurrence or the importance of Eureka! experiences. But it is important to try to specify their role in a new way. I suggest three points. First, the occurrence of an insight indicates a certain degree of mastery of a domain, something comparable to being able to speak a language with spontaneity. Everyone would agree that skillful speaking is controlled by processes that are in some sense unconscious: we don't know how we select the words in a sentence, or exactly how it will end. Every sentence is a surprise and a miracle. Second, insights often represent a moment of consolidation or confirmation, a sort of re-cognition of what one already almost knows. Third, when the insight occurs, it is affectively laden in a way that accentuates the experience. This leads the person to preserve and pursue the new idea. Often the pursuit leads to further change: the idea in its original form is displaced by its derivatives.

The famous story of Kekulé discovering the structure of the benzene ring while in a hypnogogic state—that wonderful and much-traveled image of the snake biting its tail—illustrates all three points. For him to see atoms dancing about and forming interesting configurations was not an isolated event, but one of his accustomed ways of thinking about structural problems in chemistry. Indeed, in the same lecture in which he retold the benzene ring story (years after the event), he also told of a similar imagistic event 12 years earlier still, in which he had made another important discovery. Finally, Kekulé was at no point making isolated discoveries: he was one of an international community of chemists who were very deliberately and self-consciously constructing the foundations of structural chemistry (Benfey, 1966; Gruber, 1981b).

Unconscious Work. It might seem as though the occurrence of unconscious activity would argue against the thesis of purpose in creative work. Not necessarily. Rothenberg (1979) gives a good account of the way the creative person can steer unconscious work so that it moves in the person's chosen direction.

Yeats expressed his interest in involuntary activity in many forms. In the following passage he gives an idea of how he thought it could be put to work.

> The purpose of rhythm . . . is to prolong the moment of contemplation, the moment when we are both asleep and awake, which is the one moment of creation, by hushing us with an alluring monotony, while it holds us waking by variety, to keep us in the state of perhaps real trance, in which the mind liberated from the pressure of the will is unfolded in symbols. (From "Symbolism in Poetry" written in 1900, cited in Stallworthy, 1963)

Lest it be thought that liberation "from the pressure of the will" produced outpourings of untrammeled spontaneity, be it noted that Yeats was an extremely deliberate writer. He "followed a pattern of composition which was to vary little for the rest of his life: prose draft, rough verse drafts, fair copy, magazine publication, and then further revisions for the first printing in book form" (Stallworthy, 1963, p. 4). And on a longer time scale, one of his biographers stresses "the tremendous organization that informs the poems and the poet; every crisis is mastered, and every poem comes out of years of preparation" (Ellmann, 1948, p. 295).

Insights and Stages. Can we make better sense out of this complexity by reducing it to some simplifying scheme such as Wallas's well-known four-stage description of the creative process: preparation, incubation, illumination, verification? In a sense, Wallas was expressing a point of view similar to ours, dethroning the Eureka! experience and viewing the undeniable phenomenon of sudden illumination in a developmental perspective. Wallas's scheme was intended to apply to the development of the individual creative project, not to the longer enterprise of which each project is a part, and certainly not to the creative life.

In fact, when Wallas's often serviceable scheme is applied to the creative life, the result is not so simple. If the person has a number of projects going, they may all be in different stages of development. An insight in one project may reawaken a dormant enterprise. A new skill mastered in the interests of one enterprise may suddenly become relevant elsewhere in the tangle. One project's period of incubation will be another's opportunity for demonic activity.

At the level of the individual creative project, Wallas's scheme is incomplete at both ends. He omits the early stages of problem-finding (Arlin, 1986) and of the formation of an "initial sketch" that guides the work. Arnheim's (1962) reconstruction of Picasso painting the mural *Guernica* gives a valuable picture of the role of the initial sketch. Wallas omits also the late stage of expansive application of the creative achievement.

At the level of the creative life, Wallas's scheme is silent, since it deals only with the genesis of single projects. Seen in proper perspective Wallas's developmental scheme is not a template to be applied routinely to every instance. Rather, it cries out for the determined and sensitive application of the case study method. If we elaborate the scheme by correcting the omissions noted above, and complicate it by recognizing the multiplicity of enterprises and projects, all at different stages of development, we can arrive at an image of sufficiently entangled intricacy to represent the creative person at work.

Stage Theories and the Creative Life

Our case studies of creative work have, of necessity, a narrative form. It is certainly tempting to conceive of a narrative as divisible into stages. Once that step is taken, a next step becomes plausible—to examine *creative lives in general* for common stage-wise progressions.

But I believe that this is not the correct approach. In the history of psychology, the major stage theories have been unilinear. That is, all individuals are considered to follow the same developmental pathway, to pass through the same stages in the same sequence. This is true of Piaget's theory of child and adolescent development, of Freud's and Erikson's theories of psychosexual and psychosocial development, and more recently of Levinson's account (Levinson et al., 1978) of adult personality development. Albeit with considerable latitude, these unilinear stage theories also suggest that all individuals pass through the same stages at approximately the same ages.

I do not wish to enter here into the vigorous contemporary debate about the validity and utility of stage theories in psychology. Elsewhere, Vonèche and I have argued that even Piaget's use of the stage concept was primarily descriptive and not essential to his theory (Gruber and Vonèche, 1977). In the present context, the key point to consider is the applicability of *any* theory of uniform stages to the development of creative lives.

A theory of uniform stages has its greatest promise when the task is to describe and explain behavior that is typical of the species as a whole. The case for uniform embryological, infantile, and juvenile stages is strengthened by the consideration that in some respects all individuals share the same environment and undergo similar developmental constraints. Certainly, the fetal environment is a miracle of constancy and uniformity; every new parent can experience the miraculous result: 10 fingers, 10 toes, and so on.

But as life goes on, developmental pathways increasingly diverge, even despite the strenuous efforts most people make to conform to well-beaten paths (Gruber, 1986). On evolutionary grounds, there would be little reason to suppose that our species had evolved a normative developmental pattern for individuals past the age of 40, since that is near the end of the reproductive period and was, only 2 or 3 millenia ago, about the average age of death.

When we consider the developmental patterns of *creative* individuals, the picture necessarily becomes more individualized, since we are not dealing with species-wide adaptations but with unique and original patterns. Even if creators are like other people in some respects, we would expect the interweaving of normal development and the novel aspects of each creative life to take a special form in each case. This theme is elaborated by Wallace in the next chapter.

Look at the different patterns displayed in the lives of the three major proponents of stage theories. Freud was a promising neurologist until the age of 29, when his visit to Charcot in Paris started him on a series of deviations from that path that led him to psychoanalytic theory, perhaps 10 years later (Sulloway, 1979). Piaget was a precocious biologist from the age of 11, and was firmly set in his scientific pathway by the age of 25 (Gruber and Vonèche, 1977). Erikson was a wandering artist until the age of 25, then accidentally became involved as a teacher in an experimental school that brought him into contact with prominent psychoanalysts, leading him later to his own career as innovative analyst (Coles, 1970). Thus we have one case of rather straightforward continuity (Piaget), one case of a series of deviations leading to a rather gradual reshaping of a career (Freud), and one case of a sharp break with a youthful past (Erikson).

To take an even more striking example, consider some of the great poets. Among the Romantics, Keats and Shelley were dead by the time they were 30; Wordsworth began his greatest poem, *The Prelude,* when he was 28 and finished it some 30 years later. Blake wrote all his best poetry before he was 40, but he made his best engravings and designs after he was 60. From another era, Milton began *Paradise Lost* when he was about 40, put it aside until he was 60, and finished it then.

Does this critique of the idea of unilinear developmental pathways and uniform stages mean that we must reject the idea of stages altogether? Not at all. But if we accept the idea that our starting point in the study of creativity must be the unique creative person at work, then we must look for the stages of development in the individual, and we must consider the personal developmental history as a whole: a belief system and way of working that functions as a transitional state for one person may well be another's life work.

To understand the points of cleavage between stages, and the dynamics of movement from stage to stage, we must look ever more deeply at the individual. And that is why the evolving systems approach is so intimately linked with the case study method.

REFERENCES

Amabile, T. M. (1983). *The social psychology of creativity.* New York: Springer-Verlag.

Arlin, P. K. (1986). Problem finding and young adult cognition. In R. A. Mines & K. S. Kitchener (Eds.), *Adult cognitive development.* New York: Praeger.

Arnheim, R. (1962). *Picasso's Guernica: The genesis of a painting.* Berkeley: University of California Press.

Bartlett, F. C. (1932). *Remembering: A study in experimental and social psychology.* Cambridge: Cambridge University Press.

Benfey, O. T. (Ed.). (1965). *Kekulé centennial.* Washington, D.C.: American Chemical Society.

Bloom, B. (1985). *Developing talent in young children.* New York: Ballantine.

Campbell, D. T. (1960). Blind variation and selective retention in creative thought as in other knowledge processes. *Psychological Review, 67,* 380–400.

Coles, R. (1970). *Erik Erikson: The growth of his work.* Boston: Little, Brown.

Darwin, C. (1868). *The variation of animals and plants under domestication* (2 vols.). London: Murray.

Darwin, C. (1871). *The descent of man, and selection in relation to sex* (2 vols.). London: Murray.

Darwin, C. (1958). *The autobiography of Charles Darwin.* London: Collins (Original expurgated publication 1887)

Ellmann, R. (1948). *Yeats: The man and the masks.* New York: Dutton.

Feldman, D. H. (1980). *Beyond universals in cognitive development.* Norwood, N.J.: Ablex.

Feldman, D. H. (1986). *Nature's gambit: Child prodigies and the development of human potential.* New York: Basic Books.

Gardner, H. (1983). *Frames of mind: The theory of multiple intelligences.* New York: Basic Books.

Gruber, H. E. (1976). Créativité et fonction constructive de la répétition. *Bulletin de Psychologie de la Sorbonne* [*Numéro spécial pour le 80ᵉ anniversaire de Jean Piaget*], *30*(327), 235–239.

Gruber, H. E. (1980). "And the Bush Was Not Consumed": The evolving systems approach to creativity. In S. Modgil & C. Modgil (Eds.), *Toward a theory of psychological development.* Windsor, England: NFER Publishers.

Gruber, H. E. (1981a). *Darwin on man: A psychological study of scientific creativity* (2nd ed.). Chicago: University of Chicago Press. (Original work published in 1974)

Gruber, H. E. (1981b). On the relation between "aha experiences" and the construction of ideas. *History of Science, 19,* 41–59.

Gruber, H. E. (1982). On the hypothesized relation between giftedness and creativity. In D. H. Feldman (Ed.), *Developmental approaches to giftedness and creativity.* San Francisco: Jossey-Bass.

Gruber, H. E. (1985). From epistemic subject to unique creative person at work. *Archives de Psychologie, 53,* 167–185.

Gruber, H. E. (1986). Which way is up? A developmental question. In R. A. Mines & K. S. Kitchener (Eds.), *Adult cognitive development* (pp. 112–133). New York: Praeger.

Gruber, H. E. (1988). Networks of enterprise in creative scientific work. In B. Gholson, A. Houts, R. A. Neimayer, & W. Shadish (Eds.), *Psychology of science and metascience.* Cambridge: Cambridge University Press.

Gruber, H. E., & Davis, S. N. (1988). Inching our way up Mount Olympus: The evolving systems approach to creative thinking. In R. J. Sternberg (Ed.), *The nature of creativity.* Cambridge: Cambridge Uuniversity Press.

Gruber, H. E. & Vonèche, J. (Eds.). (1977). *The essential Piaget.* New York: Basic Books.

Holton, G. (1973). *Thematic origins of scientific thought: Kepler to Einstein.* Cambridge, Mass.: Harvard University Press.

Jackson, D. N., & Rushton, J. P. (Eds.). (1987). *Scientific excellence: Origins and assessment.* Newbury Park, Calif.: Sage Publications.

Koestler, A. (1967). *The act of creation.* New York: Dell.

Levinson, D. J., Darrow, C. N., Klein, E. B., Levinson, M. H., & McKee, B. (1978). *The seasons of a man's life.* New York: Knopf.

Manuel, F. E. (1979). *A portrait of Isaac Newton.* Washington, D.C.: New Republic Books. (Original work published in 1968)

Maruyama, M. (1963). The second cybernetics: Deviation-amplifying mutual causal processes. *American Scientist, 51,* 164–179.

Merton, R. K. (1985). *On the shoulders of giants: A Shandean postscript.* New York: Harcourt Brace Jovanovich. (Original work published in 1965)

Miller, A. I. (1981). *Albert Einstein's special theory of relativity: Emergence (1905) and early interpretation (1905–1911).* Reading, Mass.: Addison-Wesley.

Miller, G. A., Galanter, E., & Pribram, K. H. (1960). *Plans and the structure of behavior.* New York: Holt, Rinehart and Winston.

Neisser, U. (1982). *Memory observed: Remembering in natural contexts.* San Francisco: Freeman.

Newell, A., Shaw, J. C., & Simon, H. A. (1962). The processes of creative thinking. In H. E. Gruber, G. Terrell, & M. Wertheimer (Eds.), *Contemporary approaches to creative thinking.* New York: Atherton.

Newell, A., Simon, H. A. (1972). *Human problem solving.* Englewood Cliffs, N.J.: Prentice-Hall.

Perkins, D. N. (1981). *The mind's best work.* Cambridge, Mass.: Harvard University Press.

Piaget, J. (1926). *Language and thought of the child.* London: Kegan Paul. (Original work published in 1923)

Piaget, J. (1952). *The origins of intelligence in children.* New York: International Universities Press. (Original work published in 1936)

Piaget, J. (1954). *The construction of reality in the child.* New York: Basic Books. (Original work published in 1937)

Piaget, J. (1951). *Play, dreams and imitation in childhood.* New York: Norton. (Original work published in 1946)

Plato (1910). Ion. In *Five Dialogues of Plato Bearing on Poetic Inspiration* (Percy Bysshe Shelley, Trans.). London: Dent.

Poincaré H. (1952). *Science and method.* New York: Dover. (Original work published in 1908)

Prickett, S. (1970). *Coleridge and Wordsworth: The poetry of growth.* Cambridge: Cambridge University Press.

Rosenzweig, S. (1986). Idiodynamics vis-à-vis psychology. *American Psychologist, 41,* 241–245.

Rothenberg, A. (1979). *The emerging goddess: The creative process in art, science, and other fields.* Chicago: University of Chicago Press.

Rushton, J. P., Murray, H. G., & Paunonen, S. V. (1987). Personality characteristics associated with high research productivity. In D. N. Jackson & J. P. Rushton (Eds.), *Scientific excellence: Origins and assessment.* Newbury Park, Calif.: Sage Publications.

Simon, H. A. (1969). The architecture of complexity. In H. A. Simon, *The sciences of the artificial* (2nd ed., 1981, pp. 193–229). Cambridge, Mass.: MIT Press.

Simonton, D. K. (1984). *Genius, creativity, and leadership.* Cambridge, Mass.: Harvard University Press.

Simonton, D. K. (1988). Creativity, leadership, and chance. In R. J. Sternberg (Ed.). *The nature of creativity: Contemporary psychological perspectives.* Cambridge: Cambridge University Press.

Spelke, E., Hirst, W., & Neisser, U. (1976). Skills of divided attention. *Cognition, 4,* 215–230.

Stallworthy, J. (1963). *Between the lines: Yeats's poetry in the making.* Oxford: Clarendon Press.

Sulloway, F. J. (1979). *Freud, biologist of the mind: Beyond the psychoanalytic legend.* New York: Basic Books.

Tolman, E. C. (1932). *Purposive Behavior in Animals and Men.* Berkeley: University of California Press.

Van Gogh, V. (1963). *Van Gogh: A self-portrait. Letters.* Edited by W. H. Auden. New York: Dutton.

Wallace, D. B. (1985). Giftedness and the construction of a creative life. In F. D. Horowitz & M. O'Brien (Eds.), *The gifted and talented: Developmental perspectives* (pp. 361–385). Washington, D.C.: American Psychological Association.

Wallas, G. (1926). *The art of thought.* New York: Harcourt Brace.

Wertheimer, M. (1945). *Productive thinking.* New York: Harper.

Westfall, R. S. (1980). *Never at rest: A biography of Isaac Newton.* Cambridge: Cambridge University Press.

Wiener, N. (1948). *Cybernetics, Or control and communication in the animal and the machine.* New York: Wiley.

Wiener, N. (1953). *Ex-prodigy: My childhood and youth.* Cambridge, Mass.: MIT Press.

Wiener, N. (1956). *I am a mathematician: The later life of a prodigy.* Cambridge, Mass.: MIT Press.

Wordsworth, J., Abrams, M. H., & Gill, S. (1979). *The Prelude, 1799, 1805, 1850, William Wordsworth.* New York: Norton. (The passage cited is from the 1805 version.)

Wordsworth, W. (1909). Preface to Lyrical Ballads. In T. Hutchinson (Ed.), *The poetical works of William Wordsworth.* Oxford: Oxford University Press. (Original work published in 1801)

2

Studying the Individual:
The Case Study Method
and Other Genres

DORIS B. WALLACE

Things have not happened to me: on the contrary it is I who have happened to them; and all my happenings have taken the form of books and plays. Read them, or spectate them; and you have my whole story.

GEORGE BERNARD SHAW

This is the statement of a person who does not separate life and work. His life is his work. Through it he has shaped his story. His most valued and best known qualities are those that are unique to him. If, therefore, we wish to understand what he did and how, we must study Shaw at work. And so with every creative person.

The study of single cases has a venerable tradition not only in psychology, but in medicine and physiology, sociology, economics, literature, law, and the history of science. Often the study of a single case has acted as a kind of watershed in a field: Stratton's (1896, 1897) reports of his own responses to wearing an inverting lens and Itard's (1801/1962) study of the development of the wild boy of Aveyron are examples in the fields of perception and human development respectively. In research on memory, Ebbinghaus (1885/1964) and Luria (1968) each made their path-breaking discoveries through the study of a single individual. But the study of individuals does not necessarily aim at understanding their uniqueness.

This chapter addresses the issue of uniqueness from the viewpoint of the whole person. It then shows how case studies, using the evolving systems approach, are related to other, apparently similar, genres, such as biography, psychobiography, and autobiography. The overlap with and distinctions between these forms and the case study method are highlighted by considering four themes: the relationship of investigator and subject; the treatment of the work as opposed to the life outside the work; the place of childhood; and theoretical commitments, implicit and explicit.

My aim in discussing these different genres in relation to each other is twofold: to characterize the studies in this book by situating them within a wider spectrum; and to clarify the particular characteristics of the case study method by distinguishing among these different modes and taking up their different characteristics.

I use the term "case study method" to refer to investigations of creative work in which (1) one individual is being studied; (2) diverse aspects of the individual's life and work are considered together; (3) an attempt is made to move toward understanding the person as a whole; (4) emphasis is placed on understanding the development of the work itself; and (5) the goal is to elaborate a psychological theory of creative work.

The Issue of Uniqueness

It has been said (Murray & Kluckhohn, 1950) that any individual is like all others in some respects, like some others in some respects, and like no others in some respects. Let us call these three aspects of the individual Alpha, Beta, and Gamma.

What then makes up the individuality of the *whole person,* the qualities that make someone unique? I contend that it cannot only be Gamma (like no others). The qualities in Alpha, Beta, and Gamma are not parceled out to be mutually exclusive; by residing in the same person, they grow into a coherent whole. Individuality lies in the particular nature of the *configuration* of Alpha, Beta, and Gamma. This aspect, emphasizing the *evolving whole* rather than single elements, I shall call Delta. When we chop a person up (conceptually!) into elements and study them separately, as we often do in experimental psychology to gain some understanding of parts and segments, Delta (the integrated whole) disappears.

Most research in psychology has concentrated on Alpha (like all others) and Beta (like some others) and can be included under the methodological rubric *nomothetic* (Allport, 1942). Nomothetic forms of knowledge are concerned with general principles, as opposed to "the individual happening or single event" (p. 53). The individual event or the psychology of individuality is an *idiographic* form of knowledge. This dichotomous classification

of the general and the particular has long been a topic of discussion in philosophy and psychology (Grossmann, 1986).

The case study, an instance of idiographic research, makes use of narrative, of historical description, and of reconstruction, qualities noted by Wundt (see Allport, 1942) in his distinction between *Gesetzwissenschaft* (lawful science) and *Geschichtswissenschaft* (historical science).

Often research that begins as a case study, like Stratton's, leads quickly to the formulation of general laws in which individuality—Delta—is submerged (Shapiro & Wallace, 1981). But research with one individual can have different meanings depending on the nomothetic or idiographic intentions of the investigator. Stratton and Ebbinghaus were interested in general phenomena, laws applying to all human beings. William James (1901/1961) reported only one case of each type of religious experience. He constructed a typology that might cover all of religious experience, but not by eliminating the differences.

It is noteworthy that pioneers of nomothetic, quantitative, and experimental psychology, such as Wilhelm Wundt, believed that the experimental method alone was futile, and he set the example by devoting a major effort in his ten-volume *Völkerpsychologie* (1900–20) to a study of man in society.

Psychology has a place and a need for both orientations. Even in the study of creative work, with its emphasis on the novel and the unique, there is room for nomothetic research. However, psychologists interested in creative work would be evading a major responsibility if they did not confront the issue of uniqueness. What attracts our attention to the creative individual is his or her unique achievement, and to explain it we are required to examine the extraordinary characteristics and circumstances that brought it about.

The study of an individual case is not necessarily outside science. Stratton wore a lens over one eye (the other eye was covered) which inverted and reversed the retinal image so that he saw the world upside-down and right–left reversed. His account of his responses to this state of affairs is highly subjective and individual. It is also thoroughly experimental and controlled. It is precisely this combination—of the phenomenological and the experimental—that provides the power of the account. This power is evident, for example, in Stratton's description of the psychologically disruptive and physically nauseating effects of going for a walk in an upside-down world in which he recognized at first no single landmark though he knew the terrain intimately. Stratton's study was methodologically self-conscious, subjective but not at all naive.

Stratton's most important finding was that he eventually adapted to the inverted image, that is, he saw the world the right way up; when he removed the inverting lens, the same experiences of inversion and adaptation were repeated. These findings were soon confirmed as Alpha (like all others) behavior.

A more extreme instance of this pattern in a case study can be found in Harré's (1983) account of the discovery of the chemistry of digestion. In

1822 William Beaumont, a doctor in the United States army, treated a patient, an army porter who had been accidentally shot in the abdomen. Although the wound healed, the opening never closed. Instead, a kind of fold or natural valve developed over the opening, which made bandages no longer necessary (p. 35). The porter was physically robust, recovered from his wound, and led a normal life. Realizing the opportunity provided by this case, Beaumont used it to study the chemical processes of digestion in vivo and in vitro over a period of nine years. By introducing a tube into the opening, Beaumont could extract the materials in the stomach. He measured the rate and temperature of digestion and the chemical processes at different stages. Here is his interesting conclusion:

> The gastric juice . . . is the most general solvent in nature of alimentary matter—even the hardest bone cannot withstand its action. It is capable, *even out of the stomach,* of effecting perfect digestion, with the aid of due and uniform degree of heat (100° Fahrenheit) and gentle agitation . . . I am impelled by the weight of evidence . . . to conclude that the change effected by it on the ailment, *is purely chemical.* (Harré, 1983, pp. 40–41)

This was a case study whose results, as Harré points out, were immediately assumed to apply to the stomachs of all human beings. But only one stomach was ever studied. The study of a single instance led Beaumont directly and inductively to Alpha. For him, the Gamma qualities in this case were a means only, permitting him to do the research concerning Alpha.

More recently Sacks and Wasserman (1987) described the case of a 65-year-old painter who, as the result of a car accident, lost his color vision. This case is unique because it combines being an artist with having a very rare injury. The likelihood of these two factors uniting in one person might be on the order of 1 in 10 billion.[1] Moreover, Mr. I, the painter in question, could paint what he saw after the accident, thus providing additional accurate and important subjective information to his verbal account. All these facts are good examples of Gamma (like no others).

Nevertheless, preoccupation with Gamma alone could be fragmenting. Each case would detail simply how it was unique. It would not be *about* anything except itself. The case of Mr. I demonstrates the importance of Delta. At the Alpha level: all human brains have specialized color processing centers. At the Beta level: artists are especially vulnerable when it comes to the loss of color vision. At the Delta level, this artist fought against his affliction and constructed a new life that preserved his role as an artist. It is Sacks' and Wasserman's account of Delta that makes the case interesting.

Uniqueness and Creativity

The case studies in this book exemplify the evolving systems approach. They are all examinations of aspects of creativity. Definitions of creativity usually recognize at least two criteria: novelty and value. The creative product must be new and it must be judged to have some value according to external criteria. Gruber (1980) added a third criterion, intent (see Chapter 1): creative products are the result of purposeful behavior; and a fourth, continuance. Creative work takes time. This is because creative people take on hard projects. Beethoven once wrote:

> I carry my thoughts about with me for a long time, often for a very long time before writing them down. I can . . . be sure that . . . I shall not forget [a theme] even years later. I change many things, discard others, and try again and again until I am satisfied; then, in my head, I begin to elaborate the work . . . the underlying idea never deserts me. It rises, it grows. I hear and see the image in front of me from every angle. . . . (Hamburger, 1952, p. 194)

The criterion of continuance gives special meaning to that of intent or purpose, extending creativity over time and capturing the notion of a creative life. To live a creative life is one of the intentions of a creative person, a topic I discuss elsewhere (Wallace, 1985).

Considering these criteria means that, by definition, in our case studies of creative thinking, we are dealing not only with Alpha, Beta and Gamma each taken separately, but also with Delta—the unique configuration they form in combination. Delta should be the centerpiece in the study of creative processes. Highly creative people are different from other people. Their differentness is what they are recognized and known for. Moreover, they are different from one another.

The difficulty in all this is the problem of generalization. One of the most common objections to the case study method is that one cannot safely generalize from a single instance. We have seen from Beaumont's case study that this is not strictly true. The impossibility of generalizing holds only for cases in which either Gamma (like no other) or the more complex whole configuration, Delta, is the focus.

In her case study of Shaw, Tahir (1989) discusses the problem of generalizing from a single case in the study of creative thinking. She asks:

> Is there a common characteristic among great playwrights? And if we could find a common characteristic . . . is it useful? Can we understand Bernard Shaw any better by knowing how great playwrights in general create? (pp. 2–3)

What did Einstein, Picasso, and Tolstoy have in common in addition to changing how we look at the world? The capacity for exceptionally hard work? A high aspiration level? Expertise? These are interesting, often marvelous qualities. They are Beta (like some others) qualities. They may be necessary but they are not sufficient for creativity. In other words, there are individuals with these qualities who are not creative.

The case study reflects a respect for the whole person and a respectful interest in the multiple contexts of the subject's[2] thought and work. "Wholeness" is here considered an ideal. In building a method for studying creative

processes, the initial aim is to discover and understand how parts work together. The case study lends itself well to such a task because it can deal with
many issues simultaneously.

In the ideal case, there is a responsibility for understanding the interplay
between Alpha, Beta, and Gamma, and their configuration, Delta, between
the universal and the unique and the spectrum between them. Feldman (1980)
is probably the only psychologist who has singled out uniqueness and related
it to development. He has suggested the interesting notion that all characteristics move along a continuum from unique to universal, whether it be through
the dissemination of an initially unique biological mutation or an initially
unique human invention like the microchip.

The evolving systems approach differs from Feldman's proposal in that it
is not focused on a historical or evolutionary movement between the universal
and the unique. Rather, we are interested in how the characteristics referred
to as Alpha, Beta, and Gamma lie together, how they are *entangled,* or better, interwoven to form a coherent system, Delta.

I now turn to a discussion of the case study method and related modes of
studying the individual, according to the four themes already mentioned.

Relationship between Investigator and Subject

The biography and the case study often involve years of research which bring
investigator and subject, whether the latter is living or not, into a relationship
of special intimacy and intense interest. Such an interest is a prerequisite and
a danger: a prerequisite because the work is demanding and long; a danger
because the case study demands both intimacy and distance.

What is the ideal relationship? One of complete detachment? Samuel
Johnson said, "If the biographer writes from personal knowledge . . . there
is danger lest his interest, his fear, his gratitude, or his tenderness, overpower
his fidelity, and tempt him to conceal, if not to invent" (1968, p. 114). Yet
like Boswell's biography of Johnson, many great nineteenth-century biographies were based on a personal relationship. Mrs. Gaskell was a friend as
well as the biographer of Charlotte Brontë. Walter Scott's seven-volume biography was written by Scott's son-in-law, J. G. Lockhart. The eminent historian J. A. Froude was Carlyle's literary executor and wrote a four-volume
biography of Carlyle. Edmund Gosse's famous autobiography of his childhood is also a biography of his puritanical father. If these works are biased,
they have also been greatly praised (Kendall, 1965). Personal knowledge can
be an advantage, providing a degree of understanding that is not accessible to
others.

Some very well-respected biographers have not based their work on their
personal relationships with their subjects. Richard Ellmann was not personally acquainted with James Joyce, Leon Edel did not know Henry James, nor
George Painter Proust. These authors are often cited for their objectivity
(Shelston, 1977). Paradoxically or not, they also come psychologically closer

to their subjects than did the eighteenth- and nineteenth-century biographers who often had a personal relationship with the subject.

Constant and Variable Elements

One of the similarities between biography and the case study of a creative person at work is that the investigator constructs a relationship with the subject that has both *constant* and *variable* aspects.

The *constant* aspect is the one that generally informs the work as a whole, is visible and recognizable in it, and in some sense reflects not only the investigator's personal orientation to the subject, but the sociohistorical context of the investigator's world. The constant relationship is part of the purpose of the biography. We see different kinds of constant relationships in different biographies of the same person: compare, for example, Ernest Jones's (1953–57) reverential three-volume biography of Freud and Sulloway's (1979) iconoclastic one. Freud was Jones's hero. Sulloway's orientation was to point out Freud's proper place in the history of science. This corrected the historical record and destroyed certain historical myths cherished by the psychoanalytic community. Sulloway's constant relationship to Freud was as respectful challenger.

The *variable* aspect is similar to one's personal relationships in life. It changes. Its qualities ebb and flow. It can move from admiration and respect through anxiety, irritation, reconciliation, acceptance. In the course of a study of many years, the variable aspect of the relationship does not necessarily follow some linear course but may move back and forth among a myriad of feelings and opinions.

The variable relationship may not be as visible in the finished study as the constant relationship. No finished product presents a full account of its production. But the history of the study, if we knew it, would also be a history of the variable relationship between the investigator and subject.

Investigator Roles

The issue of objectivity is just as critical in the case study as in the biography. In the case study, the investigator has two central roles, a phenomenological and a critical role, or, one could say, an inside and an outside role. In the phenomenological role, the investigator strives to enter the mind of the subject to reconstruct the meaning of the subject's experience from the latter's point of view. This is an attempt to achieve objectivity by putting aside one's own predilections, an attempt to understand and reconstruct what a given experience was like for the subject. In this role, the investigator comes as close as possible to the subject (see Table 2–1).

But the critical role is also essential for the case study. Here the investigator stands outside the subject to appraise the data of the case and to explain and interpret them. Objectivity is achieved by putting aside the *subject's* biases, by distancing oneself from the subject, and by evaluating "from a

TABLE 2-1. Case Study Method: Investigator Roles

Phenomenological Role	Critical Role
"Inside" the subject	"Outside" the subject
Objectivity achieved by setting aside own bias	Objectivity achieved by setting aside subject's bias
Close to subject	Distant from subject
Interpretive	Interpretive

height." Both phenomenological and critical roles aim at objectivity and both entail interpretation. The investigator is continually moving between these two roles.

Autobiography: Self to Self

While the relationship of investigator and subject is similar in biography and in the case study, the same theme in autobiography is radically different. In autobiography, investigator and subject are the same person. The relationship is not that of investigator to subject, but of the present self to the past self—or selves.[3] There is also an issue of change over time in autobiography because the autobiographer is representing those aspects of the past that seem relevant to the present. The subject's perception of the past moves with the present, like the moon. Erikson (1975), among others, has pointed out these different time frames: the writer's present, the writer's past, and the historical context. A nice example is provided in Koestler's (1954) autobiography, *Dialogue with Death,* in which he describes the six months he spent in Spain in 1937 during the Spanish Civil War. In comparing this description with the one he had written at the time, he realized that his revision was too tidy and logical. He saw that it would probably change again if he wrote it once more.[4]

This changing perception of the past has led some literary critics to maintain that autobiography is fiction, that the self is a fiction (Olney, 1980). At the same time, the natural subjectivity of the autobiography has been claimed as being its truth: one knows one's own life better than anyone else (Kohli, 1981). Autobiographers intend us to take autobiography as true. In the process of searching for the continuity of self as well as for lost selves, autobiographers reveal themselves.

The autobiographer's task differs *psychologically* from that of the biographer or case study investigator because of the difference in the structure of the investigator–subject relationship. But the central task of all three genres is diachronic reconstruction, and all three make use of phenomenological data as a way of understanding the subject.

The Work–Life Dichotomy

Any single life is overwhelmingly complex. The case study method always falls short of, but does not abandon, the ideal of doing justice to the whole creative person (Delta). To be effective, the focus must be on a manageable part of the creative work.

Henry James once said that when a man's work is over and he is dead, his image is simplified and summarized: "it stands, sharply, for a few estimated and cherished things, rather than, nebulously, for a swarm of possibilities" (cited in Edel, 1959). Such a concept may also apply to a person who, still alive, contemplates the past. When Wordsworth, in his famous autobiographical poem *The Prelude,* described episodes of his childhood—like stealing birds' eggs—he referred to them later as "spots of time" (see Chapter 4). They were the significant, vividly etched memories of his boyhood in nature. They counted as "estimated and cherished things" that enabled him to make links with his past self. Autobiography, after all, is an attempt to establish the self as a temporal structure. Wordsworth's boyhood episodes became "estimated and cherished things" through his own creative work. Each episode had to be claimed and reclaimed by the autobiographer during the long process of thinking through and constructing the poem.

The case study method is aimed at reconstructing the often tortuous path, including the blind alleys and abandoned ways, of the creative *work.* The case study moves within the "swarm of possibilities." The studies in this book all exemplify this point; each is concerned with the development of a particular aspect of the work. The choices made reflect a combination of factors: the salience of the topic in the creative thought and work of the person; its interest for the investigator; the availability of documents and works; and its pertinence for deepening our understanding of creativity.

Some subjects deliberately destroy information that would be useful to future investigators. This limits what a biographer or case study investigator *can* know. Freud, for example, at the age of 28—already assuming that he was destined for distinction—wrote to his fiancée:

> I have just carried out one resolution which one group of people as yet unborn and fated to misfortune, will feel acutely . . . they are my biographers. I have destroyed all my diaries of the past fourteen years, with letters, scientific notes and the manuscripts of my publications. . . . Let the biographers chafe; we won't make it too easy for them. Let each one of them believe he is right in his "Conception of the Development of the Hero": even now I enjoy the thought of how they will all go astray. (cited in Jones, 1953, pp. xii–xiii)

What Freud destroyed were professional correspondence and documents concerning his work and his thought about his work. (He had regularly done research since entering the University of Vienna 11 years earlier at the age of 17.) Written late in the nineteenth century (1884), this letter reveals

Freud's assumption that biography was primarily about the person's public, that is, "heroic," achievements. Although Boswell's life of Johnson, first published toward the end of the eighteenth century, had radically changed that tradition, most nineteenth-century biographies gave very little account of the private person. A typical example is McKendrick's biography of Helmholtz, published in 1899. It devotes all its almost 300 pages to Helmholtz's scientific achievements and inventions. Even the seven pages entitled "Childhood and Early Life" are concerned primarily with Helmholtz's learning and academic achievements as a child. Today this work would be classified as an intellectual biography.

Some 40 years after Freud's letter to his fiancée, Henry James, who was extremely secretive about his private affairs, burned his correspondence of the previous 40 years in a fire in his garden. Shrinking from revelations about his private life, James believed that "to leave everything to the biographer . . . was, so to speak, to remove one's clothes to the public gaze" (James, cited in Edel, 1959, p. 39). Although Freud and James performed outwardly similar acts, the meaning they gave them were very different. James's remark was a sign that times had changed, that biographers were interested in the private person. Indeed, one might complain that recent biographies deal with everything *but* the achievements.

Private versus Public

If the task of understanding the evolution of the work of one person is overwhelming, the task of the biographer is no less so: to depict the course of the life of a person from birth to death. That many biographies do not treat the work but depict only the life outside the work may reflect this difficulty. Such biographies have been attacked for utter neglect of the achievements that gave rise to the biography in the first place. They are a response to people's boundless curiosity about the private lives and personalities of well-known people, the desire to know the Alpha and Beta about a person who is only known for Gamma, the desire to make the private public, to bring the exalted down to the plebian level. Virginia Woolf was particularly interested in the private personality: "How did he look . . . who were his aunts, and his friends; how did he blow his nose; whom did he love, and how?" (1950, p. 227). Woolf did not consider such information trivial or undignified. On the contrary, it was revealing in a way that an account that dwelt exclusively on the person's public exploits could never be. Her interest was in portraying the neglected inner life. This was a big change from Freud's nineteenth-century notion quoted above. Lytton Strachey's (1918/1984) *Eminent Victorians* was probably responsible for initiating the turn away from the heroic in biography in the twentieth century.

The investigator doing a case study is interested in another range of private experience. He or she studies not only the published or finished works but the struggles to produce them—traced in notes, journals, letters, sketches, and the like. The aim is always to understand more about how the creative work evolved. Sometimes the published work, given a special reading, reveals private experience. The English novelist Dorothy Richardson (see Chapter 8) is an extreme instance. But even in formal scientific writing one can find traces of the autobiographical. For example, Darwin (1859/1966) on page 50 of *On the Origin of Species,* begins an important passage: "When a young naturalist," and goes on to describe certain dilemmas of biological classification encountered as one travels more widely. We know immediately that he is talking about himself.

Some biographies treat the "life and work." Understandably, such a task usually takes decades and often produces a multivolume work. If there is sufficient interest, a single-volume abridged version for the general reader is brought out. Edel's (1987) abridged version of his much praised five-volume biography of Henry James is an example of this pattern.

Other biographies, especially "intellectual" biographies, focus primarily on the work and its development. In their focus on the work, intellectual biographies are similar to the case study method: the investigator must know the subject's field. One cannot do a case study or an intellectual biography of Einstein without knowing physics.

There is, in all this, a tacit assumption that the life and work are separate—an interesting idea considering that for many creative people the life *is* the work. Shaw was certainly of this opinion, as were others, for example, Balzac. Even the relationships a creative person has that are apparently innocent of any connection with work, such as domestic arrangements for men, are shaped to facilitate the work. Shaping a creative *life* of this kind is more difficult for women, as I have discussed elsewhere (Wallace, 1985).

Some creative people integrate rather than separate their personal life and their work. For example, Picasso's children and especially the women in his life were drawn into his work and are heavily represented there. On the other hand, Bertrand Russell, philosopher and homme fatale, wrote two books about his life. One, about the development of his work, the brief *My Philosophical Development* (1959), might qualify as an autobiographical case study of creative work. The other (1987), a much longer work, is an autobiography mostly about his social and private life.

Unlike biography, which is probably at least 2000 years old, psychobiography is a creature of the twentieth century. Although any biographer makes psychological statements, a psychobiography is a systematic psychological account with a particular theoretical commitment. By applying psychoanalytic theory, psychobiography aims to give us a deeper, more subtle, and more complex grasp of a person.

Very few psychobiographies deal with the subject's work per se. The emphasis is on the personality. But the psychobiography does not dichotomize work and life. Instead, the work is seen and treated as emerging from the history of the personality. Freud's (1916/1964) study of Leonardo da Vinci's creativity concentrates on Leonardo's work—primarily on two paintings. But Freud's purpose is to identify latent forms in the paintings, interpret their meaning, and show the connection between them and Leonardo's early life, especially an infantile memory or dream.

Psychobiography has been much criticized, especially for its reductionism.

It is accused of reducing the life to psychological processes, ignoring social, economic, or political forces; of reducing creativity to pathology; and of reducing the adult personality to nothing but the outcome of childhood conflict. For a thoroughgoing discussion of the form, see Runyon (1984). But there have been attempts that do not fit this orthodox mold, such as Erikson's psychobiography of Luther (1958), which takes into account the sociohistorical period in which his subject lived.

Contextual Frames

In addition to its central focus on some aspect of the development of the person's work, the case study should take into account a series of contexts or contextual systems (Csikszentmihalyi, 1988). The first of these is the set of enterprises most directly relevant to the one being studied. The second is the person's oeuvre and overall purposes, revealed in the network of enterprise (see Chapter 1). The third context is the person's professional milieu—teachers, colleagues, collaborators, critics, and so on.

The fourth context concerns the subject's families—the family of origin and the current family—and their role in the development and support of the subject's creative life. Wordsworth had a collaborator in his sister Dorothy who also took charge of her brother's domestic needs. Many women who want to do creative independent work have had and still have great difficulties in constructing a life that supports their work and fulfills their other needs. Woolf argued this case in her *A Room of One's Own* (1929/1957), and more recently Hanscombe and Smyers (1987) have done so. The cost to women has been either to forgo other roles—those of wife or mother, for example—or to do everything with inadequate support.

Finally, a fifth context is the sociohistorical milieu, which may have an important role in the subject's work. Gruber argued (1981) that Darwin's long delay in publishing *On the Origin of Species* was due to his fear of a hostile reception. But this did not constrain his creative work, nor was he miserable because of it. Freud and many others left Hitler's Third Reich to work productively elsewhere. James Joyce left Ireland and Catholicism for Trieste in order to free himself from a constricting environment and do his work. Highly creative people may feel themselves to be marginal: they are breaking new ground, forging a new point of view that is at odds with contemporary belief systems or politics. This was the case for Galileo, Locke, Descartes. Persecution is a recurrent feature of the history of creative work. But there are creative people who have presented their work to the world and found it accepted without great travail: Poincaré, Henry Moore, Edison, Picasso, among many. The person's position in the sociohistorical period depends on the nature of the work, whether it is being made public, how loudly it speaks beyond a specialized audience to the general public, the degree of existing religious and political tolerance, and so on.

These five contexts (see Table 2-2) form a series of frames in the case study method. The subject, of course, both produces these contexts and is

TABLE 2-2. Contexts of the Case Study Method

1. Relevant work enterprise(s)
2. Work as a whole (oeuvre)
3. Professional milieu
4. Family and personal life
5. Sociohistorical period

produced by them. But the investigator, too, must be familiar with them as frames of reference for the study. Ideally, they are integrated into the case study as part of the system of thought and meaning that accompanies and affects the subject's work.

The Place of Childhood

The psychobiography gives the greatest systematic significance to childhood. Indeed, the driving interest of the psychobiography is to analyze, explain, and interpret the adult's personality as *caused by* childhood and infantile experiences. For example, in his biography of Isaac Newton, Manuel (1979) argues that Newton's life was dominated by his childhood deprivations. His father died before he was born. When he was three years old, his mother remarried and moved to the house of her new husband, Barnabas Smith, who lived in a village not far away, leaving her son behind. For the next seven years Newton lived with his maternal grandmother. When he was ten, his stepfather died and his mother returned to her original home and to Isaac. Manuel's thesis is that Newton spent the rest of his life venting his rage on people, a rage that he really felt toward his stepfather and that he had been unable to express as a young child. In a recent intellectual biography of Newton, Westfall (1980), describing these events, acknowledges Manuel's "vivid, subtle, and ingenious" *portrait*. But, he asks:

> Is it also true? It appears to me that we lack entirely any means of knowing. It is plausible; it is equally plausible that it is misguided. I am unable to see how empirical evidence can be used to decide on it, one way or the other. . . . I am not offering an alternative analysis. It would confront exactly the same problem of confirmation. (p. 53, note 36)

Westfall's argument could be applied to most psychobiographies. Many fall prey to what Runyon (1984) calls "eventism," the discovery of a turning point in some childhod episode from which subsequent events, including the person's work, are derived.

The Problem of Sparse Material

Westfall also points to gaps in the historical record concerning Newton's childhood, a problem that particularly affects psychobiography, biography, and the case study method. Often childhood is that part of the life for which the empirical evidence is sparsest. Feinstein's (1984) biography of William James, for example, contains almost no material about James before adolescence. Pais' (1982) biography of Einstein, which is subtitled *The Science and the Life of Albert Einstein,* separates personal from scientific material and devotes about 16 pages out of a total of over 500 to Einstein's childhood. Cabanne (1977), in his 600-page biography of Picasso, writes 29 pages about Picasso's first 14 years. Similarly, in Clark's (1976) biography of Bertrand Russell, 29 pages describe Russell's first 17 years; this book is over 750 pages long. The same kind of ratio can be found in Edel's (1953) biography of Henry James. The first sentence of Ellmans's recent biography of Oscar Wilde reads: "Oscar Wilde first emerges for us into articulate being in 1868, when he was thirteen, in a letter he wrote to his mother from school" (1988, p. 3).

The autobiographer, on the other hand, is in the position of being able to confer privileged meaning on the past. Cockshut (1984) claims that whereas in biography the childhood is often hurried over, the autobiographer is more likely to consider it the most important time. Whether we agree with Cockshut or not, it may be that the *quality* of the material about childhood differs in the two genres. Autobiography can describe memories of childhood and youth that are more detailed and perhaps more numerous. It can provide accounts of childhood relationships and events that are more laden with meaning than biography can ever match, lacking as it does the inside view and firsthand experience of the autobiographer. Even when the description of childhood is detached, as it is in the autobiography of H. G. Wells (1932), or excessively dry, as it is in the autobiography of the philosopher A. J. Ayer (1977), it retains the authenticity derived from the fact that the subject is the narrator.

Where the biographer often lacks material, the autobiographer is likely to select and emphasize childhood memories that seem relevant to the later life, giving short shrift to those that cannot be exploited for that purpose. The universe of what is relevant may be much larger for a literary figure than for a scientist.

The Case Study Method and Child–Adult Continuity

In this book the case studies are concerned primarily with the evolution of the mature adult work. There are several reasons for this. First, our interest includes establishing the development of the person and understanding continuity in the career. But the career only very rarely begins before adolescence. The case of Picasso is one of the very few that comes close to providing enough data to consider childhood as part of a continuous lifelong developmental process. The beginning of creative work in adolescence is much less rare. The organic chemist R. B. Woodward was on his way in early adolescence (see Chapter 12).

Second, the case study is a densely argued narrative. Some intellectual biographies are similarly detailed. But most, considering they must cover decades of work, cannot afford great density. The general sparseness of available information about childhood affects the biography as well as the case study.

Third, intention is a vital element in the thought and work of the creative person. In childhood, the person's network of enterprise, his or her organization of purpose, has not yet taken shape.

But childhood is certainly not irrelevant to the case study; nor is it disconnected from later life. There are childhood experiences—for example, enforced solitude through illness as in the case of H. G. Wells, or sibling solidarity as among the three Brontë children—that are later seen as formative in the development of the creative work (Howe, 1982).

For our case study work, we need to understand more clearly when and how the organization of purpose begins to be formed. Adolescence is likely to be an important period in this regard. Adolescence as a bridge between childhood and youth is ambiguous in its import for creativity. Many gifted children do not become creative adults. And many creative adults were not gifted children. We need to know how the chosen domain of work itself interacts with the individual personality, with the early social support system, and with chance events to facilitate or impede the development of a purposeful creative adulthood.

Conclusion: Theoretical Commitments

The genres I have been discussing are concerned with different levels of reality. The autobiography is in principle written to reveal the true person, sometimes to set straight the record of a public figure. It may be an objective search but more urgently it is a personal reconstruction. To recall one's life is to discover oneself and to recall it from the point of view of the changing present is to reconstruct it anew. Gusdorf (1980) sees autobiography as

> a work of art and at the same time a work of enlightenment; it does not show us the individual seen from outside in his visible actions but the person in his inner privacy, not as he was, not as he is, but as he believes and wishes himself to be and to have been. (p. 45)

Furthermore, for the autobiographer the future is opaque. For the biographer it is not; the subject is usually dead. The biographer's job is to give a dramatic account of the whole life at one level of reality—what really happened. The same holds true for the investigator using the case study method. Both must be aware, in taking the phenomenological role, that they are interpreting the subject's earlier actions on the basis of *their* knowledge of the subject's future. Toward this end, the network of enterprise is a useful tool in the case study method. The network of enterprise maps the course of and interrelations among the subject's various work enterprises. (By enterprise, we mean a set of goal-directed projects and tasks that endures over time, like Darwin's 50-year study of earthworms or Picasso's work in ceramics.) The network represents the organization of purpose of the person (see Chapter 1). It is useful for seeing the larger-scale pattern of the evolution of the work over time. But it also shows, at any time point, the *subject's* understanding of what is possible, of current activities and future plans.

There is, then, a sense in which the case study investigator moves between two levels of reality—in taking the phenomenological role and the critical role. Biographers may do this too.

Most psychobiographies are psychoanalytic and the psychobiographer is tightly leashed to the aim of demonstrating how the subject exemplifies psychoanalytic theory. A psychobiography may take up idiosyncratic features of the case but these must be fitted into the strictures of psychoanalytic theory. The material selected must be germane to the theory it exemplifies.

In principle, the idea of a psychological examination of a life is to be applauded. But the major difficulty with psychobiography lies in its need to pour each life into a preordained mold. The subjects of psychobiography are often highly creative people whose achievements define them as different from other people. The psychobiography seems bent on leveling these critical differences. It takes unusual people and demonstrates Alpha and Beta—how universally ordinary they are, or how human. Moreover, the root of psychobiography in a pathology-oriented theory distorts the investigation in a serious way. A theory of creativity must provide ample room for the positive factors that permit the creative person to sustain the dangers and ardors of creative work.

Like psychobiography, biography, and autobiography, the case study method entails a narrative. But it goes beyond the narrative. It tells a story but with the commitment of working toward a theory of creativity.

The case study method aims to contribute to a discipline. Unlike biography and autobiography, which rarely have theoretical goals, the case study is a means, not an end in itself.

Each of the genres I have been discussing has its place in understanding a person—on different time scales, on different levels of reality, and in different contexts. To see something of the relationships among these modes is helpful. But my argument is not a special pleading for one particular form. Rather, the very conception of Alpha, Beta, Gamma, and Delta argues for the view that to understand the whole person we need studies in different forms.

Darwin is a good case in point. He is important, monumentally well documented, and intellectually accessible to a wide audience. Documentation is available to support efforts in each genre. He wrote an autobiography. There are reminiscences by two sons, many biographies, and many special studies of different aspects of his thought. In spite of this wealth, there are many gaps. We know comparatively little about Darwin's childhood; neither the young Darwin nor the old Darwin has been closely examined; and we lack knowledge of Darwin's inner life. Apart from psychoanalytic efforts to demonstrate that his illness was psychogenic, his emotional patterns have not been studied. And there are certain important scientific enterprises that have not been studied in any detail. The case of Darwin points to the fact that even when much work has been done, inevitably there is still much that we do not know.

Furthermore, the biographical materials used in the case study method can become the materials for nomothetic studies on diverse topics: early childhood memories, personality, social networks and relationships, metaphors, and so on. The nomothetic approach deliberately isolates processes in order to study them in a precise, controlled way. The case study method entails studying the interaction and interweaving of processes in order to form a concept of the life and work. The two have need of each other.

NOTES

1. This calculation is based on the product of the probabilities of (1) being a painter, estimated at 1 person in 10,000, and (2) having acquired cerebral achromatopsia—a very rare brain damage, estimated at 1 in 1,000,000.

2. The reader should refer to the preface for our notion of "subject."

3. An interesting variant of this structure has been developed by de Waele and Harré. Spurred by concerns similar to ours, such as the desire to understand the whole person and the whole life history, these authors use an "assisted autobiography" as a psychological research tool for examining individual lives. "The construction of the autobiography," they maintain, "is conceived as a cooperative achievement between a team and the participant whose autobiography is to be generated," involving writing and rewriting in a "continuous process of negotiated reconstruction." (1979, p. 193)

4. This kind of change can occur—though it rarely does—in biography too. For example, in 1933 Wittels formally retracted certain parts of his biography of Freud, written 10 years earlier.

REFERENCES

Allport, G. W. (1942). *The use of personal documents in psychological science.* New York: Social Science Research Council.

Ayer, A. J. (1977). *Part of my life.* New York: Harcourt Brace Jovanovich.

Cabanne, P. (1977). *Pablo Picasso: His life and times.* New York: William Morrow.

Clark, R. W. (1976). *The life of Bertrand Russell.* New York: Alfred A. Knopf.

Cockshut, A. O. J. (1984). *The art of autobiography in 19th and 20th Century England.* New Haven: Yale University Press.

Csikszentmihalyi, M. (1988). Society, culture, and person: A system's view of creativity. In R. J. Sternberg (Ed.), *The nature of creativity.* New York: Cambridge University Press.

Darwin, C. (1966). *On the origin of species.* Cambridge, Mass.: Harvard University Press. (Original work published in 1859)

De Waele, J.-P., & Harré, R. (1979). Autobiography as a psychological method. In G. P. Ginsburg (Ed.), *Emerging strategies in social psychological research.* New York: Wiley.

Ebbinghaus, H. (1964). *Memory.* New York: Dover. (Original work published in 1885)

Edel, L. (1953). *The life of Henry James: Vol. 1. The untried years 1843–1870.* Philadelphia: J. P. Lippincott.

Edel, L. (1953–1972). *The life of Henry James* (5 vols.), Philadelphia: J. P. Lippincott.

Edel, L. (1959). *Literary biography.* Bloomington: Indiana University Press.

Edel, L. (1987). *Henry James: A life.* London: Collins.

Ellmann, R. (1988). *Oscar Wilde.* Harmondsworth: Penguin.

Erikson, E. (1958). *Young man Luther: A study in psychoanalysis and history.* New York: Norton.

Erikson, E. (1975). *Life history and the historical moment.* New York: Norton.

Feinstein, H. M. (1984). *Becoming William James.* Ithaca, N.Y.: Cornell University Press.

Feldman, D. H. (1980). *Beyond universals in cognitive development.* Norwood, N.J.: Ablex.

Freud, S. (1964). *Leonardo da Vinci and a memory of his childhood.* New York: Norton. (Original work published in 1916)

Gruber, H. E. (1980). "And the Bush Was Not Consumed": The evolving systems approach to creativity. In S. Modgil & C. Modgil (Eds.), *Toward a theory of psychological development.* Windsor, England: NFER Publishers.

Gruber, H. E. (1981). *Darwin on man* (2nd ed.). Chicago: University of Chicago Press.

Grossmann, K. E. (1986). From idiographic approaches to nomothetic hypotheses: Stern, Allport, and the biology of knowledge, exemplified by an explanation of sibling relationships. In J. Valsiner (Ed.), *The individual subject and scientific psychology.* New York: Plenum.

Gusdorf, G. (1980). Conditions and limits of autobiography. In J. Olney (Ed.), *Autobiography: Essays theoretical and critical.* Princeton, N.J.: Princeton University Press.

Hamburger, M. (Ed. and Trans.) (1952). *Beethoven: Letters and journals and conversations.* New York: Pantheon.

Hanscombe, G., & Smyers, V. L. (1987). *Writing for their lives: The modernist women 1910–1940.* London: Women's Press.

Harré, R. (1983). *Great scientific experiments.* New York: Oxford University Press.

Howe, M. J. A. (1982). Biographical evidence and the development of outstanding individuals. *American Psychologist, 37,* 1071–1081.

Itard, J.-M.-G. (1962). *The wild boy of Aveyron* (G. Humphrey & M. Humphrey, Trans.). New York: Appleton-Century-Crofts. (Original work published in 1801)

James, W. (1961). *The varieties of religious experience: A study in human nature.* New York: Collier Books. (Original work published in 1901)

Johnson, S. (1968). Rambler, #60, dated 13 October 1750. In *Essays from The Rambler, Adventurer, and Idler.* New Haven: Yale University Press.

Jones, E. (1953). *The life and work of Sigmund Freud* (Vol. 1). New York: Basic Books.

Kendall, P. M. (1965). *The art of biography.* New York: Norton.

Koestler, A. (1954). *Dialogue with death.* London: Collins with Hamish Hamilton.

Kohli, M. (1981). Biography: Account, text, method. In D. Bertaux (Ed.), *Biography and society.* Beverly Hills, Calif.: Sage Publications.

Luria, A. R. (1968). *The mind of a mnemonist* (L. Solotaroff, Trans.). New York: Avon Books.

Mandel, B. J. (1980). Full of life now. In J. Olney (Ed.), *Autobiography: Essays theoretical and critical.* Princeton, N.J.: Princeton University Press.

Manuel, F. E. (1979). *A portrait of Isaac Newton.* Washington, D.C.: New Republic Books. (Original work published in 1968)

McKendrick, J. G. (1899). *Hermann Ludwig Ferdinand von Helmholtz.* London: T. Fisher Unwin.

Murray, H. A., & Kluckhohn, C. (Eds.). (1950). *Personality in nature, society, and culture.* New York: Alfred A. Knopf.

Olney, J. (1980). Autobiography and the cultural moment: A thematic, historical, and bibliographical introduction. In J. Olney (Ed.), *Autobiography: Essays theoretical and critical.* Princeton, N.J.: Princeton University Press.

Pais, A. (1982). *"Subtle is the Lord . . ." The science and the life of Albert Einstein.* New York: Oxford University Press.

Runyon, W. McK. (1984). *Life histories and psychobiography.* New York: Oxford University Press.

Russell, B. (1959). *My philosophical development.* London: Allen & Unwin.

Russell, B. (1987). *Bertrand Russell: Autobiography.* London: Unwin Hyman. (Original work published in 3 volumes in 1967, 1968, 1969)

Sacks, O., & Wasserman, R. (1987, November 19). The case of the colorblind painter. *The New York Review of Books, 34,* 225–234.

Shapiro, E. K., & Wallace, D. B. (1981). Developmental stage theory and the individual reconsidered. In E. K. Shapiro & E. Weber (Eds.), *Cognitive and affective growth: Developmental interaction.* Hillsdale, N.J.: Erlbaum.

Shelston, A. (1977). *Biography.* London: Methuen.

Strachey, L. (1984). *Eminent Victorians.* New York: Penguin Books. (Original work published in 1918)

Stratton, G. M. (1896). Some preliminary experiments in vision without inversion of the retinal image. *Psychological Review, 3,* 611–617.

Stratton, G. M. (1897). Vision without inversion of the retinal image. *Psychological Review, 4,* 341–360, 463, 481.

Sulloway, F. J. (1979). *Freud, biologist of the mind.* New York: Basic Books.

Tahir, L. (1989). *The development of thought in young Bernard Shaw.* Unpublished doctoral dissertation, Rutgers University, Newark, N.J.

Wallace, D. B. (1985). Giftedness and the construction of a creative life. In F. D. Horowitz & M. O'Brien (Eds.), *The gifted and talented: Developmental perspective.* Washington, D.C.: American Psychological Association.

Wells, H. G. (1932). *Experiment in autobiography* (Vols. 1, 2). London: Victor Gollancz and the Cresset Press.

Westfall, R. S. (1980). *Never at rest: A biography of Isaac Newton.* Cambridge: Cambridge University Press.

Wittels, F. (1933). Revision of a biography. *American Journal of Psychology, 45,* 745–758.

Woolf, V. (1950). The art of biography. In V. Woolf, *Collected essays* (Vol. 4). New York: Harcourt, Brace & World.

Woolf, V. (1957). *A room of one's own.* New York: Harcourt Brace Jovanovich. (Original work published in 1929)

Wundt, W. (1900–20). *Völkerpsychologie* (10 vols.) Leipzig: Engelmann.

3

Antoine Lavoisier and Hans Krebs: Two Styles of Scientific Creativity

FREDERIC L. HOLMES

The study of creative scientific activity belongs to no single discipline. History of science, philosophy of science, sociology of science, and cognitive psychology are all prominent among the fields that claim to provide accounts of the processes involved. Despite their shared goals, practitioners in these fields are not yet fully engaged in a collaborative enterprise. They have approached problems of scientific creativity from different points of view, examined such activity at different levels, on different time scales, and have employed incommensurable criteria of evaluation. There are, nevertheless, encouraging signs that the barriers which have separated their respective endeavors are beginning to recede.

In his study of Charles Darwin, Howard Gruber (1981a) showed that the skills of the psychologist can illuminate the historical understanding of a great scientist, even as the study of a single highly creative individual can elucidate the general processes of creative thinking. More recently Gruber (1985) maintained that cognitive scientists must bring a sense of history to their work. Herbert Simon applied the techniques of computer programs to investigate the mechanisms of scientific discovery. Like Gruber, he turned to historical cases. Given data approximating those available to scientists of the past, Simon and his associates (Langley, Simon, Bradshaw, & Zytkow, 1987) found that with certain heuristics inserted into their programs, computers can "rediscover" the scientific laws that human minds originally discovered. Simon believes that the methodologies his group is developing "may prove to be a useful addition to the repertoire of the historians of science" (p. 5).

Within the philosophy of science, too, signs point toward a future rapprochement with history. At a 1978 conference on scientific discovery, several speakers noted that a generation of philosophers of science had excluded the discovery process from philosophic analysis, maintaining that only the justification process was susceptible to logical procedures. Some participants asserted that philosophers must now apply themselves to the problem of creative scientific discovery in order to give a full account of what science is about. These advocates of a philosophical examination of scientific discovery acknowledged that there could not be a universal deductive logic of discovery. Discovery could, however, be made intelligible, and philosophers could help to understand the creative process in scientific thought. The only route toward such understanding would be through accounts of *examples.* According to Marx Wartofsky (1978), an explanation of creativity in science "requires the re-enactment of the processes itself, the reconstruction of the *practices* of creation" (p. 15). Thomas Nickles (1980) wrote that "philosophers must join historians and other students of science in the descriptive task of making intelligible to reason (insofar as possible) actual cases of creative discoveries. The epistemologist's aims may not be identical with the historian's, but we are engaged in a common task of providing accounts of the discovery process" (p. 30).

Gruber, Simon, and these philosophers all recognize that the historical dimension is central to the study of scientific discovery and call for closer interactions with historians. As a historian of science who has fixed his attention on the processes of discovery for a number of years, I welcome these calls. The creative side of scientific activity is so deep a problem, so elusive, and so complex that to comprehend it will require the best efforts of historians, philosophers, psychologists, sociologists, and others. Scientific creativity is a favorable site for the convergence of these disciplines in a joint enterprise to which each can contribute special insight.

Historians of science can benefit greatly by being more attentive to the organizing ideas that emanate from studies of scientific creativity in other disciplines. Gruber's views on creativity as a growth process, on the length of time required to have an "aha! experience," and on networks of enterprise (1981a, 1981b) have helped me to place patterns I can discern in the lives of individual scientists into a broader framework. It is too early to foresee what impact the work of Simon and his group will have on historians. Many will be skeptical that computer-programmed rediscoveries can capture the richness and subtlety of historical discovery, but I am persuaded that this effort to isolate from particular historical discoveries general and domain-specific heuristics that may be applicable to other discoveries within the same domains will offer challenging ideas for historians to test against the detailed historical discovery stories they reconstruct in more conventional ways.

Philosophers of science and historians of science sometimes appear to live in separate worlds. The former draw sharp conceptual distinctions which do not appear to the latter to be applicable to the fluid nature of actual historical developments. That philosophers are now coming to acknowledge that the context of discovery cannot be isolated cleanly from the context of justification will not be overly impressive to historians, who have felt all along that scientific activity cannot be partitioned so neatly. Nevertheless, such distinctions do provide a useful general orientation for historical interpretation. The more subtle distinctions recently suggested by philosophers, like those between the generation and pursuit of a hypothesis or between preliminary assessment and final testing, or the characterization of scientific problems as structures of constraints (Nickles, 1980), are valuable devices for the historian searching for patterns within the ongoing flow of events.

If historians of science can utilize to their advantage organizing concepts drawn from other disciplines, what can they contribute in turn? Philosophers and cognitive scientists recognize the need for case histories. Can historians of science provide reconstructions of real scientific discoveries adequate to the needs of those who hope to build systematic understanding of the processes of creativity on such cases? The answer to that question depends not only on whether historians and practitioners of these other disciplines share enough of one another's languages to collaborate toward a common goal. It rests also on the pragmatic question of whether the surviving records of the scientific activity of the past are adequate for the reconstruction of creative discoveries at a level of resolution fine enough to respond to questions that psychologists, artificial intelligencers, and philosophers are asking about these processes.

Moments of Insight: Great and Small Leaps

Creativity in science, as in other areas of intellectual activity, is commonly portrayed as concentrated into relatively few momentous "flashes of insight," during which the solution of a puzzling problem, a major organizing concept, or a novel point of view appears suddenly to the scientist, who has been struggling up until then unsuccessfully within a received mental framework. If this is typical of patterns of discovery, then the historian who wishes to reconstruct the process is confronted with the difficult task of capturing events that not only are rare, but are unlikely to be preserved in the records that scientists customarily keep.

We must acknowledge, I believe, that true "moments" of insight, during which the first rudiments of novel scientific ideas are generated, are irretrievable. Whether we assume that they are produced in the subconscious mind or mark their origin at the point at which the investigator first becomes aware that he or she has "had an idea," it is inevitable that by the time the idea has been recorded on paper there will have been some further development. I have sometimes attempted to write down my own small insights as quickly as possible, in order to preserve them in their nascent form—but I have found it impossible. Even if one transfers the thought to paper within moments, subtle modifications occur during that process. The very act of writing out an idea merges the process of its generation with the initial stages of the pursuit of its implications.

The elusiveness of moments of creative insight has caused them to be regarded as intuitive, inspirational, or inscrutable. The main reason that they have appeared so, I believe, is not that they are intrinsically more mysterious than thought in general is, but that they are too ephemeral to be captured. Even the famous anecdotes of Kekulé, Darwin, Poincaré,[1] and others, record not the primordial insights that occurred to these people, but only retrospective references to the ideas involved and descriptions of the outward circumstances during which they took place. Our inability to freeze these creative instants is, however, less of a liability for our efforts to understand the genesis of creative scientific ideas than it might seem to be on the surface. If we do not have access to the initial form of an insight, we may nevertheless find recorded an idea that is sufficiently close to it for practical purposes. If we cannot reconstruct the precise psychological event of which the insight was the outcome, we can often circumscribe rather closely the conditions and considerations that probably gave rise to it. When we are fortunate, we can do so through documents recorded close to the time of the event; but we may also be able to draw conclusions about the character of the event from documents more distant chronologically, through inferences that are analogous to locating a physical object by triangulation.

There is another fundamental reason for optimism about the possibility of reconstructing creative scientific activity, if we agree with Gruber (1981a) that when the great flashes of insight are examined closely they tend to resolve into a series of smaller insights. Often the investigator forgets the secondary flashes which may precede or follow those dramatic experiences that impart a sense of immense significance accompanied by feelings that imprint them strongly in memory. My own historical experience has led me to a similar view. If we are able to retrieve from contemporary records of a scientist's work evidence for the less dramatic earlier and later experiences, we can sometimes show that a major conceptual gap that appeared at first to have been crossed in a leap of genius can be broken down into smaller gaps across which the investigator has stepped. This does not mean that the progression becomes a strictly logical one; it means only that it becomes less unfathomable. We may be able to reconstruct a series of moves that are more readily intelligible than the single great leap.

The Record of Creative Thought

These considerations lead us back to the historical documents apt to be available for such reconstructions. What kinds of records of their activity have scientists typically left behind? In the most favorable case we might hope for a combination of experimental records and notes, diaries or private journals, drafts of manuscripts, and correspondence which provides thick traces of interlocked thought and action. We are seldom fortunate enough, however, to find the full range of such sources for those individuals whose achievements we may most want to examine. For experimental scientists, the type of chronologically dense records most likely to have been kept are laboratory notebooks, which investigators maintain as standard practice. Such notebooks are normally kept regularly and fully, because they function in the investigations themselves as the repositories of data to be used in published papers and as guides for subsequent phases of the experimentation.

In recent years I have used surviving laboratory notebooks to construct accounts of the investigative activities of three different scientists—the eighteenth-century chemist Antoine Lavoisier, the nineteenth-century physiologist Claude Bernard, and the twentieth-century biochemist Hans Krebs (Holmes, 1974, 1985, in preparation). Notebook records such as those kept by these three distinguished scientists can, I have found, serve admirably as foundations for exploring the fine structure of scientific activity. At first glance they may appear unpromising—as opaque repetitions of a uniform format, as mere accumulations of data. It is not easy to "read" them in the sense that one reads ordinary texts. When one begins to interrogate them page by page, however, lurking behind the titles of experiments, the bare columns of figures, and the spare summaries of results, one can find implicit trails of daily human activity. When one examines the conditions under which a given experiment is carried out, in the light of all that has come before it, one can often infer the reasons the scientist had in mind for performing it, even if the reasons are not stated. When one has done this for an extended sequence of experiments, one can begin to sense where the scientist is heading, when he is routinely extending a previous line of investigation, when he is altering his course, when he is trying out something new. The most important advantage of laboratory notebooks over most other forms of documentation is that they can provide a nearly complete chronological backbone, around which we can create an exceptionally detailed narrative of an investigative venture.

The principal shortcoming of laboratory notebooks for this purpose is that, while they record fully the operations the scientist has carried out, they do not include systematically the thoughts that accompanied and guided what the scientist did. Some scientists write down in their notebooks their interpretations of the results of the day, reflections on the state of the problems with which they are dealing, or ideas for further experiments. Others put down little besides the data. In any case, the historian cannot count on such interpolations to explain the experimental moves that appear crucial to the reconstruction of the investigative pathway. Both the difficulty and the challenge in utilizing laboratory notebooks lie in the necessity to infer thought from traces of actions. The task is somewhat analogous to reconstructing someone's journey on foot from the nature and placement of the footprints left on the trail. There is no guarantee that it can be done correctly. I can only say that in my experience it has almost always been possible to make sense of the scientific activity whose tracks are deposited in the laboratory notebooks I have examined.

Some of what is typically missing from the notebooks can be supplied from other documents. By combining the chronology of an investigation embedded in the notebooks with knowledge of the ideas stated in the papers reporting the results of the investigation we can often infer the probable order of emergence of earlier forms of the ideas during the course of the investigation. If the scientist has carried on correspondence with colleagues, we may find nascent forms of new ideas in the letters. For Lavoisier I encountered a surprisingly rich record of the evolution of his ideas in surviving successions of drafts for the manuscripts of his published papers and in informal memoranda that preserve some of his private efforts to work out critical aspects of his scientific ideas. Neither of these last two types of document survive for Hans Krebs, but in compensation I had the opportunity to discuss his early work extensively with him, and even to go over with him page by page the portions of his notebooks most pertinent to his major discoveries. The information I could gather from these other sources enriches the picture one can construct of the scientific activity of these men; but I have found that it is nevertheless the laboratory notebook record that provides the strongest framework around which to recreate the investigative trail. That backbone record of daily activity enables one to organize a narrative dense enough to probe questions about the phases of scientific creativity at the level of intimacy that I believe can provide the most revealing answers.

A narrative account is, of course, not the only route toward understanding historic scientific discoveries. Telling a story has its own pitfalls. Moreover, we are often in the position of having no detailed chronological records available. Jerome Bylebyl (1973, 1979, 1982) was able to analyze deeply William Harvey's discovery of the circulation of the blood, despite the fact that there are only four surviving documents recording stages of Harvey's thoughts about and investigations of the heart and the vascular system over the 12-year period that it took him to arrive at his great creative achievement. From this record, from the *De motu cordis* in which Harvey made his discovery public, and from the contemporary configuration of the problem situation, Bylebyl has elicited penetrating insights concerning the reasoning and observations through which Harvey reached his discovery; but the sparseness of dated traces of Harvey's activity make it impossible to organize these insights into detailed narrative form.[2] Nevertheless, scientific discovery is a temporal process. When our documents permit it, we can make such processes most intelligible by following them as they unfold in time.

Lavoisier and the Theory of Respiration:
Slow Growth of an Idea

To illustrate the approach just described, I shall summarize some of the patterns of creativity that I have drawn from my studies of Antoine Lavoisier and Hans Krebs. Narrative accounts providing the level of detail required for the purposes I have outlined cannot be compressed into the bounds of a

FIGURE 3–1. Detail of the painting of Antoine Laurent and Marie-Anne-Pierrette Lavoisier, 1788, by Jacques Louis David. Purchase, Mr. and Mrs. Charles Wrightsman gift, 1977. (1977.10).

compact essay. I can only touch here on topics that I have described at length elsewhere.

Lavoisier (1743–94) is well known as the principal architect of the great chemical revolution of the late eighteenth century. Between 1772, when he first began to carry out experiments on processes that absorb or release air, and his death in 1794, Lavoisier transformed both the methods of investigation and the theoretical structure of chemistry (see chronology at the end of this chapter). He replaced the prevailing phlogiston theory of combustion with the oxygen theory, demonstrated that acids are composed of a base combined with oxygen and that water is a combination of hydrogen and oxygen, introduced, with the mathematician Laplace, the calorimetric method for measuring the heat released in physical or chemical processes, defined the gaseous state of matter, introduced the "principle of the balance sheet" as the axiom on which chemical experiments must be based, carried out the first elementary analyses of plant substances, developed the theory of respiration that has remained central to modern physiology, devised with his colleagues the chemical nomenclature that is still, in its general features, current today, and wrote an elementary textbook that provided the pedagogical basis for the reformed science.

I have not attempted to follow the full range of Lavoisier's scientific activity, but focused on those aspects of his investigations oriented toward the chemistry of animals and plants—notably on respiration, fermentation, and the composition of plant substances. His studies in these areas have generally been regarded as applications of the methods and theories that he had already worked out within the domain of mineral chemistry. With the aid of the unpublished documents previously mentioned, I have been able to show that these were problems with which Lavoisier was concerned from 1773, when he first set out on the broad research program of examining processes that fix or release air, and that his views on respiration were integral to the formation of his general theory of combustion. His laboratory notebooks enabled me to reconstruct Lavoisier's investigative efforts in these areas fully, with the exception of his last series of experiments on respiration in 1790. Informal memoranda, drafts of memoirs, and data sheets make it possible to follow at surprisingly close range the unfolding of his views on these subjects.

The core of Lavoisier's theory of respiration, as he stated it publicly in 1778, was a very simple idea. Respiration is a process analogous to the combustion of charcoal, in which oxygen is changed to "fixed air"[3] in the lungs, releasing the heat which maintains the temperature of the animal. Its simplicity, coherence, and novelty lend this theory the character often associated with those flashes of insight in which a scientist suddenly sees, in a single mental act, the solution for a difficult puzzle. Lavoisier himself (1862) referred to the theory, in the passage in which he stated it, as an "idea"; and an idea is something that often occurs as a unit.

From the record of Lavoisier's private thoughts we can learn that this idea did not emerge all at once; it was the outcome of at least several insights spread over four years; and earlier forms of the idea provided only partial solutions to a problem that had interested him throughout that prolonged period. The earliest record of an original idea about respiration is contained in a note that I believe Lavoisier wrote down, sometime between the fall of 1773 and the fall of 1774, on a folded sheet of loose paper. Under the heading "Ideas" he first summarized the view, attributed to unnamed predecessors, that the air that animals absorb through the lungs loses its elasticity and is absorbed into the animal economy. Then he added,

> Couldn't one surmise . . . that the heat of animals is sustained by nothing else than the matter of fire[4] which is disengaged by the fixation of the air in the lungs[?] It would be necessary to prove that whenever there is an absorption of air there is heat. But isn't the air itself composed of two substances, of which the lungs bring about the separation . . . of one of the two[?] (F. 350)[5]

The tentative form of this passage, cast as a query, the lack of elaboration, and the manner in which Lavoisier made alterations (not shown here) in the statement as he wrote it out give the strong impression that it represents an incipient phase in the emergence of a new insight. We should not infer, however, that this note is the immediate expression of Lavoisier's initial flash of insight. There are many possible relations between the first written form of an idea and the earliest awareness by a thinker that he has had one.

When this idea occurred to him, Lavoisier had already carried out a number of experiments involving respiration. These consisted mainly of tests of the effects on small animals of the various "airs" that he had been examining as part of his investigation of the processes that fix or release air. There appears to be no direct connection, however, between these results and the preceding idea. Rather, it seems to have resulted from his application to respiration of a combination of two very general ideas with which he was occupied at the time. One idea is that whenever an elastic fluid becomes "fixed" in a solid or fluidy body, it releases its "fire matter" as heat. The other is that common air may not be elementary, as traditionally supposed, but divisible into portions—portions that he could not yet identify in chemical terms. The simplicity of his new idea about respiration thus reflects the rudimentary state of his ideas about heat and about the composition of the atmosphere.

In February 1775 Lavoisier wrote down, again on a folded sheet, another idea about "the respiration of animals":

> The respiration of animals is . . . only a removal of the matter of fire from common air, and thus the air which leaves the lungs is in part in the state of fixed air. . . .
> This way of viewing the air in respiration explains why only the animals which respire are warm, why the heat of the blood is always increased in proportion as the respiration is more rapid. (F. 170)

Superficially this passage appears as a further development of the idea adumbrated in the first note. To his initial insights Lavoisier has incorporated an additional phenomenon associated with respiration, the fact that animals breathe out the species of air named "fixed air" by Joseph Black. Moreover, Lavoisier now stated in a more confident, fuller form, that the heat released in the process is the source of the heat of the animal. This statement also includes, however, an element that is incompatible with the former statement. Then he had surmised that respiration separates the air into two portions by absorbing only one of them. Now he described only the separation of "fire matter" from common air. He was, in fact, applying to respiration an idea he had discussed on another side of the same sheet of paper, that common air is changed to fixed air by the removal of its fire matter. This view allows no room for one of the central features of his earlier idea, that respiration absorbs one of the two portions into which common air is divisible; and it does not explain, as the earlier one might, why an animal in a closed chamber expires when it has consumed only a part of the air in which it is placed.

Thus Lavoisier had not attained a single theory of respiration able to account for all of the relevant phenomena, but two partially incommensurable ideas, each accounting for part of the phenomena. At this stage, his mental picture of respiration was incoherent; this was also the state of his views on the whole range of problems that confronted him concerning combustion, the calcination of metals, and the composition of the atmosphere. From this and analogous situations in which Lavoisier found himself repeatedly during his scientific career, I have suggested that, in moving from an existing conceptual structure to a new one, scientists often cannot make a single leap from one coherent mental framework to another. They may have to endure, for extended periods of time, deep fissures within their mental worlds. The image of the Gestalt shift, with its implication of an instantaneous transition, might well be replaced by the metaphor of a prolonged passage from one conceptual world to another.

In 1776 Lavoisier concentrated his attention on the calcination and reduction of mercury, and by this means clarified his conception of the composition of the atmosphere, even as he demonstrated his conception by the method of analysis and synthesis. Calcination[6] of metallic mercury absorbed a portion of the air in which he performed the operation. Reduction[7] of the calx then released an air which, when he added it to the residual air left from the calcination, constituted an air indistinguishable in its properties from ordinary air. Immediately following this experiment, Lavoisier carried out an analogous experiment which shows that he associated respiration at this time closely with the process of calcination. "Vitiating" the air under a jar with his own breathing, Lavoisier added to one part of the residue one fifth part of air derived from the reduction of mercury calx. The resulting mixture appeared to him to be common air. He concluded that "respiration, in absorbing air, renders a portion vitiated." The structure of the experiment indicates that he regarded the portion absorbed as identical with the air absorbed in the calcination of metals—that is, the air he eventually named oxygen. Thus he appeared at this point to have developed the first of the two ideas about respiration that he had written down earlier, by specifying the portion of the air absorbed. His preoccupation with the analogy to calcination, however, led him to exclude from his consideration that aspect of respiration represented in the second of his two notes about respiration, the formation of fixed air (Lavoisier, 1777).

Pursuing this line of investigation, Lavoisier placed birds under bell jars to examine the effect of their respiration on the atmosphere. At first he treated the results as he had the experiment on his own respiration. Along the way, however, he was forced to notice a crucial difference between respiration and calcination. The air left by respiration "precipitated limewater, whereas the air of calcination caused no change in it." Once his attention was directed to what he had, in fact, long known, that respiration has two effects on the atmosphere, he exploited that recognition brilliantly to complete his demonstration of these effects. Absorbing the fixed air resulting from the respiration in caustic alkali, he obtained a residue exactly like that left immediately in calcination. Now adding to this residue the air derived from the reduction of mercury calx, he was able to "reestablish . . . in its original state" the air in which the bird had respired (C. R-8, ff-9-19; F. 1349).[8]

Notwithstanding the fact that he had established experimentally that respiration absorbs oxygen from the atmosphere and releases fixed air into it, Lavoisier interpreted his results in a way that took cognizance only of the first of these effects. Preoccupied with his analogy between respiration and calcination, he constructed, in the first drafts of a paper on respiration, the theory that oxygen is absorbed from the lungs into the blood, where it imparts to the blood its red arterial color, just as the addition of oxygen to mercury forms a red calx. This theory simply left out the observation that fixed air is formed in respiration. Not until after he had rewritten his manuscript several times did there emerge an alternative theory, that "the effect of the respiration is to change the oxygen of the air into fixed air in the lungs." Even then he remained for a time more enthusiastic about his first theory, and one can follow in further revisions of his manuscript his struggle to reach a balanced assessment of the two theories. In his final version he presented them, in April 1777, as "equally probable" (F. 1349).

Lavoisier's first theory eventually faded from view, and the second became his theory of respiration. Simultaneously he shifted the analogy he used from calcination to combustion, a process in which oxygen is also changed to fixed air. Even then the theory did not account for the nature of this change, for at this time Lavoisier did not yet understand the relation between the composition of oxygen and of fixed air. During the next months that relationship became clear in his mind. He then saw fixed air as a combination of oxygen with the principal constituent of charcoal, later known as carbon. Together with that clarification, his theory of respiration as analogous to the combustion of charcoal took shape. Oxygen, he wrote in his paper on combustion,

after entering the lungs, comes out again in part in the state of fixed air. In passing through the lungs the [oxygen] . . . therefore undergoes a decomposition analogous to what takes place in the combustion of charcoal.

Now in the combustion of charcoal there is a disengagement of matter of fire; therefore there ought equally to be a disengagement of matter of fire in the lungs, and it is this matter of fire which is distributed with the blood throughout the animal economy and supports a constant heat. (F. 1316, p. 10)

The development of Lavoisier's theory of respiration outlined here illustrates the general point, stressed by Gruber, that creative scientific thought is not a set of isolated acts, but a process resembling growth. Lavoisier's theory of respiration grew gradually from the primordial ideas he wrote down in 1774 and 1775 into the coherent interpretation of his experimental findings that he put forth in 1778 as an integral part of his general theory of combustion. If space permitted, we could follow subsequent stages in the growth of his theory, as he and Pierre Simon Laplace established quantitative relationships between the respiratory formation of fixed air and of heat in 1783; as he expanded the theory in 1785 to include the formation of water; and as he came, by 1790, to see that the process involved the whole material balance of the "animal economy." A growth process, as Gruber notes, is typically slow. It took 17 years for Lavoisier's first ideas about respiration to grow into the mature theory of 1790.

Another factor to which I want to direct particular attention is that the second of the two theories of respiration that Lavoisier devised in 1776 and 1777—really a synthesis of the two ideas he had put down separately in 1774 and 1775—first appeared as he was revising a paper on the subject of respiration. This episode, together with other conceptual progressions that one can find in the successive drafts of some of Lavoisier's other scientific papers, led me to suggest that there is a closer connection between scientific creativity and scientific writing than has generally been noticed. It was in the process of composing his ideas on paper that Lavoisier sometimes came fully to grasp them, to see the flaws in them, to see how they could be further developed, or to perceive alternatives to what he had previously thought. Scientific papers are not merely reports of conclusions a scientist has already reached, but an important phase in the creative process itself.

Lavoisier and Fermentation: A Creative Struggle with the Data

Lavoisier's theory of respiration provided a framework within which much of the modern investigation of the metabolic processes of life has developed. Scarcely less germinal have been the views on alcoholic fermentation that he presented in 1789 in his influential *Elementary Treatise of Chemistry*. He summed up the process in the formulation "sugar = alcohol + carbonic acid," the first example of a chemical change stated in the form of an equation. He also gave a set of elaborate tables showing a complete balance among the carbon, hydrogen, oxygen, and nitrogen in the substances present before and after the process had taken place. He took this occasion to make his most general statement of the principle on which, he asserted, "the whole art of experiments in chemistry is founded": "Nothing is created in the operations of art, or in those of nature," so that there must be "an equal quantity of material before and after the operation."

Lavoisier's mature view of fermentation, like that of respiration, was the product of a long, gradual development. Fermentation had been one of his major scientific concerns ever since he began to study processes that fix or release air. His conception of the nature of fermentation underwent profound changes during that time. When he first took up the experimental investigation of the process in 1773, he was mainly interested in the apparent fact that fermentation released an air that was reabsorbed during a later stage, when the alcohol formed is further changed to an acid (Fric, 1959). When he next returned to the topic in 1784, he had come to regard fermentation as one of "nature's operations" that decompose water (Lavoisier, 1862). By the time he wrote the chapter on fermentation for his *Elementary Treatise,* he had exchanged this conception for an interpretation of the process as a decomposition of sugar, in which one portion of the sugar is reduced to alcohol while the other portion is oxygenated to carbonic acid (Lavoisier, 1789). These changes in his interpretation of fermentation were embedded in broader developments within the structure of his chemical theories.

A close study of the growth and metamorphosis of Lavoisier's ideas about fermentation through the documentary record is more difficult than is the study of respiration. His laboratory notebooks and data sheets, however, afford an exceptionally detailed reconstruction of the interaction between his conceptual framework and his experimental efforts to corroborate his views. His investigation of fermentation comprises the most complex and most challenging of his perennial struggles to realize in practice the "balance sheet" method whose introduction into chemistry is regarded as one of his historic achievements. In staking his scientific career on what has since become known as the conservation of mass, Lavoisier embraced a myriad of practical difficulties that he could never fully overcome. His study of fermentation highlights both the severity of the problems he confronted and his resourcefulness in contending with them.

Early in his investigation of fermentation Lavoisier realized that he could not attain a rigorous analysis of the process if he used the "highly composed" fruit juices which customarily served as fermentable substances. He elected instead to utilize cane sugar, a relatively simple substance, with whose qualitative elementary composition he was familiar. He had, however, to make repeated trials under varied conditions before he was able to produce an active fermentation with sugar, employing a small quantity of yeast to induce the sugar to ferment. The next problem with which he grappled was to contrive an apparatus that would enable him to measure the products of the fermentation as well as the quantities of sugar and of water consumed. He put together a closed system consisting of a flask, into which the fermenting mixture was placed, connected to two caustic alkali bottles, to trap the carbonic acid produced, and a pneumatic vessel into which the remainder of the gas passed. His measurements were repeatedly spoiled, however, by accidents such as leaks, the frothing over of the fermenting mixture, or the production of carbonic acid so rapidly that some of it escaped the caustic alkali. Since each experiment took weeks or months to complete, his progress was tediously slow (Lavoisier, 1789; C.R.-12, ff. 25–27, 135–143).

After several such failures Lavoisier decided, in April 1787, to simplify the experiment by carrying out the fermentation in a bottle and allowing the gaseous products to escape. This procedure did not permit him to measure directly the carbonic acid formed. He had to calculate that quantity from the loss of weight of the bottle, assuming that all, or very nearly all, of the gas produced was carbonic acid. To estimate the alcohol produced he distilled the fermentation solution left in the flask, measured the specific gravity of each of the fractions received, and compared these specific gravities with those of known solutions of alcohol in water (C.R-11, ff. 60–62; C.R-12, ff. 164–181).

At this stage Lavoisier's main objective was to show that the quantity of water left at the end of the fermentation was less than that initially present, in order to confirm his belief that the operation decomposes water. Along the way, however, he expanded his aim to construct the balance sheet of all of the substances involved in the process, as well as the elements composing them. This ambitious goal required him to know the elementary composition of each of the substances. For water and carbonic acid he had established in earlier investigations proportions of hydrogen and oxygen and carbon and oxygen, respectively, which he considered reliable. He also had carried out two combustion analyses of alcohol, the results of one of which he thought were satisfactory. Sugar, however, proved to be more recalcitrant, because it resisted complete combustion. During 1787 and 1788 he tried repeatedly to analyze sugar, with a variety of methods, but with very limited success (C.R-12, ff. 169–223; C.R-13, ff. 9–44).

Bogged down both in his primary experimental investigation of fermentation and in his supporting analyses of sugar, Lavoisier applied his ingenuity with calculations to the one fermentation experiment in which he had confidence—the simplified one mentioned above—in order to extract from it usable results. It would require much more space than is available here to follow him through the strategies that he employed, calculating and recalculating, changing his methods and his assumptions, until he had finally constructed the balance sheets displayed in his *Elementary Treatise*. These balance sheets did not provide an independent confirmation of the fermentation equation, or more generally of the principle of the conservation of mass. Rather, Lavoisier relied on what was for him the axiomatic truth of the principle to adjust one result through another, until he had arrived at an internally consistent set of tables representing the process (C.R-12, ff. 168–183; F. 1452; F. 345; Lavoisier, 1789). As he often did in other investigations, he pressed his data as far as he could to make them support his understanding of the phenomena he was measuring. This does not mean that he ignored persistent signals from his data that might indicate a need to modify his understanding. When, after repeated attempts to establish the quantity of water lost in the fermentation, he found that the deficit he was seeking to calculate had vanished, he gave up his strongly held view that fermentation decomposes water. In its place he devised the theory, previously mentioned, which has endured as the foundation for the modern understanding of the process. In general, however, Lavoisier did not give in easily when his results appeared not to fit his expectations. He regularly guessed at possible sources of error and made whatever corrections he thought reasonable to bring the results more closely into line with his theoretical needs.

I have argued (Holmes, 1985) that Lavoisier's practices in this regard were not a form of cheating, but were appropriate to the circumstances under which he was constrained to operate. Lavoisier essentially invented the whole mode of quantitative experimentation in chemistry on which he had to rely, and it was inevitable that such novel methods would contain more hidden pitfalls than he could hope to eliminate. To treat results that deviated from what his theories predicted as experimental errors rather than as indications of significant effects he had overlooked was, in most instances, good scientific judgment. Moreover, he often had to make do with flawed experiments instead of repeating them, because limitations of time and money permitted him to carry out relatively few of them compared to the standards of more recent eras. In managing his data to conform to his conceptual needs, Lavoisier displayed a pragmatic resourcefulness that I believe contributed much to his great creative achievements. In a later age, after the methods he pioneered had been refined by generations of experience, the same practices would have been scientifically irresponsible.

For nearly 20 years Lavoisier pursued a set of experimental problems that were distinct, but that shared central conceptual and methodological properties. These problems included especially combustion, calcination, respiration, fermentation, vegetation, calorimetric measurements, and the analysis of plant and animal matter. He shifted directions often, dropping one problem to take up another, and returning, sometimes years later, to the problem he had left. In the short term he appeared opportunistic, but in the long run he was remarkably consistent in maintaining a broad investigative program held together by multiple links between the subproblems it encompassed. I believe that his combination of flexibility and sustained purpose, the middle road between narrow concentration and scattered attention, was a characteristic of Lavoisier's scientific style important to the overall success of his investigative enterprise.

Hans Krebs and the Discovery of the First Metabolic Cycle

Hans Krebs (1900–1981) began his experimental career almost a century and a half after that of Lavoisier ended, under the very different conditions separating eighteenth- and twentieth-century science. Nevertheless, in trying to reconstruct his investigative pathway, I have found that in a broad sense

FIGURE 3–2. Hans Krebs in his laboratory at Sheffield in 1939. Photo courtesy of Philip P. Cohen.

Krebs's creative scientific activity can be approached, organized, and understood in ways comparable to the activity of Lavoisier.

Born in 1900 in Hanoverian Germany, Krebs entered medical school in the aftermath of World War I (see chronology at the end of this chapter). After completing his medical training in 1925, he had the opportunity to become a research assistant in the laboratory of the distinguished biochemist Otto Warburg. Warburg had developed methods for measuring, with sensitive manometers, the rates of respiration of thin slices of tissue placed in a fluid medium. As he learned these methods, Krebs saw that they might be applied to a wide range of currently unsolved problems in intermediary metabolism. In 1931, when he was able to begin experimentation on his own, Krebs undertook such a research program, first for a year at a hospital near Hamburg, then more intensively at the University of Freiburg. His general goal was to identify the specific chemical steps within the major pathways of intermediary metabolism. After a few brief forays into carbohydrate metabolism, he took up the problem of urea synthesis in the summer of 1931. Within a nine-month period he had achieved a major discovery, demonstrating a closed circle of reactions through which urea is synthesized from ammonia and carbon dioxide, a sequence that has become known as the ornithine cycle. During the following years, at Freiburg, Cambridge, and then Sheffield, he applied similar methods to other problems, including the deamination of amino acids, the synthesis of glutamine and of uric acid, the decomposition of fatty acids, and the formation of ketone bodies. In 1933 he took up the central metabolic problem of how carbohydrates are oxidized.

His early efforts brought little success. Stimulated to return to the problem in 1936 after Albert Szent-Györgyi had provided new experimental and conceptual insights relevant to it, Krebs, in 1937, with the aid of a paper published by Carl Martius on the steps in the decomposition of citric acid, was able to provide an elegant solution. His evidence for the existence of a cycle of reactions which he called the citric acid cycle, but which has since become known as the Krebs cycle, was a landmark in the history of intermediary metabolism. Biographical details can be found in his *Reminiscences and Reflections* (Krebs with Martin, 1981).

Thus during the first seven years of his independent career Krebs produced two discoveries of capital importance. Together they made the metabolic cycle one of the central organizing principles of the field. For nearly 50 years more he continued to pursue lines of investigation that he had begun during these productive years. From the full set of laboratory notebooks that survive, from my conversations with Krebs, and from other sources, I have recently reconstructed the detailed, day-by-day trail of his investigative pathway from 1930 to the publication of his classic paper on the citric acid cycle. Space does not permit me to summarize Krebs's investigations. I would like, instead, simply to enumerate a few characteristics of Krebs's scientific style that can be compared with what I have described for Lavoisier. First, there are some parallels.

Like Lavoisier's theory of respiration, Krebs's theory of the ornithine cycle was one of those creative solutions to a problem that appears so elegantly simple yet novel that we might expect it to have occurred to Krebs in an imaginative flash of insight. The scheme seems to provide the only conceivable pattern in which the known elements of the problem could be fitted coherently together—a pattern of the form that one might "recognize" in a single mental act. Nevertheless, Krebs described the solution as having "developed gradually as the ornithine effect was studied in detail." Although I pressed him repeatedly to identify the point at which he saw the solution, he never identified it with a specific circumstance of time or place.

My reconstruction of his investigation suggests that for a substantial portion of the several weeks that he estimated it took between the time that he had observed the ornithine "effect" and the time he arrived at a hypothesis to explain it, he was seeking solutions unsuccessfully in different directions. Eventually he reached a point at which he concluded that ornithine acted catalytically on the formation of urea from ammonia and that this action was somehow connected to a well-known reaction in which arginine gives rise to urea and ornithine; but he was, as he put it, for some time unable to visualize this connection. The two elements of the situation, in fact, seemed contradictory, because ornithine appeared to be a *product* of the reaction yet at the same time an agent catalyzing it. The solution consisted of seeing that if ornithine gave rise to arginine through a *different* pathway, there would be a closed circle of reactions, so that the ornithine would be continuously regenerated in the arginine reaction. The pathway that Krebs initially chose to close this circle was the simplest possible one; he merely added ammonia and carbon dioxide to ornithine to give a balanced equation for deriving arginine from ornithine (a little bit later he elaborated this pathway by seeing that citrulline was an intermediate; see Figs. 3–3 and 3–4). Thus the reasoning involved appears to consist of only one or two steps.

It is hard to imagine any coherent conceptual states intermediate between the contradictory situation and the solution. The time period over which Krebs passed from the one condition to the other may have been as short as a week or two—far less than the several years of formation of Lavoisier's theory of respiration. Nevertheless, the general point is the same. A solution whose nature suggests it might have occurred all at once actually formed gradually, and the investigator was forced to endure a period in which his mental picture of the situation was not fully coherent. The single flash of insight dissolves into a series of smaller ones, none of them brilliant enough to have left a lasting trace in Krebs's memory. The cumulative effect, however, was a solution as brilliant as if it had been one of those that strikes the mind in a sudden illuminating experience.[9]

Two Styles of Thought

For Krebs, as for Lavoisier, writing scientific papers was intimately involved in the development of his thought. Krebs did not save the drafts of his papers,

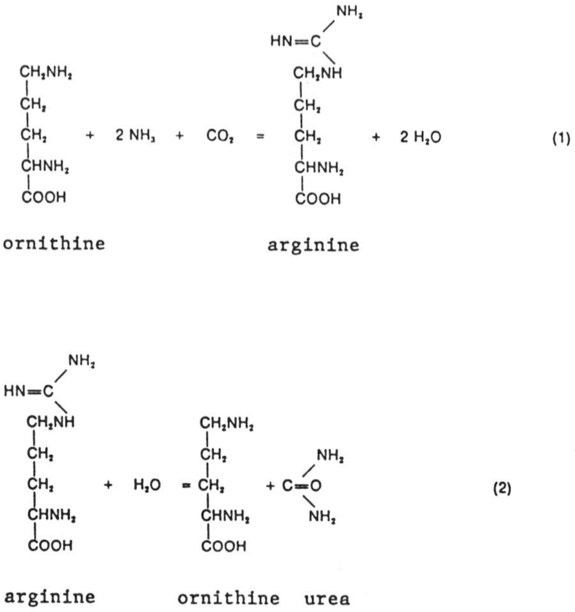

$$
\begin{array}{l}
\text{CH}_2\text{NH}_2 \\
\text{CH}_2 \\
\text{CH}_2 \\
\text{CHNH}_2 \\
\text{COOH}
\end{array}
\;+\; 2\,\text{NH}_3 \;+\; \text{CO}_2 \;=\;
\begin{array}{l}
\text{HN}=\text{C}\diagup^{\text{NH}_2} \\
\text{CH}_2\text{NH} \\
\text{CH}_2 \\
\text{CH}_2 \\
\text{CHNH}_2 \\
\text{COOH}
\end{array}
\;+\; 2\,\text{H}_2\text{O}
\qquad (1)
$$

ornithine   arginine

$$
\begin{array}{l}
\text{HN}=\text{C}\diagup^{\text{NH}_2} \\
\text{CH}_2\text{NH} \\
\text{CH}_2 \\
\text{CH}_2 \\
\text{CHNH}_2 \\
\text{COOH}
\end{array}
\;+\; \text{H}_2\text{O} \;=\;
\begin{array}{l}
\text{CH}_2\text{NH}_2 \\
\text{CH}_2 \\
\text{CH}_2 \\
\text{CHNH}_2 \\
\text{COOH}
\end{array}
\;+\;
\begin{array}{l}
\text{NH}_2 \\
\text{C}=\text{O} \\
\text{NH}_2
\end{array}
\qquad (2)
$$

arginine   ornithine   urea

FIGURE 3–3. The ornithine cycle as represented by Krebs in 1932 in H. A. Krebs and K. Henseleit "Untersuchungen über die Harnstoffbildung im Tierköper," *Klinische Wochenschrift, 11* (1932): 759.

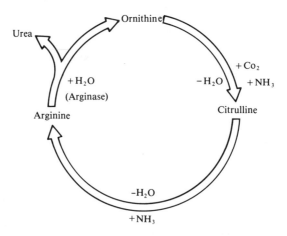

FIGURE 3–4. The ornithine cycle as represented by Krebs in 1933 in H. Manderscheid, "Über die Harnstoffbildung bei den Wirbeltieren," *Biochemische Zeitschrift, 263* (1933): 245.

so that I have not been able to reconstruct, as I could for Lavoisier, the ideas that emerged, were clarified, or were modified during the course of writing. Krebs told me, however, that he began writing his papers early in the course of an investigation. "I spent a lot of time on writing, but usually while the work was still going on. And I find in general only when one tries to write it up, then do I find the gaps. I cannot complete a piece of work and then sit down and write the paper."[10] Krebs's testimony therefore reinforces what I found in the drafts of Lavoisier's papers: scientific writing, at least for some scientists, is not merely a matter of reporting an investigation already completed or presenting a discovery already made; it is an integral part of the creative process.

The pattern of Krebs's investigative activity resembled that of Lavoisier in the contrast between short-term flexibility and long-term consistency. During his early research years he generated a repertoire of problems in intermediary metabolism that became, once he had taken each one up, more or less permanent interests. They included deamination, urea and uric acid synthesis, and carbohydrate and fatty acid oxidation. Each constituted a distinct problem, or set of subproblems, but they were linked by common methodologies and conceptual approaches. Krebs was frequently and easily diverted from one of these problems to another, interrupting himself for as little as a single set of experiments or as long as several years before returning to the investigative line dropped in the switch. He did not plan far ahead; in a sense he improvised, following up opportunities that seemed to turn up from day to day. Yet over the 50-year span of his research activity there is a remarkable continuity. The network of interrelated problems, and of similar ones that he added from time to time, constituted a broad research program that occupied his entire scientific life. And, as with Lavoisier, the combination of easy moves from one specific problem to another, with long-term steadiness of broad purpose, accounts for much of his effectiveness as an investigator. It allowed him to build up a set of methods and experience applicable to a growing range of problems that were related enough so that progress on one could often lead to progress on another; it also allowed him, when blocked on one problem, to avoid becoming bogged down by turning to another of his ongoing research interests.

There are, of course, equally prominent contrasts between the scientific styles of these two men. I will focus on just one facet of their differences in approach. Lavoisier carried out relatively few experiments on any given problem. Typically experiments were designed to support conceptual structures that were novel, deep, and persistent, in the context of the state of the fields he entered. Krebs carried out numerous experiments, day after day, most often to test out relatively simple ideas associated with a field that had grown far more complex over the intervening century and a half. The ideas that Lavoisier sought to verify were mostly aspects of an intellectual framework that he had constructed largely by himself. Krebs drew his initiating ideas mainly from a very active contemporary literature. Where Lavoisier treated anomalous quantitative results usually as errors to reason away in order to make them conform to his ideas, for Krebs anomalous results were among his most fertile sources of leads for new ideas. It was, in fact, the unexpectedly high rate of urea formation in liver tissue slices in the presence of ornithine that started him to thinking in the direction that led to one of his two most important discoveries.

Do such similarities and differences signify anything more than that scientists, like any other individuals, are alike in some ways and different in others? They can be more illuminating than that if we can connect differences systematically to differences in the circumstances under which scientists, working on problems that are in fundamental ways comparable, operated. In this case I think we can. Lavoisier could perform relatively few experiments because, with the limited technical means available in his time, they were difficult to carry out and because, with the limited social support for scientific research available in his era, he could not spend his full time on them. These limitations, the newness of the genre of experimentation he himself had invented, the fallibility of his apparatus—all made it reasonable to assume that anomalies were more likely to represent experimental errors than inadequacies in his hypotheses. Krebs, on the other hand, was the beneficiary of highly refined descendants of the experimental apparatus and procedures that Lavoisier had been the first to use. The manometric and other methods that Krebs employed enabled him to carry out many experiments, quickly and efficiently. The highly organized state of modern science enabled him to spend at least five times as much time per week on research as Lavoisier could. The precision of the twentieth-century methods made it much more likely that anomalies were not merely errors; and the ability to experiment more often and more effectively made it mandatory to repeat experiments rather than to shore up flawed results. Whereas it was most rational for Lavoisier to treat his anomalies as insignificant, or to manage them in such a way that they would not interfere with his preconceived positions, it was for Krebs most rational to treat anomalies as refutations of ideas he was testing, or as indicators of phenomena previously unaccounted for.

We should pause at the end to ask whether such comparisons between the styles of two scientific individuals—in particular between two so distant in time and temperament—are meaningful. I have no expectation that they can lead to inductive generalizations or causal accounts of scientific creativity. If, however, we accept the less ambitious criteria for fruitful investigation of scientific creativity outlined in the philosophical conference on discovery mentioned earlier—that such studies lead to a deepened understanding of the processes—then I think it is possible to claim something for comparisons of the sort I have sketched. In the long run that is for others to judge. Speaking subjectively I can only say that during my study of the investigative pathway of Hans Krebs, I have felt that I could better understand his position, or at least better situate it within the broader range of possibilities, by looking back at what I had learned from Lavoisier and from Claude Bernard.

CHRONOLOGY
ANTOINE-LAURENT LAVOISIER

1743	Born in Paris. Varied education: literature, law, science.
1764	First experiments in chemistry.
1766–67	Geological tours of France with Guettard. (Resulting theory of stratification presented to Academy in 1788.)
1768	Enters Ferme Générale, private agency collecting taxes and duties for government.
1769	Experimental proof that boiling water 100 days does not transmute water into earth (as believed by some). His first application of the idea that matter is neither created nor destroyed. Elected to Academy.
1771	Marries Marie-Anne-Pierrette Paulze, who becomes his collaborator and makes drawings and engravings for his work. No children.
1772–75	Oxygen produced, discovered, described by Scheele, Priestley, Lavoisier.
1772–78	Lavoisier's steps toward unified theory of respiration.
1773	First experiments on fermentation.
1775	Inherits father's title, buys country estate near Blois, begins agricultural experiments.
1777	His first critique of phlogiston theory of combustion.
1781–85	Studies of heat, water, and respiration.
1782–85	Collaboration with Laplace in studies of heat.
1783	Water not an element but a compound.
1785	Large-scale production of hydrogen for balloons, by recomposing water.
1785–89	Development of new chemical nomenclature.
1787	Experiments on fermentation of sugar.
1789	*Traité élémentaire de chimie* published.
1789–91	Financial work, bank director, member of commission establishing metric system.
1794	Guillotined.
1803	Lavoisier's *Mémoires de chimie* published by his widow.

CHRONOLOGY
SIR HANS ADOLF KREBS

1900	Born in Hildesheim, Hannover.
1918	Conscripted into German army. Begins medical training at Göttingen.
1925	M.D. degree, University of Hamburg.

1925–26	Hospital service, Third Medical Clinic, Berlin; first scientific publications, on cerebrospinal fluid.
1926–30	Research assistant in laboratory of Otto Warburg.
1930–31	Municipal Hospital, Altona, first independent research.
1931–33	Assistant in laboratory of Siegfried Thannhauser, University of Freiburg, discovery of ornithine cycle of urea synthesis.
1933	April: Dismissed from post by Nazi regime.
1933–35	Research in Biochemical Laboratory, University of Cambridge; discovery of synthesis of glutamine.
1935	Appointed lecturer in pharmacology, University of Sheffield.
1937	Discovery of citric acid cycle.
1938	Marries Margaret Cicely Fieldhouse. Three children, Paul, Helen, and John.
1939	Discovery of fixation of carbon dioxide in animal tissues.
1941–44	Wartime research on human dietary requirements.
1944	Establishment of Medical Research Council Unit for Research in Cell Metabolism at Sheffield.
1953	Nobel Prize.
1954	Appointed professor of biochemistry at Oxford.
1957	Discovery (with Hans Kornberg) of glyoxylic acid cycle in microorganisms.
1967	Retirement from Oxford, laboratory at Radcliffe Hospital in Oxford.
1981	Death in Oxford.

NOTES

1. Darwin related in his autobiography, concerning the problem of divergence in organic beings: "I can remember the very spot in the road, whilst in my carriage, when to my joy the solution occurred to me" (1958, pp. 120–121). For Kekulé and Poincaré, see Gruber (1981b).

2. Jerome J. Bylebyl, personal communication. For selected aspects of his study of Harvey, see Bylebyl 1973, 1979, and 1982.

3. "Fixed air" was the term used at this time to designate an "air" that Joseph Black had obtained in 1756 from *magnesia alba* and other mild alkalis. It was the first "air" recognized as specifically distinct from ordinary atmospheric air. When Lavoisier and his associates devised a new chemical nomenclature in 1787 they renamed fixed air carbonic acid gas. In the era of the atomic theory it was further identified as carbon dioxide.

4. Lavoisier believed, as many others in his time did, that heat was a subtle, weightless substance. At the time he wrote this note he called the substance "matter of fire." In the new nomenclature he named it "caloric."

5. F. 350 refers to the number of the "fiche" (sheet) by which Lavoisier's manuscripts are classified in the Archives of the Académie des Sciences in Paris.

Further references to the fiches in this essay are designated F. followed by the number, and a page number in cases where the manuscript is paginated. Titles of documents to which Lavoisier gave titles appear also in the references.

6. Calcination designated in eighteenth-century chemistry the action of fire on mineral or metallic substances. Often the substance acquired a white color and became powdery. See Eklund, 1975.

7. Reduction was the eighteenth-century term for a process that restored a metal or mineral to its original condition. See Eklund, 1975.

8. C. designates one of Lavoisier's cahier notes, catalogued in the Archives of the Académie des Science, Paris, as R-1 through 12. "ff" refers to folio (page) numbers. Further references to the cahiers will be given as C. R- .

9. I have given an account of the preliminary version of the discovery in *Federation Proceedings* (Holmes, 1980). A fuller account will appear in Holmes, F. L., *Hans Krebs: The formation of a scientific life* (in preparation).

10. Hans Krebs to F. L. Holmes, recorded conversation, April 29, 1977.

REFERENCES

Bylebyl, J. J. (1973). The growth of Harvey's De Motu Cordis. *Bulletin of the History of Medicine, 47*, 427–470.

Bylebyl, J. J. (1979). The medical side of Harvey's discovery: The normal and the abnormal. In J. J. Bylebyl (Ed.), *William Harvey and his age* (pp. 28–102). Baltimore: Johns Hopkins University Press.

Bylebyl, J. J. (1982). Boyle and Harvey on the valves and veins. *Bulletin of the History of Medicine, 56*, 351–367.

Darwin, C. (1958). *The autobiography of Charles Darwin.* London: Collins. original work published in F. Darwin (Ed.) (1887) *Life and letters of Charles Darwin.* New York: D. Appleton.

Eklund, J. (1975). *The Incompleat Chymist: Being an Essay on the Eighteenth-Century Chemist in his Laboratory, With a Dictionary of Obsolete Chemical Terms of the Period.* Washington, D.C.: Smithsonian Institution Press.

Fric, R. (1959). Contributions a l'étude des idées de Lavoisier sur la nature de l'air et sur la calcination des métaux. *Archives internationales de l'histoire des sciences, 12*, 161–167.

Gruber, H. E. (1981a). *Darwin on man: A psychological study of scientific creativity* (2nd ed.). Chicago: University of Chicago Press.

Gruber, H. E. (1981b). On the relation between "aha experiences" and the construction of ideas. *History of Science, 19*, 41–59.

Gruber, H. E. (1985). From epistemic subject to unique creative person at work. *Archives de Psychologie, 53*, 167–185.

Holmes, F. L. (1974). *Claude Bernard and animal chemistry.* Cambridge, Mass.: Harvard University Press.

Holmes, F. L. (1980). Hans Krebs and the discovery of the ornithine cycle. *Federation Proceedings, 39*, 216–225.

Holmes, F. L. (1985). *Lavoisier and the chemistry of life.* Madison: University of Wisconsin Press.

Holmes, F. L. (in preparation). *Hans Krebs: The formation of a scientific life.*

Krebs, H., with Martin, A. (1981). *Reminiscences and reflections.* Oxford: Clarendon Press.

Langley, P., Simon, H. A., Bradshaw, G. L., & Zytkow, J. M. (1987). *Scientific discovery: Computational explorations of the creative process.* Cambridge, Mass.: MIT Press.

Lavoisier, A. (1777 [Paris, 1780]). Expériences sur la respiration des animaux. *Mémoires de l'Académie des Sciences,* 186–187.

Lavoisier, A. (1789). *Traité élémentaire de chimie* (2 vols). Paris: Cuchet.

Lavoisier, A. (1862). Sur la combustion, en général. *Oeuvres de Lavoisier* (Vol. 2). Paris: Imprimerie Impériale.

Lavoisier, A. (1862). Mémoire dans lequel on a pour objet de prouver que l'eau n'est point une substance simple. *Oeuvres de Lavoisier,* vol. 2, pp. 357–359. Paris: Imprimerie Royale.

Lavoisier, A. (n.d.). Expériences sur la décomposition de l'air dans le poulmon, et sur un des principaux usages dans l'économie animale. Fiche 1349, *Archives of the Académie des Sciences,* Paris.

Lavoisier, A. (n.d.). Materiaux de la fermentation. Fiche 345. *Académie des Sciences,* Paris.

Lavoisier, A. (n.d.). Sur la combustion. Fiche 1316, *Archives of the Académie des Sciences,* Paris.

Lavoisier, A. (n.d.). Sur la fermentation spiritueuse. Fiche 1452, *Académie des Sciences,* Paris.

Nickles, T. (1980). Introductory essay: Scientific discovery and the future of philosophy of science. In T. Nickles (Ed.), *Scientific discovery, logic, and rationality* (Boston Studies in the Philosophy of Science, Vol. 56). Dordrecht: D. Reidel.

Wartofsky, M. W. (1980). Scientific judgment: Creativity and discovery in scientific thought. In T. Nickles (Ed.), *Scientific discovery: Case studies* (Boston Studies in the Philosophy of Science, Vol. 60). Dordrecht: D. Reidel.

4

Writing and Rewriting Poetry: William Wordsworth

LINDA R. JEFFREY

Repetitive activity is as essential in creative work as it is in everyday life. Repetition sometimes reflects simply the practical need to do the same thing yet again (like eating). Sometimes it is undertaken deliberately as part of an exploration of a complex enterprise. Each time we re-view something we re-vise it, seeing new aspects of the same thing.

In writing poetry the reviewing and revising are compounded since a form of repetition—reiteration—is a major poetic device for bringing home a point or strengthening an emotional effect.

In effect, exact repetition is almost impossible. Read a sentence aloud to a friend and ask her to repeat it. If it is longer than about 12 words, some variation in the wording will almost surely creep in, not to speak of innumerable variations in timing, stress, and inflection. Bartlett, in his book on *Thinking* (1958), analyzed thinking as a skilled act in much the same way. When we try to do exactly the same thing, we do it from the standpoint of the present, which includes every nuance of *this* moment, even including the fact that we have just done "it" before. So "it" evolves.

Repetition is a central idea in Piaget's discussion of the growth of the mind (Piaget, 1963). The baby tries to exercise already established schemata, for example, by trying to make an interesting sight reappear. Inevitably differences occur and the deviations from the previous version, or, better, from

FIGURE 4–1. William Wordsworth. From the drawing by W. Shuter, April 1798.

the established schema, are assimilated into the schema, thus nourishing and enriching it.

Gruber (1976) illustrated the point with a simple experiment in which observers looked at a three-minute filmed sequence of the motion of geometric objects (see Heider & Simmel, 1944) to which all viewers impute humanoid characteristics. In the experiment, the observers looked at the film three times and gave their interpretation of it at each viewing. Within the first moments of viewing observers began to develop a schema that served as a framework into which the rest of the film was assimilated. In subsequent presentations the observers attended to new themes, noticed new details, and modified their earlier formulation. Thus repeated contact with ideas or images enables a person to discover new meanings and to reorganize previously formulated views, reordering, elaborating, and condensing them. In this sense, revision is a systematic exploration of the multiform potentialities of a thing.

The main aim of this chapter is to explore how we can apply these ideas about the constructive function of repetition to an example of creative work, Wordsworth's composition of poetry. I shall be drawing on my analysis of the revisions involved in the two earliest versions of *The Prelude* (Jeffrey, 1983).

A key feature of William Wordsworth's poetry is its naturalism. He was among a few poets of his epoch who made the first break with previous poetic tradition—by trying to write in natural language about natural things. He was also a nature poet because he literally went into "Nature" in order to describe it. His walks were almost as much a part of his composing as were his words.

Among his contemporaries was John Constable, who was trying to do in painting what Wordsworth was doing in poetry. The two men had other features in common: they saw their childhoods as deeply rooted in a certain landscape to which they were passionately attached and which they considered the wellspring of their creative imagination. A natural phenomenon—the rainbow—resonated for both men and connected them: Wordsworth wrote a famous poem about the rainbow;[1] Constable made several paintings of rainbows and, moreover, copied Wordsworth's poem in his own hand. Although the rainbow is there for every one of us to see, in Wordsworth's time it was also an object of intense philosophical debate, for in some sense it is not "there" at all. Considering the optics of the rainbow brought home to the Romantics how reality results from the interaction of man and nature (Prickett, 1970).

Thus this naturalism was not achieved by simple spontaneity. It required a great deal of deliberate, knowing self-criticism and revision. In the course of writing his poetry, Wordsworth sometimes noted the need for revision. For example, in *The Prelude,* next to one passage he wrote "This is heavy and must be much shortened" (Wordsworth, Abrams, & Gill, 1979, p. 171).

The Prelude, a long autobiographical poem, is a story of revision at several different levels. Unpublished during Wordsworth's life, it exists in manuscript in three major versions now known by their approximate dates of composition spread over half a century—1799, 1805, and 1850.² But the earliest drafts, recorded in MS JJ,³ were composed in 1798, a year before the 1799 version.

In the evolving poem Wordsworth reflects on the origins of his own creativity and the role of Nature in the development of his mind. *The Prelude* is subtitled "The Growth of the Poet's Mind." Within each version there were changes. The poem itself is in good part about the reexperiencing of similar events with similar feelings under a variety of circumstances. Commentary or reflections are especially subject to change. For example, here is Wordsworth thinking about the origins of his own creativity. These four different versions (all drawn from Wordsworth, Abrams, & Gill, 1979) give some idea of the constants and variations of a passage:

1. *1798* (MS JJ)
The soul of man is fashioned and built up
Just like a strain of music. I believe
That there are spirits which, when they would form
A favored being, open out the clouds
As at the touch of lightning, seeking him
With gentle visitation; and with such,
Though rarely, in my wanderings I have held
Communion.   (p. 492)

2. *1799*
The mind of man is fashioned and built up
Even as a strain of music, I believe
That there are spirits which, when they would form
A favored being, from his very dawn
Of infancy do open out the clouds
As at the touch of lightning, seeking him
With gentle visitation—quiet powers,
Retired, and seldom recognized, yet kind,
And to the very meanest not unknown—
With me, though rarely, in my boyish days
They communed.   (p. 3)

3. *1805*
The mind of man is framed even like the breath
And harmony of music. There is a dark
Invisible workmanship that reconciles
Discordant elements, and makes them move
In one society.   (p. 46)

4. *1850*
Dust as we are, the immortal spirit grows
Like harmony in music; there is a dark
Inscrutable workmanship that reconciles
Discordant elements, makes them cling together
In one society.   (p. 47)

In MS JJ and 1799, the two opening lines with the musical metaphor for mind are followed immediately by another thought, that from the beginning of his life he had been selected as "a favored being" who had received "the touch of lightning." By 1805, the first part is expanded to five lines, the idea of conflict (discordant elements) is introduced, and the favored being passage (not quoted) is brought in later. In the 1850 version, the whole tone

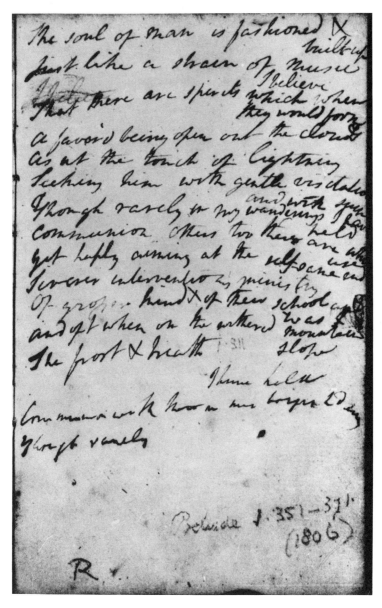

FIGURE 4–2. "The Soul of Man," page from MS JJ, 1798.

is much darker. The passage begins with "Dust as we are," "mind" has become "immortal spirit," "invisible" has become "inscrutable," and the favored being (in later lines not quoted) is now someone craving and earning a "calm existence."

Thus the constructive function of repetition is central to Wordsworth's philosophy of poetry and to his whole poetic experience. It works at three main levels: recollection, revision, and reiteration. Wordsworth's comment that poetry is "emotion recollected in tranquility" is an example of his beliefs about one such level.

Wordsworth in Goslar

The 1799 *Prelude* is a two-part poem of 978 lines. Initial worksheets for the poem are found in 24 pages of MS JJ written during the four and a half months from October 6, 1798 to February 23, 1799 that Wordsworth and his sister Dorothy spent in Goslar, Germany. In that winter of recollection and reflection, far from his beloved English Lake District, he thought long and deeply about memories of his childhood.

Wordsworth had planned to spend his time in Germany traveling and studying with his friend the poet Coleridge. The Wordsworths had spent the previous year in close contact with him, and the two poets had collaborated in the production of *Lyrical Ballads*. This volume of poems contains Coleridge's "The Rime of the Ancient Mariner" and Wordsworth's "Tintern Abbey." The trip to Germany was in part an effort to continue this productive intimacy.

Soon after their arrival in Germany in October 1798, the Wordsworths found that they could not afford to travel. They decided to remain in Goslar while Coleridge moved on to visit various universities.

During October and November of 1798, Wordsworth wrote drafts of *The Prelude*. They lived in the house of a widowed linen-draper. Provincial Goslar possessed few charms, as depicted in Dorothy's letter to their brother Christopher:

> Goslar is not a place where it is possible to see any thing of the manners of the more cultivated Germans, or of the higher classes. Its inhabitants are all petty tradespeople; in general a low and selfish race; intent upon gain, and perpetually of course disappointed. They cannot find in their hearts to ask a stranger a fair price for their goods. The woman of this house who is a civil and good kind of respectable woman *in her way* could not refrain from cheating us of halfpence and farthings when we first came. (Hill, 1985, p. 31)

In a letter to Mary Hutchinson, who would later become Wordsworth's wife, Dorothy described their life in Goslar:

> We are not fortunately situated here with respect to the attainment of our main object, a knowledge of the language . . . for there is no society in

Goslar, it is a lifeless town. . . . So we content ourselves with talking to the people of the house, etc. and reading German. . . . We have plenty of dry walks; But Goslar is very cold in winter. (DeSelincourt, 1935, pp. 202–203)

Entering society was difficult in Goslar for a man traveling with his sister. The Wordsworths were looked upon with suspicion because "sister" was a German euphemism for mistress (Margoliouth, 1953). Moreover, as Dorothy wrote to their brother Christopher (Hill, 1985, p. 30), the costs of returning social favors required funds they did not have.

Dorothy's complaint about the lack of society suggests that the Wordsworths were disappointed in their isolation. There is a sense, however, in which William and Dorothy thrived in relative isolation. For a brother and sister, theirs was a relationship of unusually complex and passionate affection. Wordsworth wrote these lines about his sister:

> My hope, my joy, my sister, and my friend,
> Or something dearer still, if reason knows
> A dearer thought, or in the heart of love
> There be a dearer name
> (cited in Beer, 1978, p. 155)

Thus, although the Germans among whom they lived did not offer much social stimulation, the Wordsworths still had each other.

In Goslar Wordsworth followed his usual pattern of frequent long walks. In his poetry, however, he did not describe the German scenes surrounding him, but rather drew upon childhood memories of the English Lake District. Reflective solitude and introspection characterized the Goslar period. Brett and Jones (1963) suggest that it was this period of his life he was thinking of when he wrote that poetry arises from "emotion recollected in tranquility." However, Dorothy's description of his state of mind in Goslar in the letter to Mary Hutchinson suggests that he was more disquieted than tranquil, and that the poetry did not emerge without struggle: "William is very industrious; his mind is always active; indeed, too much so; he overwearies himself, and suffers from pain and weakness in the side" (DeSelincourt, 1935). The compulsive quality of Wordsworth's efforts is further suggested by his statement in a letter written to Coleridge from Goslar, "When I do not read I am absolutely consumed by thinking and feeling and bodily exertions of voice or of limbs, the consequence of those feelings" (quoted in Parrish, 1977, p. 8).

MS JJ: The Beginning of an Enterprise

The 24 pages of drafts in MS JJ constitute the initial worksheets for Part I of the 1799 *Prelude*. About 30% of Part I of the 1799 version (143 lines) first appear in MS JJ and are included unchanged in the 1799 version. Another 52 lines appeared in their initial form in MS JJ but were reworked before being included in the 1799 version.

After these drafts were written, the Wordsworths left Goslar, traveling for a period in Germany before returning to England in early May. They then settled at Sockburn, the home of Wordsworth's future wife, and Wordsworth began writing again. By the end of 1799, approximately a year after the MS JJ drafts were begun, Wordsworth had completed the two-part *Prelude.*

In 1801 he began to revise and extend the two-part version, and by 1804 he had nearly completed a five-book version. In 1805 he wrote a 13-book version, but before long he was again at work. In 1839 he prepared a 14-book version, which was eventually published posthumously. Thus this unpublished poem occupied his attention intermittently for 40 years.

The poem was never definitively named during Wordsworth's lifetime. It was referred to as "the poem to Coleridge" by the members of Wordsworth's circle. In MS JJ drafts, however, he addressed his reflections to Dorothy, as he had in "Tintern Abbey."

MS JJ: Earliest Drafts of the 1799 Prelude

The theme of the MS JJ drafts is Nature's formative role in Wordsworth's development. They consist of approximately 420 lines. By my count only 26 of these did not bear fruit for the 1799 *Prelude,* for a later version, or for some other poem. Of lines that reached paper, at least, Wordsworth discarded very little. Lines or fragments that did not serve current purposes were saved for later.

Lines composed early in the MS JJ drafts became the opening of the 1799 *Prelude;* lines composed toward the end of the drafts became the conclusion of Part I. Thus the broad outline of Part I as a whole was worked out in MS JJ. There are over a hundred revisions in these drafts, mostly instances in which Wordsworth substituted a word, phrase, or line for another. Rarely did he delete material without replacing it.

Individual pages vary markedly in their number of revisions, ranging from 12 to none with an average of about four. The number of revisions declined as composition proceeded, suggesting that an interactive process developed between the poet and his poem. The growing structure of the poem both guided his composition and limited his alternatives. As the plan for the poem became more clearly worked out, Wordsworth made fewer revisions.

Echoes of Childhood

On what is probably the first page of MS JJ (Parrish, 1977, p. 115), Wordsworth began an exploration of his childhood memories of the river Derwent, the stream that ran behind the Wordsworth house in Cockermouth, his birthplace. Wordsworth used the sound of the river as his initial metaphor for the shaping force of Nature in his development:

> was it for this
> That one, the fairest of all rivers,
>   loved
> To blend his murmurs with my nurse's song
> And from his alder shades and rocky falls
>   t ⎫
> And from his fords and shallows send   ⎬
>   ⎭
>   a voice
> To intertwine my dreams

The image of the Derwent's sound blending with other sounds had already figured in two unpublished sonnet fragments Wordsworth had written before 1798. These fragments may be among the first sources for *The Prelude* (Jaye, 1969, p. 47). In the first of these, he had written the lines:

> Derwent again I hear thy evening call
> Blend with the whispers of these elms that meet
> [a] ~~with~~ in shadowy glen through wh[ich]
> Round this dear lodge nor as the moon I greet
> That scene to rock as rock their ?summits tall
> ⎧ And ⎫ ⎧ T   ⎫
> ⎨ But ⎬ ⎨ Think ⎬ how I have watched the leaves that fall
> ⎩   ⎭ ⎩   ⎭
>   (Jaye, 1969, p. 46)

In both the Derwent lines of MS JJ and this fragment from years earlier, the gentleness of the sounds, their pleasant harmony, and their associations with home and hearth are recalled. He uses similar words in the two accounts to describe his memories. Sensory impressions of the river and its setting remained with Wordsworth as salient memories and he drew upon them as he began to compose in MS JJ.

In a second fragment, also written before the 1798 drafts, Wordsworth again invoked images of the river and surrounding elms and mountains:

> Yet once again do I behold the forms
> Of these huge mountains and yet once again
> Standing beneath these elms I hear thy voice
> Beloved Derwent that peculiar voice
> Heard in the stillness of the evening air
> Half-heard and half created.
>   (Jaye, 1969, p. 49)

Here, as in the MS JJ draft, the sound of the river is a "voice." This auditory image becomes a statement of Wordsworth's sense of his creative relationship with Nature. The voice of the Derwent is "half-heard and half created." Nature, in other words, sends her shaping, formative message to an active mind.

Further elucidation of the schema underlying the initial MS JJ *Prelude* drafts may be achieved by comparing them with a second fragment and "Tintern Abbey," the poem Wordsworth wrote just before he traveled to Germany. They are all similar in important ways. In the fragment the poet "yet once again" beholds the scene of mountains, elms, and a river. In the opening stanza of "Tintern Abbey" the poet reiterates the words "again" and "once again" four times, including the line "Once again I see. . . ." Memories of the Derwent appear in the fragment and the initial page of MS JJ while recollections of the "sylvan Wye" unify "Tintern Abbey." Moreover, the phrase "half-heard and half created" from the fragment is echoed in these lines from "Tintern Abbey":

> Therefore am I still
> A lover of the meadows and the woods,
> And mountains; and of all that we behold
> From this green earth; of all the mighty world
> Of eye, and ear, —both what they half create,
> And what perceive . . .
> (Hutchinson & DeSelincourt, 1967, pp. 164–165)

Over an extended period Wordsworth used similar vocabulary to represent the childhood memories that were of great sensuous richness and of philosophical importance to him. As he began to compose in MS JJ, he used an image which had already been expressed in previously written poems, and which had already been used to symbolize his theory of the role of Nature in the development of his mind. He began MS JJ with phrases reminiscent of his earlier representations of the river Derwent: "blend his murmurs," "from his alder shades," and "sent a voice / To intertwine my dreams." These phrases are recorded in MS JJ without revision. However, at the point where the similarities to the earlier fragments end, fair copy ends also, and drafting with revision begins.

Writing Backward: A Strategy for Moving Forward

One of the striking features of Wordsworth's MS JJ worksheets is the apparently convoluted sequence in which he wrote them. He did not simply begin with the first page and write on succeeding pages in sequence. Rather, starting at the back of the notebook, he proceeded forward to a fresh page, sometimes using the next unused recto, sometimes skipping to the facing verso (Parrish, 1977). Although this zigzag procedure appears at first glance chaotic or indicative of disorganized floundering, a closer examination reveals an underlying pattern. Wordsworth's characteristic procedure in MS JJ was to skip two pages, write on the third, and work backward, filling in the pages until the previously written material was reached. An example of this sequence would be the following:

Order of notebook page: 1 2 3 4 5 6
Sequence of writing: 3 2 1 6 5 4

His pattern of page use helped him to proceed in an exploratory fashion even if he did not have a firm notion of the destined length or specific contents of the poem. Page-skipping allowed him to proceed in tentative steps while at the same time establishing structural limits. He could be tentative but not paralyzed by indecision.

In effect, he carved out three-page segments which he could expand and link together as the poem grew. The fact that he allocated a certain amount of space and then worked backward, filling up the pages, indicates that although he may not have known precisely what he was going to write, he probably had a sense of how much he wanted to say about each segment. If he decided to increase this amount, he would either elaborate a previous segment or create a new one. Either of these moves was signaled by the page-skipping action.

Implicit in this procedure of skipping two pages to begin on the third is a special role for the third page as the first page of new composition separated from previous drafts by two blank pages.

Poetic Reiteration

Very early in the worksheets a pattern emerges in which Wordsworth describes dramatic memories of his childhood in the lakes and mountains of Cumbria followed by commentary describing the role of Nature in the shaping of his mind. These memories are introduced by the question "Was it for this?" The "this," according to Parrish (1977, p. 6), was a "powerful disturbance of mind occasioned by a superabundant flow of inspiration" expressed in the first page of MS JJ as:

                                    trances of thought
          And mountings of the mind compared
                                    to which
          The wind that drives along th   autumnal
                                    lefa
          Is meekness
                         (Parrish, 1977, p. 117)

Such a disturbance of mind is consistent with his and Dorothy's descriptions in their letters while he was writing the MS JJ drafts. In effect, he was asking "Was it for this powerful burst of poetic inspiration that Nature shaped my mind in childhood?"

Wordsworth's repeated question led him to particular memories in his boyhood. Later he was to call these memories "spots of time," and he would think of them not only as "links with a past self, but [as] sources of adult confidence and creativity" (Wordsworth, Jaye, & Woof, 1987, p. 79).

Each childhood memory was followed by commentary in which Wordsworth thought further about the meaning of these events in his development and their connection with his current self—an issue he had already raised in "Tintern Abbey." By repeating the scheme of childhood-memory-plus-commentary, each time with a different memory, he clarified and elaborated the significance of the memories as he constructed the poem. Through this repeated cycle of reviewing and reflecting, the poem evolved.

Each of the multiple memories Wordsworth evoked is an example of a childhood encounter with the shaping forces of Nature. Thus each is a re-exploration of the same theme. At the same time, each varies markedly in individual detail. To exploit repetition in this way Wordsworth made use of rich experience and feeling, an organizing scheme, childhood-memory-plus-commentary, and the refrain "Was it for this?" I include two examples from the 1799 *Prelude* of memories of this kind. The first describes the boy Wordsworth, at night, robbing traps set for woodcocks:

> . . . scudding on from snare to snare I plied
> My anxious visitation, hurrying on,
> Still hurrying, hurrying onward, how my heart
> Panted: among the scattered yew-trees and the crags
> That looked upon me, how my bosom beat
> With expectation. Sometimes strong desire
> Resistless, overpowered me and the bird
> Which was the captive of another's toils
> Became my prey, and when the deed was done
> I heard among the solitary hills
> Low breathings coming after me and sounds
> Of undistinguishable motion, steps
> Almost as silent as the turf they trod.
>
> (Parrish, 1977, p. 44)

This episode was not much revised from version to version. It illustrates a pattern Wordsworth often used: event and commentary, in this case illicit adventure then guilt. The second illustration describes a boat-stealing episode. Again, it was night:

> . . . It was an act of stealth
> And troubled pleasure . . .
> Small circles glittering idly in the moon,
> Until they melted all into one track
> Of sparkling light . . . twenty times
> I dipped my oars into the silent lake,
> And, as I rose upon the stroke, my Boat
> Went heaving through the water, like a swan—
> When from behind that rocky steep, till then
> The bound of the horizon, a huge Cliff,

> As if with voluntary power instinct,
> Upreared its head: I struck, and struck again,
> And, growing still in stature, the huge cliff
> Rose up between me and the stars, and still
> With measured motion, like a living thing
> Strode after me. With trembling hands I turned,
> And through the silent water stole my way
> Back to the cavern of the willow-tree.
> (Parrish, 1977, pp. 45–46)

Both these episodes were acts of "troubled pleasure." The description of his emotional reaction in the boat-stealing episode is more elaborate and complex. The repetition of "struck" and the reference to "trembling hands" express the boy's panic. In both episodes Nature is animistic, personified.[4] Both show how the boy Wordsworth experienced Nature as a domain in which to do things but also as a Being scrutinizing his acts. Thus the boyish freedom he enjoyed in his beloved landscape was coupled with its price, guilt.

In the boat-stealing episode, Wordsworth's commentary describes the lasting emotional impact of the experience:

> . . . huge and mighty forms, that do not live
> Like living men, moved slowly through my mind
> By day, and were the trouble of my dreams.
> (Parrish, 1977, p. 46)

The emotional impact of the trap-robbing episode is powerfully increased in the more complicated account of the boat-stealing. While the footsteps of the trap-robbing episode were escapable, retribution for the boat-stealing is represented by an omniscient Nature, inescapable and ominous. Taken together, the two episodes intensify the emotion and elaborate the scheme of Nature as a moral force.

Revision

Wordsworth's use of multiple memories, variations on a theme, illustrates the constructive role of repetition in the creative process. This role is also evident in MS JJ at another level: where Wordsworth makes repeated attempts with the same passage. For example, the emotional description of the looming pursuing cliff as the embodiment of his wrongdoing and his punishment was composed in two steps. In the first version the lines are ordered as follows (the numbering is mine):

1. I struck and struck again
2. And growing still stature the huge cliff
3. With measured motion like a living thing
4. Strode after me

5. Rose up between me & the stars & still
6. With measured motion like a living thing
7. Strode after me

In the second version of this passage, the phrases are ordered:

1. I struck & struck again
2. And growing still in stature the huge cliff
3. Rose up between me and the stars & still
4. With measured motion like a living thing
5. Strode after me

Omitting the first "with measured motion like a living thing" and the first "strode after me" makes the image of looming more direct and powerful: "the huge cliff / rose up between me and the stars." This sets the scene for the menacing sequel, the cliff "like a living thing / strode after me."

An analysis of Wordsworth's drafts of another childhood memory, the raven's nest episode, also reveals the use of revisions in the evolution of an individual passage. He describes a time in spring when he would roam the mountains, climb to a vantage point above a raven's nest, and cling to the rocks as the winds blew all around him. The winds seemed so strong that it was as if they supported him as he clung to the rock face. The 1799 version of this passage reads:

> . . . Oh, when I have hung
> Above the raven's nest, by knots of grass
> Or half-inch fissures in the slipp'ry rock
> But ill sustained, and almost, as it seemed,
> Suspended by the blast which blew amain,
> Shouldering the naked crag, oh, at that time,
> While on the perilous ridge I hung alone,
> With what strange utterance did the loud dry wind
> Blow through my ears! the sky seemed not a sky
> Of earth, and with what motion moved the clouds!
>   (Parrish, 1977, p. 44)

A plausible reconstruction of Wordsworth's efforts to compose these lines can be made from the evidence left in the MS JJ worksheets. We begin with the following draft from MS JJ:

{ W
{ [?]ith what strange utterance did
                          wind
                          ~~the loud dry~~
Blow through my ears, ~~what colours~~
                          ~~what motion did~~
                          ~~The co~~   ~~the cloud~~
                          ~~the lou~~

```
                                    the colours of the sky
                                             ⎧ not
      Wh                          The sky was ⎨ then
                                             ⎩ no sky
```
Of earth & whith what motion move the cloud,
As on the perilous brink cliff

(Parrish, 1977, p. 109)

To describe the sound of the wind, its "strange utterance," he initially chose the adjectives "the loud dry." Even though this phrase appears in the 1799 version, it apparently did not satisfy him at the outset, and he drew a line through it.

When he tried to describe the sky, he vacillated between two aspects, the motion of the clouds and the colors of the sky. "What colours" was rejected for "what motion did," which was in turn rejected for "The co," probably the beginning of "the colours" again. "The cloud" was followed by "the lou," probably the beginning of another attempt at "the loud dry." This was deleted in favor of "the colours of the sky." As Wordsworth struggled to express his experience of the scene, he thus fluctuated between two of its features in the following progression:

Feature	*Wordsworth's Line*
color of the sky	what colours
motion of clouds	what motion did
color of sky	The co
clouds	the cloud
sound and feel of wind	the lou
color of sky	the colours of the sky

At this point in the drafts he had drawn a line through the phrase "the loud dry," which would later appear in the 1799 *Prelude,* and had left undeleted the phrase "the colours of the sky," which is not found in the 1799 version. His drafts reveal that his memory for this event included a sensation of a particular way the sky appeared, which did not find expression in the poem. Thinking about the color of the sky, and repeatedly trying to describe its hue, however, probably helped him to construct the lines "The sky was no sky / Of earth." Thus a descriptive detail that was discarded nevertheless played a part in describing the memory of his experience. The constructive efforts apparent on this page of drafts support, in the domain of writing, Arnheim's statement about artistic creation, "A picture is not thought out and settled beforehand. While it is being done it changes as one's thoughts change" (1962, p. 30).

Wordsworth drew a line to separate this passage of drafts from the revisions of the passage that follows: the last line of the first section of drafts, "As on the perilous brink cliff," becomes the first line of the new version and indeed is placed there in the 1799 *Prelude.* He generated "brink" and "cliff" in succession, as if he wanted to see both possibilities on the page before him.

Having drawn the line below the first passage, and having begun again, Wordsworth changed the line to read:

ridge cliff   alone
While on the perilous ~~edge~~ I hung
(Parrish, 1977, p. 109)

In this new variation he eliminated "brink," kept "cliff," and added "ridge" and "edge." Again he wrote the variants in succession. The adjective that appears in the 1799 version of the line was the second to last variant, "ridge." While "ridge" was selected by Wordsworth as the best variant, his decision was based on a progression of thought involving the other variants. His practice, from time to time, of generating a number of alternatives seems to resemble divergent thinking, that is, the random production of alternatives, with the work of selection deferred. However, it is important to note that the alternatives were related to one another, and each enabled him to clarify the image he was trying to represent. Each alternative contributed to the final selection. This is an example of constructive repetition in which directed variation leads to clarification of meaning.

The idea behind a collection of "spots of time" is that of a psychological device of a very high order. It allows the reliving of the complex experiences constituting a life. Each spot is a train of thought, extended in time as an event, as Wordsworth relieved it and reviewed its meaning. Such spots can flick across the mind in an instant or can be deeply probed as Wordsworth did.

Collaborative Revision

Wordsworth's living arrangements facilitated bringing others into the process of reworking. This was true of his collaborative relationship with Coleridge and more pervasive and longlived in his relationship with his sister Dorothy.

Dorothy was an extremely sensitive observer and recorder of the Lake District landscape scenes where she and her brother lived and walked. Wordsworth's famous poem "The Daffodils," composed in 1804, finds its source in the vocabulary and images of Dorothy Wordsworth's *Journal* where she describes the daffodils she and her brother had seen on a walk together. Wordsworth's poem begins:

I wandered lonely as a cloud
That floats on high o'er vales and hills,
When all at once I saw a crowd,
A host of golden daffodils—
Along the lake, beneath the trees,
Ten thousand dancing in the breeze.
(Hutchinson & DeSelincourt,
1967, p. 149)

Dorothy had described the scene in her *Journal* in April 1802:

I never saw daffodils so beautiful they grew among the mossy stones and about them, some rested their heads upon these stones as on a pillow for weariness and the rest tossed and reeled and danced and seemed as if they verily laughed with the wind that blew upon them over the lake, they looked so gay, ever glancing, ever changing. (Moorman, 1985, p. 109)

Thus one of the best known of English poems begins with a joint experience, a scene observed by William and Dorothy. It was subsequently reviewed and transformed, at least into another medium, by Dorothy when she wrote her *Journal* entry. Wordsworth, using Dorothy's description, as well as his own recollection of the experience, transformed the experience again. The poem concludes:

> The waves besides them danced, but they
> Outdid the sparkling waves in glee—
> A poet could not but be gay
> In such a laughing company.
> I gazed and gazed, but little thought
> What wealth the show to me had brought.
>
> For oft when on my couch I lie,
> In vacant or in pensive mood,
> They flash upon that inward eye
> That is the bliss of solitude,
> And then my heart with pleasure fills
> And dances with the daffodils.

As he had often done before, Wordsworth included a comment on his experience, since he was, as ever, interested in its current impact on his mind and in moving from the sensuous to the reflective. This, then, was a further revision of the original event, a transformation of the experience by the "inward eye."

What Is Poetry?

As we have seen in the drafts of *The Prelude* all this revision, reflection, and reworking was not for the purpose of eliminating or reducing emotional impact. The idea that poetry has its origin in "emotion recollected in tranquility" does not, after all, mean that *poetry* is tranquil. On the contrary, "poetry is passion," Wordsworth said. He added, "It is the history or science of feelings" (Wordsworth, Jaye, & Woof, p. 63). As we shall see, he had other things to say on the subject.

For Wordsworth, writing was a form of thinking. The three R's—recollection, revision, and reiteration—were the carriers of a larger process of reflective abstraction through which primordial experience was both recaptured and transformed. Some distance in time and space from the original events which are the subject of his poetry is necessarily imposed. This helps to make sense of the fact that *The Prelude* was begun during a stay in Germany, and not in a scene connected with his boyhood haunts.

In *The Prelude* Wordsworth said that he needed this time between raw experience and composing, that it was not his custom to "make a present joy the matter of my song" (Prelude 1805, Book I, line 56; Wordsworth, Abrams, & Gill, 1979, p. 30). This was of course an echo of his more famous dictum in the preface to *Lyrical Ballads* that poetry "takes its origin from emotion recollected in tranquility." But a fuller reading of the same passage shows how conscious he was of the role of prolonged contemplation and reiteration in reviving the original experience in all its power:

> I have said that poetry is the spontaneous overflow of powerful feelings: it takes its origin from emotion recollected in tranquility: the emotion is contemplated till, by a species of reaction, the tranquility gradually disappears, and an emotion, kindred to that which was before the subject of contemplation, is gradually produced, and does itself actually exist in the mind. In this mood successful composition generally begins, and in a mood similar to this it is carried on. (Owen & Smyser, 1974, p. 148)

But this is not to say that the poem so composed does nothing but reconstitute the original event. Wordsworth aspired to be a philosophical poet, to find some system of meaning through the contemplation of experience. In the same preface, in an equally celebrated passage, he wrote:

> For all good poetry is the spontaneous overflow of powerful feelings: and though this be true, Poems to which any value can be attached were never produced on any variety of subjects but by a man who, being possessed of more than usual organic sensibility, had also thought long and deeply. For our continued influxes of feeling are modified and directed by our thoughts, which are indeed the representatives of all our past feelings; and as by contemplating the relation of these general representatives to each other, we discover what is really important to men, so, by the repetition and continuance of this act, our feelings will be connected with important subjects. (p. 126)

The original experience to which he refers was not only the sensory and motor life of childhood. As Wordsworth tells it, for example, in the trap-robbing and boat-stealing episodes cited earlier, the child—at least the child favored by the touch of lightning—experiences Nature, to be sure, as the source and scene of his pleasures, but also as a moral force. The boyish exploits he recounts would not amount to any more than just that, were they not transmuted by this moral sensibility and brought to a new level of abstraction in the course of years of reflection.

To what has already been said a new dimension might be added. During a stay in revolutionary France, Wordsworth had experienced a passionate love affair and fathered a child, Anne Caroline, born in Orléans in 1792, when Wordsworth was 22. In effect, Wordsworth abandoned the mother, his first great love, and the child. It has been suggested by Herbert Read (1968) that an enduring sense of remorse grew upon Wordsworth after a delay of some years. Thus, the hypothesis runs, Wordsworth was at the height of his poetical powers from about 1797 to 1807 and then suffered a decline during the rest of his life, although not without intermittent bursts of successful creativity. Whether the whole of Read's hypothesis is true or not, in 1798, when Wordsworth began to compose *The Prelude,* his lost child was about six years old. It is not far-fetched to say that memories are grouped and regrouped according to their emotional coloration (Bower, 1981), that the dramatization of boyhood guilt was also a projection of the remorse he was currently feeling.

As an autobiographical poem, *The Prelude* is Wordsworth's attempt to make sense out of his life as a whole. Today, we are moving from attempts to understand individual acts of creation toward explaining the working of a creative life as a whole. We need to connect our interpretation of what the poet said about his life with our knowledge of how he lived it.

CHRONOLOGY
WILLIAM WORDSWORTH

1770   Born in Cockermouth, Cumbria.

1771   Dorothy Wordsworth born in Cockermouth, Cumbria.

1787   Goes to St. John's College, Cambridge.

1791–92 Receives B.A.
        Goes to France, meets Annette Vallon.
        Birth of daughter.

1793   First visit to Tintern Abbey.

1797   William and Dorothy move to Nether Stowey, near Coleridge.
        Dorothy Wordsworth begins *Alfoxden Journal.*

1798   *Lyrical Ballads* published.
        Wordsworths and Coleridge go to Germany.
        Wordsworths stay in Goslar.
        Wordsworth writes *Nutting* and other poems, begins drafts of 1799 *Prelude.*

1799   Wordsworths return to England, *Prelude* drafts completed.
        Wordsworths move to Dove Cottage, Grasmere.
        Dorothy Wordsworth begins Grasmere *Journal.*

1801   Wordsworth composes *Rainbow.*

1802   Wordsworths visit Annette Vallan and William's daughter in Calais.
        Wordsworth marries Mary Hutchinson.

1804   Completes *Daffodils,* working on *Prelude.*

1805   Finishes 13-book *Prelude.*

1831   Revising *Prelude.*

1834   Coleridge dies.

1839   Last revision of *Prelude.*

1843   Appointed Poet Laureate.

1850   Dies. *The Prelude* published.

NOTES

1. My heart leaps up when I behold
   A rainbow in the sky:

   So was it when my life began,
   So is it now I am a man,
   So be it when I shall grow old,
     Or let me die!

   The child is father of the man;
   And I could wish my days to be
   Bound each to each by natural piety.
       William Wordsworth, *The Rainbow*
       (Hutchinson & DeSelincourt, 1967,
       p. 62)

2. The version known as "1850" was mainly composed in 1838–39. It was published in 1850 after Wordsworth's death by his widow, Mary, who named it *The Prelude*.

3. MS JJ is the name given to Wordsworth's "MS Drafts and Fragments," which contains the first drafts of *The Prelude* of October 1798 to February 1799.

4. This personification of Nature in Wordsworth's work later became known as the "pathetic fallacy"—the attribution of human emotions or characteristics to inanimate things.

REFERENCES

Arnheim, R. (1962). *The genesis of a painting.* Berkeley: University of California Press.

Bartlett, F. C. (1958). *Thinking.* New York: Basic Books.

Beer, J. (1978). *Wordsworth and the human heart.* New York: Columbia University Press.

Bower, G. H. (1981). Mood and memory. *American Psychologist, 36,* 129–148.

Brett, R. L., & Jones, A. R. (Eds.). (1963). *Lyrical ballads.* New York: Barnes & Nobles.

DeSelincourt, E. (Ed.). (1935). *The early letters of William and Dorothy Wordsworth (1787–1805).* Oxford: Oxford University Press.

Gruber, H. E. (1976). Créativité et fonction constructive de la répétion. *Bulletin de Psychologie de la Sorbonne [Numéro spécial pour le 80ᵉ anniversaire de Jean Piaget], 30,* 235–239.

Heider, F., & Simmel, M. (1944). An experimental study of apparent behavior. *American Journal of Psychology, 57,* 243–259.

Hill, A. (Ed.). (1985). *Letters of Dorothy Wordsworth: A selection.* Oxford: Clarendon Press.

Hutchinson, T., & DeSelincourt, E. (1967). *Wordsworth: Poetical works.* London: Oxford University Press.

Jaye, M. (1969). *The growth of a poem: The early manuscripts of William Wordsworth's The Prelude.* Unpublished doctoral dissertation, New York University.

Jeffrey, L. (1983). *The thinker as poet: A psychological study of the creative process through an analysis of a poet's worksheets.* Unpublished doctoral dissertation, Institute for Cognitive Studies, Rutgers University.

Margoliouth, H. (1953). *Wordsworth and Coleridge 1795–1834.* London: Oxford University Press.

Moorman, M. (Ed.). (1985). *Journals of Dorothy Wordsworth* (2nd ed.). New York: Oxford University Press.

Owen, W., & Smyser, J. (1974). *The prose works of William Wordsworth* (Vol. 1). Oxford: Clarendon Press.

Parrish, S. (Ed.). (1977). *The Prelude, 1798–1799 by William Wordsworth.* Ithaca, N.Y.: Cornell University Press.

Piaget, Jean. (1963). *The origins of intelligence in children.* New York: Norton.

Prickett, S. (1970). *Coleridge and Wordsworth: The poetry of growth.* Cambridge: Cambridge University Press.

Read, H. (1968). *Wordsworth.* London: Faber & Faber.

Wordsworth, J., Abrams, M. H., & Gill, S. (1979). *The Prelude, 1799, 1805, 1850, William Wordsworth.* New York: Norton.

Wordsworth, J., Jaye, M. C., & Woof, R. (1987). *William Wordsworth and the age of English Romanticism.* New Brunswick, N.J.: Rutgers University Press.

FIGURE 5–1. Michael Faraday (1791–1867). A contemporary drawing from *Fraser's Magazine*, February 1836, p. 233, artist unknown.

5

Fields of Enterprise:
On Michael Faraday's Thought

RYAN D. TWENEY

Michael Faraday, the English physicist (1791–1867), is best known for his discovery of electromagnetic induction. He was one of the first thinkers to break from classical physics and to move toward modern field conceptions in physics (see, e.g., Berkson, 1974; Einstein & Infeld, 1938; Miller, 1984; Nersessian, 1984). The recent surge of interest in Faraday also rests on the fact that his diaries, notebooks, and correspondence form a historical record that is perhaps more complete than that left by other scientists. Faraday is thus a natural testing ground for understanding the process of scientific thought from historical, philosophical, sociological, and psychological points of view (Tweney, Doherty, & Mynatt, 1981). The richness of the surviving Faraday documents is exemplified well in the collection of papers edited by Gooding and James (1985). My own approach to Faraday has been based on cognitive psychology. In other articles, I explored the nature of his experimental strategy (Tweney, 1984), his use of an organized knowledge base (Tweney, 1985), the procedural underpinnings of his thought (Tweney, 1987), the microstructure of some of his research (Tweney & Hoffner, 1987), and, using Faraday as a case study, presented a general framework for a cognitive analysis of science (Tweney, 1985, 1988). This chapter traces the creative evolution of some of Faraday's theoretical views, providing, as I hope to show, a fine perspective from which to appreciate the nature of Faraday's creativity.

There is poetic justice in considering the life and work of Michael Faraday from the standpoint of the evolving systems approach. Gruber (1974/1981) was among the first to emphasize the potential value for an understanding of creativity of the "chancy interaction" among seemingly disparate aspects of a person's thought. "Only connect" is the message for the scholar seeking insight into creative genius as well as for the creative thinker: to understand creative products we must connect together seemingly disparate activities and show their relation to the person whose product they are. Faraday's aptness as a case study of this sort reflects his position in the history of physics; he too emphasized the interrelatednes of disparate parts. By showing the intimate connection between electricity and magnetism, by showing their relation to the nature of light, by extending and confirming the view that electricity is involved in the fundamental construction of all matter, and, last but not least, by challenging the particulate ("Newtonian") view of physical reality with a persuasive alternative (space-filling fields of force), Faraday too is saying "only connect."

The evolving systems approach shows how the concept of networks of enterprise can clarify creative endeavors (Gruber, 1988; Wallace, 1985). For the case at hand, is the approach that is the focus of this book a useful framework? I will attempt to show that it is by considering Faraday's work from two distinct points of view, each of which will then be shown to reflect a common basis. On the one hand, I will describe the evolution of Faraday's field concept from its earliest manifestations to its later, fully developed form. Here we will see the inner coherence displayed by the evolution of the concept of field, and we will see its consistency with Faraday's metaphysical presuppositions. On the other hand, I will describe the evolution of his scientific methodology, again from its earliest manifestations. Finally, I will show that the two descriptions, of theory and of method, complement each other in a surprising fashion: Faraday's methodology and his field concepts are in fact different manifestations of a single developing world view, a product of Faraday's fundamental reliance on a procedural epistemology fully consistent with his ontological assumptions. For Faraday, knowledge was anchored in concrete action; "abstract" knowledge was a secondary, derived entity. In the same way, physical reality for Faraday was anchored in concrete forces; "matter" was a secondary, derived entity.

The Context: Faraday's Life and Milieu

At the beginning of the nineteenth century, the triumph of Newton's approach to physical science was at its peak. Newton's *Principia* (1687/1942) was revered as the very model of science, and the conceptions of physical reality which Newton developed were seen by many as a key to understanding all of the phenomena of the universe. For Newton, matter, time, space, and force were givens. His system was astonishingly successful at describing the relationships among these concepts, but it did not explicitly justify the assumed essential nature of any of them. Matter was seen as hard and impenetrable, the ultimate reality of the universe. Material bodies ɾ ˙ted on each other through forces that acted in straight lines and were instantaneously transmitted through the intervening space: "action-at-a-distance" was central. The inverse square law precisely expressed the mode of action of such forces. What the forces were in any absolute sense was not specified, tractable though they were mathematically. The remarkable success of Newton's conception in explaining planetary motions using gravitational forces led to attempts to reduce all physical phenomena to similar processes. By the end of the eighteenth century, models of electricity, for example, were based on the motions of hypothetical fluids following Newtonian laws. It seemed plausible at the time because, after all, even electrostatic charges attracted and repelled each other in ways that confirmed the inverse square law (Heilbron, 1979). If such models could be made to work, then the Newtonian concept of action-at-a-distance would be further supported (Williams, 1966).

Even so, there was a fair amount of discomfort associated with the notion of action-at-a-distance. Newton's views implied that matter was hard and impenetrable, that "ponderable" (roughly meaning "weighable") matter was the opposite of "empty space." But if so, how were forces propagated? Many scientists sought to develop theories that relied on "imponderable" matter (an ether) as a way out of this difficulty. Unfortunately, no such model met the rigorous criteria of observational and experimental support that Newton's own system had established as an ideal. In this context, it is not surprising to see the variety of metaphysical gymnastics that flourished in the late eighteenth century around this issue. Humphry Davy, Faraday's mentor and among the most revered British scientists in the first years of the nineteenth century, was such a gymnast. A committed Newtonian, Davy nonetheless was heavily influenced by distinctly non-Newtonian ideas derived from the neo-Kantian views of Coleridge, Priestley, and Boscovich (Forgan, 1980). Unlike his school-trained peers, however, Faraday did not feel constrained by Newtonian notions. While many felt uncomfortable with action-at-a-distance, Faraday simply rejected it altogether. To account for this requires a look at Faraday's life.

The rags-to-riches story of Michael Faraday, a blacksmith's son and lowly bookbinder's apprentice who rises to a prominent position in science, has been told many times; there is a Horatio Alger quality to Faraday's life that has attracted readers since the last century (see especially Thompson, 1898; Tyndall, 1868; and Williams, 1965). Born in 1791 of humble parents, Faraday received only a rudimentary education at a day school before being apprenticed to a London bookbinder at the age of 14. While he successfully carried out his assigned tasks, Faraday was an unusual apprentice in that he liked to read books as well as bind them. Soon launched on a deliberate program of self-education, he became well versed in science and in 1812 was given a ticket to attend four lectures by Humphry Davy at the Royal Institution. Having taken careful notes, he expanded them into full sentences and carefully bound them. Hearing later that Davy needed a bottle-washer, Faraday sent the bound notes to Davy asking for the position. In 1813 Faraday was employed as Davy's assistant, and began, in effect, an apprenticeship in science. By 1816, at age 25, he was publishing his own scientific papers and had begun his career as a creative scientist (see chronology at the end of this chapter).

Clearly possessed of both talent and willingness to work, Faraday rose rapidly, eclipsing his mentor's substantial reputation. In 1821 he published a paper on the rotation of a current-carrying wire in a magnetic field (the first "electric motor") and in 1831 made his monumental discovery of electromagnetic induction. His career is divisible for our purposes into four broad periods: (1) the 1820s, the period of his first researches on electricity and magnetism; (2) the 1830s, when he discovered induction and explored its consequences (3) the 1840s, during which he publicly elaborated his theory of the nature of fields and supported it with further discoveries; and (4) the 1850s and 1860s, a relatively inactive period, closed by his death in 1867.

Events in his early life have consequences for Faraday's creativity, particularly for his unique approach to thinking about science. Thus, perhaps because he was self-educated, he never mastered the use of mathematics as a tool for the further understanding of physics. This gave him a peculiar advantage in an era when the occasional straitjacketing effects of a formal approach were often overlooked, and when mathematical representations were accepted as prerequisites for research and for theoretical insight. Faraday's religious beliefs as a Sandemanian Dissenter may also have had profound consequences for the development of his scientific strategies: there was a religious warrant for the moral imperative to read "the Book of Nature," but there was also a warrant for the possibility that one could easily misread it (Cantor, 1985). This, as we shall see, justified Faraday's unusual appreciation of the dangers of confirmation bias (see below). Finally, the fact that Faraday was apprenticed as a bookbinder is not irrelevant. His work gave him access to texts that a person of his social and economic status could not otherwise have afforded. In this way he first learned about electricity from the *Encyclopedia Britannica* and about chemistry from an 1809 copy of Jane Marcet's *Conversations on Chemistry*. Further, binding is a skilled manual craft and there is reason to believe (from the surviving examples of his work) that he was extremely good at it. Here we perhaps see the origins of his "hands-on" approach to knowledge.

Faraday's field theory was the first to dispense, in a productive way, with the notion that physical reality is primarily a manifestation of the properties of matter. For him, fields of force were the primary reality, and "matter" a secondary or derived phenomenon. To understand his creative life, then, we must acknowledge his position as a revolutionary, as someone who demonstrates the practicality of a world view completely different from the prevailing one, and who does this not by metaphysical argument but by a series of compelling experimental demonstrations of such conceptual force that they cannot be ignored.

Faraday was a prolific experimenter; the laboratory was an almost continuous way of life. He left notes on an estimated 30,000 separate experiments (an average of about two per day), among which are dozens of momentous discoveries: electromagnetic induction, the "ice pail" experiment, "Faraday's law" of electrolysis, diamagnetism, and the magnetic rotation of polarized light (the "Faraday effect"), to name just a few. Experimentation is the epitome of hands-on science. By placing his drive to learn by doing in the service of his presuppositions, Faraday was able to develop and refine those presuppositions until some of them reached the status of finished scientific concepts. Faraday's creativity was thus no idle flash of insight, nor was it achieved without an enormous amount of work. To see this requires a close look at the development across several decades of his scientific views on the nature of fields and forces.

The Development of Field Theory

As Gruber (1974/1981; 1988) made clear, a network of disparate enterprises provides the elements of a creative rearrangement and an underlying sense of the continuity and purpose of the network. If we trace the evolution of a particular system through the mental life of the creator, these aspects can become manifest. In the case of Faraday I shall focus on his conception of field and show its increasing elaboration across time as well as his slow recognition of the unity of the conception among diverse experimental problems.

Defining Faraday's notion of field is, of course, the first requisite, one that, as shown by Nersessian (1985), has sometimes been a problem for scholars. The difficulty arises in part because Faraday himself often hedged his true beliefs, being wary of asserting claims that he could not conclusively demonstrate experimentally. In any event, for the purpose of this chapter, Faraday's concept of field will be taken to include the notions that matter is an epiphenomenal consequence of force (Faraday, 1844), that forces are manifested as substantive (but nonmaterial) lines of force varying in intensity, direction, and number. These forces are capable of penetrating ordinary matter and are infinitely extendable (Faraday, 1852a). As corollaries, Faraday held that there was no action-at-a-distance and no ether in the sense of an imponderable but material medium serving as the vehicle for the transmission of force. Faraday believed that all forces were interconvertible (though he demonstrated this only in the case of magnetic and electric forces).

From the earliest stages of his career, aspects of the mature field conception were present. Thus as early as 1816 he may have regarded matter as a property of force (rather than the reverse). He had little to go on at this time beyond Davy's demonstrations of electrolytic decomposition: if a current is passed through a solution containing a dissolved salt, the elemental constitu-

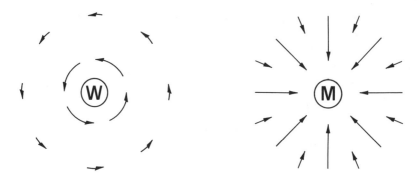

FIGURE 5–2. Left: transverse forces surrounding a current-carrying wire W, shown in cross section. Right: radial forces surrounding a gravitational mass M.

ents of the salt can be separated out (Davy, 1812; Fullmer, 1980). This suggested that electricity was somehow involved in the construction of matter.

In 1820 the Danish scientist Hans Christian Oersted demonstrated that electric currents produced magnetic fields. When a current is passed through a wire, the wire acts as if it were a magnet. Heavily influenced by *Naturphilosophie,* Oersted described his discovery in the context of a unity-of-force world view which Faraday, perhaps under the influence of Boscovich and certainly through the influence of Davy, found quite congenial.

Nevertheless, anomalies remained. In particular, why were the induced magnetic forces in Oersted's experiment not directed radially but transversely? If one passes an electric current through a wire that penetrates a card and sprinkles iron filings on the card, the filings line up in regular ways. But instead of pointing toward the wire—as one would expect if the magnetic forces are directed radially, that is, toward the wire (see Fig. 5–2, right)—the filings form concentric circles on the card (Fig. 5–2, left). The magnetic forces induced by an electric current thus seemed to be directed transversely, not radially. This seemed to violate every prior conception of how forces worked. Gravitational forces were inverse square forces directed radially from a source. The same was true for electrostatic forces acting between like or unlike charges. But induced electric and magnetic forces differed. Why? A good deal of mathematical ink was spilled in attempting to solve this problem. In particular, within weeks of Oersted's discovery the French scientist and philosopher André-Marie Ampère developed a theory of ordinary magnetism as the result of rotating electrical currents within solids: magnetic forces were only apparently curved, a by-product of their origin. The resolution offered by Ampère found many followers, in part because it seemed to rescue the Newtonian action-at-a-distance character of force (Williams, 1965, 1966).

Electromagnetic Induction and the Focus on Transients

If electricity could produce magnetism, why not the reverse? Why shouldn't magnetism also produce electricity? There was nothing in Ampère's theory (or anyone else's) that seemed to rule this out. For the next 10 years this was one of the hottest problems in European science. It was resolved in 1831 when Faraday discovered electromagnetic induction: changing magnetic fields produced electrical currents in nearby conductors (Faraday, 1832a). Even prior to this discovery, however, Faraday had put his unusual conception of force to good use.

The notion of fields has early origins in Faraday's thought, origins closely tied to his first notions of force. His earliest notebooks show a preoccupation with the problem of understanding forces. How could the earth attract the moon when there is apparently nothing intervening? How could a lodestone attract an iron nail? Why did some charges attract and others repel? In a notebook kept in 1809–10, the young bookbinder's apprentice copied out many journal and magazine articles that reflect such concerns. In 1816, in his commonplace book, the young scientist wrote the following under the marginal heading "Questions":

"Bodies do not act where they are not" Query—is not the reverse true? Do not all bodies act where they are not; and do any of them act where they are? (1816b, p. 324)

Later he quoted Laplace, under the heading "Philosophy":

The true march of Philosophy consists in rising by the path of Induction and calculation from phenomena to laws and from laws to forces. (1816b, p. 335)

In a series of lectures on chemistry given during the same year, Faraday explicitly identified forces as properties of matter (the usual conception, but one he must have felt uncomfortable arguing) but he was just as explicit about the central explanatory role of force (Faraday, 1816a): the forces of gravitation, electricity, and magnetism explained observed attractions and repulsions as well as all manifestations of cohesion and affinity such as chemical combination. Perhaps this accounts for his predominantly chemical interests during the 1820s. Chemistry was the key to understanding the role of force in cohesion and affinity. Even better, action-at-a-distance can be ignored in chemistry—a field in which, by and large, "bodies do not act where they are not."

Oersted's discovery in 1820 reawakened Faraday's speculations about forces. In an 1822 "idea book" he developed his ideas in the form of a number of experimental questions, many of which he tried in later years (Faraday, 1822). The primary idea was, of course, the great issue of whether magnetism could induce electricity, but we also see reflections on the possible induction of electricity by gravitational forces, by heat, and by solar rays. The *unity* of force was clearly on his mind. In 1821 and 1822 he published a three-part "Historical Sketch of Electro-magnetism" (Faraday, 1821–22) in which a good deal of space was given to Ampère's attempt to reduce magnetic effects to the action of electrical forces. Also in 1821 Faraday published his first scientific papers on electricity, a lovely series of experiments in which a current-carrying wire was made to rotate in a magnetic field and even in the earth's magnetic field. He was relatively silent about the larger consequences of these studies, though he did explicitly argue that the experiment proved that the forces were truly transverse, not radial. An 1823 entry in his laboratory diary clarifies the importance of his finding. In discussing certain further rotational experiments, he wrote:

> It appears the action does not regard the material substance at the centre but simply the current of electricity or the magnetic pole, the substance merely giving locality to the power. (January 21, 1823, in Faraday, 1932–36, vol. 1, p. 93)

This comment implies an important advance in his thought: material substances provide a locality for the operation of forces, but forces have an independent reality and are not reducible to mere attributes of matter.

By 1823 Faraday still did not have the empirical support needed to demonstrate, even to his own satisfaction, a sufficiently strong rationale for such a conception of force. If he was correct, Faraday should be able to show something about the properties of these immaterial but physically real entities. Gooding (1985) showed that Faraday typically moved from vague "construals" through explicit "proving experiments," to "demonstration experiments" suitable for the lecture hall. Such experiments were not available until the great discovery in 1831. In that year, Faraday showed that passing a current through a coil could induce a current in another coil held nearby, but only during the instant when the current in the first coil was either being switched on or being switched off. It took a *changing* current—that is, a changing magnetic force—to produce induction. Similarly, holding a bar magnet stationary near a wire induced no current, but a current could be detected if the magnet was in motion.

Why did Faraday not discover induction until 1831? Raising this question allows us to see with fascinating clarity the mechanism of the discovery itself. Faraday (and many others) had repeatedly tried to generate electricity from magnetism, but all of the attempts failed because everyone was looking for steady-state currents. The 1831 discovery has sometimes been cited as an example of a sudden flash of insight on Faraday's part, as if it suddenly occurred to him to look for transient currents. In fact, however, Faraday's research just before August 1831 shows that he was preoccupied with transient effects in a variety of domains: acoustics, auroral phenomena, spontaneous ignitions in hot gases. A focus on transients was the last piece of the puzzle needed to make the discovery, and by August all of the pieces were available to Faraday (Tweney, 1985). Here we see a series of enterprises in which relevant "scripts" and "schemata" come together in what appears to be a "chancy interaction" to produce a new result. Yet the result is hard to construe as *merely* chance, since Faraday's entire way of thinking about physical reality contributed to the result. The appearance of transient themes in all of his enterprises in 1831 signals a cross-fertilization with his work on induction.

After an initial short-lived attempt to explain induction by postulating a special state of matter, the "electrotonic state" (Faraday, 1832a), he instead considered the curved lines in which induced currents acted and reified the curves:

> When an electrical current is passed through a wire, that wire is surrounded at every part by magnetic curves, diminishing in intensity according to their distance from the wire, and which in idea may be likened to rings situated in planes perpendicular to the wire. (Faraday, 1832b, in Faraday, 1839–55, vol. 1, p. 67)

For Faraday, the curved patterns of force became real curves, immaterial but substantial entities that can be cut by a moving conductor (thus inducing a current), can be considered as moving or at rest, and can be considered as possessing numerosity—the more curves cut, the greater the induced current.

Lines of Force

Faraday's 1831 discovery was followed by two major research efforts, one to establish the identity of the different forms of electricity (static, voltaic, and induced), and one to develop a deeper understanding of the process of electrolytic decomposition. Each seems like a diversion from the grand program of field theory, yet each was an important step. No unity of force conception (and hence no satisfactorily simple field theory) was tenable unless it could first be shown that we were dealing with a single set of phenomena. These identity experiments (Faraday, 1833) have been held up as a model of the scientific demonstration of unity amid seeming variety (Harré, 1981). Following this, Faraday conducted a brilliant series of studies on electrolytic decomposition in which the end result was a precise law: "For a constant quantity of electricity, whatever the decomposing conductor may be . . . the amount of electro-chemical action is also a constant quantity" (1834, in Faraday, 1839–55, vol. 1, p. 145). We see here the transition from phenomena to law spoken of by Laplace. For the notion of fields, the result is even deeper; Faraday had shown that the usual action-at-a-distance theory of electrolysis was wrong (Williams, 1966). Electrolytes did not decompose because the *electrodes* acted on the molecular substances from a distance but because the *electric field* acted directly on each decomposed molecule. An electrode represented the locus of something—the lines of force—which had a tangible existence in the decomposing substance itself: "Bodies do not act where they are not." This result was critical because it showed that an apparent action-at-a-distance may in fact be something quite different.

Quantifying the forces he was dealing with was an important part of Faraday's research program because in it lay the path toward the formulation of laws. Faraday was mistrustful of the use of mathematics as an abstract analytical tool, but he was not mistrustful of numbers as representations of the magnitude of physical quantities. Cantor (1985) pointed to a religious warrant for this: Sandemanians placed great stock in certain numbers which they regarded as divine manifestations. Church seating, for example, was determined by lot. But they mistrusted any attempt to transform numbers because this could be seen as tampering with God's natural signs. In Faraday's case, we see *no* uses of formal mathematics in any of his research. On the other hand, we do see, for example, "Faraday's law," the precise quantitative relationship between the quantity of electricity and the amount of chemical substance altered in electrolysis. Once he was able to quantify the relationships involved, Faraday felt more comfortable in developing the notion of lines of force.

Quantification aside, however, there were serious theoretical reasons why Faraday needed to be cautious after 1831. Gooding (1981, 1982, 1989) and James (1985) discuss in detail the difficulty facing the notion of lines of force before it was accepted by the scientific community as something more than just an analogy. Two disturbing issues needed to be clarified before the claim could be advanced: (1) the asymmetry between the universality of electricity and the apparent restriction of magnetic effects to only a few metallic substances; and (2) the need to cope with the concept of a material ether which, though of great concern to optical theorists in the 1840s, Faraday had difficulty accepting. The first issue was resolved in 1845 by Faraday's discovery of diamagnetic phenomena (Faraday, 1846b); in fact, all substances *are* affected by magnetic fields. When suspended in a field, paramagnetic materials such as iron orient themselves with the field, whereas diamagnetic substances such as glass orient themselves across the field, at right angles to the lines of force. With this result, Faraday could safely argue that both electricity and magnetism were somehow fundamentally involved in the nature of matter. The relation of electricity and magnetism to light was resolved by Faraday's discovery (also in 1845) that a polarized light ray was slightly rotated if passed through a magnetic field (Faraday, 1846a). As James shows, the effect was not consistent with the prevalent opinion about a possible ponderable ether, and Faraday later argued just this point. Instead of an ether, Faraday was able to argue for the physical reality of the lines of force connecting two material bodies. On this view, the important aspect of matter is that it serves as a center of force—force becomes primary and matter secondary.

Though his discovery of induction was widely heralded, Faraday's claims about the lines of force were not generally accepted by other scientists. After 1832 his publications played down the role of lines of force, becoming drier and more empirical. In the 1850s he tried once again to advance his conception (e.g., Faraday, 1852b). The 1845 discovery that a strong magnetic field could rotate the axis of a plane-polarized ray of light seemed to Faraday to offer strong support for the notion that lines of force were "something real" apart from the matter in the vicinity. In addition, he had by then amassed a good deal of quantitative evidence showing that the lines of force notion could be made relatively precise. Yet Faraday failed once again to gain acceptance for his ideas, though a young Scottish scientist, James Clerk Maxwell (1855), became intrigued by the claim and sought to reconcile it with the predominantly mechanistic and highly mathematical physics that dominated British science. By using a mechanical analogy and a consistent mathematical framework, Maxwell was able to derive the relation between light and electromagnetic fields—a relation later confirmed experimentally by Hertz.

A Universe of Force

What becomes clear in this account is that Faraday's network of enterprise functioned on several levels, with his concept of field emerging slowly across time. All of the elements are present early in his career, but they lacked the kind of empirical support that he needed to argue them publicly. But Faraday did not merely use his preconceptions as a criterion for deciding when to publish; instead of using experiment in the service of revered hypotheses, he used hypotheses in the service of experiment. The case of Ampère provides us with a useful contrast here (Williams, 1985). Ampère, in 1822, had in fact generated electrical currents from a moving magnetic field. He rejected his own findings, however, because he could not reconcile them with his theoretical views. For Ampère, theory was primary and experiment was secondary. Faraday, on the other hand, conceived himself as being "in nature's school" (Gooding, 1985); he used experiment as a means for testing theory and his preconceptions as a *guide* to theory. If experiments could not be performed or if they disconfirmed the theory, so much the worse for the theory and the preconceptions. Faraday's God did not guarantee human truth, and Faraday's ideas, as he knew well, were fallible.

The boldness of Faraday's thought here is striking. It was one thing to accept on metaphysical grounds a vague Boscovichian force-centered universe, and quite another to attribute reality to the imaginary curves surrounding a current-carrying wire. In doing so, Faraday manifested an evolving system which, like his magnetic curves, was expanding outward and intersecting more and more aspects of his world view. The scope of his thought is remarkable here—he saw these curves as space-filling on an astronomical scale (as indicated by his experiments on currents induced by terrestrial magnetism). The universe became a force-filled plenum, matter being merely the stage on which the forces manifest their effects.

Force and Matter, Action and Thought

Knowledge, as already implied, is the product of ideas and activities. In science, the activity becomes formalized as both a discovery procedure and a test of truth. Faraday unified these dual aspects of the knowledge process in a thorough fashion. In another context (Tweney, 1984), I examined the nature of his experimental heuristics. At first glance there appears to be a kind of "confirmation bias" at work in the way Faraday pursued experimental questions. In his 1831 experiments on induction, he ignored a great deal of apparently disconfirming evidence. Yet this is a distorted picture. On the evidence of his diaries, we can see that Faraday ignored disconfirming evidence only in the early stages of his work, when the ideas were new and fragile. After he had obtained a fair amount of support for a hypothesis, he subjected it to deliberate and rigorous attempts to disconfirm. When these failed, he published.

Ultimately, this explains why Faraday was not rigid in his preconceptions. The primary warrant of truth was not in the realm of disembodied ideas, not logical truth, but rather in the realm of the fit between ideas and actions. The ideas could therefore change, and we see many instances of otherwise astonishing changes in his thought. Thus at the end of his career he even accepted a possible role for an ether concept, arising out of his experimental researches on the transmission of light by thin gold films (James, 1985). Similarly, in spite of repeated attempts, he was never able to demonstrate a relation between gravity and electric or magnetic effects, and hence he remained puzzled about the nature of gravity until the end of his life. No matter how he tried, he could not fully exorcise action-at-a-distance from physics.

There is a close relation between Faraday's epistemology and his ontology (Tweney, 1987). Forces become manifest by their actions on matter: needles rotate, light rays bend, magnets point north. In the same way, true ideas become manifest by their consequences when tried: induction occurs when we look for transient effects, the effect of magnetic fields on diamagnetic matter becomes evident when we look for any motions, not just those characteristic of iron. Faraday's fields of force extended through the universe, filling all space, just as he tried to extend his ideas through all possible consequences. Psychologically, the concept of force is rooted in experiences of pushing and pulling; matter cannot act where it is not. Faraday was close to this primitive perceptual level that ties us directly to the world; but his research was in no way the passive accumulation of sensory data. It is not surprising then that his concept of field had such unique properties. Lines of force existed for him, matter being merely a stage on which their effects are acted out. Because they preserved the psychological reality of his beliefs about knowledge, it was easier for him to conceive of the reality of such lines than it was to accept a Newtonian universe of hard material particles acting on each other with no intervening contact.

That Faraday integrated action and idea becomes clear when a detailed analysis of his experimental procedure is carried out. It is possible to construct a protocol analysis of Faraday's diary entries along the lines suggested by Ericsson and Simon (1984) for the analysis of "think-aloud" protocols. Such an analysis makes clear the close fit between Faraday's ideas and his experimental manipulations (Tweney & Hoffner, 1987). Only a very small number of elements are needed to make such an approach work: a set of states, corresponding to the particular content he is working on, and a set of operators, corresponding to the actions taken that transform one state into another. Throughout the diaries, there is a continual interplay between these two. Although the analysis seems to divide thought and action, in effect it unifies them; no operator is manifest except in the context of some state and vice versa. Faraday works simultaneously on a concrete sensorimotor level and on a seemingly abstract level of ideas. Is it too much to suggest that we see in this a key to the astonishing creativity of one of the greatest scientists of his century?

CHRONOLOGY
MICHAEL FARADAY

1791   Born at Newington, Surrey, son of a blacksmith.

1805   Apprenticed as bookbinder.

1812   Attends Sir Humphry Davy's lectures at Royal Institution.

1813   Employed as Davy's assistant at Royal Institution.

1816   First scientific publication.

1821   Discovery of electromagnetic rotation (foundation of electric motor).

1823   Elected Fellow of the Royal Society.

1825   Director of the laboratory of the Royal Institute.

1831   Discovery of electromagnetic induction.

1834   Discovery of "Faraday's Law" of electrolysis.

1845   Discovery of magnetic rotation of polarized light.
       Discovery of diamagnetic action.

1862   Last experiments, on relation between magnetism and light.

1867   Dies in London.

ACKNOWLEDGMENTS

Portions of the reported research were supported by grants from the Faculty Research Committee, Bowling Green State University. Thanks are due to Michael Bradie, Michael Doherty, Howard Gruber, Nancy Nersessian, and V. Frederick Rickey for their comments on earlier drafts, and to the staffs of the Royal Institution of Great Britain and the Institution for Electrical Engineers for their assistance with archival materials.

REFERENCES

Berkson, W. (1974). *Fields of force: The development of a world view from Faraday to Einstein.* New York: Halsted Press.

Cantor, G. N. (1985). Reading the book of nature: The relation between Faraday's religion and his science. In D. Gooding & F. A. J. L. James (Eds.), *Faraday rediscovered: Essays on the life and work of Michael Faraday, 1791–1867.* New York:/London: Stockton/Macmillan.

Davy, H. (1812). *Elements of chemical philosophy* (Part 1, Vol. 1). London: J. Johnson.

Einstein, A., & Infeld, L. (1938). *The evolution of modern physics.* New York: Simon & Schuster.

Ericsson, K. A., & Simon, H. A. (1984). *Protocol analysis: Verbal reports as data.* Cambridge, Mass.: MIT Press.

Faraday, M. (1809–10). *A philosophical miscellany.* Unpublished manuscript, in the collection of the Royal Institution of Great Britain, London, England.

Faraday, M. (1816a). *Chemistry lectures.* Unpublished manuscript, in the collection of the Institution of Electrical Engineers, London, England.

Faraday, M. (1816b). *Common-place book* . . . Unpublished manuscript, in the collection of the Institution of Electrical Engineers, London, England.

Faraday, M. (1821). On some new electro-magnetical motions, and on the theory of magnetism. *Quarterly Journal of Science, 12,* 74–96.

Faraday, M. (1821–22). Historical sketch of electro-magnetism. *Annals of Philosophy, 2,* 195–200, 274–290, and *3,* 107–121. (in three parts)

Faraday, M. (1822). *Chemical notes, hints, suggestions and objects of pursuit.* Unpublished manuscript, in the collection of the Institution of Electrical Engineers, London, England.

Faraday, M. (1832a). Series I. On the induction of electrical currents . . . *Philosophical Transactions, 122,* 125–162. (Based on a paper read November 24, 1831; reprinted in Faraday, 1839–55, Vol. 1)

Faraday, M. (1832b). Series II. Terrestrial magneto-electric induction . . . *Philosophical Transactions, 122,* 163–194. (Reprinted in Faraday, 1839–55, Vol. 1)

Faraday, M. (1833). Series III. Identity of electricities derived from different sources . . . *Philosophical Transactions, 123,* 23–54. (Reprinted in Faraday, 1839–55, Vol. 1)

Faraday, M. (1834). Series V. On electro-chemical decomposition . . . *Philosophical Transactions, 124,* 425–470. (Reprinted in Faraday, 1839–55, Vol. 1)

Faraday, M. (1839–55). *Experimental researches in electricity* (3 vols.). London: R. & J. E. Taylor.

Faraday, M. (1844). A speculation touching electric conduction and the nature of matter. *Philosophical Magazine, 24,* 136–144. (Reprinted in Faraday 1839–55, Vol. 2)

Faraday, M. (1846a). Series XIX. On the magnetization of light and the illumination of magnetic lines of force. *Philosophical Transactions, 136,* 1–20. (Reprinted in Faraday 1839–55, Vol. 3)

Faraday, M. (1846b). Series XX. On new magnetic actions and on the magnetic condition of all matter. *Philosophical Transactions, 136,* 21–40. (Reprinted in Faraday, 1839–55, Vol. 3)

Faraday, M. (1852a). On the physical character of the lines of magnetic force. *Philosophical Magazine, 3,* 401–428. (Reprinted in Faraday, 1839–55, Vol. 3)

Faraday, M. (1852b). Series XXVIII. On lines of magnetic force. . . . *Philosophical Transactions, 142,* 25–56. (Reprinted in Faraday, 1839–55, Vol. 3)

Faraday, M. (1932–36). *Faraday's Diary . . . 1820–1862 . . .* (7 vols.). (T. Martin, Ed.). London: Bell.

Forgan, S. (Ed.) (1980). *Science and the sons of genius: Studies on Humphry Davy.* London: Science Reviews.

Fullmer, J. (1980). Humphry Davy, reformer. In S. Forgan (Ed.), *Science and the sons of genius: Studies on Humphry Davy.* London: Science Reviews.

Gooding, D. (1981). Final steps to the field theory: Faraday's study of magnetic phenomena, 1845–1850. *Historical Studies in the Physical Sciences, 11,* 235–275.

Gooding, D. (1982). A convergence of opinion on the divergence of lines: Faraday and Thomson's discussion of diamagnetism. *Notes and Records of the Royal Society of London, 39,* 229–244.

Gooding, D. (1985). "In nature's school": Faraday as an experimentalist. In D. Gooding & F. A. J. L. James (Eds.), *Faraday rediscovered: Essays on the life and work of Michael Faraday, 1791–1867.* New York/London: Stockton/Macmillan.

Gooding, D. (1989). "Magnetic curves" and the magnetic field: Experimentation and representation in the history of a physical theory. In D. Gooding, T. Pinch, & S. Schaffer (Eds.). *The uses of experiment.* Cambridge: Cambridge University Press.

Gooding, D., & James, F. A. J. L. (Eds.). (1985). *Faraday rediscovered: Essays on the life and work of Michael Faraday, 1791–1867.* New York/London: Stockton/Macmillan.

Gruber, H. E. (1981). *Darwin on man: A psychological study of scientific creativity* (2nd ed.). Chicago: University of Chicago Press. (Original work published in 1974).

Gruber, H. E. (1988). Networks of enterprise in creative scientific work. In B. Gholson, B. Houts, A. Neimayer, & W. Shadish (Eds.), *Psychology of science and metascience.* Cambridge: Cambridge University Press.

Harré, R. (1981). *Great scientific experiments.* Oxford: Phaidon.

Heilbron, J. L. (1979). *Electricity in the 17th and 18th centuries: A study of early modern physics.* Berkeley: University of California Press.

James, F. A. J. L. (1985). "The optical mode of investigation": Light and matter in Faraday's natural philosophy. In D. Gooding & F. A. J. L. James (Eds.), *Faraday rediscovered: Essays on the life and work of Michael Faraday, 1791–1867.* New York/London: Stockton/Macmillan.

Maxwell, J. C. (1855). On Faraday's lines of force. *Transactions of the Cambridge Philosophical Society, 10,* 27–83.

Miller, A. I. (1984). *Imagery in scientific thought: Creating 20th century physics.* Boston: Birkhäuser.

Nersessian, N. (1984). *Faraday to Einstein: Constructing meaning in scientific theories.* Dordrecht: Martinus Nijhoff.

Nersessian, N. (1985). Faraday's field concept. In D. Gooding & F. A. J. L. James (Eds.), *Faraday rediscovered: Essays on the life and work of Michael Faraday, 1791–1867.* New York/London: Stockton/Macmillan.

Newton, I. (1947). *Mathematical principles of natural philosophy* (A. Motte, Trans.; rev. by F. Cajori). Berkeley: University of California Press. (Original work published in 1687)

Oersted, H. C. (1820). Experiments on the effect of a current of electricity on the magnetic needle. *Annals of Philosophy, 16,* 273–276.

Thompson, S. P. (1898). *Michael Faraday: His life and work.* London: Cassell.

Tweney, R. D. (1984). Cognitive psychology and the history of science: A new look at Michael Faraday. In S. Bem, H. Rappard, & W. van Hoorn (Eds.), *Studies in the history of psychology and the social sciences* (Vol. 2). Leiden: Psychologisch Instituut van de Rijksuniversiteit Leiden.

Tweney, R. D. (1985). Faraday's discovery of induction: A cognitive approach.

In D. Gooding & F. A. J. L. James (Eds.), *Faraday rediscovered: Essays on the life and work of Michael Faraday, 1791–1867*. New York/London: Stockton/Macmillan.

Tweney, R. D. (1987). Procedural representation in Michael Faraday's scientific thought. In *PSA 1986, Volume 2. Proceedings of the 1986 Biennial meeting of the Philosophy of Science Association*. East Lansing, Mich.: Philosophy of Science Association.

Tweney, R. D. (1988). A framework for the cognitive analysis of science. In B. Gholson, A. Houts, R. A. Neimayer, & W. Shadish (Eds.), *Psychology of science and metascience*. Cambridge: Cambridge University Press.

Tweney, R. D., Doherty, M. E., & Mynatt, C. R. (Eds.). (1981). *On scientific thinking*. New York: Columbia University Press.

Tweney, R. D., & Hoffner, C. E. (1987). Understanding the microstructure of science: An example. In *Program of the Ninth Annual Conference of the Cognitive Science Society*. Hillsdale, NJ: Lawrence Erlbaum.

Tyndall, J. (1868). *Faraday as a discoverer*. London: Longmans Green.

Wallace, D. B. (1985). Giftedness and the construction of a creative life. In F. D. Horowitz & M. O'Brien (Eds.), *The gifted and talented: Developmental perspectives*. Washington, D.C.: American Psychological Association.

Williams, L. P. (1965). *Michael Faraday: A biography*. New York: Basic Books.

Williams, L. P. (1966). *The origins of field theory*. New York: Random House.

Williams, L. P. (1985). Why Ampère did not discover electromagnetic induction. *American Journal of Physics, 54*, 306–311.

6

How Charles Darwin
Became a Psychologist

ROBERT T. KEEGAN

He who understand[s] baboon would do more toward metaphysics
than Locke.

CHARLES DARWIN

Charles Robert Darwin (1809–82) recorded this thought in a private notebook in August 1838. What would bring a young naturalist to make such a
bold assertion? Had the nickname "Philosopher," which Darwin acquired
during his years aboard the *Beagle,* gone to his head? If not born of sheer ar-
rogance, there must have been a compelling reason for him to challenge the
wisdom of the great English philosopher with regard to "metaphysics"—a
term Darwin used to refer to a set of issues we might now label "psychological" or "epistemological": questions about the nature, origin, and development of mind and knowledge. The central problem for this chapter is both
historical and psychological: how did the intellectual development of this
young naturalist equip and require him to take up psychological problems?

To answer this question, I first introduce the idea of *thought-form* and
describe the development of one of Darwin's major thought-forms during a
period of his life when his primary concerns were in the field of geology and
understanding the earth. I then describe and discuss the development of Darwin's thinking about psychological matters. I distinguish five aspects of his

FIGURE 6–1. Charles Darwin, aged 51. Courtesy of Down House and The Royal College of Surgeons of England.

development as a psychologist, his efforts to (1) understand the earth, (2) understand the baboon, (3) understand the baby, (4) understand the bee, and (5) understand mankind. Historically, linking geology with these other fields is not so surprising. Charles Lyell, Darwin's mentor, began his celebrated *Principles of Geology* (1830–33) with the remark that this science is the study of the history of the earth and of its inhabitants.

The Thought-Form

The concept of the thought-form is proposed here to provide a means for describing and explaining the intellectual functioning of a specific individual. The emphasis in psychology has been nomothetic, aiming to describe thinking and cognitive development in general. For the present task, we need a new approach and new terms. For example, if we ask "What enabled Darwin to be a creative thinker?," it would be inadequate to reply that he had acquired the logical schema of formal operations typical of well-functioning adolescents and young adults. Those schema may be necessary, but they are not sufficient for creative thought. I propose that creative thinkers make use, in a highly personal way, of a repertoire of thought-forms. In this chapter I explain this idea and examine in detail the functioning of one such form.

The development of a creative thought-form is a two-step process. First the thinker acquires expert knowledge in a field. Second, he or she applies the expert knowledge in the attempt to understand new areas—to use the expert knowledge as the basis for analogy. So the concept of thought-form embraces ideas about cognitive development, cognitive structure, and cognitive function (e.g., analogical thinking).

Understanding the Earth

At the age of 22 Darwin left England aboard the British naval ship HMS *Beagle* (see chronology at the end of this chapter). The ship's main mission was to chart accurately the coast of South America and to make a series of longitudinal measurements while circumnavigating the globe. During the five-year voyage Darwin served as the naturalist of the ship. In later years he wrote, "The voyage of the *Beagle* has been by far the most important event in my life and has determined my whole career" (Barlow, 1969, p. 76). During the voyage Darwin did indeed carve out a *career* and become an expert in at least one field, geology.

Why was the acquisition of expert knowledge in geology so important to the development of Darwin's overall thinking? Because in learning geology Darwin ground a conceptual lens—a device for bringing into focus and clarifying the problems to which he turned his attention. When his attention shifted to problems beyond geology, the lens remained and Darwin used it in exploring these new problems. Darwin's self-transformation into an expert geologist is the point at which this analysis of his thinking begins.

Uniformitarianism

When Darwin left England on December 27, 1831 he had with him the first volume of Charles Lyell's landmark work, *Principles of Geology*. In this work Lyell gave a clear and compelling statement of the "uniformitarian" perspective in geology: that the earth's physical features were produced by geological forces operating across immense periods of time. The forces that could be observed acting in the present were the same as those that had acted in the past in producing the physical features of the earth. There was no need to invoke unique, cataclysmic events (e.g., the "Great Flood") to explain the earth's appearance. In Lyell's view, all geological change occurred *gradually*. The great topographical features of the earth were built through the slow accumulation of small changes that occurred over vast stretches of time.

This idea had a strong and immediate impact on Darwin. Within six months of leaving England, Darwin wrote to his friend and mentor, the Reverend John Stephens Henslow, stating that the appearance of the Cape Verde Islands provided evidence in favor of Lyell's view that the crust of the earth was continually undergoing gradual vertical movements caused by the migration of heated fluid magma under the crust. Darwin was already using a Lyellian lens to understand the formation of the features of the earth and would continue to do so provisionally until he became convinced of its correctness.

In August 1834 Darwin discovered marine shells high in the Andes; he interpreted this as unequivocal evidence for slow, long, continued elevation of this region from ocean bed to mountain top. In February 1835 Darwin measured the effect of an earthquake on the elevation of land in the area of the Bay of Concepción in Chile. He calculated that an elevation of two to three feet had occurred, great and cataclysmic on a human scale but minuscule on a geological scale of time and space. In May 1835 Darwin visited the geological formation known as the "terraces" of Coquimbo on the coast of Chile. He concurred with Lyell that these terraces were ancient marine beaches, further evidence for the gradual elevation of this landmass from the sea. This period may be thought of as Darwin's apprenticeship from afar with the master, Charles Lyell. But Darwin would soon produce his own masterpiece in geology.

Coral Reefs

Toward the end of the *Beagle* voyage, Darwin sketched out a theory of coral reef formation. This work marks an important transitional event in Darwin's intellectual development. It reveals a confident Darwin, assured that he has learned his geological lessons well.

Both Lyell's earlier proposal and Darwin's new theory assumed that the coral reef is composed of the skeletal residue of many millions of minute coral organisms. Lyell had proposed that different types of coral formations (e.g., islands and atolls) have distinctive histories. Darwin proposed a unified explanation for the formation of different forms of reef. When a landmass is stable, a "fringing" reef can begin to form slightly offshore in the ideal shallow water conditions. If the land and fringing reef then subside, the best environment for coral growth would be on the outside edge of the fringing reef because the water would be shallow but moving. Coral organisms on the inside would die, leaving only their skeletons. This process, if continued, would lead to the gradual widening outward of the reef while the land sank; the result would be a coral formation known as a "barrier" reef. When the top of the landmass finally sank below the surface of the water, a circular reef with a still water lagoon would remain—an atoll! What Lyell had thought were geological formations with different histories, Darwin conceived of as the same formation in different phases of its history. Darwin's theory was comprehensive and coherent, and it led to predictions about vertical movements of the crust of the earth that were beyond the scope of Lyell's theory (Herbert, 1986).

The coral reef theory shows that Darwin had become an expert in one field. The first phase in the development of a thought-form was now complete. The central idea in Darwin's understanding of geology was "gradualism"— that great things could be produced by long, continued accumulation of very small effects. The next phase in the development of this thought-form would involve his use of it as the basis for constructing analogies between geology and new, unfamiliar subjects.

Earthworms

Darwin presented his theory of coral reef formation to the London Geological Society on May 31, 1837, eight months after the return of the *Beagle.* In a new paper read to the society on November 1, 1837, Darwin took what he had learned about the potential of "trivial" organisms to produce gradual change and applied it to the problem of how topsoil is formed. It was well known that the top few inches of soil were finer and richer than the soil that lay below, but why this condition should exist was not understood. One widely held notion was that the top level was composed primarily of decaying organic matter such as leaves, plants, and grasses, and hence the term "vegetable mould" was used to describe it. Darwin (1840/1980) credited his uncle Josiah Wedgwood with solving this puzzle. Wedgwood suggested that earthworms ingest vegetable material as they burrow and later excrete castings of fine particles at the openings of their burrows. Darwin agreed, and he realized that in this way small amounts of fine particles would be continually brought to the surface. Darwin also thought that a similar process was responsible for the formation of chalk deposits through the digestive action of marine animals on coral. He was thus successfully extending the basic theme of gradualism to new areas.

Glen Roy

In June 1838 Darwin visited Glen Roy in the Scottish highlands. This area was similar to the Coquimbo area of Chile, which Darwin had seen during the *Beagle* voyage. Both regions contained terraces, called "parallel roads" at Glen Roy. In fact, in the third volume of *Principles,* Lyell explicitly compared Coquimbo to Glen Roy. Darwin proposed that the parallel roads of Glen Roy were ancient sea beaches, just as he had explained the terraces at Coquimbo. But in contrast to the many marine fossils he had found at Coquimbo, Darwin found no marine fossils at Glen Roy. Why then did he propose a theory of marine origin when no supporting evidence could be found? Confidence—or overconfidence. He had come to believe in the power of his own thinking, especially in the pattern I have identified as the thought-form of gradualism. The absence of supporting evidence and other difficulties with this marine theory could be explained away by ad hoc proposals, a procedure he later regretted since his specific explanation proved to be incorrect. The terraces are now believed to have been beaches formed by glacial lakes, a theory that combines both gradual and abrupt changes.

When Darwin completed his work on Glen Roy, he had developed two distinct ways of understanding the process of gradual change in the geological features of the earth. His measurement of the immediate effect on land elevation following the Chilean earthquake of 1835 and his direct observation of terraces at Coquimbo and Glen Roy convinced him that gradual change could occur in a stepwise fashion, episodes of stasis alternating with episodes of accelerated change. The formation of coral reefs and topsoil, however, revealed no such record of episodic change, only smooth, insensibly gradual modification. Change appeared insensibly smooth when organic agents played a major role in the process. Thus when Darwin turned his attention to the question of evolution, gradualism was well established in his thinking. He would, however, have to explore the question of whether species evolved in a manner that was insensibly smooth or whether evolution was characterized by stepwise change.

Understanding the Baboon

Darwin had amassed an impressive collection of fossils and specimens of living species during the voyage of the *Beagle*. When he returned to England in October 1836, he distributed his collection among a number of experts in various fields of natural history. Darwin began to learn that classification was not simply a matter of examining the physical features of a specimen. His collection of birds was examined by the ornithologist John Gould, and their exchange of ideas was particularly important in directing Darwin's explicit attention to the "species question"—whether new species could arise from other species (Sulloway, 1982). Darwin discovered how important descriptions of the *behavior* of his specimens were in Gould's efforts to classify the specimens. It was this contemplation of behavior that eventually forced Darwin to consider problems of a psychological nature. He was well aware of theories maintaining that a change in behavior could *produce* a new species in time, such as the evolutionary views of his own grandfather, Erasmus Darwin, and of the French naturalist Jean Baptiste Lamarck. Might these theories be correct despite the fact that they were held in such low regard at the time?

The B Notebook

In July 1837, just four months after his exchange with John Gould, Darwin opened his first notebook on the "transmutation" (Darwin's term for evolution) of species.[1] Having become convinced by March 1837 that transmutation had occurred, Darwin began to search for a mechanism that could explain it. Among the various lines of speculation running through this notebook was one concerning the possible role of "mind" in producing morphological change. Here Darwin used Lamarck as a whipping boy. He understood the core of Lamarck's thesis to be that the wish of an organism brought about a morphological change, which in turn was passed to offspring. For example, an adult giraffe, through an act of will, repeatedly stretches its neck to procure leaves high up in trees; this activity results in a slight elongation of the neck, and this acquired characteristic is transmitted to the offspring, yielding a new generation of slightly longer necked giraffes than the parent generation.

The "wishing" or "willing" aspect of Lamarck's thesis particularly disturbed Darwin since it restricted transmutation to the so-called higher animals, creatures capable of "willing." Darwin believed that "lower" animals and plants had been transmuted. His gradualist thought-form led him to reject the idea of a great gulf in nature in favor of a view that stressed continuity of development. This is why he wrote statements such as "My theory very distinct from Lamarck's" (B notebook, p. 214) and "With respect to how species are formed, Lamarck's 'willing' doctrine absurd" (B notebook, p. 216). In this notebook, nevertheless, Darwin continued to mull over the possible connection between mental activity and transmutation because he recognized the important connection between the behavior of an organism and its physical features.

The C Notebook

Darwin filled the B notebook by February 1838 and immediately opened a new one, known as the C notebook. About six weeks later he recorded an idea that I believe was of central importance to the development of his thinking. He wrote, "The believing that monkey would breed (if mankind destroyed) some intellectual being though not MAN,—is as difficult to understand as Lyell's doctrine of slow movements" (C notebook, p. 74). Here is an *explicit* analogy in which Darwin compared the evolution of an *intellectual*

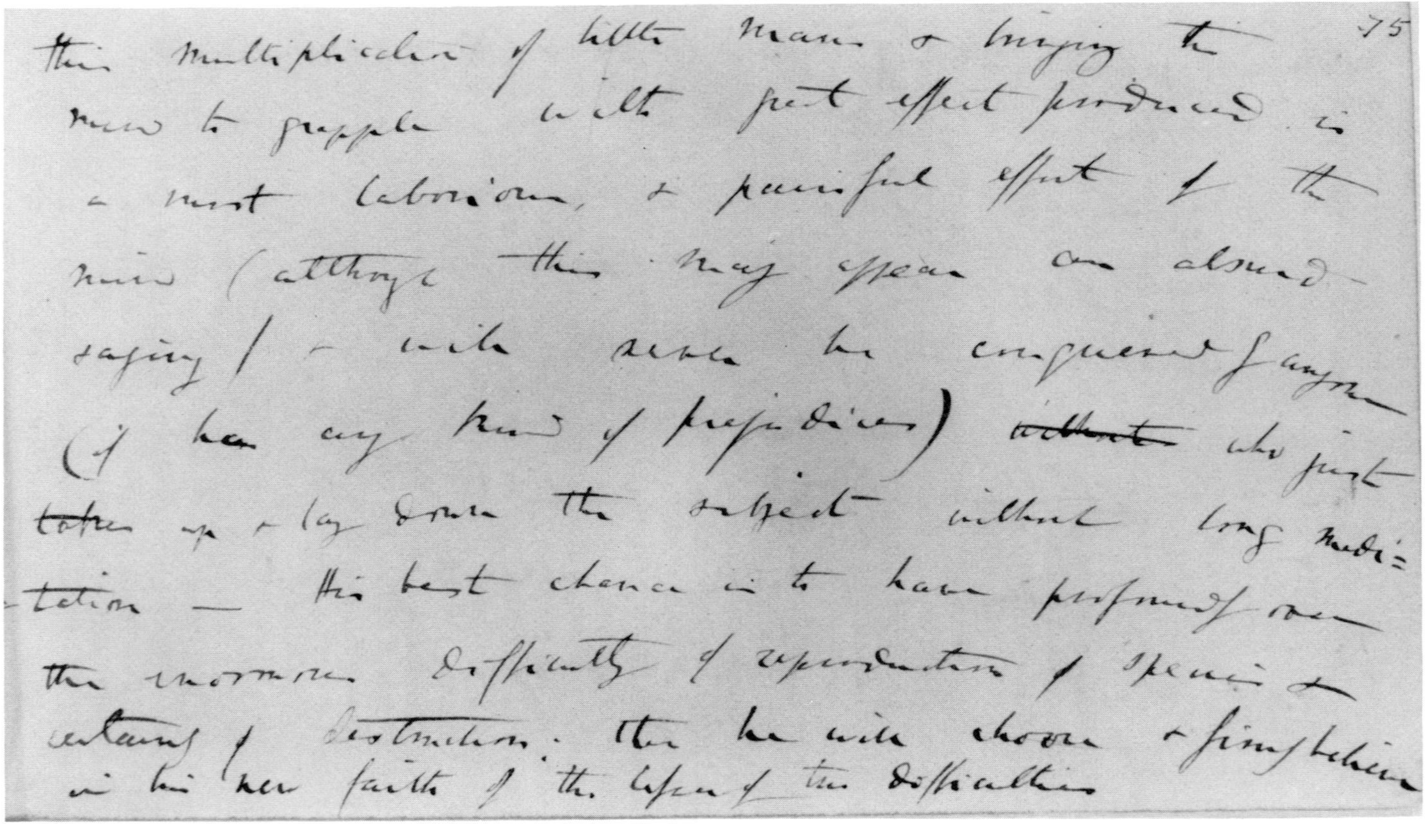

FIGURE 6–2. Page 75 of Darwin's C notebook on transmutation. By permission of the Syndics of Cambridge University Library.

being to the process of geological change. Could the mind of *Homo sapiens* have formed through a slow accumulation of small changes? Reflecting on this insight, Darwin wrote his most explicit and concise statement of the nature and utility of his gradualism thought-form: "This multiplication of little means & bringing the mind to grapple with great effect produced is a most laborious & painful effort of the mind" (C notebook, p. 75). He recognized that it took patience and discipline to discover the "little means" that were responsible for great effects. With the necessary effort, however, this gradualism thought-form could become the vehicle for explaining many remarkable phenomena in geology, biology, and even psychology.

Darwin continued to speculate in the C notebook on the possibility that a *mental* mechanism was involved in transmutation. He came to realize how rich, complex, and controversial this line of inquiry could become. When he completed the C notebook, he decided to separate his speculations about mental functioning from those about biological and geographical mechanisms of transmutation. When he began the third transmutation notebook (D) in July 1838, he also began a notebook on "metaphysics" known as the M notebook.

The M Notebook

The M notebook along with its sequel, N, can be viewed as Darwin's outline for a project for a scientific psychology explicitly devoted to a full investigation of the role of mind in the evolution of life.[2] A simple listing of some of the topics addressed in these notebooks should convey an impression of their diversity, richness, and boldness: the nature and causes of mental illness, the function of dreams, the processes involved in memory, the question of whether free will exists, the mental functioning of insects, the role of effort in mental functioning, the expression of emotion, the relationship between language and thinking, and so on.

The M notebook, together with the D transmutation notebook, preserves Darwin's last speculations about evolution before he had his insight about natural selection.[3] An idea that had emerged in the C notebook was continued in the M notebook. It concerned a theory of "hereditary habit" as a mental mechanism of evolution: (1) a frequently repeated activity would become habitual; (2) a habit would produce a morphological change, in particular, a neurological change; (3) a neurological change produced a lasting change in behavior, an instinctual change that could be inherited; (4) over time a new species could gradually be produced by this process. This theory reflects the same "insensibly smooth" process of change that we saw in Darwin's explanation of coral reef formation and vegetable mold production. After 10 pages of intense speculation on the possible role of habit formation in evolution, he confidently wrote, "Origin of man now proved.—Metaphysics must flourish.—He who understand[s] baboon would do more toward metaphysics than Locke" (M notebook, p. 84). Darwin believed that he had come a long way in understanding the baboon. Since in Darwin's evolutionary scenario all creatures were related, understanding the baboon would provide a scientific basis for understanding mankind—and that is why "metaphysics must flourish."

Two similar statements from the M notebook reflect Darwin's growing confidence in an evolutionary explanation of human nature. In writing "Our descent, then, is the origin of our evil passions!!—The Devil under form of Baboon is our grandfather" (M notebook, p. 123), Darwin had thrown down the gauntlet not only to metaphysicians but to theologians as well. "Evil passions" were remnants of our nonhuman past, not the promptings of demonic spirits. Darwin again pressed an evolutionary, naturalistic explanation of human nature when he wrote, "Plato says in Phaedo that our 'necessary ideas' arise from the preexistence of the soul, are not derivable from experience.—read monkeys for preexistence" (M notebook, p. 128). It must be emphasized that these bold statements were written *before* Darwin had hit upon the idea of natural selection. They were based on his speculations concerning a hereditary habit mechanism.

The N Notebook

Darwin began the N notebook a few days after his discovery of the mechanism of natural selection in September 1838, but it would take him many years to work through the problems and implications of this new idea. Darwin recognized that a potentially devastating flaw in his concept of natural selection was the failure to explain *how* variations arose. One had to accept the idea that small variations appeared spontaneously without being able to specify the cause. This introduced a small but abrupt element of change into the process of evolution.

This concept of evolutionary change was analogous to the gradual but *stepwise* change Darwin had recognized in the process of geological change when volcanic action or earthquakes were involved in land elevation. In contrast, as discussed above, the earlier hereditary habit mechanism, which Darwin had been elaborating in the previous notebooks, provided a model of *insensibly smooth* transition. Darwin was puzzled at being confronted by these two equally plausible mechanisms for transmutation—by the Lamarckian inheritance of acquired characteristics and by natural selection:

> An habitual action must some way affect the brain in a manner which can be transmitted.—this is analogous to a blacksmith having children with strong arms.—The other principle of those children which *chance* produced with strong arms, outliving the weaker ones, may be applicable to the formation of instincts, independently of habits. The limits of these two actions either on form or brains very hard to define. (N notebook, pp. 42–43)

Each explanation of transmutation had its strong points and weak points. The hereditary habit mechanism explained *how* variations arose, but as Darwin recognized, this sort of explanation of evolutionary change had already been proposed by Lamarck. In reviewing Lamarck's chapter on the origin of instinct in *Philosophie Zoologique* (1809), Darwin wrote that he considered Lamarck's ideas to be "almost identical with my theory, no facts, & mingled with much hypothesis" (N notebook, p. 91). But what about Darwin's earlier negative appraisals of Lamarck's theory? Could he do no better? Natural selection offered a reasonable and novel alternative, but it did not explain *how* variations arose. At this time Darwin could not reject one idea in favor of the other. It would take him several years to recognize the full power of his theory of natural selection and he would never completely abandon the notion that habit formation played some role in evolution.

The M and N notebooks reflect Darwin's belief that the subject matter of psychology could be approached through the method of natural history and could best be explained by a theory of evolution. While his entry into the field of psychology was largely motivated by the rather restricted aim of determining whether mental activity could serve as an engine of evolutionary change, the notebooks show that Darwin's inquiries and concerns rapidly enlarged as he realized that a theory of evolution would transform long held ideas about the origin, nature, and function of mind. An event in his personal life provided him with a new opportunity to continue his inquiry into mental phenomena.

Understanding the Baby

On December 27, 1839 Charles Darwin's wife, Emma, gave birth to their first son, William. Darwin immediately began a diary of his son's development. As the last entry in the M notebook reveals, the diary is a direct continuation of the investigation of mind begun in the M and N notebooks:

Natural History of Babies

Do babies start (i.e. useless sudden movement of muscles) very early in life Do they wink, when anything placed before their eyes, very young, before experience can have taught them to avoid danger Do they know frown when they first see it? (M notebook, p. 157)

Darwin's use of capital letters suggests the working title for a proposed work: *The Natural History of Babies*. Questions to be addressed in the work are listed beneath this title. They reflect his interest in determining which behaviors in the infant are instinctual and which are acquired through learning, as well as a host of other issues. The birth of William, also referred to as "Doddy" in the diary, presented Darwin with the opportunity to observe the "natural history" of one infant's development.

The diary shows his first use of the gradualism thought-form to understand *individual,* ontogenetic development. Darwin saw Doddy's development as a process of gradually increasing competence in motor, cognitive, and moral functioning. A new skill does not appear full blown but emerges from a rudimentary pattern of behavior that foreshadows it. Darwin's view of cognitive development can be illustrated by tracing his record of Doddy's continuing experiences with a single object, a mirror.

Self Reflections

Darwin's first entry about his son's encounter with a mirror occurred when Doddy was four and a half months old: "Three or four days ago smiled at himself in glass . . . Smiled at my image, & seemed surprised at my voice coming from behind him, my image being in front" (p. 18).[4] Just two months later, Doddy's reaction was substantially different: "When looking at mirror, was aware that the image of person behind, was not real & therefore, when any odd motion or face was made, turned round to look at the person behind" (Diary, pp. 21–22). Doddy had solved the major puzzle of the mirror, but Darwin, with characteristic thoroughness, continued to note his son's reactions to surfaces that reflect.

Darwin recognized that something newly acquired is fragile and cannot always be generalized to slightly different situations, as Piaget's investigations of children's concepts showed many years later. Just two weeks after Doddy learned to look behind to find the person connected with the image in front of him, Darwin observed, "Towards the end of July [Doddy] seemed puzzled at seeing me first through one window & then through another.—did not appear to know whether it was reflection in mirror or reality" (Diary, p. 22v). Looking through a window sometimes yields two images: the image of the outside world and a reflected (mirror) image we eventually learn to ignore.

Over the next two months, Doddy's idea of mirrors consolidated. When Doddy was nine months old Darwin reported, "When one says to him, 'where is Doddy?' [he] turns & looks for himself in looking-glass" (Diary, p. 23). Doddy had come to associate his image with his name, thus displaying a sense of self.[5] A week later Doddy showed definite signs that his experience with mirrors could be generalized and applied to very different situations. On October 2, 1840, Darwin wrote, "He was aware that the shadow of a hand, made by a candle, was to be looked for behind, in same manner as in looking glass" (Diary, p. 23). A principle had been learned that applied to seemingly different phenomena, mirror images and shadows: images in front of you may be caused by objects behind you.

Darwin saw parallels between ontogeny and phylogeny and used them to stimulate his thinking. In his view, both revealed a process of gradual yet substantial change. His next significant contribution to the field of psychology, however, would not entail the direct application of the gradualism thought-form, but rather the introduction of an innovative modification of it.

Understanding the Bee

During the decade between 1844 and 1854 Darwin did not aggressively pursue the investigation of psychological questions. His major project was a study of barnacles that resulted in the publication of four volumes on the subject.

Although in its published form nothing appears about evolution, nothing in this work caused Darwin to doubt his theory. To the contrary, according to the biologist Michael T. Ghiselin, Darwin used his evolutionary thesis as a guide in making judgments about the classification of barnacles into different biological groups. Ghiselin (1969) characterized Darwin's volumes on barnacles as "a rigorous and sweeping critical test for a comprehensive theory of evolutionary biology" (p. 129).

Among the many valuable things Darwin learned during this endeavor, his recognition of the "correlation of growth" is most important in the development of his psychological ideas because of its later role in the solution of a particularly vexing problem in mental evolution. In its simplest form, the concept expresses the idea that "different parts of the body may evolve as a unit" (Ghiselin, 1969, p. 128), so a correlation of growth reveals a correlation of interdependent *parts* within a coherent system. This proposition considerably opens up Darwin's evolutionary thesis, making it less deterministic. For example, if features A, B, and C are correlated, the natural selection of feature A, because it conveys an advantage in survival, results in an animal not only with feature A, but also with correlated features B and C, features that may have no immediate adaptive functions. In this view, the mechanism of natural selection does not strictly determine every feature of an organism's system.

Different Levels of the System

Darwin had long been sensitive to the idea that nature was comprised of a *system* of interactions among different organisms, and among organisms and all the conditions of life. In fact, his idea of one particular type of interaction—struggle—became a central component in his theory of natural selection. Darwin's eight-year study of barnacles broadened his understanding of the idea of a system. It enabled him to understand the complexity of the system at the level of the individual organism, how the different parts of this system were coordinated. It also enabled him to see the constituents of an individual organism as systems, for example, the interrelationship among the external plates of a barnacle. So the experience with barnacles helped Darwin appreciate how conceptual lenses of different power could be selected to analyze a problem: one could see systems within systems within systems, and so on. It also helped him to focus on relationships of coordination rather than struggle within systems and provided the key to the next major advance in his thinking about the evolution of mental characteristics.

In 1856 Darwin began work on a book in which he planned to explain the theory of natural selection, a manuscript now known as *Natural Selection*. During the summer of 1857 Darwin began writing a chapter on the "special difficulties" with his theory. One particularly vexing problem involved the instincts of neuter insects such as worker bees. Since neuters cannot breed, they cannot transmit their instincts to the next generation (Richards, 1981). After considering a number of possibilities, Darwin wrote: "I concluded that natural selection might act on the parents, & continually preserve those which produced more & more aberrant offspring, having any structure or instinct advantageous to the community" (in Stauffer, 1975, p. 510). Here was a "correlation of the parts" where the "parts" were individual organisms in a *system* which was the hive! Selection worked *indirectly* on the neuters through the direct selection of the parents. Parents (or queens) producing offspring that helped the system (hive) to survive thrived and left offspring. The hive was the system or level at which natural selection became relevant.

How had Darwin recognized that a level "higher" than the individual organism might be the one at which natural selection operated? Darwin had come to see a strong analogy between the *artificial* selection practiced by breeders and *natural* selection. While preparing *Natural Selection*, Darwin reviewed the work of a cattle breeder, William Youatt, entitled, *Cattle: Their Breeds, Management, and Disease.* The historian of science Robert Richards (1981) summarized an important aspect of this work: "When breeders wanted a herd with particular characteristics, they would select animals from several families for slaughter and then, for example, inspect the meat for the desired marbling. When this was found, they would breed from the family of the butchered beast" (p. 224). The breeder would select the *parent* that produced the most valuable variant. Darwin recognized that Youatt's explanation of "family selection" was analogous to the problem of the instincts of neuter hive bees: "This principle of selection, namely not of the individual which cannot breed, but of the family which produced such individual, has I believe been followed by nature in regard to the neuters amongst social insects" (Stauffer, 1975, p. 370).

If a queen bee in a given hive produced variants with instincts that were helpful in the smooth functioning and defense of the hive, this hive would gain an advantage over other hives in the struggle for existence. Thus the hive becomes the system upon which natural selection acts.

During the 1840s and 1850s Darwin became more aware of the subtleties and complexities of natural selection, recognizing that the individual organism is not the only system upon which natural selection works. His work on barnacles revealed that individual anatomical features could be correlated and change as a unit when natural selection chooses one feature for its adaptive utility. Such a unit is obviously subordinate to the system of the individual organism. On the other hand, Darwin's familiarity with animal breeding gave him a key for understanding how a level superordinate to the individual organism, the parents, could serve as the system upon which selection works. This was not just a clever ad hoc solution to a particular special difficulty with his theory, but it became a powerful new element in the gradualism thought-form, as will be made clear in the following section.

Understanding Mankind

On the Origin of Species (Darwin, 1859–1964) was published two years after Darwin's elegant solution to the problem of the instincts of neuter insects.

While one of the handful of truly revolutionary books in the history of science, *Origin* does not include much psychology. It contains one modest chapter on instinct but omits all discussion of the other intriguing psychological questions raised in the M and N notebooks and in Darwin's diary of his son. Recognizing the inevitable resistance that would greet his theory, Darwin chose to deemphasize its most controversial aspect, the natural evolution of higher mental faculties in our species. Still, he could not refrain from hinting at his views on this subject in one celebrated passage in *Origin:*

> In the distant future I see open fields for far more important researches. Psychology will be based on a new foundation, that of the necessary acquirement of each mental power and capacity by gradation. Light will be thrown on the origin of man and his history. (p. 488)

Though there were a number of books written by others (some of whom Darwin knew and respected, such as Lyell and Huxley) on human evolution following the publication of *Origin,* no definitive work on the evolution of the human mind appeared. Darwin published his personal point of view about the role of evolution in human psychology in *The Descent of Man* (1871/ 1981) and *The Expression of the Emotions in Man and Animals* (1872/ 1965). In these books Darwin made his most extensive public comments on psychological issues, but he still did not exploit the scope and richness of the psychology he had outlined in the M and N notebooks.

Both books embrace the idea that the mental traits of our species gradually evolved over time. *Expression* is the more focused work, elaborating an argument that Darwin believed to be especially persuasive in displaying the continuity between mankind and other animals: the common ways in which we express similar emotional states. *Descent* is the more important work from the perspective of psychology because it presents Darwin's scenario for the mental evolution of mankind.

Darwin confronted a tricky problem in *Descent*. He had to demonstrate the continuity of our species with the rest of nature, and at the same time account for the recognizably large gap between the mental capacity of human and nonhuman species. The human mind seemed to represent a discontinuity in nature, a thing far removed from anything else in nature, even from the mind of the chimpanzee. Darwin believed that "mind" was no more than a function of brain. Could the remarkable and unique capacities of the human mind be understood to have evolved through a straightforward process of gradual evolution? The answer to this question must be yes and no. Yes, the mind/brain of humans evolved gradually; Darwin did not introduce any nongradual, abrupt, or miraculous element into his explanation of the evolution of the human mind. No, the process of human mental evolution was not a *straightforward* gradual process. When Darwin had confronted the task of explaining the existence of anomalous mental traits—the instincts of neuter social insects—his clever modification of gradualism involved shifting the action of natural selection from the individual organism to the level of the hive. Darwin utilized the same modification in explaining the evolution of another anomaly in nature, the human mind:

> Natural selection sometimes acts indirectly on the individual, through the preservation of variations which are beneficial only to the community. In regard to certain mental faculties . . . these faculties have been chiefly, or even exclusively, gained for the benefit of the community; the individuals composing the community being at the same time indirectly benefited. (1871/1981, p. 155)

Since Darwin cast the tribe as one of the levels at which natural selection operated in the evolution of mankind, he had to describe the evolution of those mental abilities that promoted social cohesion, facilitated the effective functioning of the group, and enabled the tribe to survive. In *Descent* Darwin described human language and morality as prime examples of faculties that had particular survival value for the tribe. With respect to language he wrote:

> If it be maintained that certain powers, such as self-consciousness, abstraction, & c., are peculiar to man, it may well be that these are the incidental results of other highly-advanced intellectual faculties; and these again are mainly the result of the continued use of a highly developed language. (1871/1981, p. 105)

In this bold statement, self-consciousness and abstraction, the quintessence of human intellect, were treated as *indirect* or "incidental" results of other processes.

Darwin's account, in *Descent,* of the acquisition of a moral sense also highlights the fundamental importance of the shift to the group as the primary level at which selection operates for social animals. Darwin believed the moral sense arose from "parental or filial affections" that had evolved because of the survival value in having a child remain with the parents for a long period of time. These affections were gradually extended to other members of the tribe. If members of the immediate group receive aid and sympathy from each other, their individual survival chances are enhanced indirectly, because of the more efficient functioning of the group.

On Turning Points in Evolution

Darwin conceived of the shift in the level of selection as occurring gradually. He did not believe that there was abrupt change or an "explosion" of brain development, or a threshold dramatically crossed. It is not as though the addition of a small quantity of language capacity or of a moral sense produced a "critical mass" in the brain/mind that abruptly yielded a new and substantially enhanced product. Darwin's concept of evolutionary change involved gentle but significant turning points. If a ball is rolling along a surface, a very gentle sidewise nudge will not dramatically change its immediate condition, but the long-term result will be that the ball travels a very different path. Now conceive of the rolling ball as the process of mental evolution and the nudge as the acquisition of language and social instincts. I believe this metaphor accurately represents Darwin's point of view about the process and pace of evolution. The idea that novelty and uniqueness could arise in a flash, as though crossing a threshold, was incompatible with the gradualism thought-form that had been the basis of Darwin's thinking during his long scientific career. Although modern theorists have recognized the possibility that small changes in *complex* systems can evoke significant acceleration in the evolutionary pathways of certain organisms, Darwin's emphasis was always on the gradual pace of change. He recognized that the rate of change could differ for different species and that complex systems may change more quickly than simple ones, but the rates he specified can be labeled "slow," "slower," and "slowest":

> During early periods of the earth's history, when the forms of life were probably fewer and simpler, the rate of change was probably slower; and at the first dawn of life, when very few forms of the simplest structure existed, the rate of change may have been slow in an extreme degree. (1859/1964, p. 488)

Darwin's idea about a gradual shift in the level at which natural selection operates provided him with a means for understanding the evolution of seemingly anomalous productions of nature, such as the human mind, without abandoning gradualism. Ideas such as correlated change and the indirect consequences for the individual of being part of a social group allowed Darwin to understand the evolution of organisms and behaviors that eventually appeared to be discontinuous with the rest of nature without invoking the idea of abrupt events.

The concept of thought-form proposed in this chapter helps to explain the underlying unity in Darwin's thinking. I have outlined a sequence in which Darwin first acquired expert knowledge in one area (geology). He then used this knowledge as the basis for understanding new subjects by constructing analogies between his domain of expertise and novel domains. This case study of Darwin strongly suggests that the acquisition of expert knowledge in at least one domain is a prerequisite for creative thinking.

CHRONOLOGY
CHARLES DARWIN

1809 February 12: Born at Shrewsbury, England.

1825 Enters University of Edinburgh.

1827 Begins studies at Christ's College, Cambridge University.

1831 April 26: Receives B.A.
      December 27: *Beagle* leaves England.

1834   August 14: Finds marine shells in Andes at 1300 feet.

1835   February 20: Experiences earthquake while in Chile.
        May 14: Arrives at the terraces of Coquimbo, Chile.
        September 17: *Beagle* lands in Galapagos Islands.

1836   October 2: *Beagle* returns to England.

1837   May 31: Theory of coral reef formation presented at Geological Society
        of London.
        July: Begins first notebook on transmutation.
        November 1: Theory of formation of vegetable mould presented at Geo-
        logical Society of London.

1838   June: Travels to Glen Roy in Scottish Highlands.
        July: Begins first notebook on metaphysics.
        September 28: Reads Malthus and has insight into natural selection.

1839   January 29: Marries Emma Wedgwood.
        December 27: Birth of first child, William.
        Begins diary.

1857   Recognized significance of "family selection."

1859   *Origin of Species* published.

1871   *Descent of Man* published.

1872   *Expression of Emotion* published.

1882   April 19: Dies at Down House, Downe England.

ACKNOWLEDGMENTS

The author wishes to thank Marion Keegan for her generous help in the preparation of this chapter.

NOTES

1. The B, C, D, and E notebooks on transmutation were published together in
de Beer, Rowlands, and Skramovsky (1960). Citations in the text from these notebooks are from this publication and use Darwin's pagination. A new and more
complete edition of Darwin's notebooks has recently been published (Barrett,
Gautrey, Herbert, et al., 1987).

2. The M and N notebooks have been transcribed and annotated by Paul H.
Barrett (1980). Citations from these notebooks appear in the text and use Darwin's pagination. The inspiration and methodology for my own study of Darwin
stems directly from Howard E. Gruber's analysis (1981) of Darwin's life and
work during the period in which Darwin wrote the transmutation and "metaphysical" notebooks.

3. On September 28, 1838 Darwin wrote a passage in the D notebook (pp.
134–135) in which he clearly recognized the importance of Malthus's ideas on
population and grasped the idea of natural selection.

4. All citations from the Diary in this chapter come from the unpublished
original "Biographical Sketch of a Child," item DAR210.17 in the Darwin manuscript collection at Cambridge University Library. Page numbers follow Darwin's

pagination. The letter "v" (for verso) following a page number indicates that the citation comes from the page to the left of the numbered page in the diary. My transcription of the diary can be found in Keegan (1985).

5. For a discussion of modern research on the use of mirror experiments to assess the self concept, see Gallup (1983).

REFERENCES

Barlow, N. (Ed.). (1969). *The autobiography of Charles Darwin, 1809–1882.* New York: Norton.

Barrett, P. H. (Ed.). (1980). *Metaphysics, materialism, and the evolution of mind: Early writings of Charles Darwin.* Chicago: University of Chicago Press.

Barrett, P. H., Gautrey, P. J., Herbert, S., Kohn, D., & Smith, S. (Eds.). (1987). *Charles Darwin's notebooks, 1836–1844: Geology, transmutation of species, metaphysical enquiries.* Ithaca, N.Y.: Cornell University Press.

Darwin, C. (1964). *On the origin of species.* Facsimile of first edition, with an introduction by Ernst Mayr. Cambridge, Mass.: Harvard University Press. (Original work published in 1859)

Darwin, C. (1965). *The expression of the emotions in men and animals.* Chicago: University of Chicago Press. (Original work published in 1872)

Darwin, C. (1980). On the formation of mould. In P. H. Barrett (Ed.), *The collected papers of Charles Darwin* (Vol. 1, pp. 49–53). Chicago: University of Chicago Press. (Original work published in 1840)

Darwin, C. (1981). *The descent of man, and selection in relation to sex* (Vol. 1). Princeton: Princeton University Press. (Photo reproduction of the first edition, published in 1871)

de Beer, M. J., Rowlands, M. J., & Skramovsky, B. M. (Eds.). (1960). Darwin's notebooks on transmutation of species. *Bulletin of the British Museum (Natural History) Historical Series, 2, (2, 3, 4, 5).*

Gallup, G. G. (1983). Toward a comparative psychology of mind. In R. L. Mellgren (Ed.), *Animal cognition and behavior.* Amsterdam: North Holland Press.

Ghiselin, M. T. (1969). *The triumph of the Darwinian method.* Berkeley: University of California Press.

Gruber, H. E. (1981). *Darwin on man: A psychological study of scientific creativity.* Chicago: University of Chicago Press.

Herbert, S. (1986). Darwin as a geologist. *Scientific American, 254,* 116–123.

Keegan, R. T. (1985). *The development of Charles Darwin's thinking on psychology.* Unpublished doctoral dissertation, Rutgers University.

Lamarck, J. B. (1809). *Philosophie zoologique* (2 vols.). Paris: Dentu.

Lyell, C. (1830–33). *Principles of geology* (3 vols.). London: John Murray.

Richards, R. (1981). Instinct and intelligence in British natural theology: Some contributions to Darwin's theory of the evolution of behavior. *Journal of the History of Biology, 14*(2), 193–230.

Stauffer, R. C. (Ed.). (1975). *Charles Darwin's natural selection, being the second part of his big species book written from 1856 to 1858.* Cambridge: Cambridge University Press.

Sulloway, F. J. (1982). Darwin's conversion: The Beagle voyage and its aftermath. *Journal of the History of Biology, 15*(3), 325–396.

FIGURE 7–1. William James, c. 1873. By permission of the Houghton Library, Harvard University.

7

Ensembles of Metaphor in the Psychology of William James

JEFFREY V. OSOWSKI

> At a certain stage in the development of every science a degree of vagueness is what best consists with fertility.
>
> WILLIAM JAMES

William James (1842–1910) made this comment in the early days of the science of psychology. The combination of vagueness and fertility in his own thinking found dramatic expression in his use of metaphors. Indeed, James is famous for a single metaphor—the stream of consciousness—which was eventually borrowed to describe a literary genre and entered the intellectual language of the twentieth century.

But an examination of James's use of metaphor does not turn on a single item. On the contrary, it reveals an intricate hierarchic structure of *ensembles* of metaphors. Each ensemble is made up of families of metaphors, and each family has a central metaphor and other individual metaphors. The articulation of members of the ensemble, each with its special function, produces a coherent whole.

My focus is on James's use of these ensembles of metaphors in the development of his *Principles of Psychology* (1890/1950). James had trained as a physician, getting his M.D. from Harvard in 1869. In the following decade, as well as teaching anatomy and physiology at Harvard, he taught philosophy and, later, psychology (see chronology at the end of this chapter).

Once *Principles* was published, James stepped into the front rank of psychologists. The metaphors in this two-volume work are a thought-form and thus provide a lens for examining the creative process. I give central attention to metaphors that are inextricably bound to the theory of consciousness, or mind, that James was developing. These are metaphors that Boyd (1979) calls "theory constitutive metaphors" and that Gruber (1988) refers to as "images of wide scope." Indeed, like many metaphors, they are vivid images, and I shall often refer to them as images; they also range widely both in the multiplicity of their meaning and in the extensive way James uses them in *Principles*. In a final section, in order to see more clearly how they evolved, I map these metaphors onto the 12-year period—from 1878 to 1890—during which James was developing and writing *Principles*.

The Role of Different Levels of Metaphor in the Evolution of Theory

In analyzing the metaphors of a creative person, one immediately encounters a body of data far too large to analyze. The realm can be limited to a workable size by selecting for analysis only those metaphors defined as "images of wide scope."

Images of Wide Scope

Gruber (1988) introduced the notion of images of wide scope as part of the evolving systems approach to creative work. He considers an "image wide when it functions as a schema capable of assimilating to itself a wide range of perceptions, actions, ideas" (p. 135). These are the metaphors that are most durable, most comprehensive, personal, and of greatest influence in the individual's thought process.

In attempting to understand the role of metaphor in theory change, Boyd (1979) examined the concept of theory-constitutive metaphors. This class of metaphor is fundamental to science and is used to introduce theoretical terminology where none previously existed. According to Boyd, such metaphors play a role that is "constitutive of the theories they express, rather than merely exegetical" (p. 360). Such metaphors become the property of the entire scientific community, variations on them are explored, and their cognitive content cannot be made fully explicit.

What characteristics do images of wide scope share? First, they are figures of thought, not merely expressive devices. In this sense, they are or come to be irreplaceable constituents of the theory. Second, they provide models for reasoning within a large domain. They may be used to generate hypotheses, in turn generating theories. Third, they direct the development of theories, in this sense functioning as regulatory schemas. Fourth, they are not only wide, but deep (in that they thoroughly explore the complexities of any one concept). Finally, images of wide scope, although highly personal, may also be shared by a community or a particular scientific discipline.

Ensembles of Metaphors

Research on metaphor has generally been narrowly focused. Often a single metaphor is analyzed at a single point in time and the role of the individual generating the metaphor is underemphasized. Most of this research comes down to semantic analysis, attempting to uncover the structure and meaning of isolated metaphors. Richards's (1936) analysis of a single metaphor into components of tenor and vehicle and Black's (1962) similar method are examples of this type.

The psychological literature includes three exceptions to this focus on single metaphors, none of them commanding wide attention and none relating its subject to the general study of creativity. Hersch (1932) examined Bergson's metaphors and related them to his system of thought in a way similar to the present venture; Gilmore (1971) studied James's use of metaphors in his later philosophical writing, that is, after *Principles;* and Nash (1963) made a brief study of the metaphors of McDougall and Freud. Unlike this chapter, in none of these works is the subject's ensemble of metaphors viewed as part of an evolving system of thought. There is, however, a new study of the development of Freud's ensemble of metaphors during an early period in the history of psychoanalytic thought (Bruchez-Hall, 1989).

In the case of William James, one must begin with the observation that James formed his metaphors into interactive ensembles. My major focus is therefore on James's ensemble of metaphors for his theory of consciousness including *stream of thought, flight and perching of a bird, fringe of felt relations,* and *herdsman.* Together they form the ensemble of metaphors that gives his theory of consciousness, as described in *The Principles of Psychology,* its texture. I use "ensemble" to mean a set of metaphors that are different but are articulated together to form a theory. Within each ensemble there are related clusters, or families, of metaphors.

There is an even larger context that must be analyzed to understand the meaning and function of metaphor—the evolving interactive ensemble of metaphors. The ensemble may be mapped over time to capture the evolving organization of thought.

I shall thus be discussing metaphors at several levels of analysis: (1) individual metaphors, (2) families of metaphors, (3) ensembles of metaphors, (4) the evolution of the ensemble of metaphors, and (5) the cognitive economy as a whole or the development of the entire theory including the relationship between metaphors and ideas.

William James's Theory of Consciousness

James described the important characteristics of consciousness or of the thought process. First, every thought tends to be part of a personal consciousness. There are no thoughts or states of mind unless they are attached to a person, to a you or an I. There is a sense of unity and identity to consciousness.

The second characteristic of consciousness is that within each personal consciousness thought is always changing. No mental state can recur identically; hence there is constant change in mental life.

Third, within each personal consciousness thought is sensibly continuous. According to James, one is able to observe this continuity in one's thought both over time and at any one point in time, both in longitudinal section and in cross section. As thoughts proceed, there is overlap in the *stream of consciousness*. This is also evident in a cross section of the *stream of consciousness* in that any thought is surrounded by other thoughts.

The fourth characteristic of consciousness is that "human thought appears to deal with objects independent of itself; that is, it is cognitive, or possesses the function of knowing" (vol. 1, p. 271). For James, the thought of an object and the object itself are independent of each other.

James's fifth characteristic of consciousness is that thought "is always interested more in one part of its object than in another, and welcomes and rejects, or chooses, all the while it thinks" (vol. 1, p. 284). Consciousness is active. Selective attention, interest, and deliberate activity are the mechanisms of the choosing function as the mind works on the data it receives.

James listed these as the five major characteristics of consciousness in *Principles,* but as he developed the theory he gave relatively little attention to one—objectivity—and he presented still another—the relationships among elements of consciousness are as important as the elements themselves.

I shall refer to these characteristics of consciousness that form the center of James's theory of mind as follows:

Personal consciousness
Change
Continuity
Objectivity
Selectivity
Relations

The Interactive Ensemble of Metaphors in
The Principles of Psychology

The network diagram in Figure 7–2 shows the five characteristics of thought and the corresponding four major families of metaphors in James's theory of mind as described in *Principles*. The metaphors—*stream, fringe, flight,* and *herdsman*—are oversimplified in this diagram. Each represents the central metaphor in an extensive family of its own. In this sense, they are family names. All four metaphors are theory-constitutive images of wide scope.

Several characteristics should be noted in this diagram. First, one could cut through Figure 7–2 in many ways—to view the interrelationships among the metaphors, the interrelationships among the ideas or propositions, clusters of metaphors and propositions, and so on.

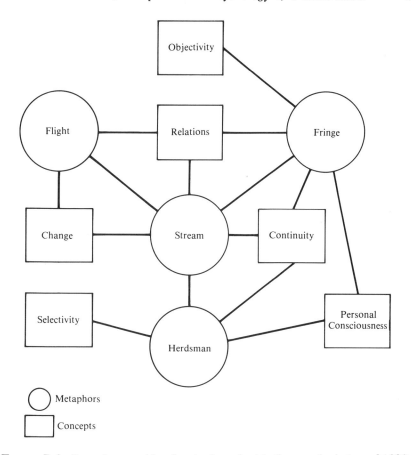

FIGURE 7–2. James's ensemble of metaphors for his theory of mind as of 1890.

Second, any one metaphor may subserve more than one idea or concept. For example, the *fringe* metaphor subserves the notions of continuity, personal consciousness, objectivity, and relations.

Third, connections are not all the same. Some, for example, those between *herdsman* and personal consciousness, are much stronger than others, such as those between *herdsman* and continuity. The strength or privileged nature of certain connections is a function of the importance of that particular metaphor to the meaning of the concept.

Finally, this diagram illustrates one of the most basic assumptions of the evolving systems approach, that thought takes place in a system. In an ensemble and in a family of metaphors or concepts, all constituents are connected in an interrelated system.

Each of the four major families of metaphors in Figure 7–2 is discussed below. Each family is introduced through its parent metaphor: *stream, fringe, flight,* and *herdsman*.

Stream of Thought

The *stream* is, without doubt, James's most comprehensive and best known metaphor. The *stream* family is a central family of metaphors around which all others were organized. The following other metaphors or images were part of the *stream* family: *train, chain, path, current* (both *water* and *electric*), *channel, line* (with *segments*), *procession, kaleidoscope,* and *fabric.* Through the *stream* family of metaphors, James was able to capture the concepts of continuity, constant change, direction, connectedness, pace, rhythm, and flow, all of which were important characteristics of thought or consciousness.

Stream/Chain/Train. James amplified the *stream* metaphor by contrasting it, in a variety of contexts, with two similar, yet strikingly different, metaphors—the *chain* and *train.* Until James, the psychology of consciousness was dominated by the British empiricists perhaps best represented by the associationist atomistic view of Hume in which the thoughts comprising consciousness were viewed as connected in linear and segmental *chains.*

In contrast, James represented consciousness as a fluid structure. In introducing the *stream* metaphor, he contrasted his own image with those of the associationists:

> Consciousness, then, does not appear to itself chopped up in bits. Such words as "chain" or "train" do not describe it fitly as it presents itself in the first instance. It is nothing jointed; it flows. A "river" or a "stream" are the metaphors by which it is most naturally described. *In talking of it hereafter let us call it the stream of thought, of consciousness or of subjective life.* (vol. 1, p. 239)

A *stream* is obviously a very different organizational metaphor from a *chain* or *train* in several ways. Constant change and movement are integral parts of the *stream,* as is continuity. Also, the idea of connection between elements of consciousness takes on a new meaning. The elements of consciousness or ideas are *related* to each other in varied and important ways, not just joined or simply linked. Real relationships do exist and they are as important as the elements of thought themselves. For James, complex thoughts could not simply be built by chaining simple thoughts. Like the *stream,* consciousness is continuous, flowing, there is constant change, much diversity, variability, and a certain connectedness in which there are no separate or discrete parts.

Throughout most of *Principles* James used the *train* and *chain* metaphors as examples of exactly what consciousness is *not.* He built upon the *stream* and related metaphors as he developed his theory of mind, its function, the self, identity of the self, and more. It is interesting to note, however, that he also used the *train* and *chain* metaphors to describe key components of his own theory of mind, specifically, the functions of association and the neural machinery. We see, in this oscillating use of these two metaphors, James's attempts to deal with apparent contradiction. The neural machinery appears to function like a *chain,* association like a *train,* but subjectively, conscious-ness appears to function like a *stream.*

James chose not to capitalize consistently on the similarities between the *train* and *stream* metaphors. His comparisons were made mainly to point out the differences. He used the *train* and *chain* images as examples of an incor-rect description of consciousness or thought. He repeatedly drew parallels be-tween the brain and the mind, but was unable to do the same with the images he chose to represent those theoretical structures—the *train* and the *stream.* James was apparently unable to find one unifying image that would fully resolve the inherent conflicts between his theories of neural functioning and of subjective consciousness.

James was undoubtedly aware of this omission and he probably accepted the different functional and structural metaphors for the two concepts that he tried so hard to wed—the brain and the mind. But he still used one meta-phor—the *train*—in antithetical ways. The *train* became two images for James. His mechanical or operational *train* metaphor, used in his theory of association, was very different in content, intent, and emphasis from the structural *train* metaphor, used to contrast with the *stream* image.

Stream/Path/Current. James often used this family of similar yet dif-ferent metaphors—*stream, path, current*—to explore further the notions of continuity, change, and connection. We must ask: What did the new meta-phors add to the ensemble? How did he capitalize on the similarities and the differences among the metaphors?

To answer these questions, the theoretical problems with which James was struggling and which found expression in this particular ensemble of meta-phors must be understood. He was trying to resolve the potential contradic-tion among the notions of continuity, change, and connection—this time in relation to a different theoretical problem, again James's notion of the rela-tion between brain and mind.

What are the essential similarities and differences among these meta-phors—*stream, path, current?* Some important characteristics of a *stream* are that it flows, is continuous, is nonlinear, has movement, has pace, is in con-stant change, and is unified because there are no separate parts. A *stream* may have, within it, a *channel* or a *current.*

A *path* is similar in that it is continuous, but in a different way from the *stream.* Although a *path* may be branching in its form, James did not stress this aspect. We may therefore consider James's *path* image to be a linear structure. A *path* has three main characteristics. It is a way or a route; it is beaten or trodden by the feet of men or animals; something generally moves along it.

James used the *current* metaphor in two interesting ways—as the move-ment of a portion of a larger body of *water* (as within a *stream*) and as the flow of *electricity.* The difference in meaning is important. *Current* must be considered as not one, but two distinct metaphors. James carefully used these in the development of his arguments regarding the brain–mind relation.

The question of the relationship between the brain and the mind can be viewed as a problem in reconciling two sets of competing, and potentially contradictory, models of mental functioning—structural versus dynamic. The *path* metaphor helped James deal with the structure of the physiological machinery and also served as a bridge between the *stream* and *chain/train* metaphors. The *current* metaphors were dynamic in nature largely because both *water* and *electric current* follow certain laws or rules of functioning such as summation and water pressure.

In the following two passages in *Principles,* James used the *path* and *current* metaphors to restate the brain–mind problem:

> The brain is essentially a place of currents, which run in organized paths. (vol. 1, p. 70)

and

> Our sensations and thoughts are but cross-sections, as it were, of currents whose essential consequence is motion, and which no sooner run in at one nerve than they run out again at another. (vol. 2, p. 526)

The brain and mind have an organized *structure* (*paths*) and *movement* (*currents*). In the *stream/path/current* family, which was most evident in volume 2 of *Principles,* the *stream* metaphor, so dominant in volume 1, played a much more passive role. While it was the most fitting metaphor for use in the phenomenological analysis of consciousness, it could not adequately be used in the formation of a theory that included not only subjective consciousness, but also neural functioning.

The *path* metaphor was used by James to represent his description of both phenomenological and physiological processes. It added new and important dimensions to the ensemble in that it was an intermediary image between the *stream* and the *train/chain* metaphors and one of a critical triad of metaphors—*path, electric current, water current*—that James developed to describe the neural machinery.

James capitalized on the double meaning of the *current* metaphor, hydraulic and electric, using the two sometimes interchangeably in a single passage. In the the following passage, the *water current* metaphor is used to describe the way incoming stimuli might stop rather than cause bodily movement:

> There are probably no exceptions to the diffusion of every impression through the *nerve-centres.* The *effect* of the wave through the centres may, however, often be to interfere with processes, and to diminish tensions already existing there; and the outward consequences of such inhibitions may be the arrest of discharges from inhibited regions and the checking of bodily activities already in process of occurrence. When this happens it probably is like the draining or siphoning of certain channels by currents flowing through others. When, in walking, we suddenly stand still because a sound, sight, smell, or thought catches our attention, something like this occurs. (vol. 2, p. 373)

Draining, siphoning, channels—these are all clearly hydraulic aspects of the *current* image. They were used by James for the electrical image as well, expanding meaning and creating flexibility in the theoretical structure.

The electrical aspects of the *current* metaphor allowed James to expand his argument on the facts of neural physiology; combining it with the *water current* metaphor allowed him to move to some degree toward resolving the brain–mind issue. In the following passage James described the neural process in hallucination:

> We have seen that the free discharge of cells into each other through associative paths is a likely reason why the maximum intensity of function is not reached when the cells are excited by their neighbors in the cortex. . . . The idea is that the leakage forward along these paths is too rapid for the inner tension in any centre to accumulate to the maximal explosion-point, unless the exciting currents are greater than those which the various portions of the cortex supply to each other. . . . *If, however, the leakage forward were to stop,* the tension inside certain cells might reach the explosion-point, even though the influence which excited them came only from neighboring cortical parts. (vol. 2, p. 123)

Three points are noteworthy in this passage. First, James is clearly discussing neural physiology. Second, the *current* metaphor is electrical in nature, with characteristics such as explosion-point (e.g., excitation or threshold), discharge of cells, intensity (as opposed to tension due to damming in the *water current* metaphor), excitation from neighboring areas (e.g., irradiation), and leakage forward. Third, this passage immediately precedes another in which the description is more phenomenological and the metaphor of choice is *water current*.

It may be concluded that the *electric current* metaphor was formed by James to fit his model of neural physiology, while the *water current* metaphor was formed to fit his model of subjective consciousness or mind. His use of *current* as a generic metaphor with double meaning was a deliberate attempt to resolve the differences and contradictions between brain and mind as he saw them.

The *stream* family of metaphors helps to explain the role of metaphor in the development of a theory. By choosing a set of metaphors with multiple meanings—*electric* and *water current*—James was able to move toward resolving a conflict inherent in the brain–mind issue. The overlap in meaning of these metaphors served to bring together disparate concepts. Laws of functioning in *hydraulic* and *electric current* are similar yet different, mirroring James's view of the laws of functioning in the brain and the mind. James did not resolve the brain–mind issue and he recognized that the science of his time did not have the tools or knowledge to approach this problem adequately. However, this did not stop James from attacking the problem, one of his most valued weapons being this particular family of metaphors.

Flight and Perching of a Bird

The family headed by the *stream* metaphor provides a broad synthesis of concepts (continuity, change, movement, flow, connectedness, circuitry). But it does not provide a clear representation of unity in consciousness, nor does it contain a mechanism by which discrete thoughts are linked or connected. The *stream* family represents continuity and change in a gross structural sense, but it does not effectively deal with the inner articulation of the continuous, ever-changing consciousness. How are apparently discrete thoughts related? What are the mechanisms of connection? James here attacked the associationist atomistic view of consciousness, this time from a different perspective. Through a new family of metaphors headed by the image of the *flight* and *perching* of a bird, he stressed the fact that relationships among elements of consciousness are as important as the elements themselves:

> When we take a rapid general view of the wonderful stream of our consciousness, what strikes us first is the different *pace* of its different portions. Our mental life, like a bird's life seems to be made of an alternation of flights and perchings. The rhythm of language expresses this, where every thought is expressed in a sentence, and every sentence closed by a period. The resting-places are usually occupied by sensorial imaginations of some sort, whose peculiarity is that they can be held before the mind for an indefinite time, and contemplated without changing; the places of flight are filled with thoughts of relations, static or dynamic, that for the most part obtain between the matters contemplated in the periods of comparative rest. *Let us call the resting-places the "substantive parts," and the places of flight the "transitive parts," of the stream of thought.* (vol. 1, p. 243)

For James this was a retreat from the *stream* image in that the *flight* metaphor represents connectedness, but not unbroken continuity. It is sequential and segmented; the *stream* is not. James used the *flight* image to emphasize the relations between the elements of thought as well as the pacing and alternation among substantive and transitory aspects of thought.

As regards the transitory characteristic of thought, the *stream* and *flight* images are similar. Both are fleeting, moving, and have inherent pace. The *stream,* however, has no nodes as in the *perching* of the bird after flight. It is all movement. In the *flight* and *perching* metaphors, the image is segmented; activity is followed by a pause. When the *stream* image could not capture all of the concepts within the theoretical structure, James developed this new yet related image.

Could he have chosen a single unifying image? Perhaps; but in fact, his argument gained scope through the use of the two images, particularly in the synthesis of potentially conflicting notions.

Fringe of Felt Relations (or Halo)

The *stream* and *flight* families of metaphors, in combination, deal effectively with the mechanisms of continuity and connectedness in thought. But James wanted to describe other kinds of relationships among thoughts. Objects in the world are discrete. In consciousness, however, all is one. How does this happen? How can the discreteness of the external world and of the mechanisms of thought, like words and images, be presented by something as continuous and unified as consciousness? To answer these questions, James developed another family of metaphors centered around the *fringe of felt relations:*

> This is all I have to say about the sensible continuity and unity of our thought as contrasted with the apparent discreteness of the words, images, and other means by which it seems to be carried on. Between all their substantive elements there is "transitive" consciousness, and the words and images are "fringed," and not discrete as to a careless view they seem. (vol. 1, p. 271)

This passage provides the bridge from the *flight* to the *fringe* image. The *fringe* family of metaphors extends the notion of transitions among ideas by describing the mechanisms of meaning, relation, and context. Consciousness is not internally comprised of a simple linking of isolated images. There is a sense of belonging together of images in consciousness. The *fringe* and the overlap of *fringes* among successive images are what defines the relatedness among these images.

In the passage that follows James synthesized several important concepts in his theory of mind, bringing together the ideas of continuity, discreteness, and overall belongingness of consciousness:

> The traditional psychology talks like one who should say a river consists of nothing but pailsful, spoonsful, quartpotsful, barrelsful, and other moulded forms of water. Even were the pails and the pots all actually standing in the stream, still between them the free water would continue to flow. It is just this free water of consciousness that psychologists resolutely overlook. Every definite image in the mind is steeped and dyed in the free water that flows round it. With it goes the sense of its relations, near and remote, the dying echo of whence it came to us, the dawning sense of whither it is to lead. The significance, the value, of the image is all in this halo or penumbra, that surrounds and escorts it,—or rather that is fused into one with it and has become bone of its bone and flesh of its flesh; leaving it, it is true, an image of the same *thing* it was before, but making it an image of that thing newly taken and freshly understood. (vol. 1, p. 255)

This is a most critical passage. Without the *fringe* image James lacked a firm statement of the way that substantive elements of thought along with their transitory aspects were combined to form a unified, continuous, flowing consciousness. These notions were provided for, to varying degrees, in the family of metaphors with *fringe* at the center.

In this transition passage we see a fusing of the *stream* metaphor (movement, flow, change, continuity, connection) with the *halo* image (separation, connection, gradation, relation). "Surrounds" is applicable to both the *stream* and the *halo*. "Escorts" is applicable only to the *stream,* but not to the *halo.* The *stream* lacks a center of focus or the substantive aspect; the *halo* lacks the characteristic of movement.

Herdsman

Two basic and important characteristics of consciousness have yet to be described: *personal* consciousness and *selectivity.* James formed a family of metaphors, with the image of the *herdsman* as its center, to represent these two important characteristics as well as the notions of unity and identity in consciousness. Personal identity is defined as a feeling that there is a self, a center to which all things, ideas, and images adhere. This feeling of identity or ownership is achieved only because there is a unity of self; all our selves, over time and in cross section, are united because they are continuous with each other. Finally, the self, for James, was an active selective mechanism.

James interwove the *herdsman* metaphor with the existing ensemble of metaphors: how is consciousness, with all its diversity, connected and united into a *single personal consciousness?*

> Our recent simile of the herd of cattle will help us. It will be remembered that the beasts were brought together into one herd because their owner found on each of them his brand. The "owner" symbolizes here that "section" of consciousness, or pulse of thought, which we have all along represented as the vehicle of judgment of identity; and the "brand" symbolizes the characters of warmth and continuity by reason of which the judgment is made. There is found a *self*-brand, just as there is found a herd-brand. Each brand, so far, is the mark, or cause of our knowing, that certain things belong-together. No beast would be so branded unless he belonged to the owner of the herd. They are not his because they are branded; they are branded because they are his. . . . For common-sense insists that the unity of all selves is not a mere appearance of similarity or continuity, ascertained after the fact. She is sure that it involves a real belonging to a real Owner, to a pure spiritual entity of some kind. Relation to this entity is what makes the self's constituents stick together as they do for thought. (vol. 1, p. 337)

Thought is both continuous and united into a single personal consciousness because there is an owner, a medium, or proprietor of the thought—the *herdsman.* Continuity derives from the stability of the self. This stability derives, in turn, from a sense or feeling of ownership, the "characters of warmth and continuity." The *herdsman* was introduced into the *stream* because James could not conceive of the *stream of consciousness* without a medium or unifying force, the vehicle of personal identity.

James was positing here a self, which was absent in associationist psychology. Resemblance and continuity in the *stream of consciousness* were not enough to explain personal identity and unity. The notions of active judging and ownership were introduced in the *herdsman* image to fill this gap in the theoretical structure.

The Evolving Ensemble of Metaphors
for James's Theory of Mind

Much of the material in *Principles* was published in the form of journal articles during the 12-year period (1878–90) James spent writing the two volumes. The earliest known reference to *Principles* is in a letter from James to publisher Henry Holt in June 1878 in answer to an invitation to write a text on psychology for a science series (Burkhardt, 1981). James agreed to have it completed in two years. This commitment could not be maintained; the final manuscript was presented to Holt in May 1890.

It is possible to determine with some assurance when the component articles were written and thereby to trace the evolution of James's major psychological tenets and the respective ensemble of metaphors. Material in 20 of the 28 chapters of *Principles* was published in no fewer than 20 articles before 1890.

Analysis of these articles is the key to understanding the maturing and orchestration of James's thought over this 12-year period. For reasons of space only a very compressed account is given here (for a full discussion see Osowski, 1986).

As we have seen, James formed an elaborate interactive ensemble of metaphors in *Principles,* including the four major families *stream, flight, fringe,* and *herdsman.* This represents his theory as of 1890, the year in which *Principles* was published.

Principles can also be examined as a process, as a theory evolving over a period of 12 years. Table 7–1 shows all of the major metaphors used by James in this 12-year period and the dates of their first appearance.

The table presents a number of additional points. First, not all of the characteristics of consciousness have equal numbers of corresponding metaphors. Continuity is by far the most heavily represented, followed by change. These are the two central characteristics in James's theory of mind; hence they get the most attention. Perhaps continuity was the most troublesome concept in the theory, thus needing all that metaphor could provide to clarify it.

There is also a pattern of appearance and disappearance of major metaphors. For example, two of the characteristics of his theory of mental life, selectivity and objectivity, were developed early, then became less the center of concern, and were revived in the 1890 version.

James did not begin to formulate his ideas about the personal nature of consciousness until very late. The family of metaphors for this characteristic of mental life was important but small.

TABLE 7–1. Major Metaphors for James's Theory of Mind

Characteristic			Year of Publication			
	1878	1879	1880	1884	1887	1890
Personal consciousness						Herdsman Warmth/intimacy Judging thought
Change	Bud out	Sprout out	Sprout out Unroll Current Flow	Stream Fringe Halo Penumbra Procession	Current Plasticity	Stream Flight Current Specious present Kaleidoscope Flow
Continuity	Chain Procession Bud out Lifted along	Sprout out	Train Chain Unroll Sprout out Awaken	Stream Fringe Procession	Fringe	Stream Fringe Chain Train Bamboo Log jam Specious present
Objectivity				Fringe	Fringe	Fringe Stream
Selectivity		Sculptor Accentuating finger Helmsman Loaded dice	Presiding arbiter			Herdsman Sculptor Log jam Judging thought Loaded dice
Relations				Stream Fringe Flight Halo Penumbra	Fringe	Stream Fringe Flight

Table 7–1 shows that the development of a theory and of an ensemble of metaphors can take a long time. In 1878 we see the first appearance of a metaphor for continuity, *procession*—a rather primitive image when compared to the complex family of metaphors for the same concept in *Principles*. James did not arrive at the *stream* image in a single flash of insight. It developed from *procession* through *sprout, unroll, train, awaken, path*, to *stream*.

This conclusion that James's images and ideas were developed slowly and laboriously challenges the more popular understanding of James as a remarkable and facile prose writer whose images spilled out as he wrote. But while he was prolific in his writing, he struggled in developing his theories and metaphors. His progress in writing *Principles* and developing the ensemble of metaphors within that work was anything but steady; there were periods of great productivity and spontaneity followed by lengthy spells of painfully slow effort.

Finally, Table 7–1 demonstrates a great deal of overlap, as did Figure 7–2. Some metaphors were used to serve more than one concept. For example, *stream* was used to elucidate the ideas of change and continuity; *herdsman* and *fringe* each appeared in two components of the theory. By means of this overlap, James could bring together diverse concepts. He purposely used the ambiguity and elasticity in metaphor to integrate the important components of his theory of mental life. He taught us that connections between ideas are as important as the ideas themselves. Metaphor thus provides the necessary flexibility to connect diverse ideas. One of the major functions of metaphor in the cognitive economy is that it allows one representation to have more than one meaning.

Conclusions: The Various Functions of Metaphor in Creative Thinking

A survey of mental metaphors in psychological articles from 1894 to 1975 by Gentner and Grudin (1985) provides a benchmark for comparing James with other psychologists. The mean number of metaphors per article was three. James's article included in the survey—"President's Address: The Experience of Activity" (James, 1905)—included 29 metaphors. Metaphor, both as a thought-form and as an expressive device, was clearly critical to James.

Theory-constitutive metaphors or images of wide scope, which James formed into families and ensembles, were important components of his theory of consciousness. The analysis of these ensembles of metaphor and their evolution reveals several major functions of metaphor in the creative thought process.

Substantiation of Vague or Elusive Ideas

The theorist works at different levels of abstraction. In general, James's use of metaphor increased and intensified as the topic became more abstract. This may reflect James's need to concretize highly abstract thoughts. His metaphors and images are relatively concrete and, in many ways, easier to understand than the abstractions they represent. By giving substance to abstract or elusive thoughts metaphors make them available for inspection. Metaphors are memorable, meaningful, and repeatable, especially when they express ideas that are difficult to grasp. Beyond this, metaphor may provide a means to express an idea for which the language may not have any literal terms available (Ortony, Reynolds, & Arter, 1978).

In this sense, metaphor serves a framework function, a concrete structure upon which concepts, abstractions, or theories may be built or hung. The major metaphors listed in Figure 7–2 became the framework upon which the major components of James's theory of consciousness were built.

Metaphor is thus an important structural device allowing the thinker to operate simultaneously at various levels of abstraction.

Generation of New Ideas or New Organizations of Knowledge

Each organization of knowledge represents only a plateau in the evolution of the cognitive economy. Each plateau is organized in such a way that new questions are asked at the same time that others are answered. Metaphor serves an important function in this generative process.

Metaphors can represent the unknown as well as the known. That is, while a metaphor may in some respects accurately represent a particular concept, that same metaphor may in other respects be a false or incomplete representation of the concept. Thus a metaphor creates productive or generative tension.

For example, James's *stream* metaphor answered many questions and, in its elaboration, through the generation of the family members, James was able to develop and draw together many strands of meaning. Equally important, however, were the strands of meaning in James's conceptualization of thought that were *not* adequately represented or captured in the *stream* image. This gap in meaning was, in a very real sense, created, perceived, and confronted through the elaboration of the *stream* metaphor, and it led to the generation of several new hypotheses, concepts, and metaphors.

A metaphor, then, is both true and untrue in its relationship to a concept or set of concepts in a theory. Metaphors may also be ambiguous, and that ambiguity creates tensions that serve to drive the thinker forward in an effort to resolve it. The same is true of the contradictions frequently created when a metaphor is formed. James, in fact, purposely created contradiction and ambiguity. Just when it appeared that he had established a stable organization of knowledge, he would do something to upset the equilibrium.

When used in this way, metaphors can provide energy and allow the thought process to be self-generating. Leondar (1968), in noting this generative function, called metaphor the "agent of discovery."

Testing the Theory

Hoffman (1984) noted that phenomena can be examined through metaphors that act like models to see if the phenomena behave in accordance with the theory. In this sense, metaphor can be used to verify a theory but also to generate falsifiers that serve to test the theory and its limits. It provides a way to demonstrate how the theory might be wrong and if it is, to identify how the theory has to be modified.

James frequently tested his ideas by forming metaphors and groups of metaphors. In his use of the *train* metaphor as a representation of his own theory as well as a representation of the theory he was criticizing (associationist atomism), James was testing limits. He found, for example, that while the *stream* image was adequate as a representation of the phenomenological side of his theory, it could not adequately or apropriately represent his ideas about neural physiology. In this testing out of metaphors, the movement from single metaphors to families and ensembles becomes inevitable.

Organization of Knowledge

In a study of William James, master of synthesis, it is important to focus on the ways he organized his ideas to form a coherent theory. For James, metaphor was an indispensable thought-form, a representational tool that served to organize knowledge, to relate old information to new concepts, and to expand the scope of the theory. The very scope of James's theory guaranteed a perpetual and generative movement between the single metaphor of the moment and the larger metaphoric structure of his thought.

Kuhn (1979) noted the role metaphor plays in relating perception to conception. New metaphors provide new ways both to cut up the world and to create relatedness among concepts. By forming the metaphor, the individual can manipulate the joints or relationships among concepts, thus creating new organizations of knowledge. Using metaphor as a model, the individual can inspect the new proposed organization of knowledge, develop hypotheses about relationships, and modify as appropriate. Through this process, the individual can create new perspectives and achieve novel views of a domain (Black, 1979).

Through a family of metaphors including *fringe,* James was able to organize many ideas and facts for which the relationships were unclear. He was able to describe continuity across time and in the momentary cross section of consciousness. James knew that consciousness has elemental thoughts that are related to one another in some way. He was able to define the relationship between these two notions or the "joint" in the system of ideas through the formulation of the *fringe of felt relations* metaphor.

Metaphor opens the realm of inquiry and allows the creative individual to step outside institutional or disciplinary constraints (Rudwick, 1977). Because there is a lot of free play in metaphor, meaning can be manipulated to bring together diverse concepts. Creative individuals such as James carefully construct their metaphors and form them into families and ensembles in ways that allow the individual to manipulate meaning, generate hypotheses, test syntheses of ideas, and form new organizations of knowledge. Metaphor provides the ability to move, without too much constraint, from the known through the unknown to new organizations of knowledge. None of this would be possible if the thinker were restricted to a single metaphor. Creative work requires skilled navigation through the chosen realm, which in turn requires the construction and use of an ensemble of metaphors.

CHRONOLOGY
WILLIAM JAMES

1842	January 11: Born in New York City.
1843	Brother Henry James born.
1855–58	James family sojourn in Europe.
1859–60	Again Europe. William studies art in Geneva.
1861	Abandons career as painter. Enters Lawrence Scientific School, Harvard.
1864	Enters Harvard Medical School.
1865–66	Assistant to biologist Louis Agassiz in expedition on the Amazon River.
1869	Receives medical degree at Harvard.
1869–70	Prolonged depression, recovery.
1873	Instructor in anatomy and physiology, Harvard.
1875	Begins teaching psychology, Harvard.
1876	Appointed assistant professor, Harvard.
1878	Marries Alice Howe Gibbens. Signs contract to write *Principles*.
1879	Begins teaching philosophy, Harvard.
1885	Appointed professor of philosophy, Harvard.
1890	Publication of *Principles of Psychology*.
1895–1903	Active in Anti-Imperialist League (vice president for a time).
1897	Publication of *The Will to Believe and Other Essays on Popular Philosophy*.
1899–1902	Breakdown in health. Two years in Europe.
1901	Gifford Lectures in Edinburgh, later published as *The Varieties of Religious Experience*.
1906	Lowell Institute Lectures, later published as *Pragmatism*.
1910	Publication of *The Moral Equivalent of War*.
1910	August 26: Dies at Chocorua, New Hampshire.

REFERENCES

Black, M. (1962). *Models and metaphors*. Ithaca, N.Y.: Cornell University Press.

Black, M. (1979). More about metaphor. In A. Ortony (Ed.), *Metaphor and thought*. Cambridge: Cambridge University Press.

Boyd, R. (1979). Metaphor and theory change: What is metaphor? In A. Ortony (Ed.), *Metaphor and thought*. Cambridge: Cambridge University Press.

Bruchez-Hall, C. (1989). *Freud's metaphors during an early period in the history of psychoanalytic thought*. Doctoral dissertation, University of Geneva.

Burkhardt, F. H. (1981). (Ed.). *The works of William James: The principles of psychology* (3 vols.). Cambridge, Mass.: Harvard University Press.

Gentner, D., & Grudin, J. (1985). The evolution of mental metaphors in psychology: A ninety year retrospective. *American Psychologist, 40*(2), 181–192.

Gilmore, L. G. (1971). *The educational significance of the thought and metaphor of William James*. Unpublished doctoral dissertation, Boston University.

Gruber, H. E. (1988). Darwin's tree of nature and other images of wide scope. In J. Wechsler (Ed.), *On aesthetics in science* (2nd ed.), Boston: Birkhäuser.

Hersch, J. (1932). Les images dans l'oeuvre de M. Bergson. *Archives de Psychologie, 23*, 97–130.

Hoffman, R. R. (1984). Some implications of metaphor for philosophy and psychology of science. In R. Dirven & W. Paprotte (Eds.), *The ubiquity of metaphor*. Amsterdam: John Benjamins.

James, W. (1905). The experience of activity. *Psychological Review, 12*, 1–17.

James, W. (1950). *The principles of psychology* (2 vols.). New York: Dover. (Original work published in 1890).

Kuhn, T. S. (1979). Metaphor in science. In A. Ortony (Ed.), *Metaphor and thought*. Cambridge: Cambridge University Press.

Leondar, B. (1968). *The structure and function of metaphor*. Unpublished doctoral dissertation, Harvard University.

Nash, H. (1963). The role of metaphor in psychological theory. *Behavioral Science, 8*, 336–345.

Ortony, A., Reynolds, R. E., & Arter, J. A. (1978). Metaphor: Theoretical and empirical research. *Psychological Bulletin, 85*, 919–943.

Osowski, J. V. (1986). *Metaphor and creativity: A case study of William James*. Unpublished doctoral dissertation, Institute for Cognitive Studies, Rutgers University.

Richards, I. A. (1936). *The philosophy of rhetoric*. London: Oxford University Press.

Rudwick, M. J. S. (1977). Historical analogies in the geological work of Charles Lyell. *Janus, 64*, 89–106.

FIGURE 8–1. Dorothy Richardson, aged 44 (1917). By kind permission of Sheena Odle, Literary Executrix, Dorothy M. Richardson Estate.

8

Stream of Consciousness and Reconstruction of Self in Dorothy Richardson's *Pilgrimage*

DORIS B. WALLACE

. . . perpetually haunted by the mutability of ideas.
DOROTHY M. RICHARDSON

Dorothy Richardson's pilgrimage was a long walk back and forth between the self and the earlier selves. Her life and work show how the artist, by creating life, changes it. She wrote about herself, reconstructing her own past and thus her identity. The very fact that no one knew of the autobiographical nature of her novel *Pilgrimage* gave her more latitude, both for revelation and for blending the lived life with the created one. The fact, also, that she wrote this very long novel over a 40-year period and lived with the central character—herself—all that time strengthened the fusion of the two levels of reality. Untangling these two skeins to make plain their relationship as part of the creative process is one of the aims of this chapter.

Although it has been my task to untangle these threads, it was Richardson's to interweave them. This was not at all an intellectual conceit but an attempt to accomplish her life's goal of creating a literature of feminine realism. How she did this is also the subject of this chapter.[1]

Dorothy M. Richardson (1873–1957) wanted to depict immediate subjective experience, to write a novel, as she said, of "feminine realism." In her 13-volume autobiographical *Pilgrimage,* she pioneered the stream-of-consciousness genre in the English novel; she was the direct forerunner of James Joyce and Virginia Woolf. Her importance in the history of the English novel has been widely acknowledged (Allen, 1976; Edel, 1972; Fromm, 1977; Hanscombe & Smyers, 1987; Hansford-Johnson, 1963; Humphrey, 1955; Rosenberg, 1973; Sinclair, 1918; Woolf, 1923). Still, she remains the least well known of the important stream-of-consciousness writers.

Although the phrase "stream of consciousness" was invented by a psychologist and obviously refers to psychological processes, it has received more attention in the domain of literature than in psychology. One of the goals of this chapter is to reinsert the idea into the psychology of creativity, with special attention to the issues of self-definition that it raises.

"Stream of consciousness," as used here, describes both content and technique. The content depicted in the stream-of-consciousness novel is inner psychic existence and functioning, especially its inchoate and incoherent qualities. It is in this sense that it differs from other psychological fiction. Several techniques have been used to convey this content, for example, indirect and direct interior monologue and free association. Robert Humphrey (1955) provides a useful discussion of the works of Richardson, Woolf, Joyce, and Faulkner. All have in common a changed relationship between author and reader and between author and characters. All tried to represent essentially private processes. The puzzle of making something public while retaining its private quality was resolved by technique. In France, Edouard Dujardin (1887/1968) was the first to use the stream-of-consciousness genre.

Pilgrimage was published beginning in 1915. Marcel Proust began writing his seven-volume novel *A la recherche du temps perdu* in 1909; it was translated and published in England in 1922. Proust's purpose was subjective remembering. By the foregoing definition, he was not a stream-of-consciousness writer. Similarly, Henry James, who often described the psychological content of the mind, was concerned with its rational qualities. He did not treat its free-flowing elliptical contents. James Joyce spent 10 years (mostly in Trieste) producing *A Portrait of the Artist as a Young Man,* which appeared in England in serial form in 1915, the same year as the first volume of *Pilgrimage,* but was not published as a book until 1916—in the United States. But it was not until *Ulysses* that Joyce exploited the new genre. *Ulysses,* which was banned in England and Ireland, did not appear until 1922. *Finnegans Wake,* which was the culmination of stream of consciousness in Joyce's work, appeared in 1939. Virginia Woolf, with whom Richardson's name is also often coupled, began using the stream-of-consciousness technique in her third novel, *Jacob's Room,* published in 1922. But here again, Woolf did not fully exploit the genre until later, in *Mrs. Dalloway* (1925), *To the Lighthouse* (1927), and *The Waves* (1931).

What did Richardson mean by "feminine realism"? How did she depict subjective experience and evolve a new genre in *Pilgrimage?* Why did writing the novel over half a lifetime assume a different pace and rhythm at different periods? Why did she call it a novel when it was so closely autobiographical?

Richardson's elected task demanded that she think psychologically. Her purpose—to depict inner experience directly—led her to quarry the processes of her own mind. This undertaking also preoccupied her contemporaries in the new field of psychology. Wundt (1904), at Leipzig, believing that the study of mind had to be a "science of experience," examined through introspection the controlled observation of consciousness. Titchener's (1899) aims were similar. He took the experiencing organism as his universe of discourse. In their attempts to gain experimental control over their data, psychologists such as Titchener sought to identify the fundamental *elements* of consciousness—sensations, images, feelings. William James, on the other hand, described consciousness as indivisible, personal and individualistic, a stream forever changing, sensibly continuous, and selective.

In describing the personal nature of consciousness in his famous chapter "The Stream of Thought" (1950), James said:

> No other thought even comes into direct *sight* of a thought in another personal consciousness than its own. Absolute insulation, irreducible pluralism, is the law. . . . Neither contemporaneity, nor proximity in space, nor similarity of quality and content are able to fuse thoughts together which are sundered by the barrier of belonging to different personal minds. The breaches between such thoughts are the most absolute breaches in nature. (p. 226)

Here James spoke to Dorothy Richardson's condition. But in spite of the insulation of indvidual minds, the absolute breach that James claimed is precisely the one she wished to bridge. The elements of sensation, image, and feelings, identified by the early elementarists, loom large in *Pilgrimage* and in other Richardson works. But it was James, the premature "wholist," who identified her immediate datum—the personal self.

Richardson wanted to depict inner experience as it appears to the experiencing person, often unorganized and unselected. To communicate this disorder, she invented a new literary genre and techniques that changed the relationship between writer and reader. Where psychologists, as scientists, were intent on establishing general laws, Richardson's purpose dictated that she describe the experience of an individual. She used introspection toward that special end. This is why *Pilgrimage* is autobiographical fiction, a novel in which Richardson reconstructs her own past.

Brief Biographical Background

Richardson, the third of four daughters, was born in 1873 in Berkshire, England (see chronology at the end of this chapter). She tells us that her parents badly wanted a son and that after the birth of the fourth daughter, her father, Charles Richardson, began referring to Dorothy as his son. Richardson (1943/

1959)[2] also attributed this habit of her father's to her own boylike willfull-ness and unruliness.

Charles Richardson was the son of a well-to-do tradesman. As soon as his father died he sold the family business. He aspired to be a rich gentleman, to have no need to work, and to pursue his interests in science and art. A member of the British Association for the Advancement of Science and an enthusiastic Darwinian, he cultivated acquaintances in academic, scientific, and artistic circles. He had little or no financial acumen, was deeply extravagant, and eventually went bankrupt. But when he had money the family lived extremely well.

There is little record of jollity, love, or play in this man. Richardson describes him as a descendant of Puritan forebears, fastidious and disciplined, but an epicurean. His Chartreuse was warmed on the tiles in front of the fireplace, he arranged musical soirées at home, and he took one of his daughters to hear the first performance in England of Wagner's opera *Lohengrin*. He was the master of the family and the household, which he bent unquestioningly to his own interests.

Dorothy Richardson's mother was of a different temperament and background. Unlike her scientifically minded husband, she distrusted "facts." Coming from an enormous country family of 22 children, she began marriage with a lighthearted, gay disposition. But she was psychologically fragile and became a semi-invalid when Dorothy was six years old. Her periodic depressions gradually grew worse and her state of health became a source of increasing anxiety and oppression. Eventually she committed suicide while she and Dorothy, who was 22, were alone at a seaside resort where they had gone for Mrs. Richardson's "nerves." Guilt over her mother's death and the trauma of discovering her pursued Dorothy for many years.

Dorothy perceived the incompatible differences between the personalities of her parents as a cause of recurrent strain in their relationship. They were also a source of deep conflict for her. She identified with both her parents and believed that she had inherited the fundamental features of each of their personalities. This idea, that the character traits of antagonistic or incompatible ancestors are inherited, was common at the turn of the century. William James discusses it in his exploration of the "divided self" in *The Varieties of Religious Experience* (1901/1958). Richardson, too, was a divided self. She internalized her father's masculine character and his dislike of women, but she also identified with her mother as a woman destroyed by a man's world. At an early age, she had been given the powerful message that she ought to have been a boy but was instead the third, unwanted girl. The male model in her life, her father, was the patriarchal ruler and shaper of the family, but he was also weak and a poor manager of the family finances. Thus Richardson's reference (1943/1959) to her "very happy childhood" included experiences of incompatibility, ambiguity, and split identity. These problems play a part in Richardson's theory of gender, which I discuss elsewhere (Wallace, 1988). Alfred Kazin (1979), reflecting on the functions of autobiography, remarked that "personal history is directly an effort to find salvation, to make one's own experience come out right" (p. 79). Richardson's autobiographical novel has the cast of such a project.

Her formal, and excellent, education ended when she was 17 and her father's finances were moving into their final downward spiral. From the time she finished school until a few years before her death, she was poor. Her working life began at 17 as a teacher in a finishing school in Hanover, Germany. After about six months she returned to England and continued working as teacher and governess until shortly before her mother's death. After that the family dispersed.

Richardson went to London in 1896, soon after her mother's death. She worked there for a fashionable dentist. She sought out and explored a variety of political, artistic, and literary groups. Among her friends was a young woman with whom she had gone to school who had recently married a writer, H. G. Wells. Dorothy visited the Wells's on weekends. Wells fascinated, attracted, and disturbed her. Except for his compelling and beautiful eyes, he was physically undistinguished with a small, high-pitched voice. But his personality was powerful and masculine, and he was a superb talker. At the Wells's house Dorothy met members of literary and political circles. Wells in 1896 was at the beginning of a highly successful and often notorious career. He and Richardson differed often, especially about the abilities of women, of which Wells had a low opinion. But he admired her for standing up to him in argument and for her intelligence and quickness. After their brief affair (for Wells one among many), they remained good friends.

Richardson and Wells are a study in contrasts. Wells was a kind of "externalist," a polymath with a passion for rationality and action. He believed— at least in the late 1890s when he met Richardson—that science could save the world. Richardson, an "internalist," distrusted science and disliked facts. She was an intellectual drawn to the irrational and to inner worlds. Perhaps the greatest contrast between them was in their literary products. Wells's *The Invisible Man,* the embodiment of masculine fantasy, is a story about an invisible man who tries to use his power of invisibility to rule the world. In Richardson's *Pilgrimage* it is the author who is made invisible in order to enrich experience.

In 1906, after about 10 years in London, Richardson began to write. She wrote and published book reviews, essays, short stories, and eventually a regular column of commentary. She gave up her job. She had become a writer. Having earlier rejected an offer of marriage from a prosperous doctor, in 1917, at the age of 44, she married Alan Odle, an artist who was 15 years younger than she. Odle was a member of an artistic circle that included Augustus John, Jacob Epstein, and Wyndham Lewis.

Like other women writers of her era, Richardson did not seek or adopt the conventional roles of wife and mother. In her correspondence she recounts that Odle and she were drawn to each other by their mutual dislike of women. He was tubercular and an alcoholic; when she married him, he was not expected to live very long. However, Odle stopped drinking and their marriage lasted until his death in 1948 left her profoundly bereaved. This unusual relationship and the role of her marriage in her life and work are discussed in Fromm (1977) and Wallace (1982).

In addition to reviews and articles in well-known literary publications like *Saturday Review* and *Life and Letters,* Richardson wrote for *Vanity Fair,* for the feminist *Egoist,* and for other specialist journals. I discuss her whole network of writing enterprises, including her nonfiction books, in my essay "Giftedness and the Construction of a Creative Life" (Wallace, 1985).

In 1912, at the age of 39, Richardson began her life's work, *Pilgrimage.* In the years before beginning it, she had written some short pieces which, in their fine-grained descriptions, anticipated the stream-of-consciousness genre. But for the most part she constructed and developed the genre over several years, much as Joyce and Woolf were to do later. The first 12 volumes were published between 1915 and 1938; the thirteenth and last was published in 1967, ten years after Richardson's death. She had spent 40 years writing it, from age 39 to a few years before her death. *Pilgrimage* was never a commercial success but it brought renown to Richardson. Greatly praised in the early years, including an ecstatic review in *The New York Times* in 1928, she was overtaken by other writers in the genre.

Pilgrimage is a novel about the development of a woman, Miriam Henderson, whose mind is the sole filter through which the novel flows. Miriam in many ways is Dorothy Richardson. She is 17 when the novel begins, and when it ends its author is about to begin writing it.

Feminine Realism

Richardson's central purpose was to write a novel of what she called "feminine realism," which she considered a "feminine equivalent of the current masculine realism" (Richardson, 1938). What did she mean by this elliptical statement?

Masculine realism, in Richardson's mind, meant adherence to a clear linear structure, including a well-defined plot with beginning, middle, and end. Richardson believed not only that these were the conventions of novels by men (and by women who, she thought, wrote like men, such as George Eliot), but also that they were men's habits of thought, deeply ingrained in them as a *gender*. The demands on men are for action. Men value themselves and each other for what they do, whereas women focus on being and value themselves for what they are. The poet and novelist Robert Graves, taking up this theme, was to call one of his novels *Man Does, Woman Is* (1964).

This characterization of the male as do-er and the female as be-er is a central feature of Richardson's theory of gender. It reflects a nineteenth-century arrangement of the industrialized English middle class, in which private and public life had been separated. In the home woman was the preeminent being; the world of work and action was man's domain. They were not only distinct, but often hostile institutions (Aries, 1962; Houghton, 1957; Rowbotham, 1976).

Thus Richardson was a product of the late nineteenth century in several ways. Like other psychologists of that era, she was interested in experience. Like other artists of the period, for example, the Impressionists, she wanted to depict immediate experience as accurately as possible. Her developing concepts of the psychological differences between men and women also had their roots in the nineteenth century. But in her feminism she was a twentieth-century radical. Unlike the suffragettes, she did not aim to change political and social institutions. Through her writing, she wanted to attack the still firmly entrenched idea that women were physically and mentally inferior to men.

Her artistic revolution was to free the novel from "masculine" realism in which authors provided detailed descriptions of their characters but always from the outside. She was also rebelling against literary traditions that presented a male, and therefore inaccurate, view of women. The psychologically real had never been captured in novels of male realism. Virginia Woolf (1923) described Richardson's innovation in stylistic terms, emphasizing its positive female qualities:

> She has invented . . . a sentence . . . of a more elastic fibre than the old, capable of stretching to the extreme, of suspending the frailest particles, of enveloping the vaguest shapes. . . . It is a woman's sentence, but only in the sense that it is used to describe a woman's mind by a writer who is neither proud nor afraid of anything she may discover in the psychology of her sex. (p. 229)

Richardson's Insight

Richardson, 39 years old, was alone in a cottage in Cornwall, beginning her major life task, when she had a great insight, a turning point in her work. Such a moment was possible only because of her earlier struggles. The comment that chance favors the prepared mind was made by Pasteur, a scientist. But the same is true of literature. If insight is an abrupt reorganization of previous thought, the matter that is "previous" is certainly as important as the insight. Such work is usually extensive, built up over years. It develops and expands the knowledge and capacities that make the insight possible. So it was with Richardson.

For several years some time after 1908, well before she began *Pilgrimage*, Richardson had thought of writing a novel. The following unpublished notes give some account of her struggles with traditional approaches:

> Each founded on "an idea." Somehow too easy, utterly distasteful & boring when thought of as being written with the idea close clasped in the hand. Very difficult to do, perpetually haunted by the mutability of ideas. Giving no satisfaction to a growing desire to express the immutable. . . . Deliberately composed narrative, incidents and figures. Became aware of the mass lying unexpressed behind any way of presenting I had met. Except Bunyan and the mystics. To write what one knows, regard-

less. The novels to date exclude the essential: first hand life. Assume life.
     1909. Wrote a mass of material each part expanding in the mind un-
manageably, choked by the necessities of narrative. Close narrative too
technical, dependent on a whole questionable set of agreements and assumptions between reader and writer. (Richardson, n.d.-a)

Richardson did not want to take an idea a priori and shape a novel around
it. But her goals were complex. On the one hand, her phrase "perpetually
haunted by the mutability of ideas" meant that, minimally, ideas change depending on the point of view from which they are considered. On the other
hand, her "growing desire to express the immutable" refers to consciousness.
Richardson's view of consciousness was *not* that it was a constant flux. In fact
she disliked the phrase "stream of consciousness" which was later applied to
her work. She believed that consciousness was a steady, immutable state, like
the core of awareness or the continuous ego or self:[3]

The mind may be, or may become, anything from a ragbag to a mad-
house. It may wobble continuously or may be more or less steadily focused. But its central core, luminous point . . . tho more or less continuously expanding from birth to maturity, remains stable, one with itself
thruout life. (Kunitz, 1933, p. 562)

Richardson wanted to capture the unchanging nature of the self as well as the
stream of subjective experience. When she tried the traditional forms she
knew, she found that the most important material—continuous inner life—
was left unexpressed. She refers to Bunyan because he had found a way,
through the allegory of *Pilgrim's Progress,* to express his thoughts "regardless," that is, however bizarre or repugnant they might seem.[4]
     When Richardson had her insight in 1912, preparing to begin *Pointed
Roofs,* the first volume of *Pilgrimage,* she was well read in Russian, French,
and English literature, and she had certainly read the novels of Tolstoy, Flaubert, Balzac, Conrad, Henry James. She was familiar with men's depiction of
the psychology of women. Flaubert certainly believed that he was "inside"
Emma Bovary's mind (he said he *was* Emma Bovary). Tolstoy, in *Anna
Karenina* and in *War and Peace,* lapses once or twice into a fragment of interior monologue. Dostoyevsky, Conrad, and Henry James had all explored the
inner minds of their characters, depicting nuances of mood, issues of identity,
and other subjective matters. But the basic posture of these writers was almost always that of an author standing back and telling a story. Although
Richardson greatly admired some of these novelists (especially Conrad and
James), they did not treat what she had in mind. Henry James perhaps came
the closest. In James's *The Ambassadors* (which Miriam Henderson was to
discover in *Pilgrimage*), the authorial "point of view" was of intense interest
to her. This was the idea that, once inside a given mind, the reader can have
only the point of view of that particular mind. In his preface to *The Ambassadors* James discusses this technique, pointing out that the reader knows
some of the characters in the novel only through Strether (the main charac-

ter) and is subject therefore to Strether's gropings about them. The same is true in *Turn of The Screw,* in which the narrator is the governess; through this technique, James directly exposed the workings of her mind. But James never tried to render unorganized, inchoate thought.

This, then, is where Richardson had arrived when she found herself alone in Cornwall. Her solitude there was almost total. She had borrowed a cottage belonging to friends and saw no one except a cleaning woman who came once a week to bring provisions. She had written copiously, a "mass of material," making repeated attempts over a period of about four years, 1908–12.

By her own account, Richardson was not consciously searching for a new form. Her struggles were with established narrative, which did not work to her satisfaction:

> When I first began writing *Pilgrimage* I intended no kind of fresh departure in method. Then in Cornwall, in solitude, when the world fell completely away, and when focusing intensely, I suddenly realized that I couldn't go on in the usual way, telling *about* Miriam, describing her. There she was as I first saw her, going upstairs. But *who was there to describe her?* It came to me suddenly. It was an extraordinary moment when I realized what could and what could not be done. Then it became more and more thrilling as I saw what *was* there. (Morgan, 1931)

This passage, from an interview years later, describes her insight. Note that the insight occurred while Richardson was "focusing intensely" on her task. In this it differs from the well-known cases. Archimedes' famous insight occurred while he was having a bath, Poincaré's when he was stepping onto a bus, Kekulé's during a reverie, and Darwin's while reading "for amusement" (see Gruber, 1981, for an analysis of these "aha! experiences"). Furthermore, one part of Richardson's insight was finding a question: *Who was there to describe her?* Her insight was to find the *problem* and not, as in the cases above, the solution. The way to the solution, as she indicated, was immediately implicated in the discovery of the problem.

Richardson's insight was a two-stage phenomenon. First she "suddenly realized" that she could not use the traditional form, in which an author tells a story "about" a character. She saw that it was not inexperience or lack of skill but the literary *form* that had prevented her from expressing "the mass lying unexpressed." Her visual image of Miriam going upstairs led to the second stage of the insight. The first sentence of *Pointed Roofs,* the first volume of *Pilgrimage,* begins "Miriam left the gaslit hall and went slowly upstairs." "Who was there to describe her?" put the problem squarely as one of form concerning the position of the *author.* The first, global stage of the insight was differentiated and concretely specified. Thus in Richardson's case a closer examination of the "moment" of insight reveals it to be a more prolonged and intricate affair than the familiar sudden flash would lead us to believe.

To improve our understanding of the "aha" or "eureka" phenomenon, we should examine the relationships among different experiences of the same thing. Richardson, in her struggle to write a novel in a new way, found differ-

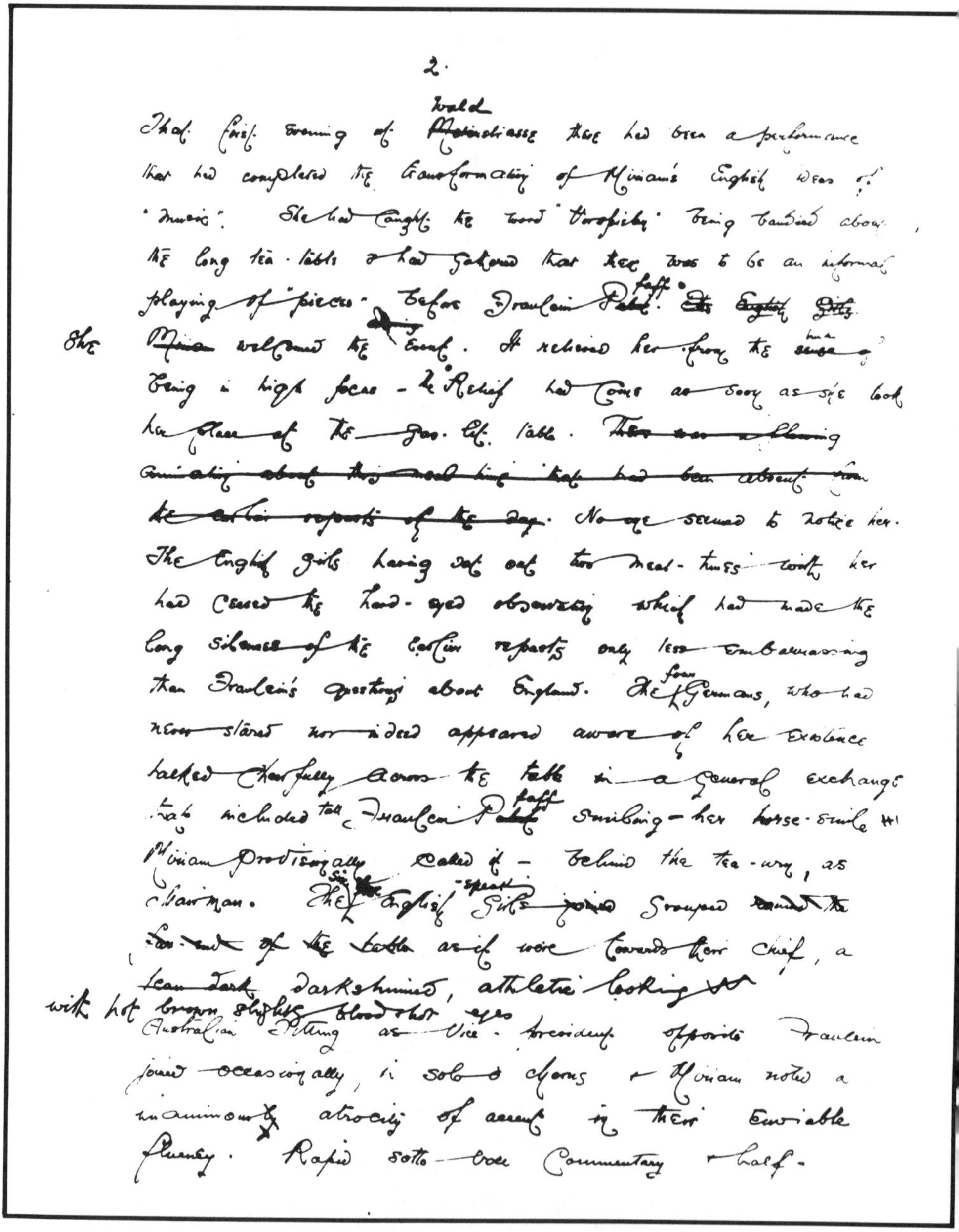

2.

FIGURE 8–2. Handwritten page from the manuscript of *Pointed Roofs*. Courtesy of the Beineke Rare Book and Manuscript Library, Yale University.

ent ways of knowing a domain. She had read a great variety of novels. She had written in different styles and for different purposes, from book reviews to short stories, essays, and commentary. She had tried to write a novel using traditional narrative. This entailed trying things out which she later rejected. A multiple perspective grows slowly, is achieved through hard work, and sets the stage for what Gruber called "the *re*-cognition we experience as a new insight" (1981, p. 58).

Meaning Versus Truth

In *Pilgrimage* Richardson gives herself another name, Miriam Henderson, but it is like her own (same number of syllables and same ending). Like Miriam's name, the "facts" in the novel—her family, the jobs Miriam has, the men she falls in love with, where she lives, where she goes—are the same facts, barely disguised, as those of Dorothy Richardson's life. But Richardson was interested in these facts in a special way. She was not interested in what *was* but in what it was *like*. Meaning, to her, was a more important, a "higher" truth than the truth of objective fact.

Taking the material of actual experience and reconstructing it by fusion with imaginary material is fundamental to the creative process in art. Christopher Isherwood (1954) became famous for his book *The Berlin Stories,* which was supposedly a documentary account of the lives of the people he knew as a young man in Berlin just before Hitler came to power in 1933. In his autobiography, written when he was 70, Isherwood (1976) revealed that many things in *The Berlin Stories* were untrue. But Isherwood's revelations of dissimulation add nothing to the experience of reading *The Berlin Stories,* which is still a marvelous book. However fabricated the stories are, they seem more real than the truths he reveals in his autobiography.

Anthony Powell (1975), through a character in one of his novels, makes the same point when he says, "People think because a novel's invented, it isn't true. Exactly the reverse is the case" (p. 84). He goes on to say that biography and memoirs can never be wholly true since they cannot include every circumstance of what happened. But novels reveal their authors. Powell claims that we know more about Balzac and Dickens from their novels than about Rousseau and Casanova from their *Confessions.*

Whether or not we agree with him, Powell's point is that the novelist is free and can, with impunity, reveal rather than conceal himself or herself. And, indeed, I believe that Richardson called *Pilgrimage* a novel and created Miriam Henderson in order to write freely, if covertly, about her past. I say "covertly" because until Fromm's (1977) biography, the extraordinarily close parallels between the lives of author and character were not known.

The death of Richardson's mother is a case in point: this event is treated with covert freedom in *Pilgrimage*. Through Miriam, Richardson could express and work through her own conflicts about her mother's death: that it set her free and simultaneously chained her to remorse and guilt. In the novel, this event ends the third volume, *Honeycomb*. Richardson builds up gradually and with increasing tension to Miriam's mother's death. She describes the mutual suffering of the two women together in their boarding house by the sea in winter as her mother becomes more ill, irrational, and desperate. Miriam tries, and fails, to get help. Night after night in the same room with her insomniac mother, there is an escalation of human despair and incipient violence. Waking very early one morning, Miriam finds her mother talking to herself and laughing:

> Forcing herself to be still, she accepted the sounds, pitting herself against the sense of destruction. The sound of violent lurching brought her panic. There was something there that would strike. (1967, vol. 1, p. 487)

And again, she wakes

> to the sound of violent language, furniture being roughly moved, a swift angry splashing of water . . . something breaking out breaking through the confinements of this little furniture-filled room . . . the best gentlest thing she knew in the world, openly despairing at last. (1967, vol. 1, p. 488)

The last paragraph of the book is the one where we realize that Miriam's mother is dead. We can only surmise what happened from the following:

> The bony old woman held Miriam clasped closely in her arms. "You must never, as long as you live, blame yourself. . . . Miriam had not heard her come in. The pressure of her arms and her huge body came from far away. Miriam clasped her hands together. She could not feel them. . . . Everything was dream; the world. I shall not have any life. I can never have any life; all my days. There were cold tears running into her mouth. They had no salt. Cold water. . . . Moving her body with slow difficulty against the unsupporting air, she looked slowly about. It was so difficult to move. Everything was airy and transparent. Her heavy hot light impalpable body was the only solid thing in the world. Weighing tons; and like a lifeless feather. There was a tray of plates of fish and fruit on the table. She looked at it, heaving with sickness. . . . I am hungry. Sitting down near it she tried to pull the tray. It would not move. I must eat the food. Go on eating food till the end of the my life. Plates of food like these plates of food. . . . I am in eternity . . . where their worm dieth not and their fire is not quenched. (1967, vol. 1, pp. 489–490)

The techniques here are multileveled. Richardson uses third-person description by an omniscient author, first-person narration, and direct and indirect interior monologue. Note too that in the last passage quoted above the reader and Miriam experience different levels of comprehension. The reasons for Miriam's sensations and feelings are only too clear to her but must be unraveled or filled in by the reader.

Epistemological Considerations

In *Pilgrimage* Miriam Henderson is both object and subject. She is object in the sense that Richardson, as author, is in control of Miriam, creating her and presenting her objectively, without authorial comment or interpretation. Only Miriam can analyze and comment. Miriam is also Richardson's subject for they are, at least in part, the same person: Richardson is observing the processes of her own mind for her material, and she is reconstructing her past self through Miriam; but she is doing so from the point of view of *her own* changing present.

The examination of the mechanisms of her mind and its activity was a *professional* project. Richardson's compelling determination to depict subjective experience directly without an intervening authorial presence was a serious public endeavor. Her reconstruction of the events and the meaning of her own past, on the other hand, was a *private* project. As novel *Pilgrimage* represents the public task; as autobiography *Pilgrimage* is a search for the earlier self, for the person who slips through the fingers, no longer existing as before, who must be reconstructed.

A major point Richardson is making is that real life is inside and not outside. Miriam's experience is indication that most lives are inconsequential to others but not to themselves. Richardson may dwell for several pages on a single sensory event that Miriam is experiencing, for example, her perception of her room and the play of light in it. She shows that a sensory event can affect the mind as powerfully as any dramatic external event and also that an apparently simple experience like this is, upon examination, extremely dense and complex.

Richardson knew that all this made new demands on the reader. Because the angle of regard is always Miriam's, the reader is implicated directly in the text, not talked to by the author. In the traditional novel, the author stands above the characters, maintaining a distance from them. It is the author who describes the characters' histories, what they look like, what they do and feel. Extending the distance further, the author sometimes comments to the reader about the characters. Richardson was closing this gap between author and characters and, as a result, between author and reader. By speaking through Miriam, not about her, she spoke to the reader without an obtrusive intervening authorial presence.

To enter into the novel, the reader had to fill in. Much to the surprise of many readers, this was not difficult to do. In some undated notes, probably written in the early twenties, Richardson commented:

> the reader is so very much more than a result, an appendage, so to speak, of the author. To do anything like full justice to their relationship, we need a composite word, something like the telegraphic name of a firm, expressing both partnership and collaboration. For the bond closer than all other arts. (n.d.-b)

Richardson considered the reader an active partner, a donor in the author–reader relationship. Although the author brings the reader into existence as it were, the reader is active in several ways. First, the reader is the author's "counterpart." Without the reader, the author does not "exist." Second, the bond between writer and reader is unique because, unlike that in other arts, they share a medium that is familiar to both: language. This is what Richardson meant by her comment "For the bond closer than all other arts." Finally, the reader is a partner or collaborator because of the demands the new form made. The reader had to work in a new way with the writer—to accept the unexpected, to tolerate ambiguity, and to get used to the absence of conventional anchors such as knowing from the outset what time of year it is, the age and exact appearance of a person, or where in a sequence of events a passage is occurring. At the same time, the reader was never left for long without essential information: it always came through Miriam.

The author's task in all this was hard. In a letter to an old friend who was attempting to write in the same genre, Richardson comments on the manuscript sent to her:

> If you let Mary tell the story you must see nothing but what she sees and you must not describe what she sees in language she would not use. If you take leave to use your powers of description you must tell Mary's story throughout and then the thing becomes narrative and has not that sensed current experience that I think you are aiming at. (Richardson, 1928)

This excerpt gives some idea of the demands of the method and Richardson's control over what she is doing. The amateur is often unaware of the craft of the artist. One is drawn into the work without necessarily knowing how this is achieved.

In an article on the nature of the novel written in 1948, Richardson said that the orthodox novel, like science, is restricted because in the effort to supply a story "complete with beginning, middle, climax and curtain," it must ignore what she called "the always unique modifications of contingency" (1948, p. 191).

Miriam's experiences put the reader into a position of participating in the contingent experience of the everyday life of one person. We are not in the presence of some absolute or symmetrical order, but we are privy to Miriam's ostensibly arbitrary viewpoint and timepoint. *Pilgrimage,* in the large, is like a flow of "detail" views in art where the viewer is made forcibly aware of the detail and density of a *part* of a painting (Galassi, 1981). When we then see the detail again as a part in a whole and not as a "whole" presented alone, we are aware that we know it in a different way and this changes our way of cognizing both part and whole. In thinking about the novels she hoped would be written, Richardson said:

> The interest in any part is no longer dependent for the reader upon exact knowledge of what has gone before or upon a frothy excitement . . . as

to what next will happen. Such novels may be entered at any point, read backwards, or from the centre to either extremity and will yet reveal, like a mosaic, the interdependence of the several parts, each one bearing the stamp of the author's consciousness. (1948, p. 192)

Within Two Time Frames

Richardson's life can be divided into two parts: the 38 years before she began writing her novel and the 40 years she spent writing it. Her work and her life, therefore, have an unusual, enduring, and intertwined relationship.

Pilgrimage is a *Bildungsroman,* a psychological novel about the formation and education of the artist, a self-portrait of the artist in the process of becoming an artist. This is an implicit and private structure in *Pilgrimage,* not grasped at all by reviewers of the novel. Richardson was communicating the course of her development in a new way; but because the reader experiences everything *with* Miriam Henderson and *through* her, her development is less perceptible. It is not explicitly pointed out. We must construe it for ourselves from Miriam's experience.

Richardson did not wish to be an author who "conducts a tour of the proceedings" as a tour guide, and she therefore did not describe Miriam's development as a plot, a series of discrete but explicitly connected events. This is one of the reasons why *Pilgrimage* seems like a book in which nothing happens, a comment which the novelist May Sinclair (1918) made in a praising review of the first three volumes. In the same review Sinclair gave the new genre its famous "stream-of-consciousness" label:

> To me these three novels show an art and method and form carried to punctilious perfection. . . . In this series there is no drama, no situation, no set scene. Nothing happens. It is just life, going on and on. . . . In identifying herself with this life, which is Miriam's stream of consciousness, Miss Richardson produces her effect of being the first, of getting closer to reality than any of our novelists who are trying so desperately to get close. (Sinclair, 1918, p. 58)

Other reviewers were irritated and reproachful about the absence of plot, as if it was something an author owed, a kind of moral obligation:

> For "Pilgrimage," unlike for example, "The Forsyte Saga," cannot be called a novel. Except for length, it has none of the characteristics of the type . . . it is essentially without a plot. . . . It should be taken only a little at a time, for every surrender to [Richardson's] method involves a really painful demand upon the imagination and the attention. (Aldrich, 1928)

In reply to a letter from an admirer, who professed both enthusiasm and confusion over *Pilgrimage,* Richardson (1944) wrote:

Within the text of my book . . . the handing out of direct information is equally excluded. This, in one direction, is a severe handicap, but also the necessary price of what I have tried to do.

There are actually hundreds of events in *Pilgrimage* but, because Miriam is experiencing them, is *in* them, they are not labeled *as such*. We do not ordinarily label or explain events as they are happening to us; we register and respond to them. This is a basic structural feature of the novel that determines its fabric. But it is true that *Pilgrimage* has no plot in the terms that readers were accustomed to, that is, as sequenced dramatic action.

The Question of Time

We think of individual development as an advance. Whatever may be its serpentine route, its qualitative leaps, discontinuity, or uneven path, development is progression (Shapiro & Wallace, 1981). The passage of time is inherent in this concept. The peculiarity of the present case is that Richardson lived much of her life within two time frames, much as a clinical case of dissociation might. Phenomena of dissociation, in which a single self was allegedly split into two selves, were of particular interest to psychologists and psychiatrists of the era (James, 1890/1950; Janet, 1890/1950).

The period covered in the novel, which I shall call *novel time,* is about 21 years, from 1891 to 1912. The second time period of immediate relevance is *writing time*—the 40-year period during which the novel was written, from 1912 to about 1952. Consideration of these two time frames raises several questions: if Richardson was describing her own past, how far back did her memory have to reach in successive books? Did the events in Richardson's past and those depicted in Miriam's life occur during the same time periods? What is the overall relationship of these two time frames?

The answers to these questions are not easily come by. In *Pilgrimage,* since Richardson wished to convey time not chronologically but psychologically, as a flow, the novel contains few conventional references to time or date.

To answer the foregoing questions I examined the novel carefully for any datum concerning time or date and determined when the events recorded in the novel actually took place in Richardson's life. The data I used from the novel are instances where Miriam or others note that it is June, or two months past Christmas, or that Miriam has been at a certain place for 15 months. On several occasions she considers her age, for example, that she is 17 or 25. Finally, external events alluded to, like the trial of Oscar Wilde (1895), provide information about chronological time. Biographical data anchor this information. Comparison of novel time with biographical information also identifies discrepancies.

The distance between Richardson's present and the past she was writing about ranges from 19 to 40 years. The shortest distance that her memory had to span was for volumes 6, 7, and 8 (19 years); the longest was for the last volume, *March Moonlight* (40 years). Without *March Moonlight,* the distance ranges from 19 to 29 years.

What conclusions can we draw from these facts? The psychological literature on memory over the life span has so far dealt little with continuous memory over long periods in a person's past. Research on memory for early childhood deals with very long-term memory but is not necessarily a good guide to long-term memory of an older adult about young adulthood. However, Bartlett's (1932) ideas about remembering are highly compatible with some of Richardson's statements. Ever since Bartlett, psychologists have conceived of memory not as a passive recording, but as an active process of reconstruction compatible with the person's current organization of knowledge and the world. This idea is central in the currently burgeoning literature on autobiographical memory (cf. Rubin, 1986). It means that the past *and its meaning* are being continually remade in the interests of maintaining inner coherence.

At the end of *March Moonlight,* the last volume of *Pilgrimage,* Miriam makes a similar statement:

> When I write, everything vanishes but what I contemplate. The whole of what is called "the past" is with me, seen anew, vividly . . . the past does not stand "being still." It moves, growing with one's own growth. (Richardson, 1967, vol. 4, p. 657)

Richardson, through remembering, reconstructed her own past and rendered it, often in minutely detailed descriptions of what Miriam thinks, sees, hears, feels, and so on. But Richardson obviously could not, even had she wanted, depict the whole of her experience.[5] She had to *select* from her past, deciding what to leave out or withhold, as well as what to include. Furthermore, the detail that her purpose required meant that she had to *fill in* the material she selected and rearrange it. However good her memory was—and it was said, by Wells, for example, to be extraordinary—it seems impossible that she would have remembered her past with the kind of continuity and detail that is everywhere in *Pilgrimage.*

But Richardson's intense contemplation of her past was not on the order of a passive recollection of what was. It was an active reconstruction, involving a dynamic reciprocal relationship between the *meaning* of past and present. Richardson was aware of the influence of her present consciousness on her perception of her past experience. Perhaps that is one of the reasons why she called *Pilgrimage* a novel. But she solicited and embraced this influence as an integral part of her artistic product. She recoiled from the passion of science for absolutely impersonal knowledge (cf. Polanyi, 1962, for the adverse effects of this passion on science). A subjective statement is what she wanted to make, though not one without discipline. The real events of her past, her episodic past, served only as the ground for the figure of her creative imagination.

Correspondence and Compression

Consideration of novel time and writing time reveals a distinct pattern and provides some answers to questions posed earlier. Miriam Henderson is younger than Dorothy Richardson actually was. In the first six volumes this age difference is on the order of months; in the next six volumes it increases to six years; in the last volume, *March Moonlight,* the age gap is closed.

The increasing discrepancy between the age ascribed to Miriam and Richardson's age over the same period could be due to the normal telescoping of memory (i.e., events happened earlier in novel time than they actually did to the young Dorothy). Paradoxically, Richardson had an opposite problem with writing time. The ninth volume, *Oberland,* is about a two-week holiday Miriam spends in Switzerland. In a letter to E. B. C. Jones, another novelist, written when Richardson was working on the next volume, she says:

> the need to condense grows with each volume . . . [about *Oberland*] each episode could have filled a single volume in the old manner but I should have been in my grave before M's fortnight was at an end and there are things calling ahead. (1927)

It is as if Richardson wanted both to catch up with time and future events and to follow her impulse to write more about less. But the age discrepancy between Miriam and the young Dorothy fades in significance when we examine the startling difference between novel time and writing time in two phases of the novel (see Table 8–1).

The first six volumes cover nine years of Miriam's life, while volumes 7 to 12 account for only three years of Miriam's life. This ratio, the number of volumes written to novel time elapsed, represents the density of the writing since the volumes are rather uniform in their length. As indicated in Table 8–1, there is a considerable difference in the density of the first six and the second six volumes: 0.67 and 2.0 respectively. Thus the second six were much more dense—or detailed—than the first.

Also presented in the table is the relationship of novel time and writing time. Writing densely entailed more writing time than did the early volumes where the writing was less detailed. Richardson took 8 years to write the first six volumes and 18 years for the next six. But other factors almost cer-

TABLE 8–1.   Volumes Written in *Pilgrimage* and Years Elapsed
in Novel Time and Writing Time

Density		Years Elapsed	
Volume	Books/Year of Novel Time	Novel Time	Writing Time
1–6	6/9 = 0.67	9	8
7–12	6/3 = 2.0	3	18
13	1/4 = 0.25	4	14

tainly entered in: she was getting older and had less energy available, especially since she had to struggle to support herself, and she was increasingly discouraged by the reception of later volumes.

The thirteenth volume, *March Moonlight,* is a special case. Richardson wrote this volume over a period of some 14 years about events in her own life that had occurred when she was between 35 and 37 years old. But events that actually took place much later are telescoped into this last volume. For example, Richardson met Alan Odle, her future husband, when she was 42, but in *March Moonlight* Miriam, much earlier, meets a Mr. Noble, whose description is almost identical to that of Odle.

Richardson was mostly in her seventies when she was writing *March Moonlight.* During this period, in a letter to Henry Savage (1947), she wrote that as we get older, we no longer see past experiences chronologically but rather "rearranged in their true sequence . . . untrammeled by . . . place or time or any other atomizing influence."

Unlike any other volume, *March Moonlight* is written entirely in the first person. It is a culmination, a multiple coming together of Richardson and Miriam: *historically,* as the young Richardson and Miriam merge; *temporally,* in that the content of the book ranges outside its temporal boundaries more than other books; and *technically,* in the consistent use of the first-person narration throughout.

Altogether, then, a three-stage development is apparent in *Pilgrimage.* In the first six volumes, Miriam and Dorothy are the same age and temporal discrepancies between actual events and events in the novel are on the order of months. In the second six, there is a radical shift in which actual events have outpaced those of the novel and the novel has entered a different time scale and is much denser, as if Richardson had exchanged her magnifying glass for a microscope. In the third stage, represented by *March Moonlight,* there is a precipitous catching up in time, and the book is far less dense. But that is a description. What is the explanation?

Richardson began *Pilgrimage* to write a new kind of novel and give an account of herself. She rapidly became a literary figure and the early books were well received. In the second stage she took a closer look at the terrrain of her life, a psychological interest that compelled her as a *private person.* It is as though she stopped giving an account of herself as a literary figure and began writing as a person interested in closely examining and reconstructing her past. During this second stage of Richardson's work, Miriam is revealed as taking the significant steps, unwittingly, unknowingly, and still in formation, that will lead to her decision to be a writer. It is during this period that Miriam, for example, struggles with the question of where her personal affiliations should be. This is the time of her life that interested Richardson most deeply and that she therefore examined in the greatest detail. It shows her writing at its densest and coincides with her increasingly masterful manipulation of the carefully limited point of view.

Richardson's later life exhibits a tension: she wanted to go deeper, although she knew she should condense and catch up. The former path proved irresistible. Consequently she did not catch up until *March Moonlight,* and perhaps only then because she knew it was the last book she would write.

An Unfinished Life

The autobiographical novel marvellously fitted Richardson's purposes. One of the peculiar features of autobiography is that it cannot report the author's death. In a sense, therefore, it is unfinished. (Of course, many creative artists left unfinished masterworks; Leonardo's *The Last Supper* is one of the most celebrated examples.) Richardson's view of what a novel should be echoes this notion: a novel with the conventional dramatic beginning–middle–end format falsifies life as experienced. In the eyes of many, *Pilgrimage* is unfinished.

Richardson used *Pilgrimage* publicly as a novel and privately as an autobiography. Her public purpose was to write a new kind of novel in which she treated subjective experience and its meaning. Her private project was to examine and reconstruct her own development and *its* meaning. Simply by withholding from the public all information about her private life, she could make whatever private revelations she chose in *Pilgrimage* under its guise as fiction.[6]

There is another sense in which combining the novel and autobiography fitted Richardson's purpose. Richardson, like other novelists, drew on her own experience; but she was opening a new territory. To depict the psychological processes demanded by the genre, she *had* to become a close observer of herself. In thus drawing information from her own psyche she became her own subject. It was Richardson as subject who also provided the raw material for her work as autobiographer. To shape her raw material into a literary work was the job of Richardson the writer and for this she became her own object. In Richardson's case, the fact that she was a woman was pivotal in her discovery of feminine realism. It provided the point of departure for the whole enterprise of writing *Pilgrimage.*

This has been an essay about the relationship between writer and person writing. In the study of creativity we are interested in understanding how the person as a whole mobilizes the energies and experiences necessary for the task at hand. Like a luxuriant and well-planned garden, Richardson's world was a microcosm that she could explore and exploit, to teach herself and others a new way of seeing.

CHRONOLOGY
DOROTHY M. RICHARDSON

1873   Born in Abingdon, Berkshire.

1884–90   Attended Southborough House School, Putney.

1891	Goes to Hanover, Germany, as teacher-pupil in girls' finished school. Father loses money.
1891–93	Teacher in private girls' school in Finsbury Park, London.
1893	Father declared bankrupt.
1895	Governess to Horace Avory family. Mother commits suicide.
1896	Goes to London; works for Dr. J. H. Badcock. Meets H. G. Wells.
1906	First writing, reviews in *Crank.*
1908	Resigns from Harley Street job. Writing essays and sketches.
1912	Begins writing *Pilgrimage.*
1917	Marries Alan Odle.
1917–31	Continues writing and publishing the volumes of *Pilgrimage,* other writing, and translating.
1937	Finishes the twelfth volume of the novel and begins the final volume, *March Moonlight.*
1938	Dent Omnibus edition published; includes all but *March Moonlight.*
1939	Moves to Cornwall.
1939–52	Continues working on *March Moonlight* and some other short pieces.
1957	Dies.

NOTES

1. My sources concerning Richardson, in addition to her published work, biographies, and other Richardson literature, are the Richardson Papers at the Beinecke Rare Book and Manuscript Library at Yale University and the Henry W. and Albert A. Berg Collection in The New York Public Library.

2. "Data for Spanish publisher," an autobiographical statement written by Richardson in 1943 for a planned translation of *Pilgrimage* into Spanish, never materialized. It was eventually published in 1959, two years after her death.

3. William James called his chapter in *Principles of Psychology* (1950) "The Stream of *Thought*" (my italics). This is a term Richardson would have had no argument with. James made no explicit distinction between thought and consciousness in this chapter, but he did treat the issue of change and continuity in identity in the succeeding chapter of the *Principles,* which he called "The Consciousness of Self." Although the matter has been argued for centuries, there is no agreed-upon definition or explanation of consciousness.

4. It is worth noting that Bunyan was labeled pathological more than once, by William James (1901/1958) and by the British historian Lord Macaulay in the 1910 edition of the *Encyclopedia Britannica.*

5. James Joyce's *Ulysses* (1934), which takes place on a single day in 1904 and is 768 pages long, also does not present the entire experience of its characters on that day.

6. For example, when asked to provide a photo to accompany an essay concerning her literary opinions, she sent a picture of herself as a baby.

REFERENCES

Aldrich, E. A. (1928, May 5). The vista of the stream (Review of *Oberland* by D. M. Richardson). *Saturday Review of Literature.*
Allen, W. (1976). Introduction to *Pilgrimage.* New York: Popular Library.
Aries, P. (1962). *Centuries of childhood.* London: Jonathan Cape.
Bartlett, F. C. (1932). *Remembering.* Cambridge: Cambridge University Press.
Bunyan, J. (1941). *Pilgrim's progress.* New York: Spiral Press.
Dujardin, E. (1968). *Les lauriers sont coupés.* Paris: Union générale d'éditions. (Original work published in 1887)
Edel, L. (1972). *The modern psychological novel.* Gloucester, Mass.: Peter Smith. (Original work published in 1955 as *The psychological novel, 1900–1950*)
Fromm, G. G. (1977). *Dorothy Richardson, A biography.* Urbana: University of Illinois Press.
Galassi, P. (1981). *Before photography.* New York: Museum of Modern Art.
Graves, R. (1964). *Man does, woman is.* Garden City, N.Y.: Doubleday.
Gruber, H. E. (1981). On the relation between "aha experiences" and the construction of ideas. *History of Science, 19,* 41–59.
Hanscombe, G., & Smyers, V. L. (1987). *Writing for their lives: The modernist women 1910–1940.* London: Women's Press.
Hansford-Johnson, P. (1963). Unpublished statement about Dorothy Richardson, dated April 25, Beinecke Library, Yale University.
Houghton, W. E. (1957). *The Victorian frame of mind, 1830–1870.* New Haven: Yale University Press.
Humphrey, R. (1955). *Stream of consciousness in the modern novel.* Berkeley: University of California Press.
Isherwood, C. (1954). *The Berlin stories.* New York: New Directions.
Isherwood, C. (1976). *Christopher and his kind, 1929–1939.* New York: Farrar, Straus, and Giroux.
James, H. (1902). *The ambassadors.* New York: Harper & Brothers.
James, W. (1950). *The principles of psychology* (Vol. 1). New York: Dover. (Original work published in 1890)
James, W. (1958). *The varieties of religious experience.* New York: New American Library. (Original work published in 1901)
Janet, P. (1950). Cited in W. James, *The principles of psychology* (Vol. 1, p. 227). New York: Dover. (Original work published in 1890)
Joyce, J. (1934). *Ulysses.* New York: Random House.
Joyce, J. (1960). *Finnegans wake.* London: Faber & Faber. (Original work published in 1939)
Joyce, J. (1975). *A Portrait of the artist as a young man.* New York: Viking. (Original work published in 1916)
Kazin, A. (1979). The self as history. In M. Pachter (Ed.), *Telling lives.* Washington, D.C.: New Republic Books.
Kunitz, S. (1933). (Ed.). *Authors today and yesterday.* New York: Wilson.
Morgan, L. (1931, October 22). How writers work: Dorothy M. Richardson. *Everyman.*
Polanyi, M. (1962). *Personal knowledge.* New York: Harper Torchbook.

Powell, A. (1975). *Hearing secret harmonies*. London: Heinemann.

Proust, M. (1952–57). *Remembrance of things past* (12 vols.) (C. K. Scott-Moncrieff, Trans.). London: Chatto & Windus.

Richardson, D. M. (n.d.-a). *Literary essays: MS on her development as a writer*. Unpublished manuscript. Beinecke Library, Yale University.

Richardson, D. M. (n.d.-b). *Authors and readers*. Unpublished manuscript. Beinecke Library, Yale University.

Richardson, D. M. (1967). *Pilgrimage* (4 vols.). New York: Alfred A. Knopf. Originally published in 11 single volumes between 1915 and 1935 by Duckworth. Collected editions are as follows: London: J. M. Dent & Sons and New York: Alfred A. Knopf 1938, 12 books in a 4-volume omnibus edition; London: J. M. Dent & Sons and New York: Alfred A. Knopf, 1967, 13 books including *March Moonlight* in a 4-volume edition; New York: Popular Library, 13 books in a 4-volume edition, 1976; London: Virago, 13 books in a 4-volume edition, 1979.

Richardson, D. M. (1927, November). Unpublished letter to E. B. C. Jones. Beinecke Library, Yale University.

Richardson, D. M. (1928). Unpublished letter to Bernice Elliott. Beinecke Library, Yale University.

Richardson, D. M. (1938). Foreword to *Pilgrimage*. London: J. M. Dent.

Richardson, D. M. (1944, January 20). Unpublished letter to Flora Coates. Henry W. and Albert A. Berg Collection, The New York Public Library.

Richardson, D. M. (1947, February). Unpublished letter to Henry Savage. Beinecke Library, Yale University.

Richardson, D. M. (1948). Novels. *Life and Letters, 66*(127), 188–192.

Richardson, D. M. (1959). Data for Spanish publisher. Joseph Prescott (Ed.). *London Magazine, 6*, 14–19. (Originally written in 1943)

Rosenberg, J. (1973). *The genius they forgot*. London: Duckworth.

Rowbotham, S. (1976). *Hidden from history*. New York: Vintage.

Rubin, D. (Ed.). (1986). *Autobiographical memory*. Cambridge: Cambridge University Press.

Shapiro, E. K., & Wallace, D. B. (1981). Developmental stage theory and the individual reconsidered. In E. K. Shapiro & E. Weber (Eds.), *Cognitive and affective growth: Developmental interaction*. Hillsdale, N.J.: Erlbaum.

Sinclair, M. (1918). The novels of Dorothy Richardson. *The Egoist, 5*, 57–59.

Titchener, E. B. (1899). *An outline of psychology*. New York: Macmillan.

Wallace, D. B. (1982). *The fabric of experience: A psychological study of Dorothy M. Richardson's Pilgrimage*. Unpublished doctoral dissertation, Rutgers University. *Dissertation Abstracts International, 42*, 11, 4565B.

Wallace, D. B. (1985). Giftedness and the construction of a creative life. In F. Horowitz & M. O'Brien (Eds.), *The gifted and talented: Developmental perspectives*. Washington, D.C.: American Psychological Association.

Wallace, D. B. (1988). Secret gardens and other symbols of gender in literature. *Metaphor and Symbolic Activity, 3*(3), 135–145.

Wells, H. G. (n.d.). *The invisible man*. London: Odhams Press.

Woolf, V. (1923, May 19). Romance and the heart. *The Nation and the Anthenaeum* [Literary Supplement].

Wundt, W. (1904). *Principles of physiological psychology*. New York: Macmillan.

FIGURE 9–1. Albert Einstein at work as a patent clerk in Bern. Courtesy Lotte Jacobi Archive, Dimond Library, U.N.H.

9

Imagery and Intuition in Creative Scientific Thinking: Albert Einstein's Invention of the Special Theory of Relativity

ARTHUR I. MILLER

Albert Einstein's (1879–1955) special theory of relativity, a monumental achievement, was the reaction of a single scientist, working alone and out of the academic mainstream, to the frontier problems of 1905, the year he published his discovery. How did this come about? What was the situation in physics in 1905? What feats of imagination did it take to make this advance?

The basic problems in cognitive studies—How is knowledge acquired? and How are new ideas produced?—are essentially the same as a basic problem in the philosophy of science—How are the statements of a scientific theory obtained from data? Thus, for example, our understanding of the invention of special relativity is incomplete unless we can unlock the black box of the mind that made it, that is, explore Einstein's thinking itself. A valuable clue for how to proceed is to take seriously an observation made by Einstein, whose research led him to investigate the process of thinking itself: "scientific thought is a development of pre-scientific thought" (1934). Some psychologists, particularly Jean Piaget, reached a similar conclusion. Inspired in large part by Piaget's writings, I decided to approach the problem of the construction of scientific knowledge by using results from historical case studies as data for cognitive theories.

In the first section of this chapter I place Einstein in the intellectual milieu in which he worked and lived. Einstein extended its emphasis on visual imagery to scientific research, conducting thought experiments that went beyond the laboratory data of 1905 and realizing concepts whose consequences go beyond the data of sense perceptions. In a thought experiment the scientist puts nature to the test in his mind's eye. The thought experiment combines the visual and abstract mathematical modes of thinking in a manner that can permit the scientist to "see" the deep structure in a problem situation.[1]

The second section is a brief investigation of Einstein's approach to the basic problems that beset the physics of 1905.

After examining the physics of 1905, I move to the principal challenge in this essay: to use the history of science as a laboratory for cognitive studies. Essentially, in the first two sections we will observe Einstein's responses to the information available to everyone, to which he generally added other "data" from thought experiments in order to formulate a new view of physical theory. We will then use results from the historical portion as data for evaluating two issues arising in two contexts, contemporary cognitive science and Jean Piaget's genetic epistemology. Cognitive science offers a means to analyze Einstein's mode of mental imagery and to further investigate the creative process. Genetic epistemology provides a framework for discussing the construction of scientific knowledge and therefore a way to explore the notion of what constitutes scientific progress. Historical evidence for a specific sequential order in which certain key scientific concepts have been constructed, in theories such as special relativity and quantum mechanics, make it tempting to offer a stage theory for scientific progress.

Einstein's Milieu and Modes of Thinking

Einstein was a product of the German cultural environment, epitomizing its finest aspects. Most important for us is his predilection for "customary intuition" [*gewöhnliche Anschauung*], the sort of visual thinking that was indigenous to scientists and engineers trained in this environment. The term *Anschauung* is rich in Kantian overtones. *Anschauung* is the visual mode of mental imagery that is based on abstractions from phenomena actually witnessed in the world of sense perceptions. For example, the visual image of magnetic lines of force was raised to an *Anschauung* by most electrical engineers in the German cultural environment. They assumed that magnetic lines of force are an integral part of electromagnetic theory, rather than just an aid to visualization as was believed by the vast majority of American and British engineers (Miller, 1981b).

The curriculum in the German cultural milieu, however, emphasized classical subjects and stressed rote learning. At a typical *Gymnasium* (academic high school) instruction in algebra and geometry did not begin until age 13. Einstein, however, had studied algebra and geometry from about the age of eight, taking extreme delight in solving problems on which he often spent long, solitary hours. He usually spent his spare time alone, and his favorite pastime was building multitiered houses of cards, sometimes as high as 14 stories. Even as a child Einstein displayed the persistence, independence, and self-reliance that would stand him in good stead in his scientific research. From the age of 12 he studied calculus. Stimulation was often provided by Einstein's paternal uncle Jakob, who had had a comprehensive mathematical education. Often Jakob would pose mathematical puzzles for Albert, who sat for hours persistently searching for a solution.[2] The influence of uncles on budding minds seems noteworthy, as Bertrand Russell also attested (Russell, 1968).

Education

Although Einstein scored high in all subjects at the Luitpold Gymnasium, Munich, he hated the rote learning and authoritarian teachers. Personality clashes abounded. A teacher who disliked Einstein's habit of sitting in the back row with a wry smile told him that his "mere presence in the class destroys the respect of the other students for the teacher." His boyhood fright at witnessing military parades had turned into a repulsion against military service, whose impending prospect added to Einstein's homesickness and dislike of school. In October 1894, for business reasons, Einstein's parents left Germany for Milan (see a partial chronology in note 3). The 15-year-old became increasingly depressed. During the fall of 1894 Einstein obtained a doctor's certificate to the effect that he was suffering from nervous disorders and he left the Gymnaisum, becoming a high school dropout. After a year of glorious wandering in northern Italy and further independent studying, Einstein received special permission to sit at age 16½ for the entrance examination at the Zurich Polytechnic (the minimum age to sit for the examination was 18). He failed because of poor grades in languages (particularly French) and history. Owing to excellent scores in physics and mathematics, Einstein was advised to complete a year (1895–96) at a *Kantonsschule* in Aarau, whereupon he would be admitted automatically into the Zurich Polytechnic.[3]

This was a lucky turn for Einstein because the school at Aarau was founded by followers of the Swiss educational reformer Johann Heinrich Pestalozzi, who emphasized the innate "power of *Anschauung.*" Knowledge, he wrote in his 1801 book, *How Gertrude Teaches Her Children,* arises from sense impressions that are "irregular, confused." Through education begun with observing the world about oneself "clear ideas" emerge, until finally one develops intuitions according to a notion of *Anschauung* analogous to Kant's. Pestalozzi realized the fecundity of visual thinking based first on a close link to objects that had actually been perceived (a close image–perception link) and then through abstraction to *Anschauungen.* The 13-year-old Einstein had been introduced to Kant's notion of *Anschauung* through Kant's *Critique of Pure Reason.* This notion was emphasized further at the *Kantonsschule* and then again at the Zurich Polytechnic. The *Anschauung* of magnetic lines of force was puzzled over throughout German-language engineering journals.

Riding Next to a Light Wave: Einstein's Thought Experiment

As Einstein recalled, his academic career was largely a "comedy." This held for the Zurich Polytechnic (1896–1900) too, where a personality clash with an important faculty member led to Einstein's being refused admission to advanced studies. He found no steady employment until 1902 when a college friend's father recommended Einstein to the director of the Swiss Federal Patent Office in Bern. In June 1902 Einstein became a patent clerk third class; he remained at the job until July 1909. The Bern period was the most creative of his life.

During this period he resolved a thought experiment he had first conceived at the *Kantonsschule* in 1895 at age 16. As he recalled much later, this experiment "contained the germ of the special theory of relativity" (Einstein, 1946, p. 53). The thought experiment of 1895 concerned the experiences of a moving observer who tries to catch up with a point on a light wave whose source is at rest. This thought experiment involves the intuition of catching up with something that at first was moving faster than the observer and the *Anschauung,* or customary intuition of light as a wave phenomenon, by which I mean that light is depicted as an entity that has properties which are abstracted from certain properties of water waves. Einstein (1946) encapsulated the experiment as follows:

> 1. According to the accepted theory of how light progagates, an observer moving alongside a light wave whose source is at rest should be able to discern the effects of his relative motion by, for example, measuring the velocity of the light wave.
> 2. It was "intuitively clear" to Einstein that the laws of optics could not depend on the state of the observer's motion.

Now, statements 1 and 2 are mutually contradictory, and so to Einstein this thought experiment revealed a paradox. To understand the incompatibility of these two statements, let us develop them further.

Some straightforward algebra reveals strikingly the mutual contradiction of statements 1 and 2. The number that you read from your car's speedometer is your car's velocity with respect to (or relative to) the road. Suppose that the car's speedometer registers 30 miles per hour. Ahead of you is another car that is moving at 50 miles per hour. Let us take v as the velocity of your car and v_2 as the velocity of the other car. The velocity of the other car relative to yours is $V = v_2 - v$. Thus initially the relative velocity is 20 miles per hour. Let us assume that the other car moves along at a constant velocity and that you increase your velocity. Soon $v_2 = v$, and so $V = 0$, which means that the two cars are side by side at relative rest but moving along the highway together at 50 miles per hour relative to the road.

Now suppose that the other car is actually a point on a light wave whose velocity relative to the ground is $v_2 = c$ (c is the symbol customarily used for the velocity of light). Then your velocity relative to a point on the light wave is

$$V = c - v. \tag{1}$$

Equation 1 is the mathematical statement of how we expect intuitively to observe relative motion. Equation 1 is the Newtonian law for the addition of velocities, from Isaac Newton's theory of mechanics. But the thought experimenter's intuition is that

$$V = c. \tag{2}$$

Equations 1 and 2 are the mathematical formulations of Einstein's statements 1 and 2. Clearly, Eq. 1 and Eq. 2 are inconsistent unless $v = 0$, which is not the case. Let us develop this inconsistency further within the historical context of the physics of 1905.

Problems in Physics in 1905

The wave theory of light was formulated in analogy with sound propagation, which requires a medium (the atmosphere) for transmission. That waves require a medium for transmission is in agreement with our intuition. After all, how could there be water waves without water? Physicists referred to the medium for the transmission of light as the ether.

Suffice it to say that the mathematics of the then accepted theory of light had to be formulated first in a reference system at rest in the ether. These ether-fixed reference systems were special because only in them was the velocity of light exactly c regardless of whether the source of light is in relative motion. Then Newton's laws of motion were applied to the fundamental equations in an ether-fixed system in order to shift the problem situation to a laboratory moving through the ether. The predicted value for the velocity of light in a moving reference system is Eq. 1.

If there is an ether, then there should be a means to detect its effects experimentally. We can draw from Eqs. 1 and 2 the basic idea of these so-called ether-drift experiments. Suppose that instead of the earth moving around the sun, we imagine that the earth is at rest and the ether is streaming by like a flowing river. Then the measured velocity of light rays will be altered by the relative velocity between the earth and the flowing ether, just as the motion of a swimmer is affected by the current in a river. The velocity of light c relative to the ether is a quantity whose value could be calculated. According to Eq. 1 measurements made on the moving earth should yield a value for the velocity of light that is other than c, where v is now the relative velocity between the earth and the ether. Yet extremely accurate ether-drift experiments were consistent with Eq. 2.

Beneath the explicit inconsistency between theory and experiment in Eqs. 1 and 2 there lurked a larger problem: if a velocity other than c were actually measured, then the laws concerning how light propagates would differ from one moving laboratory to the next. This is a serious problem for the following reason. Among the principles on which Newton's mechanics is based is a principle of relativity that is valid regardless of the velocity at which a system moves. According to Newton's principle of relativity the laws of motion are the same in laboratories that move in a straight line at a constant velocity relative to each other. Such laboratories, or reference systems, are called inertial reference systems. Einstein's statement 2 asserts that it is intuitively obvious that Newton's principle of relativity should be extended to include the theory of light too—that is, that the laws for the propagation of light should be independent of the motion of inertial reference systems.

But physicists could not consider such a straightforward solution as "simply" extending Newton's principle of relativity to include the theory of light, because it required also a drastic change in world view not unlike that of "simply" changing from a geocentric to a heliocentric universe. "Simply" extending Newton's principle of relativity to the theory of light would mean rejecting Eq. 1, thereby rendering the ether unnecessary. This was unpalatable to physicists in 1905 primarily for two reasons: there was an extremely successful theory of light based on an ether, and there was the conceptual problem of the necessity for a medium to support light in transit. Physicists preferred to remove inconsistencies between Eqs. 1 and 2 by offering various hypotheses about how moving bodies are affected by their interactions with the ether.

Newton's laws of motion are also predicated on an intuitive concept of time: time is independent of motion. For example, the time on your watch is the same as the time on the watch of someone who is riding past you in a car. Time seems to have an absoluteness. In 1895 the great Dutch physicist H. A. Lorentz offered a systematic means to remove the inconsistency between Eqs. 1 and 2 for a certain class of ether-drift experiments. Instead of using the absoluteness of time, Lorentz assumed in a purely mathematical sense that the time in a moving reference system does depend on the relative motion of this system with respect to the laboratory. Lorentz referred to this mathematical time as the local time coordinate. The real physical time was, of course, the time in Newton's laws of motion because there was no reason to assume that the time read from a clock depends on the clock's motion. Assuming the absoluteness of time, Newton's laws of motion obey the Newtonian exact principle of relativity. But by using the local time, the laws of how light propagates conform to the principle of relativity only for certain data.

To summarize, thus far, aided by his independent reading of books on current theories of light, in 1895 Einstein conceived of a thought experiment that was, in essence, a general overview of the principal problem that concerned physicists such as Lorentz.[4]

By 1900 it became clear to physicists that Newton's laws of motion could not adequately explain phenomena related to light. Nor could Newton's laws of motion explain phenomena of electric or magnetic origin. Since 1865 there had existed a theory that unified light, electricity, and magnetism (see Chapter 5, this volume). By 1892, in the hands of Lorentz, this theory had achieved astounding successes. To be sure, Lorentz's theory had its defects—for example, it was unable to explain systematically the failure of all ether-drift experiments. Nevertheless, most physicists were optimistic that any remaining defects would be removed. In 1900 a research program was proposed in which the laws of nature would be based on those of electromagnetism, and a new version of Newton's mechanics would emerge. Physicists referred to this research program as the electromagnetic world picture. The Newtonian mechanical world picture had become cumbersome and unproductive. Nevertheless, the basic concept of an absoluteness of time was maintained.

It is necessary for me to introduce one more problem, owing to its importance to Einstein's thinking about the special theory of relativity. The problem concerns the characteristics of the light that emerges from a cavity within any hot substance. It turns out that the characteristics of this light depend only on the substance's temperature and not on its constitution. Such universal phenomena fascinate physicists.

Suffice it to say that Max Planck's theory of 1900 for the characteristics of the radiation emitted from within a heated body threatened to open a Pandora's box. Although Planck's radiation law accounted for available empirical data, it violated such basic concepts of classical physics as the continuity of phenomena. So Planck's law was politely ignored by everyone—except Einstein. After having failed to adapt classical physics to Planck's law, in 1900 Einstein opted to accept the law as valid and to investigate its consequences. By the end of 1904 Einstein's unpublished theoretical investigations on Planck's law led to his realization that the electromagnetic world picture could not succeed. From correspondence and from analysis of papers that Einstein wrote during 1906–07 we know that he had deduced that light can also be comprised of particles or light quanta, a mode of light that could not be explained by Lorentz's theory.

Consequently, Einstein (1946) "despaired of discovering the true laws by means of constructive efforts based on known facts" (p. 53). By "constructive efforts" Einstein meant constructive theories which explain why phenomena occur by making assumptions on the constitution of matter. For example, Lorentz's theory explains the failure of ether-drift experiments with hypotheses that are rooted in the dynamical interaction between the ether and the constituent electrons of matter. In contrast, theories of principle do not explain phenomena. They are based on overarching principles that make no assumptions on the constitution of matter and that assert the form that physical laws must assume in order to forbid certain phenomena. An example of such a principle is the Newtonian principle of relativity, which insists that theories be formulated in such a way that the laws of nature remain the same in all intertial reference systems.

In the midst of his "despair" Einstein realized that he must turn to a theory of principle in order to go beyond the "known facts." The clues as to how to proceed lay in the 1895 thought experiment and in the process of electromagnetic induction. Electromagnetic induction is the process in which electric current is generated in a loop of wire that is in motion relative to a magnet. This is the process by which electrical dynamos function.

From Polytechnic courses, his ever-ongoing independent reading, and then as a patent clerk who had occasion to assess patents for electrical dynamos, Einstein had learned well the intimate connection between mechanics and electromagnetism for interpreting electromagnetic induction, for the laws of mechanics must be used to calculate the motion of moving parts of the system that is comprised of conductor and magnet.

But in Einstein's opinion electromagnetic theory did not adequately explain electromagnetic induction. His criticism concerned aesthetics rather than any disagreement with empirical data. Electromagnetic theory explained electromagnetic induction in two different ways, depending on whether the conductor or magnet was moving, even though the physically measurable effect (generated current) depended on a single cause (relative velocity). When the conductor moved relative to the magnet, a current flowed owing to a *force* on the conductor's electrons; in the inverse case, a current flowed owing to an *electric field* at the conductor's site. For Einstein, two explanations (force and field) for an effect that depended on only the relative velocity between magnet and conductor was more than a shortcoming of Lorentz's theory; he interpreted this redundancy in explanation as an asymmetry that was "not inherent in the phenomena" (1905).

According to Holton (1973), Einstein found the theoretical situation in electromagnetic induction so "unbearable," as he recalled in 1919, that he focused on the necessity for an equivalence of viewpoints between observers on the wire loop and on the magnet. In so doing he succeeded in linking mechanics and electromagnetism to the failed ether-drift experiments as follows. Since Newton's principle of relativity is exact, and since mechanics *and* electromagnetism are required to deal with electromagnetic induction, then a version of Newton's exact principle of relativity should cover electromagnetism and optics too, since, after all, they are unified in Lorentz's theory. With this master stroke Einstein enlarged Newton's principle of relativity to treat mechanics and electromagnetism on an equal footing, instead of attempting to reduce one to the other. But Einstein knew that a Newtonian principle of relativity covered electromagnetism only approximately.

Of all the ether-drift experiments that had been performed, the ones that Einstein deemed most important could be explained systematically by Lorentz's local time coordinate. Consequently, the local time would have to play a role in relating phenomena between reference systems. But did not everyone know this? Einstein's innovative tack was to search for a new law for the addition of velocities that agreed wth the thought experimenter's intuition. He succeeded with a derivation based on the local time coordinate.

The new addition law can be explained as follows. Although Eq. 1 agrees with the customary intuition that one is able to catch up with anything, the new velocity addition law that replaced Eq. 1 meant that the thought experimenter could never catch up with the point on the light wave, because that point always moved at the same velocity relative to his laboratory—namely, the velocity of light. The new velocity addition law produced the result in Eq. 2, when the system under investigation was light. Imagine what a mind-boggling result this is: it runs counter to intuition from the world of sense perceptions of catching up with objects. Imagine, for example, that you pull onto a highway and ahead of you is another car that was already on the highway, traveling faster than you. You step on the gas, but no matter how fast you go the other car travels at the same velocity relative to you. How can this be? We may conjecture that Einstein pondered this sort of question, and that he responded as follows.

Since the local time coordinate is the root of the new velocity addition law, Einstein asked himself whether the local time is the physical time. But this step required asserting that the times in inertial reference systems differed because the local time coordinate depends on their relative motion. Yet the absoluteness of time had always been accepted. After all, consistent with our sense perceptions there is no reason for time to depend on the motion of a clock. The thought experimenter's intuition demanded an epistemological analysis of the nature of time. Einstein recalled (1946) that he benefited from the "critical reasoning [in] David Hume's and Ernst Mach's philosophical writings." Their writings impressed on him that exact laws of nature could not be induced from empirical data or from data of the senses. The key to the paradox from the 1895 thought experiment lay in the "axiom of the absolute character of time, viz., of simultaneity [which] unrecognizedly was anchored in the unconscious" (1946, p. 53). Consequently, the new intuition that Einstein arrived at by going beyond the "known facts" was at a higher level of abstraction, one in which time is a relative quantity.

Einstein went on boldly to raise to the level of axioms Newton's principle and a second principle that the velocity of light is a definite constant independent of the relative motion between source and observer. We recall that in Lorentz's theory the second principle was valid only in an ether-fixed system; according to the failed ether-drift experiments it seemed to hold in inertial systems too.

Einstein's two principles do not attempt to explain anything—for example, why the measured velocity of light always turns out to be c. The special theory of relativity is a theory of principle.

In short, Einstein moved against the prevailing currents of theoretical physics by resolving problems in a Gordian manner, that is, by formulating a view of physics in which certain problems do not occur, a view in which the 1895 paradox becomes a mere fiction and the results of the ether-drift experiments were a foregone conclusion.

History of Science as a Laboratory for Cognitive Studies

Cognitive Science

The matrix of science, philosophy, and technology in which Einstein was educated and worked placed a high premium on visual thinking, a mode of thought that he preferred for creative thinking. In Einstein's most widely read introspection, the "Autobiographical Notes" (1946), he begins almost immediately with the question "What, precisely, is 'thinking'?" His reply is that from sense impressions "memory-pictures" emerge. A certain "picture" serves as an "ordering element" for the potpourri of memory-pictures and that picture is a "concept." Thinking is the free "play" with concepts, and words then follow. These passages also link Einstein's visual thinking to the "customary intuition" rooted in Kantian philosophy.

In Einstein's case the content of the mental representation is important. The content has a strong image–perception link. This leads me to suggest a reason why Einstein made no more great thought experiments besides those of 1895, which led to special relativity, and of 1907, which also involved a close image–perception link and which led to the generalized relativity theory of 1915.[5] The price we pay for theories that cover ever-wider domains of phenomena, wrote Einstein (1936), is a "poverty of concepts," because the higher level theories are predicated on basic statements or concepts that have increasingly ambiguous connections with phenomena in the world of perceptions. Einstein referred to his own stage theory of scientific progress as the "stratification of the scientific system" (1936). While special relativity deals with a restricted class of observers (inertial observers), the next higher level theory, which is generalized relativity, includes accelerated observers too, and so is able to combine acceleration and gravity. Among the basic concepts of special relativity are measuring rods and clocks. But in generalized relativity physical reality is shifted from space and time intervals to mathematical quantities which describe the state of gravitation that conditions the structure of space–time. On the one hand, it was possible for Einstein to begin work toward generalizing special relativity with a thought experiment based on customary intuition. On the other hand, this was not the case for Einstein's lifelong failed quest for the unified field theory that would have been the highest stratum and therefore the poorest in concepts. The basic concepts of the unified field theory would have been far removed from our customary intuitions and so not at all unambiguously connected with notions that are visualizable. In the unified theory gravitation and electromagnetism would have been unified in such a way that atoms emerge as knots in space–time.

A controversy has been raging in the cognitive science community over the legitimacy of the concept of imagery for representing thought. The efficacy of the 1895 and 1907 thought experiments is evidence that Einstein's visual imagery was functional in his thinking, thus providing support for the pro-imagery faction. Further evidence is the spatial character of the transformation of Einstein's images. For example, as the thought experimenter conceives of himself as accelerating, he measures—in accordance with prerelativistic physics—a decreasing velocity of light relative to him by noticing the steady displacement of fringes in an interferometer. Then as he catches up with a point on the light wave he observes the gradual transformation from the mode of a linearly translating vibratory state to a standing vibratory wave state when $V = 0$ in Eq. 1.

We recall that an *Anschauung* is an abstraction from primitive sense perceptions, which is appended to a theory as a visualization for its mathematics. In certain cases, such as a magnet's lines of force, an *Anschauung* is promoted to an integral part of the theory itself. The construction and dynamics of an *Anschauung* are beyond the present state of any existing theory of imagery. Nevertheless, we have found that *Anschauung* is a philosophical–cultural component of thinking. Does this not run counter to the assumption that there is a universal basic encoding in the mind? This is part of a fundamental problem in the psychology of syntax.

Studies in the history of science indicate the importance for scientific progress of such extralogical dimensions of thinking as imagery, intuition, aesthetics, and the cultural milieu. Segments of the cognitive science community object to the "fuzzy" manner in which these dimensions of human thought enter the problem of creativity (e.g., Simon, 1973). They insist that these notions can be objectified in algorithms. Yet among the rationales of scientific discovery that they offer is Norwood Hanson's (1958) "patterns of discovery," which relies heavily on a kind of intuition. Generalized relativity is wider in scope and an improvement over special relativity, which is better than Newton's mechanics. The transition from one theory to another was not accomplished by logic alone. The fact that there is such a thing as scientific progress underlies the importance of the current debate about the possibility of moving beyond the stage of formal operational thinking.[6]

Genetic Epistemology

I have found in my research in the history of science that there are hierarchical hallmarks that signal scientific advance. According to the historical scenario for special relativity there is (1) establishment of a conserved quantity ($V = c$, where V is the velocity of light measured in an inertial reference system S_r); (2) reversibility (between an ether-fixed reference system S and the inertial reference system S_r); and (3) systematization (final mathematical setting of the theory). In the theories that I have studied thus far, the sequential order of these structures is the same. The natural emergence of these hallmarks led me to turn to Jean Piaget's genetic epistemology, which is a stage theory of mental development. Piaget's theory offers a framework for exploring the dynamics of thought processes as the scientist interacts with the environment, that is, with empirical data, data of the thought experimenter, philosophical and cultural input included. Genetic epistemology also offers a means to explore scientific progress by linking it with the dynamics of the construction of prescientific knowledge and creative thinking. At least presently, I have found that these problems are difficult to investigate using leads from contemporary cognitive science.

While the analysis to follow assumes the validity of genetic epistemology, in my work I have reinterpreted certain parts of the theory and modified others, particularly the notion of a formal operational stage as the final equilibrated level of intelligence. My procedure is to use genetic epistemology as a model for understanding the genesis of special relativity. Genetic epistemology is a rich and intricately developed body of knowledge. As a first approximation in dealing with the genesis of a complex theory as it emegres from theories that are already highly developed and abstract in their own right, I will deal with a small portion of the core of genetic epistemology: the stages of mental development and the assimilation/accommodation process. We shall find that genetic epistemology is not a completely adequate framework for describing Einstein's thinking.

When Einstein began his research he had long since entered the formal operational stage of thinking. Clearly, extensions of certain notions from genetic epistemology are required to explore how in the scientist's mind a scientific theory is created and then further constructed.

I suggest the following ones:

1. Physicists deal with schemes that possess *ab initio* the proper mathematical attributes to set them in a postformal operational stage.

2. But it is the interpretation of new data and/or conflicts with theoretical puzzles that place a theory into a lower stage of genetic epistemology—for example, for Einstein the 1895 thought experiment exhibited a paradox in the current theory of light that went beyond existing empirical data.

3. A second definition of assimilation: The application of a scheme to problems involving empirical data, data from thought experiments, or aesthetic–philosophical commitments.

4. With Piaget I define structure as "the set of possible states and transformations of which the system that actually pertains is a special case" (Piaget, 1970a).

Drawing on the previous historical results we may construct the following "genetic epistemological scenario."

For Einstein the formal operational structure of classical physics was disequilibrated in 1895 and again in 1900. In 1895 he assimilated the data of the thought experiment to the structure of classical physics with no attempt at adjustment or accommodation (see level in 1 in Fig. 9–2). The "intuition" of the thought experimenter predicts that, as in classical mechanics, the laws of physics should be the same in the ether-fixed system S as in the inertial system S_r. But for the purpose of describing the behavior of light, electromagnetic theory predicted results at variance with empirical data, that is, Eq. 1.

A further anomaly in classical electromagnetic theory was revealed to

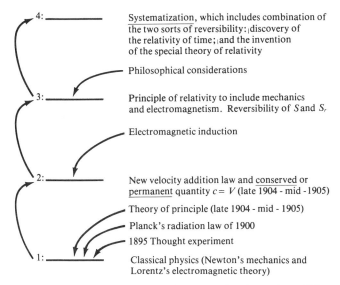

FIGURE 9–2. Assimilation and accommodation in the dynamics of Einstein's thinking toward the special theory of relativity.

Einstein through his unsuccessful assimilation of the structure of classical physics to Planck's radiation law (see level 1 in Fig. 9–2); Einstein realized that Planck's law violated electromagnetic theory and mechanics.

By early 1905 Einstein's further researches revealed that Lorentz's theory could not be the cornerstone of all of physical theory because it could not explain the structure of light. Einstein's "despair" led him to turn to the methods of a theory of principle which he assimilated to the disequilibrated structure of classical physics. This resulted in a new accommodation, the formation of a structure that contained a new addition law for velocities. This law guided him in the construction of the scheme of a conserved quantity, namely, the velocity of light in vacuum, that is, $c = V$ (see level 2 in Fig. 9–2). The equilibrium was temporary, however, because this scheme did not contain full reversibility. There is inversion because S_r with its local time also could be taken to be the resting system, that is, the reference system at rest relative to the physical system under examination. But there is no reciprocity because the reference system S can never move. One cannot, therefore, relate the subclasses of systems S and S_r to the total class of inertial systems.

Einstein made further progress by including data from electromagnetic induction whose explanation contained an asymmetry that is "not inherent in the phenomena." To alleviate this "unbearable" situation, he focused on the relation between observers on the magnet and on the conductor. This permitted Einstein to link mechanics and electromagnetism with the failed ether-drift experiments. In Piaget's terms this meant the assimilation of data (electromagnetic induction) to a scheme (new addition law of velocities that accounted approximately for the results of the failed ether-drift experiments) for which the scheme was not meant originally.

There followed a further accommodation to a level that contained the scheme of reversibility of S and S_r. According to Einstein's principle of relativity, the laws of mechanics, electromagnetism, and optics are the same in every inertial reference system. This principle was still approximate because it was based on the new addition law for velocities of whose exactness, at that point, Einstein was unsure. Since his thinking was still linked to images, both sorts of reversibility could not be used together. He had resolved in principle, but not yet mathematically, the situation of electromagnetic induction involving magnet and conductor. Here Einstein's reflective abstraction, and assimilation of the level 3 in Fig. 9–2 to his reading of, among others, Hume and Mach, convinced him that he had to reach beyond sense perceptions. The result was accommodation of level 3 to a new level of abstraction, which is formal operations (level 4, Fig. 9–2).

Having achieved this level of formal operations, Einstein realized that the mathematical group of the space–time transformations required to shift between reference systems was rich enough to include conservation of the velocity of light, and that full reversibility resolved the "unbearable" situation in electromagnetic induction. As Einstein later wrote, an important and new facet of his special theory of relativity was that the relativistic space–time transformation "transcended its connection with [Lorentz's] equations." Thus, with regard to the special theory of relativity, Einstein had achieved the level of formal operations by liberating himself from dependence on perception to locate what Piaget (1970a) at this level of thinking refers to as "reality in a group of transformations"—reality, that is, concerning the proper value for the velocity of light in vacuum. At this juncture, we may say that Einstein invented the relativity of time because the group structure implied full reversibility of S and S_r and, consequently, the physical reality of time's dependence on the motion of a reference system.

Achieving full operativity through mathematical structures agrees with Einstein's comment that his thinking was predominantly visual and that mathematical work was undertaken in the final stages of research. However, historical research provides material to suggest that Einstein never freed his further creative thinking about special relativity from images—for example, there were thought experiments that were important in Einstein's generalizing special relativity.

Nor does it seem reasonable that Einstein invented something as basic as the relativity of simultaneity only through mathematical considerations. Rather, he realized after discovering the new velocity addition law that the local time might be the physical time. Philosophical considerations followed. Moreover, Einstein's discovery of the relativity of time preceded his proposing the second axiom of relativity. These breaks in the heretofore most reasonable historical sequence points up a basic weakness in genetic epistemology's emphasis on logic in the formal operational period, in which considerations based on visual imagery are deemphasized.[7]

Figure 9–2 shows that the genetic epistemological scenario indicates that the dynamics of scientific progress is driven by the upward spiral of the assimilation/accommodation process resulting in a hierarchical series of structures in which equilibration is achieved only in part. The brain is an open system in search of a stable equilibration which the inquiring mind never achieves. If Piaget's level of formal operations was the final stage of scientific development, scientific progress would come to a halt.

Conclusion

A principal goal of this chapter has been to show how cognitive studies are essential to understanding creative scientific thinking. Whereas cognitive science is useful for exploring mental imagery, and genetic epistemology for understanding the construction of knowledge, I have found that neither theory illuminates the nascent moment of creativity. For this purpose, Gestalt psychology's stress on the discontinuous change in the field of knowledge is useful. It is likely that a combination of these three cognitive theories will reveal deeper insights into scientific creativity. As Jean Piaget aptly wrote:

> A great deal of work remains to be done in order to clarify this fundamental process of intellectual creation, which is found at all the levels of cognition, from those of earliest childhood to those culminating in the most remarkable of scientific inventions. (1970b, p. 78)

NOTES

1. There is little extant archival material on which to base a historical scenario of Einstein's invention of the special theory of relativity. Thus much detective work must be done to piece together these few materials with primary sources, secondary sources, and Einstein's own recollections as well as archival materials of other scientists. I have sketched here the most reasonable historical scenario of Einstein's thinking. For details that include a comprehensive bibliography see my earlier work (Miller, 1981a, 1986a, 1986b); information from Einstein's recently published collected papers (Einstein, 1987) support the scenario presented here.

2. For useful published biographical material on Einstein through 1905, see Holton (1973), Miller (1981a), Pais (1982), and Einstein (1987), which contains a biographical sketch of Einstein written in 1924 by his sister Maja.

3. Holton (1973) first pointed out the importance of the *Kantonsschule* for Einstein's development. I explored this episode elsewhere (Miller, 1986a).

A partial chronology of events in Einstein's life for the period under investigation (1879–1905) follows (see Pais [1982, pp. 520–530] for a detailed chronology):

1879   March 14: Einstein is born in Ulm, Germany.
1888   Einstein enters the Luitpold Gymnasium, Munich.

1894   The Einstein family moves to Italy, leaving Albert behind to finish his studies at the Gymnasium.
1895   Spring: Einstein leaves the Gymnasium to join his family in Pavia.
1895   Einstein writes his first scientific essay, which he sends to his uncle Caesar Koch.
1896   Fall: Einstein fails the entrance exam for the Zurich Polytechnic.
1895–96 Einstein attends the *Kantonsschule,* Aarau, Switzerland, where in 1895 he conceived of the thought experiment of what it is like to ride along next to a light wave.
1896   Einstein enrolls at the Zurich Polytechnic.
1900   Einstein graduates. Owing to poor recommendations from professors at the Zurich Polytechnic Einstein can obtain neither a position as a graduate assistant at the Zurich Polytechnic nor any steady employment.
1902   Einstein starts work at the Swiss Federal Patent Office, Bern, as a patent clerk third class.
1905   The special relativity paper is received at the *Annalen der Physik.*
1907   Einstein conceives of the thought experiment that is fundamental for his generalizing the special theory of relativity (see note 5).
1909   Einstein takes up his post as associate professor at the University of Zurich.

4. For example, during the summer of 1895, before entering the *Kantonsschule,* Einstein wrote his first scientific essay, which he sent to his favorite uncle, Caesar Koch. Its contents indicate that by age 16, through independent reading, he was already conversant with advanced topics in the theory of light.

5. The thought experiment of 1907 concerned an observer in free fall and the consequences of there being for him during this fall no gravitational field in his immediate vicinity (pictures only). But these pictures were not merely image-perceptual representations; they were theory-laden. For example, in this thought experiment Einstein "saw" objects that dropped with him, and thus fell at relative rest, in the context of Newton's law of motion applied to the falling observer and to an observer on the ground. Although scientists have many times "seen" objects falling side by side, Einstein "saw" the deep structure in this scene; that is, he "saw" the relation between gravity and acceleration so long as he also assumed the exact equality between gravitational and inertial masses.

6. For an excellent survey of the problem of going beyond formal operational thought, see Broughton (1984).

7. The imagery problem is especially acute in a genetic epistemological analysis of the genesis of atomic physics (see Miller, 1986b).

REFERENCES

Broughton, J. M. (1984). Not beyond formal operations but beyond Piaget. In M. L. Commons, F. A. Richards, & C. Armon (Eds.), *Beyond formal operations: Late adolescent and adult cognitive development* (pp. 395–411). New York: Prager.

Commons, M. L., Richards, F. A., & Armon, C. (Eds.). (1984). *Beyond formal operations: Late adolescent and adult cognitive development.* New York: Praeger.

Einstein, A. (1905). On the electrodynamics of moving bodies. *Annalen der Physik, 17,* 891–921. (Translated in Miller [1981a], pp. 391–415)

Einstein, A. (1934). The problem of space, ether and field in physics. In A. Einstein, *Essays in Science* (pp. 61–77). New York: Philosophical Library.

Einstein, A. (1936). Physics and reality. *Journal of the Franklin Institute, 221,* 313–347. (Reprinted in A. Einstein [n.d.], *Ideas and Opinions* [pp. 290–323]. New York: Bonanza Books)

Einstein, A. (1946). Autobiographical notes. In P. A. Schilpp (Ed.), *Albert Einstein: Philosopher-scientist* (pp. 2–94). Evanston: Library of Living Philosophers.

Einstein, A. (1987). *The collected papers of Albert Einstein: Vol. 1. The early years* (J. Stachel, Ed.). Princeton: Princeton University Press.

Hanson, N. R. (1958). *Patterns of discovery.* Cambridge: Cambridge University Press.

Holton, G. (1973). *Thematic origins of scientific thought: Kepler to Einstein.* Cambridge: Harvard University Press.

Miller, A. I. (1981a). *Albert Einstein's special theory of relativity: Emergence (1905) and early interpretation (1905–1911).* Reading, Mass.: Addison-Wesley.

Miller, A. I. (1981b). Unipolar induction: A case study of the interaction between science and technology. *Annals of Science, 38,* 155–189. (Reprinted in Miller [1986b], pp. 153–187)

Miller, A. I. (1986a). *Imagery in scientific thought: Creating 20th-century physics.* Cambridge, Mass.: MIT Press.

Miller, A. I. (1986b). *Frontiers in physics, 1900–1911.* Boston: Birkhäuser.

Pais, A. (1982). *Subtle is the Lord: The science and life of Albert Einstein.* Oxford: Oxford University Press.

Piaget, J. (1970a). *Structuralism* (C. Maschler, Trans.). New York: Basic Books.

Piaget, J. (1970b). *Genetic epistemology* (E. Duckworth, Trans.). New York: Columbia University Press.

Russell, B. (1968). *The autobiography of Bertrand Russell—The early years: 1872–World War I.* New York: Bantam.

Simon, H. (1973). Does scientific discovery have a logic? *Philosophy of Science, 40,* 471–480.

FIGURE 10–1. Jean Piaget, about 15 years old. From an undated family photograph. Courtesy Jean Piaget Archives, Geneva.

10

Self and Oeuvre
in Jean Piaget's Youth

FERNANDO VIDAL

Jean Piaget's (1896–1980) worldwide reputation is built on his work as a child psychologist. Yet he claimed to be interested less in actual children than in the "epistemic subject." The epistemic subject is made up of that which is common to all subjects at the same level of development. Thus the epistemic subject is abstract because it is not meant to correspond to any concrete individual and because Piaget insisted on describing it in abstract formal language. Not surprisingly, therefore, the most widespread image of Piaget today rests on his emphasis on logic, or formalization, as the essential tool for construing the subject of cognitive studies. Although Piaget did not deny the importance of social and affective life, he simply did not consider it central to his work.

The image of Piaget is reinforced by his self-presentation as a man motivated exclusively from adolescence by the project of elaborating a "biological explanation of knowledge" (1952, p. 240). True, he acknowledged having gone through a religious and philosophical crisis (1952, pp. 239–240). He also recalled having made the decision to devote his life to philosophy, whose central aim he then saw as the reconciliation of science and religious values (1971, p. 5). But Piaget suggested that the crisis was rapidly overcome, and that the project of reconciling science and values was just as quickly superseded by a more logical and scientific orientation akin to the theory with which he is usually identified now.

Piaget's autobiography illustrates the frequent "decontextualizing" function of the genre and its tendency to shape life-history as a destiny advancing toward the autobiographer's present. Uncritical reliance on Piaget's self-presentation would lead to a "Whig" or hindsight interpretation of the Piagetian oeuvre. Gradually, however, a less "official" picture is emerging. For example, when all of Piaget's writings are taken into account, he no longer appears as having had exclusively epistemological and scientific motivations. On the contrary, religious, moral, social, and political concerns turn out to be extremely important in his development and fully integrated into his oeuvre up to the 1930s.

As for historical context, when the situation of Swiss intellectual bourgeois youth during World War I is examined and related to the history of Protestantism in the first decades of the twentieth century, Piaget emerges as a scientific and philosophical spokesman for values rooted in a variety of liberal traditions (Vidal, 1987a).

Gruber's (e.g., 1980) "network of enterprise" concept has been central to the elaboration of such a biographical image of Piaget. First, the network idea demands that the diverse interests and productive activities of an individual be approached as an organized totality. Second, it suggests a hierarchy according to which an enterprise is a longlasting system made up of varying projects and tasks to be accomplished. Third, it highlights the importance of placing a person's intellectual development in the context of his whole life (Gruber, 1981). This approach leads to the discovery that Piaget's well-known epistemological enterprise was originally inseparable from, and sometimes even subordinate to, a moral enterprise aimed at making possible human individual and social salvation.

In this chapter I examine one feature of the early development of Piaget's network of enterprise: the way in which a self-project relates to intellectual projects. By "self-project" I mean the plans a self-conscious individual makes with personal identity in mind. I have already studied how, about 1917, Piaget's concepts of his own personality and of his own affective and intellectual development were inseparable from his first critical ideas on psychoanalysis (Vidal, 1986).

My focus here is on an earlier period, represented in particular by *The Mission of the Idea,* a 1915 poetical text in which the young Piaget's expressed self-project is closely connected to his earliest philosophical system, political ideals, and social concerns.[1]

The Social Context of *The Mission of the Idea*

In the introduction to their abbreviated translation of *The Mission of the Idea,* Gruber and Vonèche provide an excellent short presentation of Piaget's text:

> *The Mission of the Idea* is a long prose poem written at the height of the First World War to castigate a Europe afflicted with a conservative spirit, nationalism, egoism, pride, and inertia. These are the evils seen as

killing the Idea. As the work progresses, the identity of the Idea seems to change, or rather, the particulars chosen to exemplify it: justice, equality, women's rights, free expression of the human spirit in all its diversity, faith in Jesus, faith in the people, self-discipline, struggle for the good, peace, socialism, and so on. The Idea is all these things, and above all, the never-ending movement of thought toward them. The author expresses over and over his belief in the power of ideas, they "lead the world," govern action. If we must sum up his message in a few words, we can call it the outcry of youth against the smug hypocrisy of the Church and the bourgeoisie during the long suffering of the war, and a romantic, moralistic belief in Christian socialism. (1977, p. 26)

The religious drive of Piaget's poem is much stronger than this summary suggests. Indeed, the ultimate "mission of the Idea" was the "new birth of Christianity" (p. 68). This mission is construed as the mission of young people. The 19-year-old Piaget shared with many of his peers the ideal of modeling himself upon a heroic image of Jesus Christ. Since Jesus is "the Idea made flesh," the duty of the young man was to work for the realization of the Idea on earth.

Piaget's revolt against the evils that "kill the Idea" manifests the image of youth that was common in his milieu. His poem synthesizes concerns, themes, and aspirations widely shared within the Swiss Christian Students Association to which he had belonged since 1914. *Mission* was published as a special issue of the association's bulletin. The leaders of this association were liberal Protestants; most of its student members adhered to the principles of religious liberalism.

Liberal Protestantism flourished in the decades preceding World War I. Respect for historical criticism, rejection of the literal reading of the Bible, and an effort to reconcile religion with all aspects of secular culture were among its main features. It emphasized the inwardness of revelation and the immanence of God, and it tended to base religion on individual feeling rather than on obedience to a transcendental Divinity revealed in the Scriptures. It saw faith as a form of human experience, governed by the same psychological and historical laws that govern other human experiences. Every aspect of Christianity was thus humanized. Jesus, for example, became more a historical figure and a model of conduct than a redeeming Messiah and the Son of God.

Critiques of the apparent subjectivism of the liberal approach and of the intellectualism that resulted from its historical and psychological orientation were formulated even before World War I. During the war, intellectualism was often considered a betrayal of the mission of theology and judged partly responsible for the incapacity of the churches to face sociopolitical circumstances. *The Mission of the Idea* seemed to show that youth could be trusted with the task of renewing the liberal attitude. It proclaimed a subjectivist kind of religion, with a rather abstract immanent deity and a totally human figure of Jesus Christ. Contrary to neo-dogmatic trends developing at the time, the religion of *Mission* remained anthropocentric.

For several paternal figures of the student movement, Piaget's poem confirmed that youth was pure and idealistic, moved by the highest spiritual and social ideals, and the hope of a world in crisis. One reviewer wrote: "We have just read a sort of declaration of Youth looking to the new times: it is fresh, it is vigorous, it is extraordinarily alive. It should be read: by the young, so that their soul may vibrate; by the older ones, so that they may learn once more the new life, and anticipate the times to come." The review ends by thanking the young Piaget for having opened himself up, thus revealing "the heart of idealistic youth" (Pettavel, 1916).

In the Christian student milieu, youth was endowed with a redemptive mission. This, one of the main themes of Piaget's poem, is expressed in the warning, "Woe unto the young man who is not stirred by the power of the idea!" (p. 6). In *Mission,* the idea itself is young: "Honor to him who meditates, alone, in his silent room, and then thrusts into full light the young idea that will dash through the world, as the storm agitates the sea" (p. 11). The mission of the idea is to be carried out through an active identification with the model of its unique incarnation, Jesus Christ, the "young and humble man" whose "exquisite soul" tragically clashed against "the deaf obstinacy of stupid traditions" (p. 9).

Piaget's self-project at age 19 consisted of trying to become a young man modeled on Jesus, who was regarded as a human hero, and an archetypal youth. It is significant that Piaget integrated this model, as well as his own self-ideals, into an organized intellectual framework. This "system" is not so much a primeval form of Piaget's theory as an early expression of some of his major "thematic commitments," as Holton (1975) would put it. This is particularly true of Piaget's commitment to the moral goodness of nature and to evolution as a process oriented by an ideal toward which it ineluctably tends. What might be called the "system of the Idea" is, I believe, Piaget's first identifiable elaboration of a total interpretation of the world. *The Mission of the Idea* indeed expresses an outcry of youth, but this revolt gains full significance only in the context of a grand intellectual scheme.

The System of the Idea

Piaget's original French text distinguishes between "idea" and "Idea." Although "idea" is one of the most common terms in *Mission,* "Idea" appears rarely. This distinction is at the heart of the cosmogony and the cosmology contained in Piaget's prose poem.

The system of *Mission* is an idealism of clearly Plotinian overtones; it is also inspired by the notions of creative evolution and *élan vital* elaborated by the French philosopher Henri Bergson. Its framework is a hierarchy of beings made up of three levels: the Idea, the ideas (often simply "idea"), and the human formulas of the idea. This hierarchy branches down from the unique archetypal Idea to the formulas, which can be as numerous as individuals.

Particular ideas, such as freedom and justice, are seen as the motor of life, and, in accordance with Bergson's philosophy of creative evolution, are described as constantly renewing themselves. As in Victor Hugo's 1837 *Voix intérieures* (poem 1, line 2), "Partout on voit marcher l'idée en mission," toward a renewal of society that relies on the strength of the people, the poet's divine nature, and the power of the thinking man.[2]

> Launched into the world, it [the idea] goes through like a hurricane, overthrowing kings and priests, raising the masses, eliciting living and dying, deciding the outcome of battles, creating the people's strength, and guiding the whole of humanity. (p. 4)

Although "ideas" are the motors of history, they are not autonomous human creations. They derive all their power from the Idea, the supreme and almost unnameable origin.

In *Mission*'s hierarchy of beings, the Idea, which is unique, represents the absolutely living and real, whereas the very numerous human formulas and actions possess little genuine fundamental reality. Thus an increase in existential diversity is proportional to a decrease in ontological status. This ontological hierarchy is accompanied by an epistemological one, from absolute knowledge and truth at the top to subjective knowledge at the bottom. In turn, the scheme is completed by a descending order going from absolute totality to the individual parts. History is the same hierarchy, temporalized under the name of "impulse" or "march" of life (Bergson's *élan vital*), advancing "towards the ideal, the unknown, God" (p. 16).

According to the young Piaget's system, history consists of the gradual integration of the parts (human individuals) within a "'higher totality that supersedes and coordinates the different resonances [of the Ideal]" into "the ideal and absolute Humanity" (pp. 22, 23). History turns out to be identical to life, to change, and to evolution: "The idea is an organism" (p. 4); "The evolution of life and the aims of morality coincide point for point. . . . To hasten evolution is to do moral good" (p. 18); conservatives "think that they are the end of evolution, and deny all future progress" (p. 15), whereas "Jesus believed in progress" and "lived in the future" (pp. 64, 65). All those ascending movements toward integration into a unique whole define progress. They constitute the march of the Idea; as author of *Mission,* Piaget illustrates a typically late nineteenth-century version of what Kundera (1984) calls the "political kitsch" of the Great March forward.

The hierarchy of *Mission* is linked not only to human history, but also to a history of the cosmos. "In the beginning was the Idea, says the mysterious word of the Christian cosmogony" (p. 4). Ideas are brought into being through a process of "resonance" in the human soul (p. 4). Different individuals adopt different formulas to apprehend and express such resonance (Piaget, for example, wrote *Mission*) and try to act according to them. The Idea is always the essence that persists behind, above, and beyond concrete existence; it is the absolute totality toward which everything progresses; it is the final Heaven where "all struggle will have ended" (p. 7); "everything is idea, comes out of the idea, and returns to the idea" (p. 4).

Metaphysics, Poetry, and Mystical Experience

The first thing to be emphasized is that the system of the Idea is metaphysical, and that its premises are unequivocally Bergsonian. For the French philosopher Henri Bergson, metaphysics is the only way of apprehending the constantly evolving and creative essence of life. Contrary to the sciences, which use symbolic and analytic tools and break the perfectly continuous flow of time and evolution, Bergsonian metaphysics uses the method of "intuition," whereby creative evolution is comprehended without discursive intermediates. Thus, Piaget urges: "Let us give up our own selves, save morality, and apprehend the Christ, without going through the symbols of the brain" (p. 52). As he claimed:

> Metaphysics is the supreme manifestation of the idea, insofar as it remains living sympathy, rather than the dry ratiocination whose dogmatism hides the emptiness of its reasonings. Metaphysics will arouse religion from its present torpor, since in speculation Christians learn the value of truth, even when this truth is opposed to their own interests. (p. 55)

Metaphysics, however, is not just speculation. For example, when the child reaches the age of knowing, "his mother reveals to him, one evening, the secrets of his birth":

> And then, in the midst of his sacred turmoil, he experiences the pure and noble joy of true knowledge, and he thankfully adores beautiful truth. . . . Because it is the first time that he elevates himself to the sublime regions of human search, reaching the point where knowing and feeling merge into one religious act.
> Such is the nature of metaphysics. (p. 54)

Revolt against intellectualism and dry ratiocination, and a penchant for a rather mystical metaphysics, were common among pre-World War I European and American religious youth, whose battle cry was Bergson's philosophy.

In agreement with what was often proclaimed in his milieu, the young Piaget affirmed that "progress comes out of the sage's brain, not out of the arm of men of action," that "the Reform was carried out in the cloister's silence rather than in struggles and councils," that "the Revolution was made in Rousseau's promenades," and that "the future Republic is constructed in the idealists' visions" (pp. 10, 11). Yet Piaget claimed that the apprehension of the idea is not the result of mere thinking:

> The idea surges from the depth of our being, from the fertile and mysterious regions to which man never descends by himself. It surges from that vital hearth which gives out emanations only under the hold of the sublime: a night over the sea, a sunset in Autumn, or the august silence of two friends' hearts. (p. 3)

Piaget (1918a, p. 15) later criticized himself for having felt close to those religious young men "who had paid at a distance some homage to science, and then, triumphantly, took a rest and cultivated mysticism." Nevertheless, there can be no doubt about the importance for Piaget of his earlier mystical experiences.

Mysticism of the Lonely Traveler

Three years after writing *Mission,* Piaget published *Recherche,* a confessional *Bildungsroman* combined with a philosophical essay. In the confessional part of his text, Piaget (1918a, p. 42) wrote that Sebastian, the hero he identified with himself, "had philosophized since the age of reflection, starting with a vague mystique, later constructing one of those frail metaphysical structures that charm and console for an instant, and then rapidly disappoint." In *Recherche,* mysticism and metaphysics are the object of many critical remarks. Moreover, in a 1917 letter to the pacifist and internationalist French writer Romain Rolland, Piaget (1966, p. 7) wrote of his efforts to stop being a "metaphysician" and a "theologian."

In later years Piaget never mentioned the period of *The Mission of the Idea.* Nevertheless, he hinted at the existence of at least one moment of quasi-mystical elation: his discovery of Bergson, which took place about three years before the publication of *Mission.* He described his discovery as an "intellectual shock" that led him to decide he would consecrate his life "to the biological explanation of knowledge." The intellectual shock was accompanied by an emotional one. "I recall," Piaget wrote "an evening of profound revelation. The identification of God with life itself was an idea that stirred me almost to ecstasy because it now enabled me to see in biology the explanation of all things and of the mind itself" (1952, p. 240). He also had "a moment of enthusiasm close to ecstatic joy" (1971, p. 5). For the young Piaget, "biology" meant neither natural history (a discipline to which he had already devoted much time) nor any branch of experimental biology, but a Bergsonian sort of biological philosophy, of which the evolutionary idealism of *Mission* provides an early example.

I have already suggested that in *Mission* poetry, metaphysics and mysticism *combined* serve to approach the figure of Jesus Christ and to apprehend the Idea. The importance of the young Piaget's temporary predisposition to mysticism is shown by the fact that the only two passages of *Mission* where the pronoun "I" is used describe quasi-mystical episodes. The following is a partial translation of those passages:

> It was during the great year.
> And it was sunset. . . .
> An enormous weight oppressed every soul.
> And then, the bells started to ring, and the faithful crowded the Churches.

And at the same time, some men wandered alone, opening themselves to the idea. . . .

—God cries with us, thought the lonely ones; and their souls were filled with an immense love. Then, true mercy moved them to help the impotent God who moaned, unrecognized, with absolute charity forgiving the guilty and launching the idea. And I understood the sepulchral emptiness of the cults of the Church, and the beauty of the life for the idea.

And I understood the abdication of Christianity, whose silent lips for twenty centuries in vain had moved to honor the Lord. I also seized the goodness of God, whose ignored love was bleeding over our misfortunes. (pp. 42–43)

It was during the war.

One evening, a Requiem was sung. And I experienced the orthodox's terror before the anger of God. I then seized better the beauty of nascent ideas. . . .

[Piaget then includes the *Dies irae,* the Requiem prayer that implores God's mercy on judgment day.]

The choir sang *Sanctus, sanctus, sanctus, Dominus deus Sabaoth.* And I thought of the soft and subtle voice of the old prophet's God, after thunder and the elements' roar. When will the God of love and mercy destroy the "holy" and revengful God? (pp. 57–59)

Both passages place inner illumination in characteristically mystical settings. The first occurs in a section of *Mission* entitled "The Betrayal of Christianity." A melancholy sunset, the ringing of bells, and a sense of communion between the lonely contemplative individual and God make up the atmosphere in which the narrator understands the betrayal of the Christian churches. The only chronological indicator is a mysterious "great year"; what counts, however, is that the adjective "great" is used in connection with a quasi-mystical illumination narrated in the first person.

The second passage occurs in a later section entitled "The New Birth." Here, the "inductor" of the illumination is the overwhelmingly imposing music of a Requiem. The illumination itself combines a revolt against the traditional God with a realization of the beauty of nascent ideas and of the future world they would inspire. This second experience takes place "during the war," and it is clearly oriented to the future, toward the "new birth" that constituted "tomorrow's ideal."

The whole of *Mission,* including the passages in question, is marked by the literature read and written by the young Christian intellectuals of Piaget's milieu. The quasi-mystical episodes of the sunset and the Requiem are hardly original, yet they express the affective tone of the young Piaget's thinking, the emotional setting in which he elaborated the metaphysics of the Idea and the self-project of living for the Idea. The image of the lonely traveler is a further sign of mystical inclination in the Piaget of 1915:

A traveler passed, alone, on the white countryside.
Night was falling. A vague restlessness took hold of him, growing

little by little into the movement of a life . . . that would like to manifest itself in something grand and superhuman. . . . At this moment, the spirit lets itself go in an unfurling of interior life. (p. 13)

This passage occurs in the first section of *Mission,* entitled "Hymn to the Idea." In moments of mystical impulse, the lonely traveler feels his inner life most fully, and apprehends the idea. Once again, we find in this description an experience that is simultaneously affective and intellectual. The mystical moment is "sterile" because, after having let the idea bring the soul closer to God, it opens onto a void (p. 14). In an individual's "life for the idea," such a paralyzing oscillation between mystical exaltation and melancholy anguish precedes the period of revolt ("the betrayal of Christianity") and the time of elaborating a constructive project for the postwar era ("the new birth").

Piaget's self-project of modeling himself on Jesus is interwoven with his mystical predisposition. In *Mission,* the young man who experiences the mystical intuition of the Idea becomes an apostle, goes out to preach its metaphysics, and is ready to work for the construction of "tomorrow's ideal."

The Young Man's Mission

Piaget's self-project is epitomized in the idea that the proper mission of youth is to struggle for the realization of the Idea on earth. Youth must make history. Such a sense of mission is apparent in Piaget's organization of work (the writing and publication of *Mission,* for example) and in his view of himself as an arrogant yet loving and righteous apostle (Piaget, 1918a, p. 13). But it is most apparent in his conception of the young man, conveyed in the following passage from *Mission:*

> When at the beginning of his life, the young man thinks about the web of lies with which he has been suffocated, and compares it with the idea that is being born in him, he is seized by indignation and disgust. . . .
>
> Then, immensely free, and concentrating in himself everything he knows to be noble and elevated, he—a tiny unity—faces the evil-doers. And because he has not compromised, he feels in himself the power, that is, the duty, to undertake the immense struggle of clearing the way for the idea. . . .
>
> This is the truly moral period known to all men; as long as it lasts, they feel in true communion with life, with God. . . .
>
> Then, the self affirms itself, and forms its conceptions. The idea reaches its largest breadth. It raises itself to the metaphysical sphere, accumulating and coordinating all potentialities, all the beauties of true theory, all the poetry of the soul. . . .
>
> Later arrive evil, the first compromises, the first defections. . . . The conservative spirit corrodes the initial impulse. Then start slow agony, daily renunciation, suicide.
>
> Yet, here and there rises a hero, a genius appears. Genius is the crystallization of the idea in a man; heroism is this man's abandonment to the

idea, the magnificent life reserved to the powerful who, passing through with high and illuminated brows, elicit (as the spark igniting gunpowder) the anger of what is selfish, bourgeois, orthodox, conservative, in a word, reactionary.

Such is the force of the idea on the individual. (pp. 7–8)

In *Mission,* the commonplace developmental theory of youth (beginning of life, moral period, intellectual autonomy of the self, decline into adulthood) becomes part of a cosmic system where both the Idea and Jesus are young. Youth, nature, and history are all reflections of the Idea and mirrors of one another. The identification of the young man's life with cosmic rhythms confers meaning and consistency on his projects and aspirations. The sense of shared identity and heroism ranges from mystical longing for the intuited Idea to the feeling of friendship and communion with peers; it defines the apostles in terms of a population group. Men, "young and strong, different yet united in the same thrust of life" (p. 29), feel the idea in themselves, and "as long as it [the idea] lives, it gives life to an intellectual core within the sentiment and the will in which this core is immersed" (p. 4).

Emphasis on the potentialities of youth is yet another feature of this developmental theory. In *Mission,* Piaget was talking for and about himself. But he was also reproducing common ideas about adolescence and integrating them into his larger metaphysical scheme.

In *Mission*'s metonymical ideology, the young man is a microcosm, comparable to the Church, and a model for it: "Still young, the Church was pure and idealistic, because it struggled, it suffered, it created" (p. 36). Salvation and youth go together:

> When the child is about to become a man . . . [his] body is weaker, and more deserving of respect, since it is the seat of an august labor. His soul is prey to an awaiting anxiety, sometimes also to a pain rendered beautiful by its mysterious source.
> And then, this crisis bears a ripe fruit. . . .
> Thus shall be born humanity. (p. 30)

The metaphor of labor, as well as the emphasis on pain, suffering, struggle, and anxiety as the heroic sources of creation and redemption, were commonplaces in the conception of youth prevalent in the Christian student milieu. Their meaning and value, however, were intensified by the war, killer of the younger generation. Piaget's system of the Idea raised the idealist clichés about postwar salvation to the rank of metaphysical concepts: by virtue of the microcosmic nature of the young man, the birth of true humanity could take place through the realization of a sort of collective adolescence.

The mission of youth follows from the nature of youth, yet it appears as obligatory in the context of *Mission*'s social theory. The young Piaget thought that the society of his day was based on the error of emphasizing rights over obligations (p. 62). For him, "a formulated ideal becomes a duty" (p. 63). Thus, he moralized, the young generation must accept its duty:

In the supreme enjoyment of this sacred [metaphysical] research, he [the believer] experiences states that no art could afford him. The beauty of reason is a hundred times superior to the beauty of the senses.

But this enjoyment means nothing. Although it is noble and intense, we should not pursue it. There is more in the search for the idea: there is duty.

Once we have understood that the idea drives the world, and that today Christianity is giving up, we grasp the urgent mission incumbent upon post-War men: to engage themselves in the pursuit of a truth purer than the one that still nourishes us, since only through that search shall begin the new birth [of Christianity]. (p. 55)

Self-Project and the Network of Enterprise after World War I

A fundamental notion of the metaphysical system of the Idea is that there is a sort of Plotinian *circuitus spiritualis* that starts from the Idea, descends to the individual, and animates the individual's return to the unique transcendental origin. The young man's mission is to participate in this march of the Idea, which is identified with history and progress. For a young intellectual, living for the Idea implies working for the rebirth of Christianity through the metaphysical search for truth. In *The Mission of the Idea,* metaphysics is an activity of reason, yet its method is intuition; poetry and mysticism are forms of intuition, and they participate in the young man's search.

The mission that defines the young Piaget's nascent network of enterprise can be analyzed into three projects: the self-project of being a certain kind of person; the moral, social, and political project of contributing to the construction of a new Christian world out of the ruins left by the Great War; and the intellectual project of elaborating a system to back up the moral project.

This threefold organization of Piaget's "proto-network" can also be perceived in his conception of who is to carry out this mission:

Everybody's help is necessary for the rebirth of the idea. Metaphysics is not an aristocratic art. The scientist who finds hypotheses must place above them a great edifice capable of containing them; the Christian who has felt life within his heart must assimilate it through an interpretation furnished by his reason; the moral man who wants to find a life-rule in his action must construct an idea and justify it. (p. 68)

Piaget here defined three types of man and three types of activity: the thinking scientist (*savant,* which also means scholar), the believing Christian, and the acting moral man. Science, religion, and morality constitute three branches of Piaget's tree of enterprise, which he tried to combine in his own personality and productive activity.

To understand the development of Piaget's network of enterprise in connection with his youthful mission it is important to emphasize that the "rebirth of Christianity" was by no means a fundamentalist project. On the contrary, Piaget remained attached to the principles of liberal Protestantism; for him, Christianity was more an ethical than a religious ideal.

As already discussed, later Piaget condemned his early penchant for metaphysics and mysticism, omitting it from his autobiographical writings. Eventually he evolved toward the kind of cognitivist hyperrationalism with which he is usually associated today (Gruber, 1982). Yet this rationalism itself grew out of the proto-network of 1915, and its roots remained visible until the early 1930s (see Vidal, 1985, 1987a).

Piaget himself mentioned (1971, p. 5) that his early Bergsonian religion—"the certainty that God is life, under the form of the *élan vital*"— changed to an increasingly rationalistic immanentism. The transcendental Idea was replaced by an immanent Reason. Across this fundamental change, Piaget's more rationalistic arguments shared with the system of the Idea an evolutionary, naturalistic ethics. According to *Mission,* "the evolution of life, and that of morality coincide point for point. . . . To hasten evolution is to do moral good" (p. 18). In *Recherche,* written between 1916 and 1917, Piaget (1918a) claimed that "evolutionary moralities have proved that the good is life itself" (p. 173) and that "scientific morality does nothing other than confirm the views adopted by individual conscience" (p. 182). Also in 1917, he told Romain Rolland that "the great problem is to base morality on science" (Piaget, 1966). In a 1918 article entitled "Biology and War," he argued that "to struggle against war . . . is to act according to the logic of life against the logic of things, and that is the whole of morality" (Piaget, 1918b; trans. Gruber & Vonèche, 1977, p. 41).

Since the beginning of Piaget's psychological career, his faith in the "logic of life" took the form of the study of psychological development. His 1932 book *The Moral Judgment of the Child* describes children's development as the progress from heteronomous morality, characterized by obedience to apparently eternal and unquestionable rules, to autonomous morality, characterized by cooperation, reciprocity, and the creation of norms in a system of social contract.

In the social and political domain, Piaget (e.g., 1931) believed that nationalism and the arms race are fundamentally psychological, rather than economic or societal phenomena, since they result from a lack of universality of human reason and thus show that, in international relations, man is still a primitive or a child. Piaget expressed these ideas in his early reports and lectures to the International Bureau of Education in Geneva, which he directed from 1929 until 1967.

At the same time, Piaget was occasionally active as a former member of the Christian students association that published *Mission.* In talks given at the association, he argued that immanentism is the most moral and rational religious attitude—and also the one toward which mental and cultural development naturally advance (see, for example, Piaget, 1930). The achieved expression of this rationalist immanentism is the idea that God can be identified with the universal and impersonal norms of thought (e.g., Piaget, 1928, p. 36).

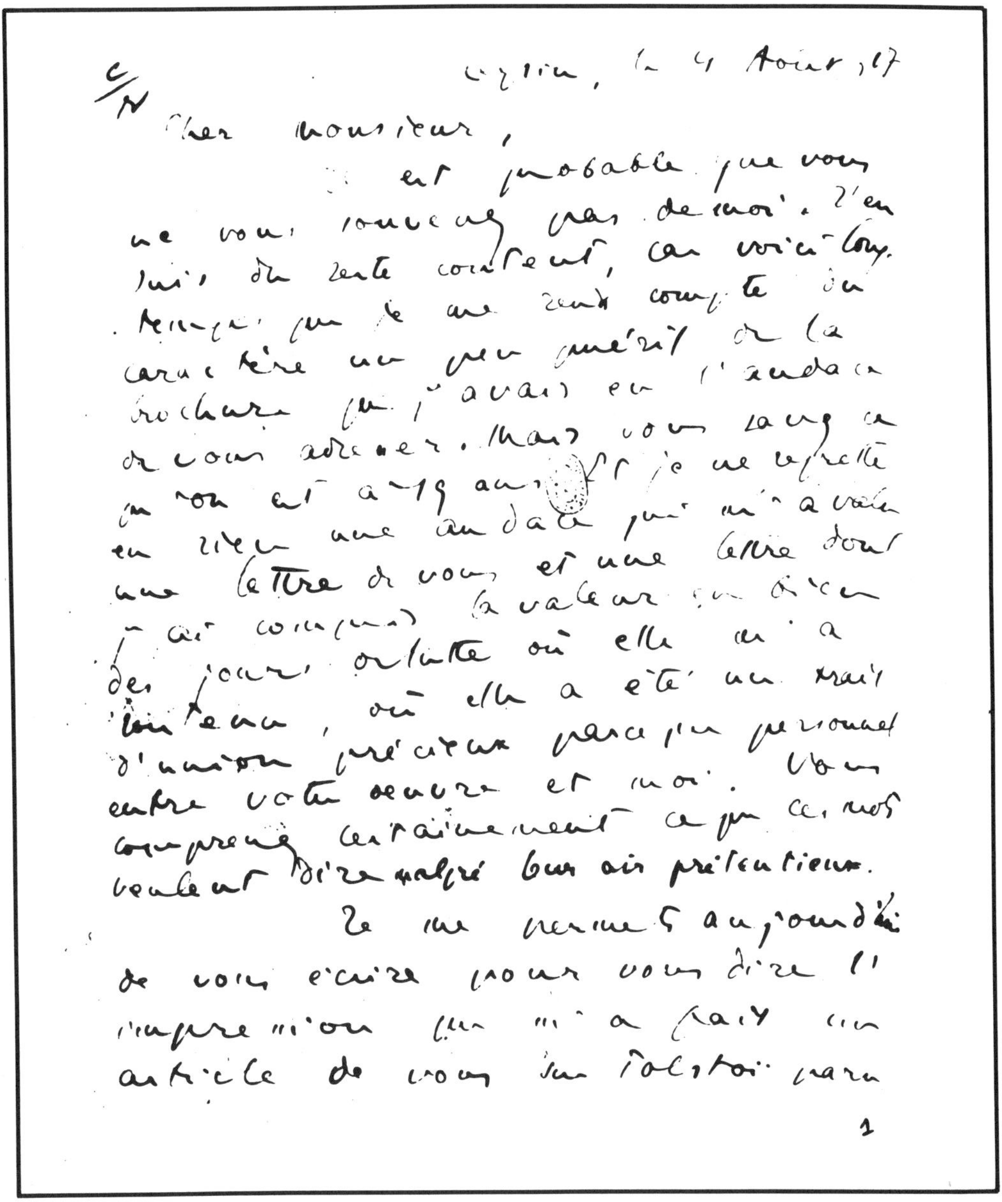

FIGURE 10–2. First page of Jean Piaget's 1917 letter to Roman Rolland. Photographie de la Bibliothèque Nationale, Paris.

Network Transformations

Piaget's ideas in the religious domain are one aspect of a more general empirical psychology of values. The following passage, taken from a talk where Piaget defends immanentism as a religious attitude, summarizes this psychology:

> From the viewpoint of morality, the ego is subjected to norms such as reciprocity or justice. These are the very norms of reason, which apply to action as much as to thought. Morality is a logic of action, as logic is a morality of thought. (Piaget, 1928, p. 37)

The Moral Judgment of the Child, published in 1932 but based on a decade of research, is Piaget's formidable argument for this position. It is the realization of his project "to base morality on science." It also represents the nonmetaphysical and nonmystical fulfillment of his youthful ideals, more identifiable now with a mission of Reason than with "the mission of the idea."

Given this development, two main issues remain to be examined: (1) the change from the mystical and idealist metaphysics of 1915 to the rationalist and psychological science of values of the 1920s, and (2) the quiescence of the "moral enterprise" after 1932 and the unflagging pursuit of the epistemological enterprise for which Piaget is universally remembered.

The transformation of the Idea into Reason reflects a change in method, as well as a sort of reorientation of affect. As is clear from *Recherche,* and as Piaget (n.d.) suggested in a 1918 letter to his teacher and mentor, the philosopher Arnold Reymond, his critique of the "mystical" period was also a revolt against what he perceived as his generation's neglect of science.

From the psychological point of view, Piaget's revolt is related to something he shared with many of his peers: an increasing dissatisfaction with the most subjectivist aspects of religious liberalism. He wanted to believe and to defend a set of values, yet he wanted to do so on an "objective" basis. The search for the Absolute narrated in *Recherche* is finally satisfied through the scientific elaboration of a developmental hierarchy of values that, at least in principle, can be replicated by independent investigators. Piaget can even be seen as a spokesman for the basic values of liberal Protestantism, which he tried to defend against the neo-orthodox movement of the 1920s on the grounds of its developmental superiority (see Vidal, 1987a).

Piaget's dissatisfaction with "mysticism" and metaphysics might also be linked to an emotional state he wished to modify. The atmosphere of *Mission* is laden with anguish, and the confessional parts of *Recherche* always connect the hero's search to a fluctuation between depression and exaltation, to crises of despair, and to fits of anxiety. But not all the affect attached to the young Piaget's projects disappeared. For example, the almost prophetic assertiveness that is often found in his writings on religious matters recalls the passion of *The Mission of the Idea.* The style, the setting, and the methodological and theoretical foundations of the arguments are different, but they all manifest a zealous pursuit.

The discontinuance of the moral enterprise after the publication of *The Moral Judgment* in 1932 can be linked to several factors. On the one hand, to the extent that it shows empirically a developmental hierarchy of values and assumes that development is always progressive, Piaget's book achieves his project of basing morality on science. Moreover, it does so in a way that is coherent with the demands of a naturalistic ethics. On the other hand, however, *The Moral Judgment* leaves open the question of the role of society in the genesis of morality.

In the 1920s Piaget was preoccupied with the relationship between the individual and society; in contrast to the French sociologist Durkheim, he wanted to show that morality is not necessarily imposed on children by the school and the family, but can evolve through the spontaneous formation of self-governing children's societies. He wished to integrate sociology and psychology, but he did not go further than to say that they constitute two mutually consistent points of view. He suggested that the development of moral judgment is an immanent psychological process, and yet he emphasized the socialization of thought as a process that advances morality toward its highest stage—that of cooperation. Perhaps Piaget realized that he needed a full-fledged "genetic sociology" in order to solve the theoretical and empirical issues raised by his enterprise and chose to suspend what might have become the work of his lifetime.

The decision to focus on the epistemological enterprise might also have been connected to the political situation of the early 1930s. *The Mission of the Idea* proclaimed Christian socialism. In a more political language, *Recherche* argued that a federalist socialism is the equilibrium point between nationalism and internationalism, bourgeois liberalism and communist collectivism. After the general strike that affected Switzerland in November 1918, Piaget (1918c) wrote that his faith in socialism was strengthened.

Starting in 1921, Piaget worked, with some interruptions, at the Jean-Jacques Rousseau Institute of Geneva. The institute reflected the so-called spirit of Geneva of the interwar years. Between 1919 and 1932, Geneva symbolized the belief that peace and security can be attained through arbitration, disarmament, and international cooperation in economics, politics, and intellectual life. The institute's most visible contribution to this spirit was its foundation of the International Bureau of Education in 1925. The educational ideals and methods advocated by the institute were imbued with internationalist and pacifist hopes (Vidal 1987b, 1988a).

Geneva, however, was not isolated from the rest of Europe. The local government, controlled by the bourgeois parties, tolerated the growth of a nationalist and fascist movement and became obsessively anticommunist. The institute was often criticized for its apparently "leftist" ideology and for poisoning youth with its "red" pedagogy. In 1933 political pressures tied to state financial support led to its reorganization. Officially constrained to limit its activities to that of an academic body for research and teaching, the institute was forced to adopt an outer and inner attitude of neutrality on questions of politics, morality, educational policy, and so forth.

In this process, Piaget was trusted by political authorities; he argued for a change in the institute's direction and supported a reorganization that was clearly favorable to him. Thus the political circumstances that neutralized the Rousseau Institute also furthered Piaget's career and were consistent with the relinquishing of his moral enterprise.

The Network of Enterprise as a Biographical Tool

The story of Piaget's network of enterprise up to the early 1930s illustrates some main features of this concept. It highlights, in my view, the important contribution the network of enterprise notion could make to the study of scientific creativity as a branch of the history of science that is increasingly aware of its own existence (cf. Holmes, 1986). (See Lenoir [1987] for the impact of the network model on the Darwin industry.)

Biography is the form that large-scale studies of scientific creativity tend to acquire; thinking in terms of network of enterprise may help solve some of the central problems of biography. As Hankins (1979) skillfully explained, these problems lie in the difficulty of making a coherent picture out of the different aspects of an individual's life, integrating this picture with the history of science and with social and cultural history.

In Piaget's case, the network of enterprise suggests that his development was more complex than is suggested by his autobiography. In turn, the network is supposed to reflect the development of an individual's total production. Thus the comparison between Piaget's oeuvre as described in the autobiography and as embodied in the ensemble of his writings suggests that the main operation of his self-description was a "network reduction," or "pruning the tree of enterprise." In this chapter I have emphasized what Piaget left out of his autobiography. For a thorough picture of his development between 1910 and 1920, however, it would be essential to show the connections among his work in natural history, his naturalistic ethics, and his Bergsonian religion (Vidal, 1988b).

A structural dimension of the network of enterprise is given by its form, by the way in which it can be analyzed into distinct enterprises, problems to be solved within an enterprise, and tasks subordinated to the problems. Since this form must be studied at different points in time, the final outcome of research on enterprise structure is a temporal series of networks. Such a series displays the development of the individual's organization of goals and productive work.

For example, the "self-project" that was supremely important in Piaget's proto-network in 1915 gave way in 1918 to the elaboration of an intellectual system. The moral enterprise that was inseparable from Piaget's philosophical, biological, and psychological research in the 1920s disappears from the network after 1932. Such modifications, made visible in the network structure, emphasize key questions about the reasons for choice and change in the individual's creation of an oeuvre, about his or her strategies of enterprise programming, about problems that seem "bracketed" or left unsolved, or about the interplay between the private and the public levels.

Another internal dimension of the network of enterprise might be called "regulative." Insofar as it embodies the total organization of purposes and work, the network contributes to the regulation of the individual's diverse activities. In other words, a network is also a sort of internal environment. In Piaget's case, it could be said that in 1915 the self-project regulated the totality of the network. Every project, every task, every research had to be adjusted to it—hence the place of the moral enterprise at the beginning of Piaget's career. The later growth of the epistemological enterprise can be interpreted as the result of a tradeoff. In the late 1920s, as it progressed toward its partial fulfillment, the moral enterprise reached a problematic point at which a choice had to be made between struggling with the difficulties it brought with it, or shifting to other important enterprises and purposes.

Finally, an external dimension must be added to the two internal ones. There is an immediate context that provides models of personal and professional identity and contributes to define what is an important project; there are political circumstances that contribute to shape a network; and there is every imaginable social and cultural factor intervening in an individual's development.

In the perspective of a study of scientific creativity inspired by the network idea, there is also the hypothesis that the community to which the subject belongs can be understood as a network of networks. Influence, discipleship and training, the division of work, the choice of general and specific research domains, the assignment of employment, the distribution of reward and punishment, the vicissitudes of competition and collaboration—all these aspects of the life of science consist largely in interactions among individuals governed by networks and by values that determine the sacrifices individuals are ready to make for their achievement.

CHRONOLOGY
JEAN PIAGET—THE FIRST 34 YEARS

1896	August 9: Born in Neuchâtel.
1911	Begins professional career in malacology.
1912	Starts elaborating a Bergsonian viewpoint in natural history and in religion.
1914	Member of the Swiss Christian Students Association.
1915	Fall: Student at the University of Neuchâtel.
	December: *The Mission of the Idea,* a prose poem.
1918	March: "Biology and War."
	October: Dissertation on the classification of mollusks.
	Recherche, a confessional and philosophical *Bildungsroman.*
	Studies in Zurich (experimental psychology, psychiatry, psychoanalysis).
1919	Fall: Studies in Paris (history and philosophy of science, logic, psychology).
	First observations of children.

1921	Research and teaching at the Rousseau Institute of Geneva. First articles on child psychology.
1923	Marriage (children born in 1925, 1927, and 1931). Publication of *The Language and Thought of the Child*.
1924	Publication of *Judgment and Reasoning in the Child*.
1925–29	Professor at Neuchâtel.
1926	Publication of *The Child's Conception of the World*.
1927	Publication of *The Child's Conception of Physical Causality*.
1928–32	Numerous articles and lectures (on logical and moral development, sociology, philosophy, religion).
1929	Return to Geneva University and Rousseau Institute. Appointed director of the International Bureau of Education. Monograph on the Lamarckian mechanisms of mollusk adaptation.
1932	Publication of *The Moral Judgment of the Child*.

ACKNOWLEDGMENTS

This chapter was in part prepared while the author was employed under subsidy no. 1535.0.82 of the Fonds National Suisse de la Recherche Scientifique. Documents from the Reymond papers are used with kind permission of Mme A. Virieux-Reymond.

NOTES

1. In the following discussion, unless otherwise noted, page numbers refer to *La Mission de l'Idée* (Piaget, 1915). All quotations are from my translation.

2. I wish to thank Jacques Vonèche, who pointed out to me the possible influence of Hugo on Piaget's notion of a "mission of the idea."

REFERENCES

Gruber, H. (1980). Cognitive psychology, scientific creativity, and the case study method. In M. D. Grmek, R. S. Cohen, & G. Cimino (Eds.), *On scientific discovery*. Dordrecht: Reidel.

Gruber, H. E. (1981). *Darwin on man: A psychological study of scientific creativity* (2nd ed.). Chicago: University of Chicago Press.

Gruber, H. E. (1982). Piaget's mission. *Social Research, 49,* 239–264.

Gruber, H. E., & Vonèche, J. (1977). *The essential Piaget*. New York: Basic Books.

Hankins, T. L. (1979). In defence of biography: The use of biography in the history of science. *History of Science, 17,* 1–16.

Holmes, F. L. (1986). Patterns of scientific creativity. *Bulletin of the History of Medicine, 60,* 19–35.

Holton, G. (1975). *Thematic origins of scientific thought. Kepler to Einstein*. Cambridge, Mass.: Harvard University Press.

Kundera, M. (1984). *The unbearable lightness of being*. New York: Harper & Row.

Lenoir, T. (1987). Essay review: The Darwin industry. *Journal of the History of Biology, 20,* 115–130.

P[ettavel], P. (1916, January 29). [Review of *La Mission de l'Idée.*] *L'Essor social, moral, religieux,* p. 3.

Piaget, J. (1915). *La Mission de l'Idée.* Lausanne: La Concorde. (Abridged translation in Gruber & Vonèche [1977])

Piaget, J. (1918a). *Recherche.* Lausanne: La Concorde. (Chapter-by-chapter summary in Gruber & Vonèche [1977])

Piaget, J. (1918b). La biologie et la guerre. *Feuille centrale de la Société suisse de Zofingue, 58,* 374–380. (Translated in Gruber & Vonèche [1977])

Piaget, J. (1918c, December 15). Unpublished letter to A. Reymond. In A. Reymond papers, manuscript department. Bibliothèque cantonale et universitaire (Lausanne/Dorigny).

Piaget, J. (1928). Immanence et transcendance. In J. Piaget & J. de la Harpe, J., *Deux types d'attitudes religieuses: Immanence et transcendance.* Association chrétienne suisse d'étudiants, s. 1.

Piaget, J. (1930). *Immanentisme et foi religieuse.* Geneva: Groupe romand des Anciens membres de l'Association chrétienne suisse d'étudiants.

Piaget, J. (1931). Introduction psychologique à l'éducation internationale. In *Quatrième cours pour le personnel enseignant. Comment faire connaître la Société des Nations et développer l'esprit de coopération internationale.* Geneva: International Bureau of Education.

Piaget, J. (1932). *Le jugement moral chez l'enfant.* Paris: Alcan. (*The moral judgment of the child.* M. Gabain, Trans. London, 1932)

Piaget, J. (1952). Autobiography. In E. G. Boring et al. (Eds.), *A history of psychology in autobiography* (Vol. 4). Worcester, Mass.: Clark University Press.

Piaget, J. (1966). Letter to Romain Rolland, 4 August 1917. Printed in *Action étudiante* (Geneva), *12,* 7.

Piaget, J. (1971). *Insights and illusions of philosophy.* New York: New American Library.

Piaget J. (n.d.). Unpublished letter to A. Reymond. Undated but written between November 1 and December 15, 1918. In A. Reymond papers, Manuscript department, Bibliothèque cantonale et universitaire (Lausanne/Dorigny).

Vidal, F. (1985). The religious roots of Piaget's thought. In S. Bem, H. Rappard, & W. van Hoorn (Eds.), *Studies in the History of Psychology and the Social Sciences* (Vol. 3). Leiden: Psychologisch Instituut van de Rijksuniversiteit Leiden.

Vidal, F. (1986). Piaget et la psychanalyse: Premières rencontres. *Le bloc-notes de la psychanalyse* (Geneva), *6,* 171–189.

Vidal, F. (1987a). Jean Piaget and the liberal Protestant tradition. In M. G. Ash & W. R. Woodward (Eds.), *Psychology in twentieth-century thought and society.* New York: Cambridge University Press.

Vidal, F. (1987b). Toward a social history of the Rousseau Institute. Paper presented at the XIX annual meeting of Cheiron, Brunswick, Maine.

Vidal, F. (1988a). L'Institut Rousseau au temps des passions. *Education et Recherche, 10,* 60–81.

Vidal, F. (1988b). Piaget adolescent: 1907–1915. Unpublished doctoral dissertation, University of Geneva.

FIGURE 11–1. Anaïs Nin operating her hand press in Macdougal Street studio, 1944. Courtesy Anaïs Nin Trust.

11

From Life to Diary to Art in the Work of Anaïs Nin

VERA JOHN-STEINER

Art always came to the rescue as the
alchemy which enriched life.

ANAÏS NIN

Anaïs Nin's life work, her writing, was the means by which she transmuted the given patterns governing her existence and created for herself a more authentically realized, fulfilled identity. While Nin is greatly admired for a group of short novels which form a flowing, interconnected, symbolist exploration of human relationships, her greatest achievement is her *Diary*. Nin was born in 1903, and by the time of her death in 1977 had produced 35,000 handwritten pages of journals. The published materials from her diaries consist at present of 10 volumes, covering the years 1914–74, from age 11 to age 71.[1]

Nin was interested in the sources of her personal artistic growth as well as in the general problems faced by women writers. While there is a rising interest in her work from a literary point of view, relatively little has been written about the development of Nin's methods of working, her way of thinking. These themes are the focus of this chapter.

The key concept governing this development is Nin's idea of transformations: that experience in one domain, coded in one particular form or language, can be transmuted or converted into another domain, code, or representation. Nin often wrote and spoke of this process. In a conversation with me, in which she was talking about the way women learn, she said "everything Otto Rank said to me *I converted at the deepest level to my own use*" (italics added). At the same time she felt conflicted about transforming experience in her works, associating such transformation with her fear of change and loss. She wrote to confront and counteract this fear (Hinz, 1975; Nin, 1968). Readers seeking to experience and evaluate Nin's work must explore these conflicts and fears to assess how well Nin met her goal of extending Freud's work of "psychological deep-sea diving," of depicting the fluidity of character, of charting the diverse paths of neurosis.

Her initial efforts were nourished by D. H. Lawrence's example. She followed his route of working from what she called an instinctive, intuitive source and his way of capturing "livingness" through the senses and through symbols. Nin wanted to capture states of mind in powerful images and to depict relationships as fluctuating and mutable. Of most immediate significance for this overriding concern are the first four volumes of her adult diaries, spanning the period 1931–47 and including some of her years in Paris and in New York. During this period Nin's early works appeared, first her study of D. H. Lawrence and then the short novels *House of Incest, Winter of Artifice,* and *Ladders to Fire,* together with a book of short stories entitled *Under a Glass Bell.*

In addition to the novels and diaries, important sources for exploring Nin's writing enterprise include her nonfiction books *The Novel of the Future* and *A Woman Speaks,* as well as my own conversations with Nin in the fall of 1971.[2] In addition, the growing literature on Nin increasingly contributes new insights into the process by which she transformed life experiences first into personal written record, a "second seeing," and then into the art form of the psychologically oriented poetic novel.[3]

Even in her erotic writings, done strictly for urgently needed cash, the themes of transformations and enrichment of experience show through. Nin was one of a number of writers providing erotic writing for an unknown wealthy gentleman. While she was first gaining experience in this genre, the message came to her by telephone, " 'The old man is pleased. Concentrate on sex. Leave out the poetry' " (*Diary,* 3, 1969, p. 69).[4] In her *Diary* Nin reacted to such remarks, "Does not the old man know how words carry colors and sounds into the flesh?" (*Diary,* 3, 1969, p. 60). Here, of course, the transformation intended is not, as in Nin's other work, from life to art but from art to life.

A knowledge of both diary and novel forms in her work is necessary to understand what Nin wanted to do in her psychological novels. She was aware of the difficulties of transforming her own experience into art, but she also believed that her journal writing gave her an essential tool for capturing moments of intense emotional reality. In this writing lay the origins of Nin's use of highly condensed images in her fiction and her systematic avoidance of historical, cultural, and political contexts in the development of her characters. These aspects of her work have been attributed solely to her reliance on psychological symbols and on her following Jung's advice, "to proceed from the dream outward." Indeed, these are some of the sources that influenced Nin's choice of certain aesthetic means, but other, equally important sources are to be found in her life history, such as frequent changes in domicile, in her friends, in the language she used (see chronology at the end of this chapter). She wrote about the first of these recurrent uprootings in her childhood diary *Linotte* when at age 11 she had to leave her father, grandmother, and her much-loved Spain for a new existence in New York: "One can't be sure of staying anywhere and if one leaves, there is too much sadness" (Nin, 1978, p. 20).

The theme of being "dépaysée"—rootless—occurs again and again in her writing. The adult Nin made some peace with this issue in her life; nevertheless, when in her sixties she described her writing from the beginning, from childhood, as a search for deeper values and an inner world "which could resist outer catastrophes, change, loss, and deprivation." Finding such deep roots in herself gave her the freedom to "identify with characters unlike myself, enter their vision of the universe" (Nin, 1968, p. 68).

Most fundamentally she identified with the plight of women generally. Her importance as a writer may lie in her success in exploring the psychology of the emerging twentieth-century woman. She also provided a full record of her own efforts to give women a voice to break through their inarticulate domesticity. Nin was aware that there were some universal approaches to the understanding of the human psyche and that Rank, Jung, and Freud had a lot to offer her in that exploration. She nevertheless believed that these approaches needed to be transformed and united with women's own knowledge of themselves as women if they were to find their own paths.

Nin saw this process as critical in her efforts to write as a woman about women; she also believed that the transformation of symbolic images into written language was essential to this task. She explained in the course of our conversations that she was always afraid of blind emotion, that is, emotions expressed without the shaping counterforce of balance and judgment; thus she searched for symbols with which to capture an event in terms of its emotional impact and its meaning, to render psychological truths in forms that readers could convert to resolve conflicts in their own lives.

The critical literature on Nin to date provides excellent background material, but it does not adequately explore the nature of her imagination, particularly her attempts to unite thought and feeling, word and image, the personal and public aspects of existence. These studies link her with either Jung or Freud, but they do not give sufficient weight to her own multilingual, multicultural experience or to her analytic work with Rank, even though Nin left us a broad range of materials for such an examination. They do not account for the means by which the theme of transformation encompasses the process of moving from experience to language, from thought to text. Nor do they convincingly demonstrate Nin's ability to convert the wisdom of others into powerful and generative ideas of her own.

Childhood and Adolescence

Anaïs Nin was born in Paris in 1903. Her father, Joaquin Nin, was Spanish, a composer and pianist with a dazzling, extravagant, charismatic personality, who filled the house with music and musicians. Nin's French–Danish mother, Rosa Culmell, was a singer and a vital, cheerful woman. According to Nin, her mother was deeply in love with her father, but as for how mutual it was: "I never knew. He once said, 'Rosa's sister was prettier, but Rosa had a strength, a courage, a decisiveness I needed' " (*Diary,* 1, 1966, p. 104).

In tracing back her memories, Nin recalled the disturbing impact of her parents' stormy and gradually deteriorating relationship on her two brothers and herself:

> The beginning of memory or the beginning of pain? . . . A French house in Saint-Cloud. . . . My father is gay and charming for visitors. In the house, alone, there is always war. Great battles. War at mealtimes. Over our heads at night when we are in bed. (*Diary,* 1, 1966, p. 217)

She remembered the many musicians who came to their house: Pablo Casals, Manén, Ysaye; how she fell asleep listening to chamber music. Her brother Joaquin later became a musician; in Nin, "music was channeled into writing" (*Diary,* 4, 1971, p. 50).

These early years were shaped, dominated by her father's powerful personality, which Nin vividly describes, including as well a hint of other women in her father's life:

> My father always moving, alert, tense, passionately laughing or passionately angry. When a door opened and my father appeared, it was a radiation. It was dazzling. . . . A gust. A mystery. . . . The neighbor woman writes me fairy tales in the form of letters and gives them to me across the hedge of our small garden: it seems that the letters were for my father, to charm my father. Suspicion. Jealousies. (*Diary,* 1, 1966, p. 218)

During these same years, Anaïs Nin first started to read books (which she did not understand) from her father's bookshelves, and to play in the shadows of these warring, glamorous, complex adults.

As her parents' marriage became more and more difficult, her father decided to leave his family, and Nin remembers her desperate efforts to hold him back, "grasping his coat and holding on to it so fiercely that I had to be torn away" (*Diary,* 1, 1966, p. 318). The significance of Nin's relationship to her father, whose daily presence she was never again to enjoy, is the traditional search for the father, in this case not by a son, but by a woman "whose quest is for the artist father she has lost, along with a way of life she yearns to recover" (Spencer, 1977, p. 125). Through men whom she met later, such as Otto Rank and Henry Miller, Nin eventually overcame her wish for dependence and assumed her responsibilities as an adult woman. When she left Europe with her mother and two brothers soon after her father had gone, and after a brief sojourn in Spain, Nin left behind an existence which had been shaped by her father's talents and extravagant tastes and took with her an image of his vivid life as an artist.

The lengthy trip in 1914 from Barcelona to New York was the start of Nin's early diary *Linotte* (1978), begun as a long "letter" to her father. In the introduction to this volume of her childhood journals, Nin's brother Joaquin refers to her diary as an "indispensable lifeline" (p. vii). Nin later described the beginning of this central enterprise in her life as one that helped to make the unbearable bearable. Her diary had as one of its purposes the reworking and transformation of past and present experience: "Even beginning a diary . . . was already conceding that life would be more bearable if you looked at it as an adventure and a tale" (*Diary,* 7, 1980, p. 266).

She wrote and rewrote her first impressions of New York, which she saw as "too big, too superficial, everything goes too fast. It is just *hell*" (Nin, 1978, p. 502). The many carefully recorded details of the voyage, the arrival in New York, the early painful years were later condensed by Nin into only a few pages in her short novel *Winter of Artifice* (1948).

In New York, Nin had difficulty in adjusting to a parochial and later to a public school, recording that she hated school as well as New York. The city was too noisy and everything struck her as "somber, shut-in, severe" (*Diary,* 3, 1969, p. vi). In later years she referred to these immigrant experiences—learning English, but feeling embarrassed about her speech, while her father criticized her mistakes in French in her many letters to him—as "the first handicaps, the first difficulties. Coming from what the social welfare calls the broken home, being uprooted, knowing what poverty is, coming to a country whose language I didn't know—all these things taught me simply to put my roots in the self" (Hinz, 1975, p. 17).

One of the ways she rooted herself was through writing *Linotte*. While the desire to capture her experiences in words was partly a need to share her world with her distant father, to whom *Linotte* was addressed, it was also an attempt to banish the sense of loneliness that haunted her in the new world. Her writing therefore had the psychological impulse and purpose of helping her gain control over her own experience.

Her mother, whose only training was in singing classical music, was facing a very difficult new life; Nin both loved and resented her. At first, Anaïs assumed all the responsibilities of the household; later she started to search for a more independent life: "I read avidly, drunkenly, by alphabetical order in the library. I had no guidance, as I rebelled against the rowdy, brutal Public School Number 9" (*Diary,* 1, 1966, p. 220).

Reading and wanting to become a writer provoked the first rifts between Anaïs and her mother. She started to question her mother's failed business ventures and the creditors who hounded them. Eventually she decided to leave home and look for work. She first took a job as an artist's model, later becoming a fashion model. Watching her mother's struggle had taught her to wish for a different life, a life of freedom for women. Many years later, after her mother's death, she recognized these ambivalent feelings and came to accept within herself parts of her mother, especially her need to care for others.

Even in the diaries written in her adulthood, Nin often recalled her adolescent years in New York. Such passages describe her sense of loss and longing for life as it used to be: "I can understand why the music that came from the house in front of us filled me with yearning, jealousy, envy, despair. It seemed to me inaccessible. It seemed to me to come from a forbidden, an impossible world" (*Diary,* 2, 1967, p. 240).

Throughout her life Nin attempted to recreate an artistic community similar to the one she had known as a child, but to shape it in ways that corresponded more fully to her own sense of values. The habit of noting down all her experiences, of analyzing her feelings, of evoking in her "portraits" the people whose lives she had shared, never faltered, ending only with her death.

Apprenticeships

Once Anaïs Nin decided that she wanted to be a writer, she immersed herself in French, English, and American literature throughout her self-taught, often lonely, adolescence. She wrote in *The Novel of the Future:* "I had intuition about what went on behind appearances, and I trusted it and spoke out, as most children do" (Nin, 1968, p. 44). The discovery of D. H. Lawrence was "the crevice in the wall," which opened a new world for her. One of Lawrence's great attractions for the young Nin was his willingness to explore the full complexity of relationships between men and women. This artistic focus revealed the heart of life to Anaïs, who even as a child showed awareness of and sensitivity to human relationships.

Though duty to her large and highly religious family governed her external existence, Nin was seeking to understand the hidden life of the senses and emotions. Her diary writing was the most private part of that exploration. She also read the Romantic poets, Shakespeare, and the great Russian novelists. But it was Lawrence's picturing of "heightened moments of living" that gave life to her literary experiments. Through him, she began to trust her own intensity. Her "unprofessional study" of this then still highly controversial English novelist and poet reveals "emotional knowledge" of Lawrence.[5]

Nin used her own intuitions in exploring Lawrence's ability "to see with the soul and the body." The book encompasses an analysis of Lawrence's methods, his reliance on reality and symbols, his interest in "the primitive" as well as his religiosity, and his study of relationships. Nin appreciated the way he gave his characters time to develop: "It was very slow, this gaining of confidence in the wisdom of the body. So Lawrence was patient, through a maze of timidities, retractions, blunders, awkwardnesses" (Nin, 1964b, p. 19). Nin saw Lawrence's characters as artists who reflected their *"creator's craving for a climax far bigger than the climaxes life has to offer"* (Nin, 1964b, p. 26). Of greatest importance for Nin's own writing was Lawrence's interweaving of dream and reality. She herself followed this path in crafting her poetic novels.

In recollecting this formative period of her life in *A Woman Speaks,* Nin described the dearth of female models for writers then (Hinz, 1975). There were some, especially Virginia Woolf and Djuna Barnes. Although she never attempted to contact Lawrence (he was what I have called in *Notebooks of the Mind* one of her "distant teachers"), she did write to Djuna Barnes, whose failure to respond was a painful blow to the young Nin.

She married Hugh P. Gailer, a banker and financial consultant, in 1923, when she was 20, and they moved to Louveciennes, near Paris, where he was employed. The atmosphere in Paris was fruitful for Nin, and she soon began to develop her own circle of friends among the surrealist artists. She met André Breton, Antonin Artaud, Max Ernst. She wrote of these encounters: "Even though I never joined the surrealist group in the thirties, surrealism was a part of the very air we breathed. Everything was surrealistic—all the paintings we saw, all the films. In a sense my writing is surrealistic only insofar as it is concerned with superimposition, with life experienced on a multiplicity of levels" (Hinz, 1975, p. 207).

During these same years, Anaïs developed her friendship with Henry Miller and with many avant-garde dancers, painters, composers, and poets. She wrote in *The Novel of the Future* that each art she became familiar with seemed to bear a relation to the art of writing. When, as an artist's model, she watched the paint being mixed and discovered the range of colors, Nin began to become more aware of and observe the colors people wore and lived with. From her brother she learned to think of people in terms of the music that expressed them; studying dancing made her aware of how people moved and handled their bodies, hands, and feet. Her experiences with artists and with different art forms sensitized her and extended the possible ways in which people, and life, could be perceived and depicted. Nin's diary descriptions of these experiences are always acute and lively.

Nin led several lives in Paris during the 1930s. In her beautiful suburban home in Louveciennes, which she shared with her husband, mother, and brother, she had "days of illuminations and fevers. I have days when the music in my head stops. Then I mend socks, prune trees, can fruits, polish furniture. But while I am doing this I feel I am not living," she wrote in the beginning of volume 1 of her *Diary* (1966, p. 5). Writing was her escape, her raison d'être, as it had been when she began her childhood diary, *Linotte.* The desire to lead a creative life was Nin's ever-present intent, and her other lives at times felt like barriers, prisons from which she needed to escape.

In Paris, Nin showed Miller the manuscript of her first novel. Although as writers they differed profoundly, his encouragement was important to her. During their intense friendship, Nin discovered more about herself, discoveries that were part of her writer's apprenticeship. She commented that writers live not one life but two, the living and the writing. The latter is a sort of delayed response, a reassimilation of experience.

At this time, another equally important kind of apprenticeship began in

Nin's life: her exposure to and lifelong reliance on psychoanalysis. She first entered therapy with Dr. René Allendy, a French analyst whose books and lectures she had admired. In the course of her therapy, she dealt with her relationship with her father, the legacy of which was still a serious and troubling presence in her young married life. Characteristically, as she gained more self-confidence, and with Allendy's encouragement, she started working on the prose poem *House of Incest*.

But Allendy did not fully meet Nin's growing needs as an artist and as a woman who had tried to design her own path instead of adjusting to male visions of female existence. The author of *Art and Artist*, Otto Rank, became her second analyst.

From the beginning of this relationship Nin felt both intellectually stimulated and emotionally supported by Rank, who saw in the struggles of the artist a critical process of ideological and personal growth. Rank wrote of artists' tendencies to immerse themselves in extremes of worldly experiences or in highly abstract symbolic concepts, and of their needs to use these materials: "The artist . . . has this feeling of *Weltschmerz* . . . [but] can use this introverted world not only as a protection but as a material; he is thus never wholly oppressed by it—though often enough profoundly depressed—but can penetrate it by and with his own personality and then again thrust it from him and re-create it from himself" (Rank, 1932, p. 377). And while Rank depicted several stages of growth within the individual artist, he also knew that artistic creation is not possible without a belief in oneself and one's power to create. It is this conviction that Rank helped Nin to achieve, and in the process she deepened her knowledge of character, of relationships, and of the meaning of her work.

Psychoanalysis remained an important part of Nin's existence. It provided tools to deal with personal conflicts and it offered insights that allowed her to develop her own blend of poetic and psychological writing. Rank's concept of the creative will in particular gave Nin an important foundation from which to think and rethink her work as a writer. In the *Diary* she discusses the support she received from Rank in defining herself as an independent, creative woman: "Rank made me finish *House of Incest*. He helped me to discover the meaning and then I was able to make a synthesis" (*Diary, 2,* 1967, p. 31).

As an experience, the process of psychoanalysis convinced Nin of the fluidity of the human psyche, and as a body of knowledge it gave her confidence to explore and capture that fluidity in her own writing. In describing her approach, she wrote:

> The conventional novel depicted character as a unity, already formed, while psychoanalysis studying the unconscious revealed the opposite, that character was fluctuating, relative, mutable, and asymmetrically developed, unevenly matured, with areas of rationality and areas of irrationality. I wanted to reveal not the fatality of character but its mysteries, its blocks, its negative aspects that interfered with fulfillment and relationship. (Nin, 1968, p. 113)

Because Nin chose to focus on the fluctuating and mobile aspects of character, her novels often seem abstract and condensed. She presents a paradox of psychological power and narrative incompleteness. What sources did she use for this form? What are the connections between her use of psychoanalysis and her reliance on a certain group of symbolist and surrealist artists as her mentors?

Cities of the Interior

Cities of the Interior (1974a) brings together in one volume five of Nin's short novels: *Ladders to Fire,* previously published in 1946; *Children of the Albatross,* originally published in 1947; *The Four-Chambered Heart,* previously published in 1950; *A Spy in the House of Love,* published privately by Nin in Amsterdam in 1954; and *Solar Barque,* first published in 1958 and later revised and published in 1961 as *Seduction of the Minotaur.*

In *Cities of the Interior,* rather than plotting traditional stories Nin explores the adventures of the psyche. The basic theme of these short novels is the exploration of the intimate relationships of three women, depicted in condensed episodes and linked together like movements in a musical composition. These relationships take place in many settings—New York, Paris, Mexico—and the protagonists are usually artists. Each novel illustrates some barrier that a character faces: In *Ladders to Fire,* for instance, Nin describes how Lillian—one of the three women who figure in these novels—virtually breathes through her lover, lives vicariously through him, and depends on him.

"The core of creation is to summon an image and the power to work with the image," Nin told me while explaining her approach to her novels. Her images are neither fleeting sensations nor photographic glimpses. She strove to capture the symbolic aspects of reality and consequently often left interpretation to the reader.

Nin's psychological representation of her characters is always transfigured and dramatized by imagery. Her character Sabina, whose haunted and haunting existence is depicted in *A Spy in the House of Love,* is announced through the clashing strong colors of her dress, the clanging of her bracelets. The sounds of a fire engine are used to evoke her destructiveness. Hers is a persona spilling outward, touching and disturbing those around her.

Nin saw a parallel in the work of artists and psychotherapists. Both are skilled in peeling off the masks human beings wear to face the complex demands of social existence. Technically, this involved a process of distillation and reduction "to the barest essential . . . because in dealing with the chaotic contents of the unconscious it is necessary to filter, to eliminate the upholstery" (Nin, 1968, p. 25).

One of Nin's sources for her innovative fiction was the symbolism drawn from the life of the unconscious. "Proceed from the dream outward," she quoted from Jung in beginning *The Novel of the Future* (1968, p. 5). A dream that recurs in various forms in her writing is that of a beached boat. It first appears in the early collection of novelettes, *Winter of Artifice,* in which the central figure, Djuna, struggles with her complex relationship with a glamorized, idealized father:

> *This boat I was pushing with all my strength because it could not float, it was passing through land. It was chokingly struggling to pass along the streets, it could not find its way to the ocean. It was pushed along the streets of the city, touching the walls of houses, and I was pushing it against the resistance of earth.* (Nin, 1948, pp. 173–174)

Nin was often criticized by friends and literary critics for her heavy reliance on dreams and symbols. But she was clear about her need to write from the unconscious and to use the language of the unconscious, the language of symbols. In a powerful scene in *The Four-Chambered Heart,* Djuna, her most autobiographically drawn heroine, bursts out in anger, provoked not only by her lover's jealousy but also by fiction that does not recognize the complex, troubling emotions in human relationships. Rango accuses Djuna of liking the work of her friends too much. In an escalating quarrel, he picks up a book about a painter friend of hers and suggests burning it:

> "Burn them all," she said with bitterness.
> To her this was not only an offering of peace to his tormenting jealousy, but a sudden anger at this pile of books whose contents had not prepared her for moments such as this one. All these novels so carefully concealing the truth about character, about the obscurities, the tangles, the mysteries. (Nin, 1974a, p. 272)

The critics responded to the original publication of two of Nin's novels from this collection, *The Four-Chambered Heart* and *The Spy in the House of Love,* with an approximately equal mix of praise and denunciation. Their positions, whether negative or positive, were often extreme, and the negative reviews were at times bitterly scathing: Nin was criticized for the decadent eroticism of her content, for her lack of action and plot, for the superficiality and pretentiousness of her style. She wondered how, in the face of so much rejection, she would find the strength to continue, and often wrote in her journal of the difficulty of writing to an "empty hall." But Nin persisted: the encouragement of some of her friends, and her belief that her kind of psychological novel was needed in this impersonal world, kept her going. She wrote to her friend the literary critic Maxwell Geismar that she was continuing Freud's work and wanted "to change human beings at the source. That means psychological deep-sea diving" (*Diary,* 5, 1974b, p. 159).

Although Nin realized that writing poetic prose placed an unusual burden on her as well as on her readers, she loved and believed in this form of literature. She believed that poetic phrases contain mystery, provoke investigation, and crystallize meaning. In her journals she records the pleasure of a writer "hearing the music" of her work; and the anxieties, so often accompanying self-revelations, powerfully manifested themselves in her dreams. She wrote of one of her dreams, in which she delivered an exquisitely written lecture in

French to an audience unfamiliar with the language, that it exposed the writer's dread of not being comprehended by her audience.

Nin was fearful of too solid a construction in her writing; she struggled to find a form that captured the flow of existence and her psychological insights. Nevertheless, reading her novels as a connected work in *Cities of the Interior* prompts a better appreciation of her achievements than reading them singly. It is easier to situate a character, to recognize the powerful psychological insights so relevant to one's own existence, to chart the changes. It is in this way that Lillian emerges as the most fully chronicled heroine in Nin's fiction, one who reaches equilibrium in *Seduction of the Minotaur,* the last short novel in the volume. In *Ladders to Fire,* the first novel in the collection, Lillian is the jazz pianist depicted as feeling earthbound and imprisoned in the self but also as struggling against these constraints. Lillian tries to find a new identity through her numerous relationships with men and women. She leaves her husband and children and becomes enmeshed with artists. The story does not really end. We know of Lillian's struggles but little of the continuity of her existence.

The next novel in the series, *Children of the Albatross,* explores Djuna's life history. It traces her difficult childhood in flashbacks and gives glimpses of her adulthood in a beautiful house in a Paris suburb. It depicts Djuna's relationships with the airy men adolescents, Michael and Paul. (Nin never provides last names.) Again, the focus is on the interior psychological drama of the characters, who are dancers, painters, and musicians.

In *The Four-Chambered Heart,* Nin depicts a triangle of Djuna, her lover, Rango, and Rango's wife, Zora, an unhappy woman plagued by illness and defeat.

A Spy in the House of Love takes place in New York and focuses on the actress Sabina. (The first three were set in Europe.) A central symbol in the novel is the Lie Detector, a combination of detective and conscience. He follows Sabina throughout her adventures, her split life—part female Don Juan, part woman tied to an unimaginative but caring husband.

The last novel in the series, *Seduction of the Minotaur,* is again Lillian's story, this time about the resolution of her struggles in the form of a journey. The theme of the novel was foreshadowed by Nin's remark in 1951 that she wished to write of the way out of the labyrinth—"of the understanding and mastering of the neurosis" (*Diary,* 5, 1974b, p. 85). In this novel Lillian has an engagement in a night club in Mexico, a country she finds strange and beguiling. Of great importance in her adventures there is the figure of Dr. Hernandez, who provides his healing insights about Lillian's search. His death leaves Lillian with full responsibility for her journey. The journey succeeds.

Through the conflicts portrayed in these five novels, to which Nin gives dramatic personae and progression, receptive readers can obtain psychological insights into their own conflicts. Such journeys toward increased self-knowledge and the resultant self-acceptance express Nin's vision of the attainment of mature life, "and that something so seemingly simple is in fact so difficult is the message of Nin's first five novels" (Franklin & Schneider, 1979, p. 146).

The Modalities of Creative Work

Many art forms, each with its special functions, played a role in Nin's work. For example, the world of motion, expressed in dance, symbolized freedom for Nin (Spencer, 1977). "From every form of art there is something that I wanted to include in writing, and I wanted writing, poetic writing, to include them all" (*Diary,* 7, 1980, p. 264). In one novel, for instance, *Ladders to Fire,* a key scene, the entire chessboard and Chess Player sequence, was inspired by one of Martha Graham's dances (Knapp, 1978, p. 110).

Among the arts, however, music played the most significant role for Nin. Her life started with music, as both parents were musicians, and it ended with music. The last entry in the *Diary* reads:

> My attitude toward music was always nostalgic. Emotional. I was never cold or detached or intellectual about music. I never tried to explain the feeling of exile. I accepted the weeping. . . . Yes, music indicates another place, a better place. . . . One should think of this place joyfully. Then if it follows death, it is a beautiful place. A lovely thing to look forward to—a promised land. So I shall die in music, into music, with music. (*Diary,* 7, 1980, p. 342)

Nin wrote in her diary in 1946 that her work was like musical composition, beginning with a word or phrase and building variations and improvisations, "always in an effort to extract the largest possible meaning" (*Diary,* 4, 1971, p. 151).

The Careful Shaping of a Creative Life

My journey through Nin's writings was similar to that of many of her readers. I first read the published volumes of the *Diary* and years later read *Cities of the Interior.* The contrast between these two kinds of work intrigued me—the condensed, imagistic novels on the one hand and the flowing, detailed journals on the other. It was after the publication of the diaries and their extraordinary impact on her public that Nin succeeded in uniting her private and public selves, the diarist who explored the labyrinth of her psyche and the artist who sought to render in words that had meaning for others the underlying truths of her personal struggles and growth. In communicating with this audience Nin fully realized her role as "artist in life."

When I met Nin in 1971, she was enjoying the fame that the publication of the first volumes of her *Diary* had brought her. Her success did not make her aloof; she responded warmly to the young women and men who wished to know her better. Her own experience of rejection and criticism after the publication of her short novels shaped her commitment to young artists. During her many lecture tours in the sixties and seventies, Nin traveled with a large woven bag filled with the unpublished manuscripts of people who had approached her for comments. She answered these requests on her travels, in planes and hotel rooms. It was one of her ways of maintaining human connections while in these impersonal settings.

She attended to this public deed as she attended to her personal quest for growth by writing the diaries. Journal writing was her literary workshop for examining her growing sense of a new female identity. She battled against the mute power of female masochism and inarticulateness, burdens she had seen in her mother and grandmother. Otto Rank's observation that women had not yet found a way of fully communicating their experiences also guided her. She struggled against the silence of pain, against woman's fear of creative work and of neglecting other more traditional responsibilities. She spoke of a capacity for feeling and intuition that is instilled in the inner speechlessness of privacy; it is against this silence that men build their active engagement and articulate their understanding of the human experience.

I questioned Nin about these observations, as they did not immediately ring true to me, to my generation. In response, she described some of the women she had known when she—and they—were quite young, how they were driven by blind emotion, "where all things begin: in nature, at the roots" (Franklin & Schneider, 1979, p. 64). Writing had helped her to find her way out of this female labyrinth, but it was not always enough. Her conflict, when she first sought out Otto Rank, was that she felt oppressed and trapped by her condition as a woman—trained for devotion, service, and loyalty to a personal world, and wanting all that, but yearning at the same time to maintain her separate identity, her difference.

"[Rank] focussed on the strongest element in my divided and chaotic self. No matter what disintegrating influences I was experiencing, the writing was the act of wholeness. . . . He was challenging my creative will" (Nin, 1976b, pp. 59–60).

In her diary, Nin revealed her struggle to overcome and go beyond the traditional, dutiful role of womanhood through art and psychoanalysis. When the first volume of the *Diary* was published in 1966—"which erased all the past disappointments"—Nin described her journal as the record of a thousand years of womanhood, and of a thousand women (*Diary,* 6, 1976a, p. 400).

Nin's enterprises were to capture womanhood in transition, both in her detailed journals and in her condensed novels. Like some of her predecessors, for example, Dorothy Richardson (see Chapter 8) and Virginia Woolf, she believed that the characterization of women in novels by men was not always accurate. Nin thought that such characterizations were those of men who loved women too much or not enough, or who hated women. Nin identified with the women she wrote about (Nin, 1968, p. 70). Her own journey toward integration and balance was the groundwork for her novels, and her close friendship with women painters, musicians, actresses, filmmakers, and psychologists provided some of the models for her fictional characters.

Her contribution to a new literature by and about women has been stressed by all the literary critics who have addressed her work. Each of the novels is concerned with the barriers that women face in their efforts toward fulfillment.

And Nin's diaries document her own struggles against maternal self-sacrifice, emotional depletion, and masochism. Only when Nin achieved a sense of balance in her life and relationships, reconciling "earth and imagination," was she able to chronicle a fictional heroine's journey to self-discovery. In *The Seduction of the Minotaur,* Nin describes Lillian's homeward journey, her ability to address and resolve conflicts. At the time when she herself had achieved this new balance, Nin finished her continuous novel. She published only one more volume of short fiction, entitled *Collages* (1964a), thereafter devoting herself exclusively to her diary. Thus she wrote in 1962, "I am starting now as a diary writer and realist. For the rest of my life I will be at work on this" (*Diary,* 6, 1976a, p. 298).

Editing the diaries for publication required sustained and focused work. This task engaged Nin during the final years of her life. In addition to the difficult job of editing, Nin also had to face her fears of self-revelation represented by the publication of the diaries. Soon after the first volume appeared she was discovered by a new audience, the women and men who had reached maturity in the sixties and seventies. These young people were looking for alternatives to the female lives they had observed, and they found a model in Nin, whose development was fully recorded in the *Diary.* In addressing women's groups, Nin often reminded her audience that liberation meant the power to overcome obstacles.

In addition to its implications for the women's movement, Anaïs Nin's *Diary* also represents an important document detailing the processes of creative work. The novels are clearer to the reader who is familiar with Nin's journals. Together they reveal the development of her creative will.

In defining the role of the artist in society, Nin resisted the notion that the artist must contribute to solving the urgent problems of the moment. She wrote:

> Throughout the ages man has dreamt in order to create a larger world, and to dream he has to use language figuratively . . . to dream he has to transcend reality and he cannot be drafted into action. He has to make his own detours (to gain philosophical and psychological perspective) or he becomes a reporter. If the artist cannot practice this transmutation, then no one can. (*Diary,* 3, 1969, p. 52)

Thus the desire to be an artist in life, to be free of old roles, to transform masculine patterns into those constructed by women, were the guiding themes in Nin's life. Her greatest achievement was to share, through her *Diary,* these private struggles with the world.

CHRONOLOGY
ANAÏS NIN

1903   February 21: Anaïs Nin born in Paris to Joaquin Nin, a Spanish concert pianist and composer, and Rosa Culmell-Nin, a singer of French and Danish ancestry.

1913   Anaïs's father separates from his family; Rosa Culmell-Nin takes her children to Spain.

1914   Rosa Culmell-Nin, Anaïs, and her two brothers, Thorwald and Joaquin, settle in New York City.

1923   Nin marries Hugh P. Gailer (known as engraver and filmmaker under the name Ian Hugo) in Havana, Cuba. They move to Paris.
Begins *Waste of Timelessness* (early short stories not published until 1977).

1932   *D. H. Lawrence: An Unprofessional Study* is published.
House of Incest begun.
Psychoanalysis with Dr. René Allendy begun.

1933   Begins therapy with Dr. Otto Rank.
She has a stillborn child.

1934   Leaves Paris for New York where she works with Dr. Rank as a lay analyst.

1936   Returns to France.

1939   Returns to New York City and life in Greenwich Village.

1942   Establishes her own printing press, the Gemor Press, in a loft on Macdougal Street.
Starts analysis with a Jungian, Dr. Martha Jaeger.

1944   Prints and publishes *Under a Glass Bell,* a collection of short stories.

1946   Nin goes on a lecture tour which includes Harvard, Dartmouth, and Amherst.

1947   Nin travels again through the American West and Mexico.

1951   Starts analysis with Dr. Inge Bogner, the woman with whom she maintained a close relationship until her death.

1954   Nin lectures in some western colleges.

1958   Travels in Europe.
Publishes *Solar Baroque.*

1966   *The Diary of Anaïs Nin, Volume 1: 1931–1934* is published.

1970   Publicity tour in Europe.
Cancer treatments start.

1973   Receives honorary degree of Doctor of Fine Arts from Philadelphia College of Arts.

1974   Honored by the Institute of Women's Studies; elected to the National Institute of Arts and Letters.

1977   January 14: Dies of cancer.

NOTES

1. The first six volumes of Nin's adult diaries, covering the years from 1931 to 1966, were published between 1966 and 1976. The seventh volume, written between 1966 and 1974, was published posthumously, in 1980. Also published after her death were *Delta of Venus: Erotica* (New York: Harcourt, 1977), *Little Birds: Erotica* (New York: Harcourt, 1979), *Linotte: The Early Diary of Anaïs*

Nin, 1914–1920 (New York: Harcourt, 1980), *The Early Diary of Anaïs Nin: Vol. 2, 1920–1923* (New York: Harcourt, 1982), and *The Early Diary of Anaïs Nin: Vol. 3. 1923–1927* (New York: Harcourt, 1983).

2. I was introduced to Nin in 1971 by a psychologist, Beatrice Harris, who, as a result of writing to Nin two years earlier, had begun a lasting friendship with her. Nin generously included me in this relationship and also encouraged my own early work on creative thinking and the book I had just begun, *Notebooks of the Mind* (1985).

3. Books about Nin (Evans, 1968; Franklin & Schneider, 1979; Hinz, 1973, 1975; Holder, 1981; Knapp, 1978; Spencer, 1977) provide a comprehensive summary of Nin's writings and place her psychology in the tradition of Freud, Rank, and Jung, who deeply influenced her work. The genre of Nin's fiction is within the symbolist and surrealist movements of twentieth-century European and American literature.

4. This and all subsequent text citations to the published diaries will be as follows: *Diary,* volume number, date, and page.

5. The phrase "emotional knowledge" comes from literary historian Harry T. Moore, whose introduction to the 1964 reissue of Nin's study places this essay in its historical context.

REFERENCES

Evans, O. (1968). *Anaïs Nin.* Carbondale: Southern Illinois University Press.

Franklin, B., & Schneider, D. (1979). *Anaïs Nin: An introduction.* Athens: Ohio University Press.

Hinz, E. J. (1973). *The mirror and the garden: Realism and reality in the writings of Anaïs Nin.* New York: Harcourt Brace Jovanovich.

Hinz, E. J. (Ed.). (1975). *A woman speaks: The lectures, seminars, and interviews of Anaïs Nin.* Chicago: Swallow Press.

Holder, O. E. (1981). *Anaïs Nin's fiction: Proceeding from the dream outward.* Unpublished doctoral dissertation, University of New Mexico.

John-Steiner, V. (1985). *Notebooks of the mind.* Albuquerque: University of New Mexico Press.

Knapp, B. (1978). *Anaïs Nin.* New York: Frederick Ungar.

Nin, A. (1948). *Winter of artifice: Three novelettes.* Denver: Alan Swallow.

Nin, A. (1964a). *Collages.* Denver: Alan Swallow.

Nin, A. (1964b). *D. H. Lawrence: An unprofessional study.* Chicago: Swallow Press.

Nin, A. (1966). *The diary of Anaïs Nin: Vol. 1. 1931–1934.* New York: Swallow/ Harcourt, Brace & World.

Nin, A. (1967). *The diary of Anaïs Nin: Vol. 2. 1934–1939.* New York: Swallow/ Harcourt, Brace & World.

Nin, A. (1968). *The novel of the future.* New York: Collier Books.

Nin, A. (1969). *The diary of Anaïs Nin: Vol. 3. 1939–1944* New York: Harcourt, Brace & World.

Nin, A. (1971). *The diary of Anaïs Nin: Vol. 4. 1944–1947.* New York: Harcourt Brace Jovanovich.

Nin, A. (1974a). *Cities of the interior.* Chicago: Swallow Press.

Nin, A. (1974b). *The diary of Anaïs Nin: Vol. 5. 1947–1955.* New York: Harcourt Brace Jovanovich.

Nin, A. (1976a). *The diary of Anaïs Nin: Vol. 6. 1955–1966.* New York: Harcourt Brace Jovanovich.

Nin, A. (1976b). *In favor of the sensitive man and other essays.* New York: Harcourt Brace Jovanovich.

Nin, A. (1978). *Linotte: The early diary of Anaïs Nin 1914–1920.* New York: Harcourt Brace Jovanovich.

Nin, A. (1980). *The diary of Anaïs Nin: Vol. 7. 1966–1974.* New York: Harcourt Brace Jovanovich.

Rank, O. (1932). *Art and artist: Creative urge and personality development.* New York: Tudor Publishing Company.

Spencer, S. (1977). *Collage of dreams: The writings of Anaïs Nin.* Chicago: Swallow Press.

FIGURE 12–1. R. B. Woodward working with fibrous proteins. *Boston Herald,* June 18, 1947.

12

Art and Elegance in the Synthesis of Organic Compounds: Robert Burns Woodward

CRYSTAL E. WOODWARD

Robert Burns Woodward (1917–79) has been called the greatest organic chemist of his time. He is known for his work both in the synthesis of organic compounds and in structure determination, theory, and rules in chemistry. In 1965 he was awarded the Nobel Prize for his "meritorious contributions to the art of organic synthesis." In 1981 the American Chemical Society held a commemorative meeting that honored Woodward for demonstrating, more than anyone else, that no molecule was too difficult to synthesize and for showing great *art* in the way he constructed molecules.

In this chapter, I will focus on the issues of art, elegance, and beauty in Woodward's work in chemistry. I write as daughter to Woodward and as artist. For my discussions of chemical history and chemical fact, I rely largely on statements of his colleagues.

Woodward's work was his life. How can one know how he thought unless one knows about the medium in which he was thinking? Thus it is important to present the thinking person in the context of an account of his chemistry. To do so, indeed, is a basic tenet of the evolving systems approach to creative thinking which informs this chapter (Gruber, 1980, 1981).

Although most of his writing and lectures are highly technical, there are a few lectures or articles in a more general vein. In these instances, Woodward's observations on his own attitudes and procedures in chemistry help to make his topic more accessible to a nonspecialist. Among his papers is an unusual item, a group of some eight handwritten pages, probably written some time between 1955 and 1962, which I found in his files. These notes for a presentation on principles of how to do synthesis give a sense of how he moved in his thinking in the planning of synthetic steps.

Also in his files were the many pages of notes, mostly drawings rather than writing, in which he was working out the actual plans for his syntheses and other chemical work. These pages are covered with drawings of chemical structures. They can only be understood by those well versed in organic chemistry and, as such, provide rich material for study of Woodward's thought processes. Even without a deep understanding of chemistry, one can see him at work: the many drawings are executed with an aesthetic drawing skill, attention to detail, and perseverance. They are annotated by a few written comments showing his thinking. Indications of feelings are evident in the form of exclamation marks, underlining, red-ink additions, and, in one case, "Eureka!"

Biographical Background

My father was born in 1917, in Quincy, Massachusetts. His parents were of Scottish-English background, his mother supposedly a descendant of the poet Robert Burns. Woodward was only a year old when his father died. Although his mother remarried, she was soon abandoned by her second husband and left to support herself and her child alone. She was very frugal and had hopes for her son.

Even before he was 10 years old, Woodward had a chemistry laboratory in the basement of his Quincy home. Legend has it that by the time he was 12 he had performed all the experiments in Ludwig Gatterman's classic manual, *Practical Methods of Organic Chemistry,* a famous book that played a major role in the training of generations of young German students in experimental organic chemistry. According to Woodward, this legend "was substantially true" (Woodward, 1973, p. 13).

At about this same age, he was walking to the public library some five miles away to read chemistry textbooks. One of the authors of those textbooks also wrote mystery novels. Woodward described his reading of those mysteries as probably the origin of his appreciation of that literary genre (Woodward, 1973). His sense of the mystery and detectivelike drama of chemistry continued throughout his life.

When Woodward entered Massachusetts Institute of Technology at age 16, he already had as much knowledge of organic chemistry as a fourth-year undergraduate in the subject. He published his first scientific paper (Woodward & Hall, 1934) at age 17. He had his doctorate when he was 20.

Woodward's career was a lifelong progression and persistence along a straight path, widening in breadth and gaining in complexity, but never jumping to other themes or contradicting views he had held earlier. He was embarked on the main themes of his lifework near the beginning of his interest in chemistry.

An overview of his accomplishments can be found in the words of one of his friends and colleagues at Harvard, Frank Westheimer:

> Robert Burns Woodward will be remembered, along with August Kekulé and Emil Fischer, as one of the great organic chemists of all time. What he accomplished during his spectacular career was no less than the rationalization—the intellectualization—of the process by which organic chemists achieve synthesis of complex vital molecules.
>
> An analysis of the last hundred years in science will help us to put his achievements in perspective. During the second half of the nineteenth century the structural and stereochemical theory of organic chemistry—one of the most magnificent intellectual generalizations of mankind—was developed, principally by Kekulé, Butlerov, Couper, Pasteur, Van't Hoff and Le Bel. . . . [Yet] in the first half of this century . . . most leading practitioners paid scant attention to the struggling new area of physical-organic chemistry . . . they failed to recognize the revolution implicit in the application of reaction mechanisms to synthesis, a revolution that permitted the determination of structures and the preparation of materials so complicated as to be wildly beyond the capabilities and perhaps even the imagination of the leaders in nineteenth century chemistry.
>
> That revolution in methodology was sparked by Woodward. In totally remaking the strategy for synthesis, he not only incorporated mechanistic thinking into practical work, but he also capitalized fully on the potential of the burgeoning electronic instrumentation for which chemistry is indebted to physics. Through these major shifts in strategy he showed how to assign structures to compounds such as strychnine, to understand biogenesis such as that of the steroids and to carry out fabulous syntheses of complex natural products with only a fraction of the man-years previously needed for much simpler tasks. He illustrated the power of his methods with the syntheses of quinine, cholesterol, chlorophyll, strychnine, reserpine, vitamin B_{12} and a host of less well known but important natural products. In all of these researches, he demonstrated how to maintain precise control of the stereochemistry—the arrangement of atoms in space—for each and every step. Although Woodward is famous for these specific syntheses, his intellectual synthesis was a much greater achievement. He formed a coherent methodology for planning and carrying out the synthesis of intricate biologically active molecules. . . . After he had shown how to utilize theory and advanced instrumentation in planning and executing syntheses, many skilled chemists all over the world found that they, too, could do wonders by emulating him. . . .
>
> Even scientists who mastered his methods could not match his style. For there is an elegance about Woodward's work—his chemistry, his lectures, his publications—that was natural to him, and as unique as the product itself.
>
> His real style was most clearly expressed in the syntheses themselves, in the ways he found to put molecules together, ways that somehow feel right—each step neatly designed to prepare for the next, a kind of art that combined inevitability with surprise, as in great classical music. The

style was there, too, in his lectures . . . his Thursday night seminars
began at about 8:30 and continued, with probably the best and most
penetrating discussions of organic chemistry ever heard anywhere, far
into the night—and into the early morning. . . . A lecture on a particular synthesis would begin in the upper left hand corner of the board and
end in the lower right, with the entire surface filled with artistic formulas,
the essentials highlighted in color, and the whole looking ready to be
photographed for publication. . . .

In addition to sparking the revolution in synthesis, Woodward, together with Roald Hoffmann, made the most significant contribution to
the theory of organic chemistry of recent decades, the set of rules known
as the conservation of orbital symmetry. These rules have stimulated a
vast expansion of organic chemistry that has occupied the profession for
the past fifteen years. (Westheimer, 1979)

Historical Background

In the Cope talk of 1973, in which he reviewed the background of his orbital
symmetry work, Woodward said:

For almost 50 years now, I have been involved in an affair with chemistry. It has been throughout a richly rewarding involvement, with numerous episodes of high drama and intense engagement, with the joys of
enlightenment and achievement, with the special pleasures which come
from the perception of order and beauty in Nature—and with much
humor. (Woodward, 1973)

Chemistry and Woodward were matched for each other, so to speak. In a
way, chemistry was ripe for the mind and interest Woodward brought to it.

Following the early history of chemistry with its passage through alchemy
and vitalism, there was a second period in the history of organic chemistry,
starting in 1858 with the birth of structural theory (Cram & Hammond,
1964). In 1973, Woodward pointed out that it was Couper—and not Kekulé,
to whom credit is often given—who first presented the structural formulas that
are the most fundamental tools of organic chemistry. It was then known that
the atoms in molecules are bound together by bonds and a given atom is
characterized by having the same number of bonds in most stable compounds.
A new dimension was added to the concept of molecules in 1874 by Van't
Hoff and Le Bel, who suggested that the four bonds in most carbon compounds are directed toward the corners of a tetrahedron (Cram & Hammond,
1964).

Woodward had always found the history of chemistry absorbing and had
been "particularly entranced," as he said, by the concept of bonding in the
most general sense. In the decades after World War I, the concept of bonding
evolved. Where chemists in the classic era of structural chemistry had thought
in terms of "ball and stick" models for organic compounds, now "a more fluid
concept of the chemical bond was generated" (Cram & Hammond, 1964, p. 4),
with bonding described as a sharing of electrons.

Also characteristic of the modern period has been "a dramatic increase in

FIGURE 12–2. "Plan in detail, then carry it out." *Chemical and Engineering News,* November 1965, p. 38. Reprinted by permission of the American Chemical Society.

the understanding of organic reactions. The concepts of reaction mechanisms have provided indispensable guidance in synthesizing natural products whose structures are so complex that their syntheses were considered 30 years ago to be out of reach" (Cram & Hammond, 1964).

Woodward worked on a number of fronts. The focus of this chapter is his work on synthesis. He also made important advances in structure determination, in stereochemistry, in the nature of chemical reactions, in the use of modern physical measurements in chemistry, and in formulating the fundamental laws governing structures. Some of these subjects will be mentioned only briefly. A more complete examination would show that each of these projects or themes was pursued over long periods of time, more or less concurrently with the others, as Gruber has suggested in his work on networks of enterprise (Gruber, 1988). Together these enterprises form a coherent whole, a domain within which Woodward navigated with consummate skill.

Synthesis

Woodward's work as "artist" was apparent in all the areas of chemistry in which he was involved, but his art was developed to its "highest peak of perfection" in his syntheses (Todd, 1965, p. 254). He began thinking about and trying to "dream up" syntheses when he was a boy; by the age of 12, he had worked out a synthesis for quinine. He subsequently described trying to synthesize a "tough molecule" as the best teacher in chemistry. His independent, even idiosyncratic ways of thinking about and doing chemistry perhaps originated when he began his lifework at such a young age and essentially taught himself.

A few general comments about synthesis give perspective to Woodward's contributions:

> Synthesis of organic compounds is at the heart of science. One of the earliest ambitions of chemists was to produce in the laboratory, through rational assemblies of reactions, organic compounds discovered in nature. . . . Research chemists can frequently draw structures of compounds as yet unknown, which, when prepared, have a calculable chance of possessing a desired property. . . . Conception of organic syntheses for compounds of any complexity usually involves a stepwise procedure of "working backward" from the structure of a product to the structure of available starting materials. . . . Frequently, "blind alleys" are encountered, and other sequences must be envisioned. From this procedure usually emerges a number of possible synthetic routes, the most attractive of which is selected for trial in the laboratory. (Cram & Hammond, 1964, pp. 565–567)

In his talk "Art and Science in the Synthesis of Organic Compounds," Woodward cited the "two basic tools" of synthetic activities: "the science of chemistry," with its laws and principles, and "the body of experimental, manipulative techniques." He went on to say, "Beyond that, chemical synthesis is entirely a creative activity, in which art, design, imagination, and inspiration play a predominant role" (Woodward, 1963, p. 8). He pointed out that, contrary to the popular picture, the operations of the synthetic chemist always involve a sequence of steps or stages, often a very long such sequence. Each stage builds on the previous one and no stage can even be attempted, let alone succeed, unless all the preceding ones have previously been reduced to practice (Woodward, 1963, p. 9).

Art and Beauty in Chemical Thought

Hand in hand with chemistry's increasing capacities for synthesis was the necessity that chemistry be a language not only of description but of rigorous thinking. Synthetic activities are rarely undertaken by chance; moreover, as Woodward said, "even the most painstaking or inspired observational activities" are not enough. The step-by-step nature of chemical synthesis exacts rigorous thinking and careful planning. Woodward remarked that "the successful outcome of a synthesis of more than 30 stages provides a test of unparalleled rigor . . . of the predictive capacity of the science" (1956, p. 155). In 1963 he was writing about 50 stages; by 1972, in his vitamin B_{12} synthesis, he referred to sequences of 65 to 70 steps. The following year he spoke of 50 or even 100 or more steps. His great achievement is not only the actual synthesis of many compounds but that "he taught us how to think in chemistry" (Barton, 1981).

In 1860, Marcelin Berthelot, writing about organic synthesis and chemistry, stated:

> Chemistry creates its object. This creative faculty, similar to that of art itself, distinguishes it essentially from the natural and historical sciences . . . the experimental sciences have the power to actualize their conjectures . . . [they] create their object by discovering by thought and by verifying by experiment the general laws of phenomena. (pp. 811–812, my translation)

One hundred years later, Woodward had contributed to making this real. Thus chemistry, in its synthetic capacities, became, through him, a language of thinking and a practice; and within that practice it became a locus for art.

And yet exactly how can art be at work in the realm of chemistry? One colleague commented:

> The composition and execution of a complex organic synthesis is a human art unlike any other. In one sense, imperfection is excluded: if one step fails, there is no synthesis. But within the class of technically successful syntheses there are those in which the possibilities and sensitivities of matter are expressed in harmony, and one loses the feeling that recalcitrant molecules are being tortured into new shapes. (Cornforth, 1981, p. 655)

The aspects of art and beauty in Woodward's work are contained not only in the forms found in or built into the fixed structures of molecules. They have perhaps more to do with the way in which he manipulated the molecules, in his design of the synthetic steps, in a process that was not tortuous but harmonious, that felt right and was elegant. Thinking about and designing a chemical synthesis abetted the movement of his thought as if thought both rode on and pushed forward the sequence of steps. Some of Woodward's aesthetic pleasure in his work may have come from creating and experiencing this movement. It is important to realize that this movement and its eventual object had to correspond to a substance in the physical world. This constraint and challenge—that the created object had to match a substance in the external world—formed an important component of his aesthetic involvement in chemistry.

Corresponding to those aspects of Woodward's sense of beauty in chemistry, his work was based on the one hand on an appreciation of the "subtlety of the structural concept." On the other hand, Woodward's ability to appreciate and manipulate chemical structures depended on his knowledge of chemical reactions, those by which bonds are made and broken. I shall trace briefly how Woodward put all this together.

In 1963 Woodward explained why the structure theory was crucial to developing synthetic possibilities. Arriving at a synthetic design is based initially on appreciation of the fixed structures of a molecule. Before taking on the synthesis of molecules, the chemist must "determine their structures— what kind of atoms are present, and determine in each case the manner in which these atoms are associated together in the fixed, rigid, architectural assemblages called molecules" (Woodward, 1963, p. 5).

For example, in Figure 12–3 we see how

> the 33 carbon atoms, 40 hydrogen atoms, 2 nitrogen atoms and 9 oxygen atoms of reserpine are arranged in the molecules of that substance . . . [the] six stars attached to various of the carbon atoms . . . each . . . represents a point at which a small change in arrangement leads to an entirely different molecule, and hence to an entirely different form of matter, *without any change in the number and kind of atoms involved in the construction of the array.* (Woodward, 1963, p. 6)

Reactions and Stereochemical Control: Art

The importance of reactions is that

> chemical transformations ordinarily take place in solutions, which contain large numbers of molecules of the reacting substances, roving about at high speed, and colliding with one another in a highly random fashion. The transformations of one form of matter into another take place as a consequence of the collisions . . . much of the art of directed synthesis involves the design of ways to place constraints on molecular motion, with the aim of bringing about desired changes, and suppressing others. (Woodward, 1963, p. 11)

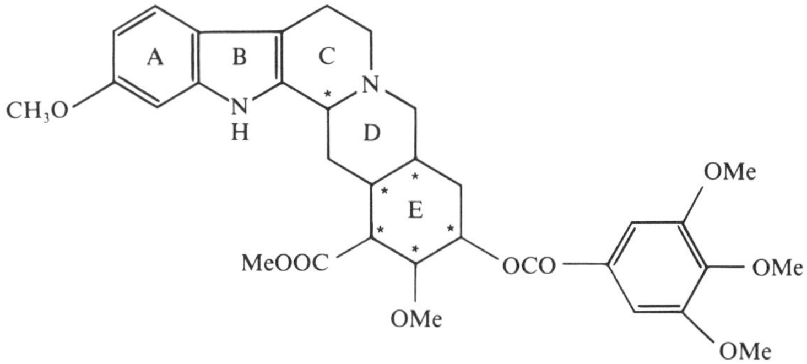

FIGURE 12–3. Reserpine. From R. B. Woodward (1963), *Art and Science in the Synthesis of Organic Compounds: Retrospect and Prospect.* Reprinted by permission of Ciba-Geigy.

As Cram and Hammond (1964) point out, organic compounds are composed of a relatively small number of different kinds of parts, which can be assembled in an almost infinite number of different ways. But most of the changes introduced in a reaction are limited to the "making and breaking of a relatively small number of bonds compared to the total number in the molecule" (Cram & Hammond, 1964, p. 15). We shall shortly see how Woodward used bonds in his art of chemical synthesis.

When Woodward was a boy there was not yet much appreciation of the three-dimensionality of molecules, but he and other chemists increasingly recognized the necessity of understanding this aspect of chemical structures. Through painstaking attention to detail, and through his extraordinary capacity for visualizing three-dimensional structures, Woodward was able to carry out the art of chemical transformations.

His art in synthesis was largely based on the particular bonds and architectural shapes he created to constrain molecular motion. The basis of Woodward's art, and of his feeling for it, existed on that fundamental level of bonding and reactions, what he referred to as "propinquitous spatial relationships." He emphasized that establishing and exploiting such spatial relationships contributed "more than any other single artifice to the power and beauty of synthetic designs" (Woodward, 1963).

That this principle of propinquity "is widely used in Nature, is indicated in the large number of ring compounds existing in Nature" (Woodward, n.d.). That is, a ring, like the bond, as an example of the principle of propinquity, can be used as a constraint on molecular motion.

The Ring Tactic and the Initial Building Block

Woodward's skill in the synthesis of natural compounds largely involved his ring tactic, making "a ring which contains the atoms needed in the target in their correct position with the correct relative stereochemistry, and subsequently to break the ring to make the final product" (Wheeler, 1982, pp. 9–10). This tactic simplified the path to the target structure so that a less reactive, more controllable system could be used. Woodward's idea was to "construct the carbon framework as quickly as possible, leaving some function (e.g. double bond) for eventual structural adjustments" (Stork, 1980, p. 284).

Woodward used this tactic in his first synthesis, that of quinine in 1944, and in subsequent syntheses of molecules with increasingly complex ring systems. He was, in this way, able to achieve the synthesis of molecules whose complexity had defied previous attempts. The use of the tactic was one of the main factors in the elegance of Woodward's syntheses, a quality particularly displayed in his syntheses of strychnine (1954), reserpine (1956), chlorophyll (1960), and vitamin B_{12} (1960–72).

In his Ciba talk, Woodward described his main procedures for constraining molecular motion. One was to construct a grouping of atoms whose bulk prevented intermolecular collisions at a particular moment in the synthesis. The second was to "introduce a grouping of atoms which . . . attracts another kind of molecule with which reaction is desired." This acts as a "platform for effecting desired changes" (Woodward, 1963, pp. 11–12). Furthermore, rather than disposing of such facilitating atom groupings once their initial purpose was served, Woodward was able to use them in later steps, thus incorporating them into his eventual target. This contributed both to the *economy* of his synthetic designs and to their elegance.

The choice of the initial building block in syntheses exemplifies a general principle, a particular architectural aspect of chemical synthesis, which Woodward described as

> the systematic aggrandizement of asymmetry. Most of the molecules of complicated naturally occurring substances represent highly asymmetric arrays, whereas the simpler starting materials which form the basic building blocks for their synthesis are much less obviously disordered. The problem of synthesis then is often to multiply this directional function, making it more cogent with each succeeding step, until the small geometric differences which existed at the outset have been developed into the greatly unsymmetrical situations represented by the final product. (1963, p. 19)

Woodward derived much aesthetic pleasure from relating previous work to a subsequent context. It must have been doubly satisfying to be able to take an item or approach that had been effectively developed in one context and use it, sometimes in combination with other earlier work, in another. So, for example, the "systematic aggrandizement of asymmetry," applied in the reserpine synthesis, was also used in his far more complex synthesis of vitamin B_{12} on which he worked from 1960 to 1972. This is a form of development in creative thinking: to invent a method and use it in increasingly complex tasks.

Similarly, Woodward's achievement of the synthesis of chlorophyll (1960) spurred his interest in the synthesis of vitamin B_{12} which is a very complicated relative of chlorophyll with a much more complex molecule. The synthesis of vitamin B_{12} took 12 years, involving 90 co-workers from 19 countries. Woodward mastered this problem through collaboration. The left half of the molecule was worked on by Woodward and his group at Harvard, and the right half by Albert Eschenmoser in Zurich.

One colleague commented that in Woodward's synthesis of vitamin B_{12}, "We are treated to a pyrotechnic display of appearing and disappearing rings which are used here to achieve control of almost all the asymmetric centers of the molecule" (Stork, 1980, p. 384).

The Sensuousness of Chemical Work

For Woodward, the aesthetic pleasure in chemistry had sensuous aspects. He demanded high standards of purity in his work, for example, in the crystallization of intermediate substances during a synthesis. Though he regarded such practical aspects of experimentation as partly a "craft" of synthesis, he nonetheless referred to them as "like all things made with care and affection, beautiful" (1963, p. 11).

His comments about crystallization in his account of the synthesis of colchicine in 1963 are telling:

> Each of the intermediates along our progression to the colchicine molecule is a beautifully crystalline substance, an entirely new form of matter. . . . It is delightful to work with such things, and the delight which the experimenter experiences in his manipulation contributes in no small measure to the skill required to create them. (Woodward, cited in Ollis, 1980, p. 213)

Woodward's view of these manipulations is one facet of a larger feeling he had for experimentation. Theory, for him, rested on experimental facts. Without experimental proof it was worthless. Ideas and theory could have an aesthetic aspect but their beauty and elegance were always tied to a concrete relationship with a physical reality. During his years as a student at MIT, he had considered studying architecture and also considered changing his major from chemistry to mathematics. His interest in structures, in transformations, and in elegance—so evident in his attitudes to chemistry—were thus expressed in more than one way. Explaining why he had not abandoned chemistry for mathematics, he said that although he loved the formal beauty, precision, and elegance of mathematics, it lacked

> the *sensuous* elements which play so large a role in my attraction to chemistry. I love crystals, the beauty of their form—and their formation; liquids, dormant, distilling, sloshing!; swirling, the fumes; the odors— good and bad; the rainbow of colors; the gleaming vessels, of every size, shape and purpose. Much as I might *think* about chemistry, it would not exist for me without these physical, visual, tangible, sensuous things. . . . Second, while in mathematics presumably one's imagination may run riot without limit, in chemistry one's ideas, however beautiful, logical, elegant, imaginative they may be in their own right, are simply without

value unless they are actually applicable to the *one* physical environment we have—in short, they are only good if they work! I personally very much enjoy the very special challenge which this physical restraint on fantasy presents. (1973)

Woodward's phrase "physical restraint on fantasy" is central. His work in chemistry did not exclude fantasy; rather, designing synthetic pathways to assemble a structure already determined both demanded and provided a context for "restraint on fantasy." Most of the compounds Woodward synthesized were natural compounds, that is, they exist in nature. Thus the known structure exists as a "target" toward which the chemist designs the synthetic steps, which are then to be executed in the laboratory; these do not duplicate the steps taken by nature in the biogenesis of the compound.

Woodward did study the biogenesis of some natural compounds; his interest was multifaceted, from the purely intellectual or aesthetic to the more practical. Such studies provided a context for his appreciation of the "beauty and order in Nature." This he placed alongside his emphasis on the importance of rigor and planning. Biogenetic studies could contribute to predicting structures, to suggesting pathways of synthesis, and to understanding the biological activity of compounds useful as antibiotics.

Imagination and the Synthesis of Entirely New Compounds

Thus nature and reality provided a "physical restraint on fantasy," even while Woodward revealed himself as an artist in favoring the imagination over copying nature. In 1956 he wrote that although nature "can be used to good effect in providing inspiration for synthetic plans . . . the advantages over permitting the imagination free rein may be doubted" (p. 171). In 1963 he said that in the synthesis of naturally occurring substances

> the final objective is rigidly set by the known existence of a molecule of a particular fixed architecture. But at each . . . stage of such syntheses the chemist is . . . creating . . . forms of matter which have never existed before. Natural quinine [Fig. 12–4] has been prepared by synthesis, but chloroquine and many related molecules which never existed in nature have also been prepared synthetically, and have been found to be superior in some respects to quinine in the control of malaria. This is an area which is entirely creative in spirit, and in which there is unlimited opportunity for art and imagination. (1963, pp. 19–20)

Woodward's first synthesis in 1944, of quinine (with Doering), generated a lot of excitement. It filled a need for a synthetic source of the substances used to combat malaria, urgent during World War II. But he also demonstrated that by slightly rearranging the structure of the quinine molecule, a number of useful different "cousins" could be made. It was some time later that chemistry extended itself to the synthesis of entirely new compounds such as chloroquine.

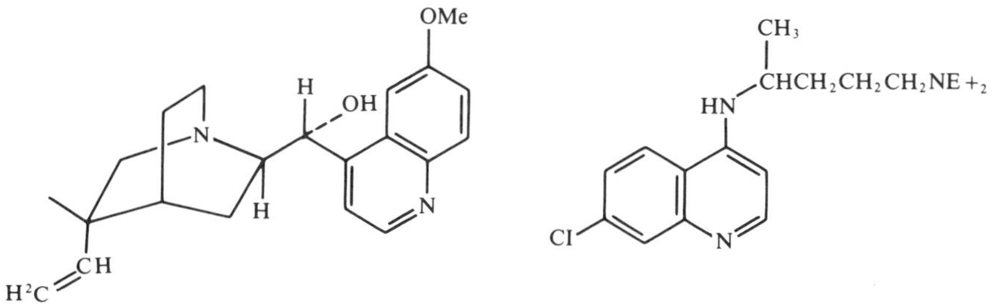

FIGURE 12–4. Quinine (left) and chloroquine (right). From R. B. Woodward (1963), *Art and Science in the Synthesis of Organic Compounds: Retrospect and Prospect*. Reprinted by permission of Ciba-Geigy.

Woodward was the first to correctly interpret the chemical reactivity of penicillin, demonstrating that the β-lactam ring structure accounted for the complex reactions of the molecule. In turn, he had been sensitized to the pertinent aspects of the lactam indirectly as he dealt with a related issue during his work on the synthesis of quinine, completed shortly before. As a consultant to the Pfizer Company, he had directed a research group working toward the structure determination of terramycin, which led him to the recognition that drugs or antibiotics superior to the naturally existing compounds could be made by chemical modification of structure. In 1965, at the Woodward Research Institute set up for him in 1962 at Ciba-Geigy in Basel, he achieved the synthesis of cephalosporin, related to penicillin. In 1971 he and his team succeeded in synthesizing a group of antibiotic substances which are not found in nature and which combine structural elements of the cephalosporin and penicillin molecules.

In his Nobel lecture in 1965, Woodward said that in the course of synthetic work, one or two key ideas often set the style, development, and outcome of the investigation, while providing "the flexibility essential for any long journey through unknown territory, beset with perils which at best can only be dimly foreseen."

His ideas were organized around themes of both practical and artistic creative value, immediately applicable as well as part of a much wider long-range vision. In fact, the development of his work over time presents a picture of rings within rings, as one project circles back to a previous one, there to connect with some relevant item, then to be linked with yet another theme.

An important component in Woodward's thinking was his extraordinary memory. Often details of work on one project or from his vast reading of the chemical literature became pertinent in a subsequent project. Co-workers and others were "constantly amazed at [Woodward's] ability to recall obscure reactions, including precise experiment conditions, which could be called into play when needed in a synthetic plan" (Wasserman, 1977, p. 8).

This also had bearing on Woodward's ability to supervise the work of others in his research group and among his graduate students and to be involved in collaborations. His extraordinary memory contributed to his unusual capacity for "directing simultaneously and in detail the work of many individuals" (Todd, 1981, p. 632).

Visualization and Movement over the Range of Areas

Woodward was able to visualize not only complex three-dimensional structures in space, but the path of possible reactions within a structure and, subsequently, the possible transformations of the structure. Such visual representations, as contrasted with verbal modes, serve important functions in scientific thinking and may be allied as well to similar processes in artistic creativity (Arnheim, 1969; C. E. Woodward, 1987).

Woodward's visualizations included both the mind and the hand and had sensuous aspects as well.

Teaching Chemists How to Think

Another facet of Woodward's art and work was his public presentation, his transmission of his knowledge, inspiring others with the beauties and mysteries of chemistry. In this area he became a legendary figure. In 1948 Woodward made his first trip to Europe, giving several lectures, with great impact on the chemical community. One colleague, present at a lecture in London, remarked,

> The occasion was electrifying. The analysis of the problem, the lucid marshalling of the evidence, the intellectual leap to the structural solution, the logical rationalization in terms of the new structure were presented with superb blackboard technique that illuminated the reasoning and the inevitability of the conclusions. (Raphael, 1979)

Derek Barton, later known for his work on conformational analysis (for which he received the Nobel Prize in 1969), related the occasion of one lecture as follows:

> It was a brilliant demonstration of how you could take facts in the literature which seemed obvious and just by thinking about them, as he so ably did, interpret them and obtain the results and then go into the laboratory and *prove* it was the right result. That we thought was the work of genius. . . . Ten years later [at Imperial College] our second year undergraduate students could do that problem, and . . . about 25% of them could get it right. Now does that mean that in 1958 we had 25% mini-Woodwards in the second year class? No, of course it didn't. What it meant was that Woodward *had taught us organic chemists how to think.* (Barton, 1981)

Woodward's trip in 1948 was the beginning of a series of honorary lectureships that took him to many countries in the course of his life. Lord Todd recounts:

One of the most striking features of Bob Woodward was the way in which he could transmit his passion for organic chemistry and his enthusiasm to young chemists. . . . I do not know nor have I ever known any other scientist who could so hold an audience; young chemists and many not so young were spellbound by him as by an evangelist. . . . He was, of course, a brilliant lecturer and withal no mean actor; his timing was always perfect [with] the famous little box containing his own set of colored [chalks], his special blackboard duster, his methodical and meticulous drawing of formulae (which at once slowed the pace and aided understanding). . . . (Todd, 1979)

Woodward showed his affection for chemistry in his writing. He wrote of nature's making "at least moderate resistance to our advances"; and of "coaxing" and "inducing" various reactions to go in the desired way (1955, p. 220). Referring to the isothiazole ring, a new substance which he developed for his synthesis of colchicine (1963), he wrote:

our investigations now entered a phase which was tinged with melancholy. Our isothiazole ring had served admirably in every anticipated capacity and some others as well. . . . Now it must discharge but one more responsibility—to permit itself gracefully to be dismantled, not to be used again until someone might see another opportunity to adopt so useful a companion on another synthetic adventure. And perform this final act of grace it did. (Woodward, cited in Ollis, 1980, p. 213)

Woodward's early resourcefulness, his ability to present his material, and his way of surprising and exciting the chemical community permitted him to create an international network of colleagues, institutions, and information—all necessary to make the advances he did in science.

Personal Life

Woodward's deepest and strongest emotional expression took place within the chemical community, particularly in his work with his research group and other colleagues. To outsiders he often seemed uninterested in human feelings. Since most of his waking hours were spent at his laboratory and office, little time was left for the family, a situation that was difficult for family members. After two marriages and four children, Woodward spent his last 10 years living alone.

He did not like vacations or interruptions from his work. He could get rather angry, at times, if he was interrupted or prevented from pursuing his work or concentration. At home, he used to call down "a little less noise there, please," not very sympathetic to the noise of children's play and havoc.

In contrast to his mind, his body was not important to him. He "loathed" physical exercise, as he put it, and slept little. It was as though his body had long since been given to his chemistry. His physical movement was curtailed and interiorized in his chemistry, there to be expressed in his extraordinary capacity for visualizing three-dimensional molecular structures. It was as though he could move, in his mind, among these structures, viewing them from all angles, even foreseeing their transformations, as he effected, step-by-step, their pathways toward new possibilities and eventual targets. This is an important example of Woodward's shifting issues of self into the arena of chemistry: in the creating, dissolving, and re-creating of structures, the opening and closing of rings and reactions, Woodward's body image was, perhaps unconsciously, being broken down and reassembled, fueling his work with a deep, probably unacknowledged dimension of aesthetic pleasure.

With his emphasis on the role of the hands and the sensuous aspects of chemistry, he gladly took part in the actual experimentation. But over the years, as he gave more of this over to his research group, he became less involved in doing the experiments. He even took to using slides in his lectures rather than drawing the structures.

Woodward enjoyed drinking at parties, and among colleagues and his research group there were occasions of hilarity, jokes, and sometimes competitive games. He had enormous energy for his work, and even after late-night festivities, he was at his office at his usual early morning hour.

Woodward was a chain smoker. This, along with his lack of rest or physical exercise, probably contributed to his dying of a heart attack at age 62.

I realized at his memorial service at Harvard in 1979 that he had to a large extent become a father in the world of organic chemistry. Perhaps his becoming a present father in chemistry had required his being a largely absent father to his family. As a child, he had experienced the absence of a father.

Woodward's aesthetic feeling did not figure only in his work. His legendary preference for the color blue extended to his blue car and the blue suit and blue tie he wore every day. He cared enough to see to the tasteful decoration of his office and, after his second separation and divorce, of his apartment. In all of this there was a distinct refinement and elegance.

Socially, the pleasure of work included existing within a supportive network which he in large part created. For example, he chose his research fellows, who often went on from their experience with him to very successful careers. And, more inwardly and centrally, there was the pleasure of similar relationships of give and take in his thinking, in his being both accountable to and creator of the myriad chemical reactions that, in their or his sequences, lead to beautiful molecular structures.

Somehow, in this conjunction between imagination and nature, which was required in the process of thinking about organic chemical synthesis, Woodward conveyed a sense of being uplifted, purified. Can we see here a curious resurfacing of the old alchemical search for the transmuting of base metals into gold, not as a materialistic goal but for the purification of the self? Woodward transmitted such a feeling to others in chemistry. As one colleague wrote:

> To be in R. B. Woodward's presence was for us much like young priests with the opportunity of having a papal audience. There was an aura of greatness as he blessed us with a sense of his creative elegance and showed us Sistine Chapels of chemical architecture. (Scheinbaum, 1979)

The aesthetic feeling, the beauties and mysteries of chemistry, had to do not only with the chemistry itself, but with this transformation and uplifting of the self.

Orbital Symmetry and the Matrix of Discovery

Woodward once commented that in synthesis the achievement of the objective—the synthesis—is less important than the fact that on the way to that objective a "matrix" for discovery is provided. An early example of this matrix for discovery may be seen in Woodward's reference to the "tough molecule" as teaching him about chemistry in his high school years. Later in his life, when he realized that he needed more detailed electronic theories of molecular structure, he sought the necessary knowledge of and collaboration in quantum mechanics. This extended him into a domain perhaps farthest from his own field of all the other areas which he had enlisted into his work in chemistry. It also led him to one of his most important discoveries, the laws of the conservation of orbital symmetry, discovered in 1965 when he was working on the synthesis of vitamin B_{12}.

Given the importance of rings, and of the ring tactic, in Woodward's work, it is of interest that this discovery was prompted when a cyclization, that is, the making of a ring of atoms, did not go as predicted at a stage in the B_{12} synthesis. His interest in the unexpected here found dramatic fulfillment. The orbital symmetry laws were recognized by the awarding of a Nobel Prize in 1981 to Roald Hoffmann, the person with whom Woodward collaborated on this project, and whose theoretical background and knowledge of quantum mechanics Woodward had sought as a necessary adjunct to understanding the new findings. Had Woodward been alive in 1981, he would almost certainly have participated in this award, thus receiving a second Nobel Prize.

The orbital symmetry laws constitute a mode of control of chemical reactions, and thus are at the heart of Woodward's description of the "art" of synthesis. Woodward came to this discovery after he had already achieved the work in synthesis that had merited his Nobel Prize in 1965 for the art of synthesis.

As I have said, as a young boy, he was already thinking about a number of issues centrally linked to his later discoveries and achievements. As he built up his network in the world of chemistry, it became more and more possible to translate his own original ideas into practice through appropriate experimentation and collaboration. When he first realized this possibility, he described a feeling of "purest pleasure" (Woodward, 1956). His boyhood fascination with bonding, his preoccupation with the Diels–Alder reaction, and later with other mysterious reactions, his interest in valence theories, and so on, were the general beginnings of his affair with chemistry. But they were also indications of his far-reaching sensitivity to the crucial issues in the chemistry of his time.

In brief, to contextualize the discovery of the orbital symmetry laws:

> Bohr developed a model for atomic structure in which electrons circulated around nuclei in orbits. . . . It was necessary to introduce a scheme known as quantum theory, according to which electrons could occupy only certain "stable" orbits. Electrons could jump from one orbit to another by absorption or emission of light energy in discrete packages known as quanta. This system of non-classical mechanics was known as quantum mechanics. [It was this more fluid concept of the atom which permitted an image of bonding as a "sharing of electrons."] . . . The motion of the electron is thought of as a standing wave . . . wave functions contain the coordinates of the electron . . . [and] are called *orbitals*. . . . The characteristics of the various orbitals provide the basis for discussions of bonding in molecules. (Cram & Hammond, 1964, pp. 119–121)

Regarding the significance of the orbital symmetry laws, Woodward remarked, "The ideas which Professor Hoffmann and I have developed represent an extension, to dynamic reacting systems, of those basic structural concepts which have served chemists so well in dealing with static systems" (Woodward, 1973, p. 12).

The importance of this work is further elucidated by a colleague:

> The summarizing paper in *Angewandte Chemie* (The Conservation of Orbital Symmetry, 1970) is probably the most cited contribution to modern chemistry. The work gave molecular orbital theory a practical role in organic chemistry which hitherto it had lacked. It systematized an enormous body of chemical knowledge. Better still, it predicted new results at a time when experimental knowledge and technique were capable of verifying the predictions. . . . If Woodward had left no other legacy, this one discovery would assure his fame. But if he had not at the time been attempting an extremely difficult synthesis, pushing to the limit his powers of prediction, he would not have come upon the set of facts that seemed inexplicable . . . it must have been a great satisfaction to him that the solution arose from his own experimental work and from the pattern of organic chemistry that he had woven in his own mind. (Cornforth, 1981, p. 637)

Childhood Imagination and Excitement Carried Over

Very early in his life, Woodward had to decide on the kind of relationship he wanted between his mind and imagination on the one hand and the external world or reality on the other. He later referred to how, when he was about 10 years old, his "imagination was engaged" with certain questions current in the chemistry of the day. Since "everyone who had given the matter any thought had his own benzene formula . . . I didn't see why I shouldn't have mine" (Woodward, 1973, p. 15). He recounted that, though he had his own benzene formula,

I was not so enamored of it that I ceased to give attention to those of others. In particular, my imagination was engaged by the relationship between the two conceptually clearly differentiable Kekulé structures [i.e., of benzene] . . . I recognized that if one were to assume the separate existence—however fleeting—of those entities, the conversion of the one into the other might be regarded as a *chemical reaction*. . . . Thus was born—in my mind—one of the first chemical reactions of my own design. (1973)

He then described a remarkable tale. During his boyhood, when he was reading chemistry textbooks he heard about the existence of chemical journals. He managed to have some sent to him and discovered the article of 1928 about the Diels–Alder reaction, which was the very reaction he had predicted!

He recounted, "Imagine my feelings at receiving these treasures," and "imagine further my feelings" on reading the now classic paper on the Diels–Alder reaction. "An idea that I had had could be reduced to reality!" (Woodward, 1973).

Perhaps in some way the relationship between the two Kekulé structures had some unconsciously felt parallel to the relationship which Woodward was beginning to create and evolve between himself and his chemistry. Mind and chemistry were, presumably, clearly differentiable, yet somehow interrelated, sharing and exchanging, pushing his thinking into tangible forms. As "chemistry creates its object" the distinction between thinking about chemistry and the object of that thinking may be difficult to maintain. At the same time, he believed that theory, or thinking, should be based on experimentation and fact. He used to say, when I asked him about certain people and their philosophical questioning, that he wasn't sure such questions were real. The feeling he conveyed was that in order to be "real," questioning and thinking should be based on testable, provable facts.

The Metaphoric Significance of Bonding

This early event marked the beginning of a lifelong interest in the Diels–Alder reaction and played an important role in the train of events leading to the discovery of the Woodward–Hoffmann rules in orbital symmetry. What evidently intrigued Woodward about the Diels–Alder reaction was its stereoselectivity; that is, unlike other reactions, there seemed to be a preferred way for the electrons to shift. Woodward published several papers on the reaction in the 1940s and 1950s and used it in a number of his syntheses. Finally, in the Woodward–Hoffmann rules, he was able to clarify the problem that had bothered him for so many years: The rules indicate how electrons are "allowed" to shift in chemical bonding (cf. Wheeler, 1982, p. 14).

Thus Woodward's discovery of the orbital symmetry rules is a culmination of his childhood and subsequent preoccupation with bonding. This discovery may reflect his sensitivity to the elusive, fleeting, mysterious dynamics connected to the close bonding or "sharing," not only between electrons but between self and non-self, subject and object, or mind and reality. The discovery also represents a lifetime of striving and a need, in accord with his belief in scientific objectivity, to divine an order and a rationale, rules for predicting and governing, for "allowing" those shifts.

The correspondence between his external preoccupations and inner aspects of self can be only speculated upon. It points to unconscious levels of affect and motivation active in his work. As I have said, the mystery of self, or of mind, shifted, in Woodward's case, into the arena of chemistry where it was both occluded and accessible—to be tapped in the resolution of complex chemical mysteries.

Being able to solve the mystery of chemical reactions meant understanding their stereospecificity, that is, how the electrons shifted in situations of bonding, and how that would affect the shapes and architectures in space of the resulting bonds among atoms and grouping of atoms.

The particular bond between himself and the world or between his mind and chemistry, which Woodward had worked out in his childhood, was to set the stage for his way of thinking about and doing chemistry. It was a bond in which rigor of reasoning and art were combined. We have seen how the early engagement of his imagination with the reality of chemistry was carried over into his later attitudes. So too that strong excitement in the face of chemical facts and of their discovery was evident in his subsequent accomplishments, as it was in the way he presented chemistry and in the atmosphere he transmitted.

This was a bond in which concern for mind had priority, with a careful balance between "reality" and "fantasy." And in this bond, social relationships were largely governed, found or created, through their relevance to chemistry. This did not imply a cold impersonality: "When he talked about chemistry, the stars in his eyes would sparkle, with a sort of childish delight . . . and he remained a perpetual youth till the end" (Tishler, 1981).

Finding and Creating

Woodward's belief in synthesis as a "matrix of discovery" includes a theme of finding and creating: the structure that is "found" and isolated from the natural world is then synthesized, or "created." In this process, new discoveries are made. Studies of childhood reveal the pertinence, to the understanding of artistic creativity, of this theme of finding and creating.

Winnicott (1971) described the first steps in building a healthy constructive relationship between reality and desire. The mother presents the baby with objects that meet its needs, first the breast, then other things. This leads to the baby's needing those very things, and this in turn to a feeling of confidence in the adequacy of the self–world relationship. Paradoxically, the baby feels "as if" it has created the object, while at the same time having found it. Winnicott called this the "transitional object" through which is born the child's love of reality and the seeds are sown for the later growth of creative imagination.

In the artist, this paradox, this coincidence of finding and creating, is maintained. The artist's creativity is nourished by the feeling "as if" in art he or she creates some part of the world. The great joy in, and devotion to, his work as creative suggests that Woodward shared this quality. Yet at the same time he presents a further paradox: not only does he proceed "as if" he creates a part of his world; he actually does so. For in his art, his created "object," the synthetic compound, *is* the naturally occurring compound. He has taken the "as if" and made it real. This distinguishes Woodward's creative process from that of other artists. The artist may permit a certain lack of differentiation between the self and the object and between the self and the world, so that finding and creating are merged. Woodward, on the other hand, emphasized the distinction between self and object—"objectivity." Similarly, as seen in his boyhood insight regarding the Diels–Alder reaction, he could see that two ways of conceiving a dynamic structure correspond to two modes of existence of the same thing. This capacity for discernment was a key to his becoming a master in the planning and control of stereospecific reactions—his "art."

Qualities of surprise and delight are usually associated with a spontaneous approach, whereas Woodward was known for his meticulous planning. However, it is through his rigorously planned and assembled "matrix" that Woodward created a space, an arena, in which beautiful surprises could arise in a context of verifiability:

> it is possible to introduce delightful elements of surprise into synthetic work. An apparently rather dull grouping of atoms suddenly, under the impact of especially chosen reactants, undergoes unusual transformations which are of great utility in progress toward the objective. The impact on an observer may perhaps be compared with that of the traveller down an uninteresting street, who turns through a hidden doorway into a delightful and charming garden. (1963, p. 16)

The impact on the chemist may be that he feels initially as though he had spontaneously found something. But at the same time he has *created* the "dull grouping" context in which the spontaneous can arise.

There is a sense of fit, as though the found unexpectedly "fits" into the created, thus to reveal or accomplish a new or perhaps already inherent interpenetration between the two items. At a series of points on the way to a synthesis, new weldings are made between the newly found and the already created.

In the realm of ideas, arriving at a sense of fit can bring a feeling of aesthetic pleasure; in the domain of molecules, the pleasure is compounded by the presence of an actual physical counterpart, in which the "fit" is embedded. Woodward's sense of beauty was bound up in his awareness of and ability to maneuver and construct the multitude of fittings-together of such component parts. It was based not only on criteria of visual appearance but on his sense of participation in manipulating levels of meaning that constitute both structure and appearance.

In synthesis, Woodward held the structure, the compound in the mind; then he visualized a number of its possible "meanings," and then he physically constructed one of those structures, having decided on one of those meanings. In making these choices and then creating the chosen structure, Woodward became a part of that structure's becoming and it, perhaps, of his becoming. Nevertheless, in the end, the synthesized compound remained outside him, separate from him. It was the created object, identical to the natural compound. He could contemplate it from a distance. This distance served to bring to completion the sense of aesthetic elegance and beauty: the compound was not himself but something separate, existing in its own right and with its own coherence.

Even within a basic position of differentiation and objectivity, he stressed the importance of imagination over copying nature, and the feeling of beauty and the delight in the sensuous aspects of such experiences as crystallizations as contributing to one's skill. The concept of the transitional object sheds further light here. Through his imagination, Woodward designed into his synthetic pathways "coherent configurations" in which self and non-self, nature and imagination, were bonded together. How much is this specifically related to the ambiguity inherent in chemistry's creating its object? Via his imagination, Woodward was able to bond, to use creatively, items that might otherwise remain opposites. Here we may see another curious resurfacing of the old alchemical idea of the "conjunction of opposites," translated into the language of chemistry of the twentieth century.

Play

These observations on the dynamic of surprise within the matrix of control and planning can be extended to the question of play. How much was Woodward's work a form of play? The evidence of his sense of humor and his jokes with colleagues and friends and his enjoyment in using the English language suggest a play element. For example, he coined playful names for newly occurring substances in his synthetic pathways, such as Christmasterol, a compound whose synthesis he completed on Christmas Day, 1953.

Yet play often presupposes an "as if" attitude, and the real world context of Woodward's goals and methods suggests that he did not place himself in a basic "as if" attitude. On the other hand, he did write "won't conceal most done for fun" in his handwritten notes concerning synthesis. And his statements that discoveries along the way to synthesis might be more important than the synthesis itself echo the role of play as a mode of discovery in the child, useful and enriching when carried over into mature forms of search and research. For him, play may have been similar to luck. About the latter he used to say, along the lines of Benjamin Franklin, that it took a lot of work to get to the point where one could be lucky.

The Self in Chemistry

In ordinary child development, the earliest "matrix of discovery" is the mother–child bond. This expands into a development matrix, an environment of social relationships, exploration of bodily movement and sensation, participation in communication, and eventually a shared verbal language, from which the child's sense of self and of objects emerge. Apparently in Woodward's development—personal, cognitive, affective, and even aesthetic—this matrix of discovery was transformed by his very early self-immersion in chemistry. From that a particular "chemistry-oriented" development of self arose. This may have been largely channeled into an indirect discovery of his mind, through the object on which it was focused, chemistry, which was particularly conducive to revealing and making real his mind's potential. The discovery of the Diels–Alder reaction is an example of this: what did he *realize?* That an idea could be reduced to reality.

Thus Woodward's sense of self was initially and throughout his life associated with chemistry. The goal was not "to have become," but to continue becoming. Woodward's development *became* his development of chemistry and in that form could continue to become. This explains his extreme dislike of interruptions in his work, his reluctance to take vacations, even his unwillingness to spend time with his family. It also ties in with the value he placed on being at the forefront of knowledge. The network of research groups and colleagues, the academic structure, chemical literature, conferences, and the community of world chemistry were like a fabric he carefully wove externally, parallel to the "pattern of organic chemistry" he wove in his mind. The inter-relating threads, in various ways, supported his work. But chemistry was not only a support, it was an object, a medium, and a language of his thinking. An interruption was like a tear, a hole in the fabric, a loss in the thread of thought, a forced hiatus in the sense of purpose in his life.

More than once it was said when Woodward accomplished a synthesis, that it was the most complex synthesis yet achieved. Woodward would then set about to accomplish the synthesis of yet a more complex molecule, or eventually to inspire and instruct others to do so. The "object" of chemistry is not only *one* synthesis, but the changing, evolving sum contained in many, and the understanding and sharpening of the tools of chemical principle which are discovered through them. Thus the object of chemistry changes over time.

From his visualization of multiple, interrelated perspectives, Woodward reached and grasped horizons; he was able to embody them into actual created objects: the intermediates first, each crystallized as visible stable landmarks along his pathway; then the completed synthesis of the organic compound; and finally the move to new horizons "indefinitely."

The Poetry of Chemistry

Having elucidated the difference between Woodward's process and that of the artist, it is important to indicate some of the ways in which their processes are similar. If chemistry can be regarded as serving as a language of Woodward's thinking, then his use of it may be akin to the poet's use of verbal language. Woodward wrote "write formula in as many ways as possible. Each way may suggest different possibilities" (Woodward, n.d.). Such procedures, along with the subtlety of the structural concept, are reminiscent of the poet's experimentation with the moving around of different letters in a word, or words in a line and in the whole poem: the slight change in arrangement brings out a different substance or meaning in both the molecular and poetic medium.

For the poet this can involve a return to modes of childhood play, exploring new combinations of sound and meaning, brought forward into the present creative process. Through this and other structural relationships, such as rhyme, rhythm, accent, and meter, aspects of bodily, sensory, and developmental experience are implicated. Such dynamics can provoke the surprise of old horizons seen from new perspectives through which self and world, language and experience, are welded into networks of new and unexpected meanings that may have been arrived at only through the art.

Or, in painting, the artist may try a number of different perspectives, rubbing out and painting over, incorporating parts of earlier layers with subsequent layers of paint. The destruction of one meaning leads to the discovery of another idea. A new meaning is built up through this conjunction of the destroyed and the new. Similarly, Woodward wrote "synthesis does not have to involve process just of building up. May well be advantageous to overbuild and then tear away" (n.d.).

Woodward's involvement in the creation of "meaning" as process and as knowledge seems to fluctuate between different levels, between the more occluded, elusive, and fleeting and the more stable, definite, and specific; between the past and the not yet found but sensed as there, up ahead, around another turn of thought or experience; between the very near and the not near enough. Woodward's sensitivity to this fluctuation may reflect sensitivity to a fluctuation in himself, between an outerdirectedness, his thinking about his object, chemistry, and an innerdirectedness of sensory, bodily, affective elements.

Woodward's art, then, lay in stabilizing this fluctuation, that is, in his "constraints on molecular motion"; and then opening it up again to fluctuation, to imagination, delight, uncertainty; then, with the help of his "physical restraint on fantasy," to stabilize it once again; and so on. Upon the achievement of a total synthesis, he could step back to see it as identical to nature, as somehow beyond time. And perhaps he was moved by the feeling that he was standing at the intersection of time and eternity, glad that he had played a part in their meeting. It was in such moments that Woodward perhaps allowed himself a sense of rest from his efforts, before moving on again.

But this is where he allowed himself an "as if." He worked "as if" he did not need much actual physical rest. Zosimus of panopolis in an alchemical text of the third century, wrote of a vision he had had in which a voice said:

> I have accomplished the action of descending the 15 steps walking toward the darkness, and the action of ascending the steps, going toward the light. The sacrifice renews me, rejecting the dense nature of the body . . . it is thus, by the transformation of the body, I have learned to become spirit. (Holmyard, 1931, p. 36)

In some ways, Woodward might have liked to "become spirit" and go on working. On a visit to Israel, to the Sea of Galilee, he joked about how he would now "walk on the water." Such jokes were shared with colleagues but might also have reflected a certain serious image he had of himself.

There was a quality about him that led a colleague to remark, "he seemed immortal; we did not think he would ever die" (Westheimer, 1981). Yet his physical body could not keep up. Neither was he indifferent to the difficulties which had gone on in his family and personal life; he too had suffered sorrow, loss. Toward the end of his life he was probably often lonely and not always happy. Aside from teaching others how to think in chemistry, he may also have taught some of us how to neglect his personal needs—for sharing, for rest.

In Woodward's work, his art in science, we can see how elements of the humanness of a person, the artist and scientist in the fullness of his life, are both occluded and fulfilled; sacrificed, perhaps, and transformed; transcended and confirmed. The elegance in Woodward's work and his ring tactic speak of this going away and coming back around by another new route, of setting out on a journey whose goal becomes the journey itself.

CHRONOLOGY
ROBERT BURNS WOODWARD

1917	April 10: Born in Quincy, Massachusetts.
1918	Father dies.
1923–33	Elementary and high school education, Quincy, Massachusetts.
1937	Ph.D., MIT, chemistry. Marriage to Irja Pullman. (Two daughters.)
1938	Junior Fellow, Harvard University Society of Fellows.
1940–42	Four papers on rules for the correlation of ultraviolet spectroscopy with molecular structure; known as the Woodward Rules.
1941	Instructor in chemistry, Harvard University.
1942	Writes early paper on the Diels–Alder reaction.
1944	Completes synthesis of quinine.

1945–56   Determines the structure of penicillin, patulin, strychnine, terramycin, aureomycin, and magnamycin.

1945   Honorary degree, D.Sc., Wesleyan University, the first of more than 25 honorary degrees.

1946   Divorces Irja Pullman.
           Marries Eudoxia Muller. (One daughter, one son.)

1950   Full professor at Harvard.

1951   Synthesis of the steroids cholesterol and cortisone.

1954   Synthesis of strychnine and lysergic acid.

1956   Synthesis of reserpine.

1960   Completes synthesis of chlorophyll, which took four years.

1961   Pope Pius XI Gold Medal, Pontifical Award, Rome.

1963   Begins work at the Woodward Research Institute in Basel under the aegis of Ciba.
           Synthesis of cephalosporin C.

1965   Awarded the Nobel Prize for chemistry.

1965–69   Development of the laws of the conservation of orbital symmetry, with Roald Hoffmann.

1972   Synthesis of vitamin B_{12} completed with A. Eschenmoser of Zurich, a project that took 11 years and some 100 co-workers.

1978   Awarded Copley Medal of the Royal Society, London.

1979   July 8: Dies.

REFERENCES

Arnheim, R. (1969). *Visual thinking*. Berkeley: University of California Press.
Barton, Sir D. R. (1981). *Some recent progress in natural products chemistry*. Paper presented at the 182nd annual meeting of the American Chemical Society, Woodward Memorial Symposium, New York.
Berthelot, M. (1860). *Chimie organique fondée sur la synthèse*. Paris: Mallet-Bachelier.
Cornforth, Sir J. (1981, November). R. B. Woodward, 1917–1979. *Biographical memoirs of the Royal Society, 27*.
Cram, D., & Hammond, G. (1964). *Organic chemistry*. New York: McGraw-Hill.
Gruber, H. E. (1980). The evolving systems approach to creativity: Charles Darwin's early thought. In E. Nickles (Ed.), *Scientific discovery: Case studies* (pp. 113–130). Dordrecht: Reidel.
Gruber, H. E. (1981). On the relation between "Aha experiences" and the construction of ideas. *History of Science, 19,* 41–59.
Gruber, H. E. (1988). Networks of enterprise in creative scientific thought. In B. Gholson, W. Shadesh, & A. Houts (Eds.), *Psychology of science and metascience*. New York: Cambridge University Press.
Holmyard, E. J. (1931). *Makers of chemistry*. Oxford: Oxford University Press at the Clarendon Press.

Ollis, W. D. (1980). Robert Burns Woodward—an appreciation. *Chemistry in Britain, 16,* 210–216.

Raphael, R. A. (1979). *Robert Burns Woodward—in memoriam.* Compilation of memorial statements about R. B. Woodward. Cambridge, Mass.: Harvard University, Department of Chemistry.

Scheinbaum, M. L. (1979). *Robert Burns Woodward—in memoriam.* Compilation of memorial statements about R. B. Woodward. Cambridge, Mass.: Harvard University, Department of Chemistry.

Stork, G. (1980, March). R. B. Woodward, 1917–1979, Obituary. *Nature,* 283–284.

Tishler, M. (1981). *Introductory remarks.* Presented at the 182nd meeting of the American Chemical Society, Woodward Memorial Symposium, New York.

Todd, Lord (1965, October). Nobel prizes for chemistry and physics. *New Scientist.*

Todd, Lord. (1979, November 9). Address. *Memorial service for R. B. Woodward, 1917–1979.* Harvard Memorial Church, Cambridge, Mass.

Todd, Lord, with Cornforth, Sir J. (1981, November). R. B. Woodward. *Biographical memoirs of the Royal Society.*

Wasserman, H. H. (1977). Profile and scientific contributions of Professor R. B. Woodward. *Heterocycles, 7.*

Westheimer, F. H. (1979, November 9). Address. *Memorial service for R. B. Woodward, 1917–1979,* Harvard Memorial Church, Cambridge, Mass.

Westheimer, F. H. (1981). *Robert Burns Woodward and the revolution in organic synthesis.* Paper presented at the 182nd meeting of the American Chemical Society, Woodward Memorial Symposium, New York.

Wheeler, D. M. S. (1982). *R. B. Woodward and modern organic chemistry.* Unpublished manuscript, Department of Chemistry, University of Nebraska, Lincoln. (Published in 1984: R. B. Woodward und die moderne organische Chemie, *Chemie in unserer Zeit, 18*[4]).

Winnicott, D. W. (1971). *Playing and reality.* New York: Basic Books.

Woodward, C. E. (1987). Art as visual language for awareness of self. *Leonardo, 20,* 225–229.

Woodward, R. B. (1955). *The total synthesis of strychnine.* Basel: Birkhäuser. (Originally presented at the 14th International Congress of Pure and Applied Chemistry, Zurich, Switzerland, July 1955)

Woodward, R. B. (1956). Synthesis. In Sir A. Todd (Ed.), *Perspectives in organic chemistry.* New York: Interscience.

Woodward, R. B. (1963). *Art and science in the synthesis of organic compounds: Retrospect and prospect.* Paper presented at Ciba-Geigy, Bombay, India.

Woodward, R. B. (1965). Recent advances in the chemistry of natural products. Nobel lecture upon receipt of the Nobel Prize in Chemistry. *Les Prix Nobel en 1965.* Stockholm: The Nobel Foundation.

Woodward, R. B. (1973). *The conservation of orbital symmetry.* Arthur C. Cope Award talk, 116th meeting of the American Chemical Society, Chicago.

Woodward, R. B., & Hall, W. J. (1934). Precipitation of barium in the copper–tin group of qualitative analysis. *Industrial and Engineering Chemistry, Analytical Edition, 6,* 478.

Woodward, R. B. (n.d., unpublished). Handwritten pages on synthesis, probably written between 1955 and 1962. R. B. Woodward Papers, Harvard University Archives.

FIGURE 13–1. Melissa Zink. Photograph by Margery B. Franklin.

13

A Convergence of Streams: Dramatic Change in the Artistic Work of Melissa Zink

MARGERY B. FRANKLIN

The work of any artist, like that of any creative individual, changes over time. Art critics and art historians, as well as psychologists, trace lines of development in artists' work, identify periods marked by changes in style or subject matter, and attempt to discern sources of change. Dramatic shifts in style or mode of work, the apparently sudden appearance of a stream of new ideas, and marked increases in level of energy and productivity are not uncommon in narratives of artistic work. Yet relatively little attention has been devoted to analyzing such phenomena. In this chapter, I examine an instance of dramatic change in the work of one artist, Melissa Zink, showing how she forged a new personal idiom at a crucial point in her career. I will argue that this event cannot be seen as a step in an orderly continuous progression but is more appropriately understood as a phenomenon of emergence, representing a radical disjuncture with what went before and, in effect, a new beginning. To account for the emergence and early development of Zink's new art, I develop the notion of "converging streams."

Melissa Zink made the commitment to being a professional artist when she was in her early forties. Over the next four years, she worked in a series of media. She first made assemblages and constructions and then turned to painting. After two years, the painting came to an end. A few months later, following a brief period of exploration, Zink began small-scale figurative ceramic sculpture. About a year after beginning in this medium, having completed more than 40 sculptures, Zink had her first one-person show in a well-established gallery of the Southwest. The show sold out almost immediately. Since that time, Zink has continued to work in the medium of sculpture. She has had a series of one-person shows, participated in numerous group shows and museum exhibitions, and has gained increasing recognition.[1]

The special interest of this case lies in the pattern of Zink's development as an artist. Zink did not set her sights early on a specific path and follow it unswervingly—a pattern often found in accounts of creative lives. Rather, she found her professional identity and artistic path in her early forties. Her effort to forge a medium that would enable the expression and development of her artistic ideas was a protracted, not always conscious, struggle. It was only after concentrated work in assemblage and painting that she turned to sculpture and began to produce extraordinary original work—mysterious, ironic, profound—that was artistically successful and received critical attention. The nature of Zink's shift to work in sculpture and the early evolution of work in the new medium are the focus of this chapter.

Approach to the Study:
The Phenomenological–Narrative Perspective

This chapter encompasses the five-year period from 1974 to 1979, from the moment when Zink dedicated herself to being a professional artist to the time of her first one-person show (see chronology at the end of this chapter). I have discussed some aspects of Zink's subsequent development elsewhere (Franklin, 1983, 1988). Three series of interviews with the artist and viewing almost all of the work completed within the four-year period comprise the empirical material of this study. The initial series of interviews was open-ended and conversational; the second series was more structured, focusing on themes emerging in the first series; in the third series, preliminary interpretations were offered to Zink for corroboration and correction. In the first and second series of interviews, every effort was made to hold in abeyance specific hypotheses and to avoid asking directive questions. The interview process follows Kvale (1983).

The approach to interviewing and to interpretation is phenomenological in the sense that every attempt is made to see or reconstruct events from the subject's point of view (Kvale, 1983; Wallace, 1985). The narrative presented here is securely grounded in the artist's experience of her work but is not the same in all respects as the story that the artist would tell. As Gruber (1980) and Wallace (1985) suggest, the task of interpretation may yield an account that differs to some degree from the subject's own.

A word must be said about the narrative perspective that guides this account. The underlying notion of narrative is the story—a tale, with plot and characters, that describes a sequence of actions and experiences, and in so do-ing gives coherence to what would otherwise be a series of isolated events. Two closely related theses of the narrative perspective can be readily identi-fied. First, analysis of human action and experience in terms of narrative structure provides forms of understanding not available through more tradi-tional approaches that rely on antecedent–consequent models of causal expla-nation (Bruner, 1986; Sarbin, 1986). In this perspective, explanation resides in presenting a coherent picture in which central entities and sequences are identified and relationships of parts to one another in the constitution of the whole are revealed. This general approach to explanation is not limited to those who endorse the narrative perspective, but it is an essential aspect of their view.

Second, narratives are constructed and necessarily interpretive. They are wholes comprised of parts that have been selected and arranged by an inter-preter. As Ricoeur (1981) emphasizes, narrative accounts involve two di-mensions. The chronological or "episodic" dimension has to do with temporal ordering: what happened? What happened next? In the construction of real life or historical narratives (contrasted with fictional narratives), objective chronology provides a guide, but it cannot determine the selection of events comprising a sequence. Freeman (1984) points out that in studies of the life course (as in historical reconstruction) we actively select from among possi-bilities to develop a coherent account, and this selection is theoretically guided. In this perspective, then, it is emphasized that establishing sequence is itself interpretive. Moreover, the activity of narrating is not just a matter of string-ing episodes together but involves the construction of meaningful wholes from "scattered events" (Ricoeur, 1981, p. 278). This is the other dimension of narrating, according to Ricoeur: constructing thematic patterns by showing relationships between the parts in addition to sequential ordering. Clearly, the two aspects of narrative construction interact: selection of events to be temporally linked is guided by ideas about meaningful configurations; on the other hand, formation of meaningful configurations may lead to reselection of events for the temporally ordered sequence. The latter point is not made ex-plicitly by Ricoeur but seems consistent with his views.

I turn now to the case study.

Searching for the Way: Assemblage and Painting

At 41 Zink separated from her first husband and entered into a relationship with a man whom she married about a year later. It was in the context of the new relationship that Zink made the commitment to being a professional art-ist. The time and setting are identified:[2]

> We went to Santa Fe on a holiday . . . and we'd gone around to all the galleries. . . . We started talking about art and artists and so forth. And I admitted that I wanted to be an artist, that that is what I wanted to

spend my life doing, that I wanted to be recognized. . . . And I had to be able to say that before I could do anything really. . . . You have to be committed, and the point is—you have to be willing to fail.

Zink's interest in art and her wish to be an artist go far back. In childhood and adolescence, Zink did some drawing and painting; in college she majored in art history. She worked intermittently at drawing, painting, and printmaking in the years following, and for a short time, took courses in art. But she did not pursue any of these endeavors in a consistent way. Over this same 20-year period, Zink became skilled in a variety of crafts and at some points used her skills to generate income. She did not identify herself as an artist in her own mind or to others.

The avowal of intent marked a crucial moment: the transformation of a submerged wish into a statement of purpose, the articulated commitment to being a professional artist. From that time forward, Zink devoted herself unstintingly to work in art. The importance of purpose as an organizing force in creative lives is a central precept of the evolving systems approach (see Chapter 1). In this case, the initial statement of purpose preceded the formulation of specific artistic ideas or the forging of specific instrumentalities for their realization. But it would be erroneous to see Zink's statement of purpose as simply representing a wish. The background of knowledge in art, experience in drawing and painting, extensive skills acquired by working in several media no doubt provided a sense of possibilities.

In 1974 Zink began to make assemblages of feathers, shells, bones, stones, and other small found objects; these were placed with galleries and sold quite well. The extent to which her experience with other crafts served as a resource in this first arts endeavor remains unclear, but it is certainly possible that assemblage was a transitional form for a person who was leaving the security of being an accomplished craftsperson and embarking on a career as a professional artist. While still making assemblages, Zink began to work on constructions made of cloth-wrapped pieces of wood assembled to form flat surfaces. These two-dimensional constructions have motifs suggestive of landscape. Shortly after this, she stopped making assemblages. The series of constructions came to an end in fall 1975, about 18 months after the initial commitment to being a professional artist. Zink describes her work with assemblage and with construction as "dead ends."

Speaking about the transition to the next phase of work, Zink ascribes an important role to her husband, Nelson Zink. During this period he gave her a great deal of support and encouragement. He also suggested that perhaps assemblage and construction were not suitable means of artistic expression for Zink. His statement, reverberating with Zink's own train of thought, provided the necessary impetus for her to "march off and buy paints, brushes, canvas and stretchers, and begin painting." As noted, Zink had studied painting some years earlier, well before her commitment to being an artist.

Zink's work in painting during the next two years, beginning in 1976, may be seen as a series of overlapping phases marked by changes in style, technique, material, and/or subject matter. In the first phase, she did a series of large paintings, using acrylic on canvas and a very limited palette. Abstract and "hard edge," these works use motifs drawn from the southwestern environment. After six months, Zink began to use another technique: painting on the reverse side of Plexiglas. After several months, she stopped painting on canvas. While continuing the work on Plexiglas, Zink made a series of constructions that she describes as "partly objects, partly paintings." Then, while making a few more constructions, Zink discontinued the paintings on Plexiglas and began a series of more abstract works on canvas. Again drawing on configurations of the southwestern landscape, she now used a wider range of color than previously, applied the paint to achieve rougher surfaces, and used shadows to create impressions of depth. As with preceding work, very few paintings sold. In fall 1977 Zink did a series of large paintings on Plexiglas that show further change of style. To some degree abstract, these paintings involve the representation of depth and are explicitly thematic. A final series of five large representational paintings on canvas includes two still lifes and Zink's only figurative work to this time. At this point, deeply dissatisfied and discouraged, Zink stopped painting. Reflecting on her work in painting, Zink says:

> You know, after I admitted I wanted to be an artist, I fooled around with assemblage but then I really came out, I put myself in the art slot. And doing art means you conform to the ruling schema, so your paintings are big and bright and hopefully impressive. . . . I wanted to be on the leading edge, but I couldn't buy it. . . . All those paintings are a mask, I wasn't doing what I would call personal work.

During the entire period from spring 1974 to early 1978, Zink typically worked 8 to 10 hours a day, producing a considerable body of work. What is the relation among the phases of work? The constructions are not similar in appearance or technique to the assemblages that preceded them, and the beginning of work in painting is rooted in explicit rejection of both these forms as suitable means of expression. In the two-year period of painting, there were marked shifts in style and technique, as well as some changes in materials and subject matter. And the phases became shorter and shorter. Considering the work itself, one is struck by the abruptness and frequency of change over the four-year period. Material from the interviews supports the interpretation that Zink was engaged in a series of relatively discrete endeavors—explorations that were successive but not cumulative. Certainly, none of these explorations evolved into a significant form of expression for Zink. But it seems that the series of explorations in a variety of media served the important function of eliminating possibilities and, at the same time, enriched Zink's artistic skills and vocabulary.

"The Chinese Gate": Beginnings and Early
Development of Zink's Sculpture

In contrast to the painting, the beginning of Zink's work in sculpture was not marked by a deliberate decision. Deeply discouraged by the fact that her paintings neither met her artistic purpose nor sold, Zink focused on producing income through her crafts. In the spring of 1978, her husband was doing some work with clay, and Zink thought of making decorative flower pots. She saw this as a viable alternative to scrimshaw, which she had done for some years and was now finding tedious. Zink's first attempts to hand build pots were not successful and almost immediately, without any particular end in mind, she abandoned these efforts and began to experiment:

> You could push pieces of junk into the clay and look at what you had made . . . and they became fragments from antiquity. In a sense, I wasn't making anything. I was finding something, like pressing a piece of transmission gear into the clay and looking at it and then saying "This is a Chinese gate." It's like what a child does when they're playing, taking one thing and saying it is something else.

From May until early July 1978, Zink experimented. Early on, she made a form that she refers to as a kind of "arched gate"; she says of this, "That's when I realized I could make places, not only people." But Zink did not yet attempt to "make places." Rather, she learned through inquiry and trial and error about techniques of firing and how to achieve colored surfaces without applying glaze. Zink was modeling small classic heads, pots like "something you might find on an archeological dig," and making impressed designs reminiscent of "other ancient things." Although she did not yet have a clear idea of where this exploration might lead, it seems that Zink was beginning to think in terms of new possibilities of artistic expression. There is no doubt that she found renewed pleasure in her work.

The problem was finding a way "to put it all together." Here, Zink appeared to be speaking literally: she could "make a lot of little things" but had not figured out how to bring parts together into a whole structure. She may be speaking metaphorically as well. Zink was at a crucial juncture, poised between open-ended experimentation and making works of art. At this point, Zink made an object formed of slabs of clay with an opening into which small bones were placed. She refers to this piece as "a shrine" (Fig. 13–2) and makes clear that its completion marked a significant moment. Making this piece involved solving certain technical problems; for example, creating particular kinds of surfaces on clay and assembling parts into a whole that could endure the firing process. Moreover, this piece—"mysterious, magical, evocative"—had an expressive power that Zink was searching for and felt had been missing in her previous work. She never put this piece up for sale. As a successful container structure, the "shrine" showed how parts could be brought together into a whole. Zink did not pursue that possibility immediately but

FIGURE 13–2. Melissa Zink. *The Shrine*. 4″ × 6″, fired ceramic, 1978. Private Collection.

found another solution to the problem of how to form a whole structure: she realized that a "wall" could be made by forming a flat piece of clay and curving it so that it would stand up, and that objects could be arranged on the wall.

The Period of the Nine Walls

The invention of the wall was a crucial event, marking the end of early explorations and the beginning of Zink's productive work in sculpture. The first sculpture, *Blind Navigator* (Fig. 13–3), was done in July 1978. In a period of a few months, Zink made another eight sculptures that utilized the same basic structure: a single curved wall with arrangements of objects on each side. I designate this first phase as "The Period of the Nine Walls." The works are entirely of ceramic; individual pieces are sculpted of earthenware, fired to maturity, and assembled to form the finished sculpture. A variety of textured surfaces is achieved through impression, incision, and brushing; pieces are immersed in water-soluble chemicals and refired to produce colored surfaces.

FIGURE 13–3. Melissa Zink. *Blind Navigator,* detail. 6″ diameter, fired ceramic, 1978. Collection of Tally Richards, Taos, New Mexico.

Some of the sculptures are smoked. The overall size of the sculptures is small, ranging from approximately 7 × 7 × 7 inches to 28 × 30 × 12 inches.

Following the pattern of her first explorations, Zink allowed the material to "suggest" something and then used this as a guiding idea. For example, of *Blind Navigator,* she says:

> At that point, I wasn't in control of what I was doing. I was exploring possibilities. . . . The title came from looking at the piece . . . the circle looked like a navigational drawing. . . . I placed the head within it. . . . The idea of a blind navigator, something very evocative about that. Most of the first ones work that way, I named them for what I saw there.

The theme of museum collections served as an important organizing idea in the early period, as reflected in titles such as "Classical Antiquities," "Chinese Collection," and "Italian Museum." Only in the final work of this group, *Black Monument,* are the two displays (one on each side of the wall structure) related to each other as parts of a whole structure. On one side of the wall, there is a group of heads and a small collection of wrapped boxes on a shelf just beneath the heads (Fig. 13–4*a*); on the other side is a flat double door that, if it were movable, would open upon the interior space shown on the other side (Fig. 13–4*b*). Zink comments: "This [*Black Monument*] is the first one in which I had in mind a picture of a place. . . . The thoughts are not too well developed, they're just feelings about old times, old days, magic

FIGURE 13–4a. Melissa Zink. *Black Monument.* 12″ × 9″, fired ceramic, 1978. Courtesy Clay and Fiber Gallery, Taos, New Mexico.

FIGURE 13–4b. Melissa Zink. *Black Monument.* 12″ × 9″, fired ceramic, 1978. Courtesy Clay and Fiber Gallery, Taos, New Mexico.

and ritual." In the subsequent phase, this sense of creating a place becomes a guiding conception.

Streams

Reflecting on the period from May, when she began experimenting with clay, to September, when *Black Monument* was completed, Zink comments:

> It's like you're walking around with this enormous suitcase full of magic and you are never allowed to open it, because the rules say that the things in that suitcase are not worthy of artistic consideration. Words, childhood memories, pretend, fantasy, archeology—all that. And so, until I could open that suitcase, I didn't really have anything to work with. It was like trying to paint with your hand tied behind your back.

In this quote, Zink provides a vivid image embodying her sense that, quite suddenly, she found access to rich resources that were previously excluded from the work stream. In schematizing this situation, I use the notion of *stream* to refer to an ongoing flow of wishes, ideas, aims, and endeavors that have some experiential unity. Thus when I speak of the "work stream," I mean an interconnected set of feelings, ideas, and activities that a person considers to be his or her work and that is experientially extended in time. The term "stream" refers to the major organizing streams of life and also to other streams of experience that flow alongside and are sometimes drawn into the major streams. For example, in the discussion to follow, I refer to a stream of experiences having to do with childhood play.

While the delineation of major streams is probably formed by culture, the role and content of such streams—and of other streams—would seem to vary greatly among individuals within a culture. Attempts to characterize the organization of individual experience from a phenomenological perspective have tended to use metaphors such as life space (Lewin, 1936), spheres of experience (Werner, 1940/1978), and provinces of meaning (Schutz, 1962). These characterizations, however powerful, lack an inherent temporal dimension. The notion of stream is proposed as an alternative formulation for describing differentiated ongoing aspects of individual experience.

When Zink committed herself to being an artist, she created a new work stream that recruited hopes and fantasies from earlier days and to some extent skills and ideas acquired in earlier artistic endeavors. But, as we have seen, the particular forms of art that Zink explored during her first four years as a committed artist did not realize her artistic goals. The stream of artistic work came to a stopping point. Zink had started using clay with the idea of making decorative flower pots, but instead began to experiment with the material and to model small objects and figures. I suggest that the beginning of Zink's new art issued from a coming together of streams previously excluded from the work stream. Most important in the initial phases—from the first explorations to the making of *Black Monument*—were the resources of childhood play and a stream of interest in (and knowledge about) archeology, art, museum collections, ancient ritual, and myth. The *childhood play* stream has to do with ways of making things, specific memories of childhood play, and feelings associated with pretending or make-believe. If the play stream—and, specifically, pretending—contributed significantly to the mode of working in the initial phases, the *archeological/art* stream provided the prime source of imagery. Equally important to the emergence of the new work were Zink's increasing skill as a sculptor and, in particular, the invention of the wall—a structure that served both technically and conceptually as a means for bringing parts together into a unified whole.

The convergence of streams took place in a context of other happenings. Two aspects of immediate context seem most salient. The first is Zink's relationship with her husband. Her commitment to being an artist was made in the context of this relationship. The second was living in parts of Colorado where "there is no art for 250 miles," at a great distance from other artists and art galleries, away from "outside influences." The "outside influences" to which Zink refers include the trends and pressures of the art world in the 1960s and 1970s, which encouraged work that was "large, bold and tough" and denigrated the highly personal, the "intimate."

Thus Zink's relationship with her husband and her artistic isolation were significant aspects of the context in which resources were liberated and a new stream of work begun. The importance of considering context from the point of view of the subject (Wallace, 1985; see also Chapters 1 and 2, this volume) becomes clear when we consider that Zink's previous place of residence was just as isolated as the place to which she moved prior to beginning the new work.

The Itinerant Potter in the Age of Discovery

In September 1978 Zink took the first nine sculptures to a gallery in Taos, New Mexico where they were well received and began to sell almost immediately. In the phase of work started toward the end of summer 1978, and extending through December, Zink developed new ways of working, discovered two new basic structures, and expanded the range of themes in her work. In the following months—from January 1979 to the time of her first show in July of that year—she continued to develop the new medium and to explore and develop possibilities opened up by her earlier discoveries. These two phases, from September 1978 to July 1979, comprise the period that I call the "age of discovery."

One of the major developments in this period is Zink's first representation of self in the person of "the itinerant potter." In this section, I shall discuss three central aspects of Zink's work in the age of discovery, showing how additional resources were integrated into the work stream during this time: the development of the medium as personal idiom, modes of working, and the evolution of themes.

Development of the Medium as Personal Idiom

The sculptured forms of Zink's medium evolved in concert with a shift in her modes of working and with the rapid expansion of thematic material. In the early period, as I have described, Zink used the "wall" as a basic organizing structure—a surface on which individual pieces could be arranged to form a display. In early fall 1978 Zink invented two additional basic structures that served organizing functions. The first of these was the generic form that I refer to as the "container"; the other was the "open setting." The container structure was first used in *Sealed Column,* a cylindrically shaped pot with an opening at the top, containing a collection of boxes. In the next work, *The Tale of End* (Fig. 13–5), a figure of a man surrounded by wrapped scrolls is inside a square-shaped structure partly open at the front; the opening is clearly a doorway. This work took shape from a story invented by Zink's husband about the "last man on earth who is there, in his cave, surrounded with old scrolls that are the record of history." The container form continues to appear in a series of works done between January and June 1979.

In the open setting structure, objects and figures are arranged on a base; walls may be present but do not form a container. This structure first appears in fall 1978. A few months later, having completed seven more pieces, Zink produced her most ambitious work to that time, *Tomb of the Great Eater* (Figs. 13–6a and 13–6b). This was the first of many works that includes the wall structure in an open setting. It represents an archeological excavation of undefined time. Toward the end of 1978, Zink utilized the open setting structure in the first of a series of explicitly autobiographical pieces, *Itinerant Pot-*

FIGURE 13–5. Melissa Zink. *The Tale of End.* 7″ × 6″ × 6″, fired ceramic, 1978. Collection of Howard and Mara Taylor.

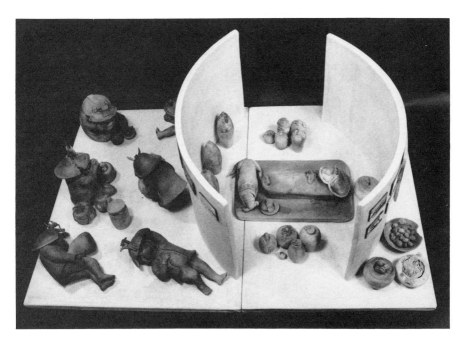

FIGURE 13–6a. Melissa Zink. *Tomb of the Great Eater.* 24″ × 14″ × 9″, fired ceramic, 1978. Collection of Jerry and Lennie Berkowitz.

FIGURE 13–6b. Melissa Zink. *Tomb of the Great Eater.* 24″ × 14″ × 9″, fired ceramic, 1978. Collection of Jerry and Lennie Berkowitz.

FIGURE 13–7. Melissa Zink. *Itinerant Potter and Faithful Companions, Dog and Valise, Seek Shelter in a Strange Monument*, 12″ × 12″ × 7″, fired ceramic, 1978. Courtesy Clay and Fiber Gallery, Taos, New Mexcio.

ter and Faithful Companions, Dog and Valise, Seek Shelter in a Strange Monument (Fig. 13–7).

In discussing artistic media, it is important to make a distinction between the material—in this case, earthenware—and the medium per se. On one level, the medium is what is done with the material. In Zink's work, clay is modeled into objects and figures; shaped to form flat pieces that are used to construct various types of structures; worked—through impression, incision, and coating—to produce a variety of textured surfaces; used to make individual parts that are assembled into whole structures. On another level, the medium is a set of processes for using the elements or forms produced at the first level. It is this second level that becomes a personal idiom. As a first step in characterizing Zink's idiom, we may note the following: (1) the use of *mimesis:* simulating real objects, figures, surfaces, spaces; (2) the use of three *basic structures*—walls, containers, and open settings—and specific forms for arranging parts, for example, juxtaposing objects on a flat surface, placing objects or figures inside containers; (3) *scale variation:* use of small scale and scale contrast, for example, a vessel of normal "everyday" size containing miniaturized figures and objects. Another distinctive aspect of Zink's work that must be included as part of her personal idiom is (4) the use of *titles:* Zink's titles are not "labels" but are integral to the central meaning of the work.

Modes of Working

In the first phase of her work in sculpture, Zink was making arrangements of individual items that gained coherence not only through their physical placement on a surface but thematically as "museum" displays. From Zink's description it seems that, initially at least, most of the work was the result of refined exploration: An individual object was formed and provided a guiding idea for making other objects, and the collection was then assembled to form a display. It was while making *Black Monument* that Zink first clearly had in mind "the picture of a place." At this point, Zink not only began to make sculptures using containers and open settings—structures that facilitate the representation of place—but engaged in active "controlled visualization" before beginning actual construction. Describing this change in her way of working, Zink made clear that she had not previously drawn on imaginative visualization in her art although it was something she had often done and had enjoyed—for example, when reading stories as a child. Imaginative visualization, perhaps because it was carried forth from childhood, served to bring forth thematic material previously excluded from the work stream. Zink comments about the relationship between imaginative visualization and the development of her particular idiom:

> I don't feel it's something I learned to do. I learned to have access to it, to control it. It doesn't ordinarily have an end result, it's just a mental activity, but you learn to manipulate it. And the medium gives you some kind of impetus to learn to move your mental images around, to concentrate, to improve them. . . . You can move things around, you can open doors.

We see that tapping into the stream of *imaginative visualization* was very closely tied to a crucial shift in Zink's mode of working: from a predominantly exploratory approach involving a part-to-whole mode of construction to an approach in which construction is guided by prior visualization of the whole. Bringing imaginative visualization into the work stream went along with a change from making displays to creating "places"—the places or worlds of Zink's imagination. Further, the critical transition from making displays to creating imaginary worlds involved visualization in connection with further use of the play stream. Positive feelings associated with play and pretend continued, but the imaginative transformation of objects (as in seeing a design as a Chinese gate) was replaced by imagining environments and scenarios—an activity that Zink relates directly to the pretend play of childhood. Zink explains that she spent a great deal of time alone as a child, and that much of this time was spent reading stories and playing—in her words, "imagining."

Beginning about January 1979, Zink began to draw more directly than before on another stream: the stream of *interest in language,* in words and phrases. From the beginning of her work in ceramic sculpture, Zink selected titles carefully and used them to communicate what her pieces were about (for example, *Italian Museum, PreColumbian Fragments*), but these titles came after the works were completed. By contrast, in subsequent periods many works were titled before construction was started or during the construction process, and in many instances titling contributed substantively to forming the concept of the work (see Franklin, 1988, on the topic of titling). For example:

> I remember lying in bed at night and thinking of the phrase "Spice Trade." And you kind of mull it over . . . and you see things. Once you begin to see jars, let's say ginger jars, and you say "well, we have all these jars . . . maybe there would be a person with those jars." And then I start building it into something I can make. I'll put it in a container. What kind of container? Well, if you want to keep on thinking about the spice trade, then you think of some kind of box in which the spices would have been shipped. And it's on two levels. It's the objects themselves, and it's the environment and the people that would nave been concerned. So it bounces back between reality and fantasy . . . the objects are real, the box is real, but the person in the box is a fantasy, and then the whole thing, the inside of it, becomes alive.

Zink's accounts of her thought processes while working include reference not only to visualization and exploring sounds and meanings of language but often to inner dialogue as well (as in the preceding excerpt). This kind of dialogue seems to serve primarily a problem-solving function for Zink, while visualizing and exploring word/phrase meanings serve basic generative functions.

Evolution of Themes

Zink's work, like that of any artist, contains many different themes often woven together without conscious intent. Certain themes come in initially and are given expression, in different form, in subsequent work. Other themes make their appearance after the initial phase, in concert with the development of the medium. In the year under consideration here, none of the themes introduced disappear.

The first series of nine works, beginning with *Blind Navigator* (Fig. 13–3) and concluding with *Black Monument* (Figs. 13–4a & 13–4b), embodies themes that are characterized by the artist as "ancient days," "ceremonies and rituals" of other cultures, "the museum, the gallery, art." Initially, these interwoven themes are represented in the arrangement of archeological fragments, costumes, masks, and other artifacts as "museum collections." In the next phase (the Age of Discovery), the themes become elaborated and are given more complex realization.

The *museum* theme as Zink uses it can be seen as a metaphor for memory itself. The museums Zink creates, particularly in the Age of Discovery when they become imagined places rather than displays, clearly embody and are intended to evoke a sense of mystery. This is often associated with reminiscence and with the sometimes acute nostalgia, even pain, of remembering, with a sense of the past in the present, with being transported to other times and other places.

Other times/other places is a theme in its own right, inextricably interwoven with memory or reminiscence but also with exploration of and play with *fantasy–reality* relationships. An early realization of the coalescence of these two themes is found in *The Tale of End,* which originated, as mentioned above, in a story of "ancient days" and represents one of the first departures from the museum format. The use of a "scene within" structure as one means of realizing the fantasy/reality theme also occurs in *The Spice Trade,* which Zink was discussing in the passage cited above.

Another theme that permeates the early museums and is given more elaborated realization soon after is identified by Zink as *ceremonies and rituals.* This can certainly be seen as part of other times/other places, but it receives sufficient attention to be identified in its own right. *The Tomb of the Great Eater* (Figs. 13–6*a* & 13–6*b*) is but one example.

Zink's first sculpture, *Blind Navigator,* described by the artist as "something you might see in a museum," embodies another theme that appears repeatedly in Zink's oeuvre: the *journey/quest.* This theme is given a more personalized expression six months later in *Itinerant Potter and Faithful Companions, Dog and Valise, Seek Shelter in a Strange Monument* (Fig. 13–7). The "itinerant potter," representing the artist, had her origins in a fantasy of Zink's from the time before she committed herself to being a professional artist. Zink says of this work:

> It was the first time I could continue a fantasy of myself as a world explorer. It gave me a way to express. . . . It's a journey through time to different places. This one is a little Eastern somehow. Perhaps a desert, and this wonderful black monument, at night. [Query about the origins of the "itinerant potter."] It came from a fantasy I had then [when the first marriage was breaking up] of being a gypsy potter, of going from village to village with my dog, supporting myself. . . . And at the same time, I could see the wonders of the world.

About six months later, in late spring 1979, Zink made two more sculptures with the itinerant potter, *The Itinerant Potter and Faithful Companions, Dog and Valise, Visit an Ancient Shrine* and *The Itinerant Potter and Faithful Companions, Dog and Valise, in the Garden of Earthly Delights.* In addition to carrying on the theme of the journey, the latter makes reference to a specific work of art (Hieronymus Bosch's *Garden of Earthly Delights*). References to art abound in Zink's work from the beginning, constituting another important theme that sometimes intersects with the museum theme—as in *Flemish Portrait Gallery.* The representation of self as itinerant potter seems to be an image symbolizing the *exploration of imaginary realms* that stands at the center of Zink's art and is inextricably tied to her sense of "finding a means of expression." The journeys recounted are a metaphor for the other journey: the journey inward. It is clear that at this point, Zink was beginning to draw more directly than she had previously on the stream of deep *personal experience,* using specific memories, feelings, and fantasies as thematic material. It is not only the journey but the self in an extended sense that now emerges as a recognizable theme.

I use the term "theme" to refer to the manifest content of Zink's work as represented in the imagery of sculptures. Where symbolic meanings of the themes are suggested, I use the term "metaphor." The dividing line between the manifest and the metaphoric may be even less clear in the visual and plastic arts than it is elsewhere, simply because the manifest does not correspond to the literal, and there is no system of precisely codified meanings as there is in language. There are grounds, then, for considering the group of manifest and metaphoric themes together as an ensemble of metaphors (Gruber, 1987) that not only reflects Zink's interests and concerns but, more importantly, plays a central generative role in her work.

In this section, I have shown how the critical transition from making displays to creating imaginary worlds depended on interaction of developments in the medium and changes in modes of working. The marked development of themes must be seen as an inherent part of the process, closely bound to the invention of forms in the medium and to the use of new modes of working. This constellation of changes involved further plumbing of streams of experience drawn upon in the first phases of work in sculpture, and, equally important, drawing upon streams previously excluded altogether from the work process—such as the stream of imaginative visualization (now used as a mode of working) and specific personal life experiences (now used as a source of thematic material). Figure 13–8 shows the initial convergence of streams that, in my interpretation, underlies the beginnings of Zink's work in sculpture and the subsequent confluence that marked the age of discovery.

Development, Emergence, and the Role of the Medium in Artistic Work: Theoretical Considerations

Until recently, the task of analyzing change in the work of individual artists has been taken on primarily within art history and criticism. Psychoanalytic theory provides a resource for many working within these disciplines or at their borders (see, for example, Gay, 1976). In addition, a number of psychoanalytic theorists have undertaken extended studies of individual artists' work and have touched upon processes of change as well as sources of themes and style (see, for example, Gedo, 1983; Liebert 1983). Spitz (1985) discusses the relevant psychoanalytic literature. Bornstein (1984) examines the applicability of nonpsychoanalytic developmental principles to phenomena of change in artistic work. The divergent principles of change considered by Bornstein are maturation, equilibration (Piaget), learning through reinforcement (Skinner), learning through imitation (social learning theory), and adaptation. Bornstein concludes that although each of these can account for some aspects of change in the work of particular artists, there does not appear to be a "monistic or even prevailing perspective available from developmental

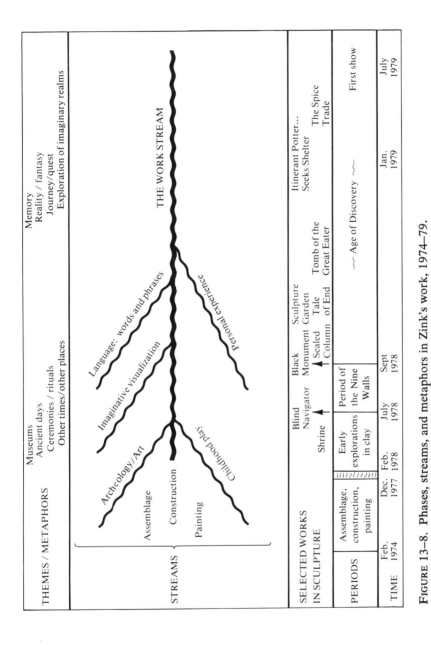

FIGURE 13–8. Phases, streams, and metaphors in Zink's work, 1974–79.

psychology that could account for artistic evolution in the individual" (p. 141). I suggest that some less well-known formulations in developmental theory may contribute to building a coherent view of change in artistic work.

In Melissa Zink's view, her sculpture marked a dramatic departure from anything she had done previously—it was a new beginning. Can we reconcile this with our view of continuity in development, with the idea that a line of sequential changes can be traced even where the conditions of change cannot be precisely identified? More specifically, should we go back to Zink's work in assemblage and painting and attempt to identify precursors of her work in sculpture?

Kagan (1983) points out that developmental psychology has long endorsed one version or another of a "connectivity" thesis. Freud's view of the inherent connection between childhood conflicts and adult behavior, Piaget's view of the evolution of logical thought, and a learning theory view of incremental change in behavior patterns all accept a notion of underlying continuity in individual human lives as in history writ large. So-called continuity theorists look for evidence of incremental change, perhaps gaining strength from the thesis of gradualism in Darwin's evolutionary theory (see Chapter 6). Discontinuity theorists assume that "underlying structures and predispositions are preserved even though the surface displays change" (Kagan, 1983, p. 43). As Kagan says, most developmental psychologists "resist the suggestion that some emergent phenomena may not have a long connected history" (p. 47).

In suggesting that the appearance of Zink's sculpture is an instance of emergence, I am proposing that it has no identifiable precursors in the earlier work and cannot be seen as evolving from it. Zink developed her skills as an artist during the phases of assemblage, construction, and painting, but the work of these phases in no sense prefigures what was to come—in form, process, or thematic material. Indeed, it seems that the repudiation—an active leaving behind—of earlier modes of work served the very important function of clearing the field. In this cleared field, Zink began to experiment and soon embarked on a new line of work. I see her new art as issuing from a radical restructuring that involved both repudiation of earlier modes of work and the convergence and interaction of streams previously excluded from the work stream. Zink's metaphor of "opening the suitcase" is helpful in understanding how she sees the resources newly drawn upon and in conveying her sense of discovery and liberation. But this image does not adequately convey the dynamics of interaction, the radical restructuring, that in my view took place.

The central idea here, of viewing at least some major developmental changes—and, in particular, phenomena of emergence—in terms of a convergence of streams, draws on Werner and Kaplan's (1963/1983) model of the emergence of language in the child. These authors see language as an emergent in the sense that it is not merely a continuation or elaboration of something that existed prior to language or a unique form that springs forth as a function of biological maturation. Rather, they hypothesize that language emerges from a convergence of depictive and referential activity, each manifest in vocal and gestural forms prior to language. When these two forms of activity coalesce, the child begins to speak—initially in single words and subsequently in more elaborated forms—in a language we recognize as our own.

This model of development provides a way of conceptualizing emergent forms and functions as the confluence and interaction of specifiable streams, rather than as totally novel and inexplicable or as outcomes of isolated antecedent conditions, as in a traditional cause–effect model. However, analysis of change as a function of converging streams is not specific to artistic development. In a case such as Zink's, we see not only the sudden emergence of new work but a sequence of interrelated changes in the ensuing period. This sequence of changes involved complex but specifiable interactions among selection and shaping of thematic material, modes of working, and evolution of the medium.

Arnheim (1962, 1974), perhaps more than any other psychologist, has pointed to the centrality of the medium in artistic work and to the nature of the connection between the development of form and meaning. His study of Picasso's *Guernica* (Arnheim, 1962) is an exemplary microdevelopmental analysis of interaction between thematic material and visual representation. For Cassirer (1942/1979) emphasis on the role of the medium in artistic work flows directly from a view of symbolizing as constructive activity through which meanings are formed, not merely expressed:

> Art is not only expression in general, in an unspecific manner, but expression in a specific medium. A great artist does not choose his medium as a mere external and indifferent material. To him, the words, the colors, the spatial forms and designs, the musical sounds are not only technical means of reproduction; they are the very conditions, they are essential moments of the productive artistic process itself. (Cassirer, 1942/1979, p. 161)

Cassirer's view of human beings as symbol-making creatures for whom the process of knowing depends on giving shape to ideas in a medium is articulated as a psychological theory by Werner and Kaplan (1963/1983). These authors see symbolization as a constructive or constitutive activity; meanings do not exist fully formed independent of a mode of expression but are realized in and through the mutual shaping of form and content. Whether or not one accepts this as a theory of mind, it provides a characterization of artistic work with which most artists would agree. Moreover, it allows us to see the evolution of an artist's personal idiom as the development of a symbol system.

In this chapter, the notion of converging experiential streams has been used in coordination with a narrative approach and a view of symbol formation as creative activity to develop an interpretation of change in one artist's work. This synthesis of perspectives provides a theoretical framework for the study of artistic development more generally.

CHRONOLOGY
MELISSA ZINK'S ARTISTIC WORK
MARCH 1974–JULY 1979

1974   March: Commitment to being an artist.
       April: Begins assemblage.

1975   February: Begins making constructions.
       March: Ends work in assemblage.
       October: Ends making constructions.

1976   January: Begins painting.

1977   February–April: Makes group of constructions; continues painting.
       December: Ends painting.

1978   February: Begins experimenting with clay: modeling small heads, parts of
       figures, miniature pots, impressing designs in clay.
       Early July: Makes "shrine."
       Mid-July: Invents "wall" and makes *Blind Navigator.*
       Mid-September: Completes ninth sculpture using wall structure, *Black
       Monument.*
       Late September: First container structure, *Sealed Column.*
       October: First open setting structure, *Sculpture Garden.*
       November: First sculpture using wall in open setting, group of human
       figures, etc. *Tomb of the Great Eater.*
       December: Completion of nineteenth sculpture, first autobiographical
       work, *Itinerant Potter and Faithful Companions . . . Seek Shelter.*

1979   January: Continues work; from January to late June, completes 24 sculp-
       tures.
       July: First one-person show, Clay & Fiber Gallery, Taos, New Mexico.

NOTES

1. Melissa Zink is currently represented by Gerald Peters Gallery, Santa Fe,
New Mexico and Dallas, Texas. Articles on her work have appeared in *American
Ceramics, Artnews, Artspace,* and *Arts Magazine,* among other publications.

2. The following and all subsequent quotations of the artist are from interview
transcripts.

REFERENCES

Arnheim, R. (1962). *The genesis of a painting.* Berkeley: University of California
       Press.
Arnheim, R. (1974). *Art and visual perception.* Berkeley: University of Cali-
       fornia Press.
Bornstein, M. (1984). Developmental psychology and the problem of artistic
       change. *Journal of Aesthetics and Art Criticism, 43,* 131–145.
Bruner, J. (1986). *Actual minds, possible worlds.* Cambridge, Mass.: Harvard
       University Press.
Cassirer, E. (1979). Language and art I. In E. Cassirer, *Symbol, myth and cul-*

ture (D. P. Verene, Ed.). New Haven: Yale University Press. (Original work published in 1942)

Franklin, M. B. (1983). Imaginary worlds take shape: A study of creative work in sculpture. *Leonardo, 16,* 212–216.

Franklin, M. B. (1988). "Museum of the Mind": An inquiry into the titling of artworks. *Metaphor and Symbolic Processes, 3,* 157–174.

Freeman, M. (1984). History, narrative and life-span developmental knowledge. *Human Development, 27,* 1–19.

Gay, P. (1976). *Art and act.* New York: Harper & Row.

Gedo, J. E. (1983). *Portraits of the artist.* New York: Guilford Press.

Gruber, H. (1980). The evolving systems approach to creativity. In S. Modgil & C. Modgil (Eds.), *Toward a theory of psychological development.* Windsor, England: NFER Publishers.

Gruber, H. (1987). Ensembles of metaphors in creative scientific thinking. In J. Montangero, A. Tryphon, & S. Dionnet (Eds.), *Symbolism and knowledge.* Geneva: Fondation Archives Jean Piaget.

Kagan, J. (1983). Developmental categories and the premise of connectivity. In R. Lerner, Ed. *Developmental psychology: Historical and philosophical perspectives.* Hillsdale, N.J.: Erlbaum.

Kvale, S. (1983). The qualitative research interview: A phenomenological and hermeneutical mode of understanding. *Journal of Phenomenological Psychology, 14,* 171–196.

Lewin, K. (1936). *Principles of topological psychology.* New York: McGraw-Hill.

Liebert, R. S. (1983). *Michelangelo: A psychoanalytic study of his life and images.* New Haven: Yale University Press.

Ricoeur, P. (1981). The narrative function. In P. Ricoeur, *Hermeneutics and the Human Sciences* (J. B. Thompson, Ed. and Trans.). Cambridge: Cambridge University Press.

Sarbin, T. R. (1986). The narrative as a root metaphor for psychology. In T. R. Sarbin (Ed.), *Narrative psychology.* New York: Praeger.

Schutz, A. (1962). *Collected papers* (Vol. 1). The Hague: Martinus Nijhoff.

Spitz, E. H. (1985). *Art and psyche.* New Haven: Yale University Press.

Wallace, D. B. (1985). Giftedness and the construction of a creative life. In F. D. Horowitz & M. O'Brien (Eds.), *The gifted and talented: Developmental perspectives.* Washington, D.C.: American Psychological Association.

Werner, H. (1978). Primitive worlds and spheres of reality. In S. S. Barten & M. B. Franklin (Eds.), *Developmental processes: Selected writings of Heinz Werner* (Vol. 1). New York: International Universities Press. (Original work published in 1940)

Werner, H., & Kaplan, B. (1983). *Symbol formation.* Hillsdale, N.J.: Erlbaum. (Original work published in 1963)

14

Creativity and Human Survival

HOWARD E. GRUBER

From *Children of Hiroshima:*

I steal a glance at my arm under the sleeve—
Death's spot is not there yet.

> From "Blood," a poem by KOICHI TOKUNO, 11th grade boy (5th grade at the time the atom bomb fell).

In the right hand we have penicillin and streptomycin; in the left hand the atom and the hydrogen bomb. Now is the time for the people of the world to consider more rationally this contradiction.

> From essay by YOSHUKO UCHIMURA, 12th grade girl (6th grade at the time of the bomb).

The study of creative work is fascinating and rewarding in its own right, but it may also provide a valuable springboard for some useful reflections on the greatest moral question of our age—how to work effectively for the survival of our species.

As the creative life unfolds, work proceeds on many fronts; this is expressed in the diversity of the creator's network of enterprise: the work is organized in hierarchical structures—problems within tasks, tasks within projects, and projects within enterprises. The creator must not only organize the work itself but must manage the diverse demands of a creative life. Work and life go forward within the bounds of constraints that can be divided into two kinds—what can be done and what should be done. These can be expressed as the claims of ability and possibility on the one hand, and the claims of morality and desirability on the other. In this chapter I explore the claims of morality on the creative person.

Unlike the other chapters in this book, this exploration is not so much about creative work itself as it is about an aspect of the creative life: how creative people manage to live with themselves in a troubled world. To be sure, the task of making something new sometimes requires withdrawal from the world, but the resulting seclusion is not something given to the creator. It is hard won and often tenuous. And, often enough, creative work goes on amid the hurly-burly.

We do not find one pattern, one special way of relating to the world, that characterizes the creative person. Here too, as with other aspects of creative work, the watchword is variability. A glance at some of the people examined in this book emphasizes this point.

Lavoisier was guillotined during the French Revolution; ironically, he was not particularly antirevolutionary. Wordsworth evolved from an ardent supporter to a bitter critic of the same revolution. He lived most of his life in relative isolation in rural England.

Darwin did his most seminal theoretical work as a young man living in London, but spent the rest of his adult life in a country home outside the city. Although he described himself as "Liberal or Radical," he was not particularly involved politically. Nevertheless, the meat of his thought was dangerous, and expressing it in Victorian England was a courageous political act.

Faraday's theoretical and experimental work made the electric generator possible, but he did not pursue the practical applications of his discoveries. When Gladston saw Faraday's laboratory demonstrations, the story goes, he asked about their utility. Faraday replied, "Of what use is a baby?"

In contrast, Woodward's chemical syntheses were of such immediate practical value that a major pharmaceutical company gave him a large laboratory in Switzerland to supplement the facilities he had at Harvard. Most likely, he could have pursued his abstract theoretical aims without doing work of direct practical significance. But he obviously had a nose for the practical, and over and over did work that bettered the human condition—all without any political or moral rhetoric or fanfare.

Einstein's work was at the outer extreme of abstractness, yet it turned out to have immense practical significance. Although for the most part he lived a life of quiet contemplation, he never forgot the world outside and was a lifelong, outspoken pacifist. William James, too, was a pacifist, and for a time vice president of the Anti-Imperialist League, mobilizing political sentiment against U.S. incursions into Latin America.

Richardson was not a political activist. But in her weekly column in the *Dental Record* she often commented on social issues. More important, her major work, *Pilgrimage,* is an explicitly feminist work, and she counted the radical suffragettes among her friends. Perhaps the turning inward that characterized her work and others' was motivated by disenchantment with the promise of ceaseless progress that had attracted previous generations.

Piaget described himself (in an interview with me) as "always on the Left." But in fact he avoided political activity, except for helping some colleagues when they had difficulties with various repressive regimes around the world. Nevertheless, his work has had important social consequences, perhaps the most important of which is our respect for the child as a thinking person.

But our examination of the social entailments of creative lives should not be limited to the fairly direct connections I have been citing. Even in its most other-worldly forms, creative work is a celebration of life. And even criticism is a form of celebration. When William Blake wrote the lines, "The Harlot's cry from Street to Street shall weave Old England's winding Sheet," his criticism of the exploitation of prostitutes was part of his veneration of love.

Nin wrote so sensuously and frankly about sexual experience that she projected a radical image. But raised in a traditional Latin Catholic family and married to a banker for many years, she was not conventionally radical or otherwise politically involved. She did, however, commit herself to two movements that have done much to influence twentieth-century culture. In the 1920s she was part of the surrealist movement in Paris, and in the 1960s she was involved in the women's movement. In the sense that she personified the 1960s' idea that "personal is political," she became a role model for many younger women.

Still others possess an extreme attitude that in times of crisis art should, above all things, mobilize people for struggle. This is suggested in a recent article about Chekhov by the Soviet poet, Andrei Voznesensky (1988): "Who has time for 'The Cherry Orchard' when the orchards near Chernobyl are turning black?"

Creativity and Morality

Our conceptions of creativity and morality are intertwined in a number of ways. First, it is widely believed that a creative person *ought* to exercise his or her gifts. Second, we often act as though creators are exempt from normal moral standards because they are driven by special inner necessities and *must* express their creative impulses. Third, there may be special kinds of creativity: extraordinary moral perceptiveness and extraordinary moral responsibility (Gruber, 1985a).

At once we see that the indispensable middle term between creativity and morality is freedom. We can hardly speak of a moral act if the actor has no choice. Creative work also requires inner freedom. Although we would like to believe, quite simply, that freedom of expression favors creativity, history makes clear that creative work often proceeds successfully under oppressive outward conditions—indeed often in conscious, active opposition to them.

Creative work must be in some ways kindred to the world, if not the world as it is, then the world as it will or might be. It flows out of that world and it flows back into it. Thus the creative person, to carry out the responsibility to self, the responsibility for inner integrity, must also in some way be responsive to the world.

Part of the creator's task, then, is to work out these sometimes conflicting demands of personal freedom and social responsibility. But there can be no permanent solution. As history shambles along, the shape of the problem changes. Both opportunities and constraints evolve. Picasso's *Guernica* is this century's great visual antiwar statement, but the destruction of a city is what made it possible (Arnheim, 1962). Today's world gives this idea of changing demands a special point. A creator working with the next generation in mind (so soon upon us!) must believe that there will be a next generation. The danger of nuclear war and other planetary threats put that belief in jeopardy.

Difficult moral problems require creative work. Every proposal that something *ought* to be done implies that it is possible. But how do we know what *can* be done? Only by pushing to the very limits of the possible (Gruber, 1985b, 1986). The problems we have in mind are not the easy ones with obvious solutions, but the most important and most intractable ones. These deserve and require our most creative efforts. Thus *"ought" implies "can" implies "create"!*

In the thermonouclear age every corner of life is called into question. The power of modern technology to threaten our home, the earth, through war and other means touches everything—the air, the sea, the forests, and every living creature. We speak of the "thermonuclear" age, because nuclear war remains the greatest single danger, but the term is really a shorthand for something much wider: the worldwide, wild, undisciplined growth of technology without corresponding social controls, the aggregate threat to life on our planet resulting from the behavior of our civilization.

The Task of Protecting Our Planet from Ourselves

The very breadth of the problem means that there are openings for every kind and every level of creative effort. The following brief discussion is intended mainly to underline the idea that almost everyone has a part to play in this effort.

Clarifying the Threat

An Unintentionally Demonic Collaboration. As long ago as 1909, Frederick Soddy, later a Nobel Prize winner in chemistry, wrote *Interpretation of Radium,* a popular account of what was then known about radiation and the enormous energy of the atom. H. G. Wells read it and in 1910 wrote *The World Set Free,* a novel about an atomic war and the destruction of civilization. In the 1930s, the brilliant Hungarian physicist, Leo Szilard, read the book, became convinced of the feasibility of making atomic weapons, and began to campaign among his colleagues against taking research in that direction. A little later, in 1939, moved by the fear that the Nazis would develop an atom bomb first, Szilard changed his ground. He was one of a few who were instrumental in framing the letter signed by Einstein that persuaded President Roosevelt to authorize the first moves that eventually led to the atom bomb. An international financier, Alexander Sachs, one of Roosevelt's advisors, helped gain access to the White House. Thus scientists, writers, politicians, and others played their part in what appeared to be a purely technical development.

Today the same broad-spectrum creative collaboration is needed to guide the course of events in another direction. But to have any chance of succeeding, it must be planful, steady work. Is it too much to imagine a "Brooklyn Project" for peace—equal in magnitude, intensity, and creativity, but not necessarily in form, to the gigantesque, military-dominated Manhattan project that made the atom bomb? The idea of naming the project for planetary survival after my birthplace stirs a primitive chord in me. I hope you name it after yours.

Escalation Processes. The familiar story of the atom bomb is one among many that illustrate how escalation works. At first Szilard, Fermi, and many of their colleagues were against work that might lead to an atomic weapon. Ultimately they changed their minds because of their perception of enemy capacities. This perception was, in turn, based largely on an extrapolation of their knowledge of friendly capacities. In 1950, a similar sequence of events persuaded some scientists to reverse their opposition to the development of the hydrogen bomb, infinitely more dangerous, and to collaborate in the project.

There is almost always, within any system for research and development, a pressure to increase human capacity to manipulate nature. If another system is perceived as "the enemy," then similar intentions and capacities will be imputed to it. Thus policies are based not only on what the potential enemy actually does, but also on what it might do—and our conception of this is based on a particular aspect of self-knowledge, our own thirst for progress. Ergo, the power of escalation that is always with us.

As we saw in Chapter 1, students of creativity are necessarily interested in systems that escalate—deviation-amplifying systems. Escalation processes are not intrinsically good or bad; they can be gloriously creative or they can be unbelievably destructive. They are, of course, bound to entail some unknown risk, since in principle they change the established order of things. Perhaps we can learn how to apply our knowledge about creative work to understand how escalation processes become dangerous, and how to redirect them.

The Image of Humanity

All of the arts contribute to our image of humanity, and not always on the side of peace. Beethoven, in the *Eroica* symphony, celebrated, as he thought, the liberating warrior Napoleon. We can agree that wars begin in the minds of men, but it is not easy to see how to change those minds. Exposing the horrors of war is clearly not adequate. In his great essay, "The Moral Equivalent of War," William James said "the horror makes the thrill" (James, 1910). And every day's television programming, with its steady stream of violent images, exploits that principle. The mood of the media is hard.

Yet there is hope. Antiwar literature like Remarque's *All Quiet on the Western Front* and Vonnegut's *Slaughterhouse Five* has found an enormous audience. Likewise antimilitarist works such as Hlasek's *The Good Soldier Schweik* and Mozart's *Magic Flute,* a Utopian tale, still delight.

What can we expect of the arts? A great outpouring of works engendering new hope and new images, world consciousness, planetary solidarity? This would help. If the artists themselves were determined enough, and if others helped in a steady, deliberate way, they might catalyze a shift toward a new mood. The Manhattan Project involved no artists. The Brooklyn Project would need them.

Ours is a great civilization. May there always be poets to sing its praises! But it is deeply flawed by a collection of social arrangements that ignores our need for harmony with nature and with each other, that accentuates the drive for power—power over other individuals, power over other countries, power over nature. In *Ozymandias* Shelley evoked the ruins of such a world:

> . . . Two vast and trunkless legs of stone
> Stand in the desert . . . Near them, on the sand,
> Half sunk, a shattered visage lies, whose frown,
> And wrinkled lip, and sneer of cold command,
> Tell that its sculptor well those passions read . . .
> And on the pedestal these words appear:
> "My name is Ozymandias, king of kings:
> Look on my works, ye Mighty, and despair!"
> Nothing beside remains. . . .
>   (Rogers, 1975, pp. 319–320)

Earth Our Home

We need to work toward new political forms, new ways of doing science and of monitoring technological change, new images of humanity that emphasize the ideal of harmony in nature rather than dominion over it.

The Home Planet (Kelley, 1988) is a book of memories and reflections by astronauts of all countries. These are people who have been where the differences between Us and Them disappear:

> The first day or so we all pointed to our countries. The third or fourth day we were pointing to our continents. By the fifth day we were aware of only one Earth. (Astronaut Sultan Bin Salman Al-Saud)

> It does not matter what country you look at. We are all Earth's children, and we should treat her as our Mother. (Astronaut Alexandr Alexandrov)

Task—Ego—World

In Chapter 1 I alluded briefly to a prime motivational distinction between task-oriented and ego-oriented behavior. Ego-orientation, or extrinsic motivation, refers to an attitude toward work that is motivated by desire for rewards not inherent in the task itself, rewards such as recognition, prestige, prizes, money, privileges, and power. Task-orientation, or intrinsic motivation, refers to an attitude toward work that is motivated by the intrinsic nature or demand-character of the task itself.

Several intellectual traditions—Gestalt theory, Piagetian developmental theory, Veblen's idea of the instinct of workmanship, and an antibourgeois rejection of the marketplace mind—all converge upon the expectation that the creative person will be primarily task-oriented. Amabile's (1983) experimental research has given strong support to that hypothesis. Once confronted with a task and committed to it, to be engrossed in it, to be caught up in the work, is a good augury. Moreover, considerable experimental evidence has indicated that, at least in the short time of a laboratory experiment, once intrinsic motivation is established it is best left alone: introducing the prospect of reward may actually undermine creative activity (Amabile, Hennessey, & Grossman, 1986). On the other hand, if we look at motivation over the time span of a creative career, we must introduce some other considerations.

As we have seen, each creative person develops a network of enterprise. In other words, at any given time a number of projects may be under way, each belonging to different enterprises. Each one will have a different motivational profile. The creator will be more invested in the finished product envisaged for one project but more intrigued by the immediate problems presented by another. He or she may expect greater immediate, short-term recognition from completing one project but a deeper long-term admiration from another. Thus the creative person must manage the relationships between motivation and conduct, continually assessing the whole situation—abilities and opportunities, progress already accomplished, and the motivational profile of each undertaking.

To these complexities I would add another. The dichotomy between task- and ego-orientations is inadequate. There is a third actor in the play of motives, the World. One is not always free to choose the most alluring task, as governed by task- and ego-orientations. Extrinsic motivation must be subdivided into two categories, ego-orientation and world-orientation.

The world makes its claim on us. True, not everyone responds in the same way. Task-orientation, ego-orientation, and world-orientation each have their appeals. Every creative person must shape his or her own motivational profile. Historically, the task-ego distinction has been thought adequate for many purposes. Now our planetary situation is more desperate and the world makes more urgent claims on creative people everywhere.

It should be emphasized that these motivational orientations—task, ego, world—are not mutually exclusive. They probably all operate together. What distinguishes individuals is not all-or-none choices of one orientation or another, but different motivational profiles. Moreover, the relative salience of motives can shift, depending on circumstances and on the work itself. Let us suppose that each of these orientations is coupled with its typical emotional tone: task—engrossment; ego—ambition; world—duty. Then we would expect that the ebb and flow of these motivational patterns would produce a changing pattern of emotional experience.

"World-orientation" may take many forms, even the simple and direct altruistic helping of another. In discussions of altruism, it is sometimes suggested that apparently selfless behavior is, in effect, a sham—that the altruist actually behaves altruistically for self-centered reasons, such as increasing self-esteem or avoiding guilt. This may sometimes be the case. But there is mounting evidence that altruistic behavior can result directly from fellow feeling for the other person, or as one study concluded, "empathic emotion evokes altruistic motivation" (Batson, Dyck, Brandt, et al., 1988).

Elsewhere (Gruber, 1987) I have argued that most altruistic behavior is limited to corrective action such as alleviating suffering. It can only occur when there is a discrepancy between the fortunes of the beneficiary and those of the benefactor, but it does not envisage eliminating this gap; it hopes only to lessen it. Indeed, part of the ordinary moral responsibility of everyday life it to behave altruistically in this sense, from time to time, when the situation demands it.

On the other hand, we can envisage and identify cases of "creative altruism," in which a person displays extraordinary moral responsibility, devoting a significant portion of time and energy to some project transcending immediate need and experience. Creative altruism, when it goes the limit, strives to eliminate the cause of suffering, to change the world, to change the fate of the earth.

What Is Possible?

The newspapers routinely carry items evoking the fear that modern civilization is less the cornucopia of marvelous technology and more the Pandora's Box of chronic warfare and untrameled destruction of nature. If one war peters out, another explodes; if one environmental threat is dampened, another comes to a boil. The task of defending the earth has become endless.

Confronted with an infinite task, the finite individual may well feel impotent. You might ask, How can anything one does make a difference? I offer some thoughts on the strategy you might adopt, a strategy that bears some resemblance to the way creative people work:

Take a developmental approach—start with what seems within grasp, then strive to expand the zone of the possible. Carve out a finite domain within which change can be detected, success identified. Try to define certain invariants, conditions that seem imperative, then look for flexible ways of maintaining these constants. There is probably no giant step that represents *the* solution, but very many one-percent steps, or even smaller. Choose a project and invent the steps that will be within your reach.

Go beyond your own limitations by finding friends, neighbors, and colleagues who also want to defend their planet. Multiply your creative resources by inventing a project together with others. Be realistic about time. If you are not prepared to devote your whole life to your project, set a definite goal, such as one-half day per week. I think of this as tithing, the custom of giving one-tenth of one's income to one's church. As one strand in my network of enterprise, the defense of my planet seems to be worth about one day per week. Perhaps the goal has infinite value and ought therefore to merit 100 percent of one's energies. But at least I can tell myself that if I am regular about one day per week, and if I work with others, a project of some worth can be pursued.

Ecologically minded people sometimes capture a similar way of thought in the phrase, "think globally, act locally." Once a certain level of world consciousness has been achieved, this is a valuable strategy. But that consciousness spreads slowly, perhaps not fast enough to counteract the exponential growth of the various maladies of the earth. I predict that a different pattern will take hold. More and more people will respond to some immediate problem in their own milieu, and that will lead them to consider the contradiction between human intelligence and civilization's crazy behavior. They will act locally, then think globally.

A word on one last troubling question. Suppose a person gets involved in using his or her creative energies to developing this world consciousness or to work on some local problem connected with planetary defense. If the problems are endless, if Pandora's Box is bottomless, then won't such a commitment simply make one miserable? Won't it drain creative energies in a futile effort?

The question calls to mind Camus' essay, "The Myth of Sisyphus," about the man who refused to die. As Camus (1955) recounts the Greek myth, Sisyphus is condemned by the gods to roll a heavy rock up a steep hill; when it reaches the top, it rolls down, and he must start over again. Camus puts himself in Sisyphus' place and wonders if there is any point in this labor, would not death be better? Camus concludes his reflection: "Sisyphus teaches the higher fidelity that negates the gods and raises rocks. . . . This universe henceforth without a master seems to him neither sterile nor futile. . . . The struggle itself toward the heights is enough to fill a man's heart. One must imagine Sisyphus happy."

REFERENCES

Amabile, T. M. (1983). *The social psychology of creativity.* New York: Springer-Verlag.

Amabile, T. M., Hennessey, B. A., & Grossman, B. S. (1986). Social influences on creativity: the effects of contracted-for reward. *Journal of Personality and Social Psychology, 50,* 13–23.

Arnheim, R. (1962). *The genesis of a painting: Picasso's Guernica.* Berkeley: University of California Press.

Batson, C. D., Dyck, J. L., Brandt, J. R., Batson, J. G., Powell, A. L., McMaster, M. R., & Griffitt, C. (1988). Five studies testing two new egoistic alternatives to the empathy-altruism hypothesis. *Journal of Personality and Social Psychology, 55,* 52–77.

Camus, A. (1955). *The myth of Sisyphus and other essays.* New York: Knopf. (Original work published in 1942)

Gruber, H. E. (1985a). Giftedness and moral responsibility: Creative thinking and human survival. In F. D. Horowitz & M. O'Brien (Eds.), *The gifted and talented: Developmental perspectives.* Washington, D.C.: American Psychological Association.

Gruber, H. E. (1985b). Going the limit: Toward the construction of Darwin's theory (1832–1839). In D. Kohn (Ed.), *The Darwinian heritage.* Princeton: Princeton University Press.

Gruber, H. E. (1986). Creative reactions to life under the nuclear sword. *International Journal of Mental Health, 15,* 314–326. (Special issue on *Mental health implications of life in the nuclear age,* edited by M. Schwebel)

Gruber, H. E. (1987). Creative altruism, cooperation, and world peace. Address at symposium on "The Greater Self," sponsored by the Institute of Noetic Sciences.

James, W. (1910). *The moral equivalent of war* (Leaflet No. 27). Association for International Conciliation. (Also published in *McClure's Magazine* and in *The Popular Science Monthly* in 1910)

Kelley, K. W. (1988). *The home planet.* Reading, Mass.: Addison-Wesley.

Osada, A. (Ed.). (1980). *Children of Hiroshima.* New York: Harper. (Original work published in 1951)

Rogers, N. (Ed.). (1975). *The complete poetical works of Percy Bysshe Shelley: Vol. 2.* Oxford: Clarendon Press.

Soddy, F. (1909). *Interpretation of radium.* London: Murray. (The book went through at least six editions.)

Voznesensky, A. (1988, November 27). Review of V. S. Pritchett's Chekhov, *A spirit set free. The New Times Book Review,* p. 3.

Wells, H. G. (1910). *The world set free.* London: Odhams Press.

Name Index

Subjects of case studies are indexed in detail in the Subject Index. Page references in italic refer to bibliographic citations.

Abrams, M. H., *24*, 71–72, 86, *89*
Aldrich, E. A., *168*
Allen, W., 148, *168*
Allendy, R., 216
Allport, G. W., 26, *41*
Amabile, T. M., 13, *22*, 284, *286*
Ampère, André-Marie, 96–97, 101
Archimedes, 155
Aries, P., 152, *168*
Arlin, P. K., 20, *22*
Armon, C., *186*
Arnheim, R., 20, *22*, 83, *88*, 240, *252*, 275–*276*, 281, *287*
Arter, J. A., 142, *145*
Auden, W. H., 15
Ayer, A. J., 38, *41*

Barlow, N., 109, *125*
Barnes, D., 215
Barrett, P. H., 124–*125*
Bartlett, F. C., *22*, 69, *88*, 163, *168*
Barton, D. R., 233, 240, *252*
Batson, C. D., 285, *287*
Batson, J. G., *287*
Beaumont, W., 28
Beer, J., *88*
Beethoven, L. van, 29, 282
Benfey, O. T., 19, *22*
Bergson, H., 129, 192–195
Berkson, W., 91, *103*
Bernard, C., 48
Bernard of Chartres, 9
Berthelot, M., 233, *252*
Black, J., 53, 66
Black, M., 129, 143, *145*
Blake, W., 4, 21, 280
Bloom, B., 15, *22*
Bornstein, M., 272, *276*
Boswell, J., 30
Boyd, R., 128, *145*
Bradshaw, G. L., 44, *48*

Brandt, J. R., 285, *287*
Braque, G., vi
Brett, R. L., 75, *88*
Broughton, J. M., *186*
Bruchez-Hall, C., 129, *145*
Bruner, J., 257, *276*
Bunyan, J., 154, *168*
Burkhardt, F. H., 139, *145*
Bylebyl, J. J., 49, *67*

Cabanne, P., 38, *41*
Campbell, D. T., 10, *22*
Camus, A., 286–*287*
Cantor, G. N., 94, 99, *103*
Cassirer, E., 275–*276*
Clark, R. W., 38, *41*
Claudel, C., vi
Cockshut, A. O. J., 38, *41*
Coleridge, S. T., 16, 74, 93
Coles, R., 21–*22*
Commons, M. L., *186*
Constable, J., 71
Cornforth, J., 244, *252–253*
Cram, D., 230, 232, 235, 244, *252*
Crovitz, H., 17
Csikszentmihalyi, M., 36, *41*

Darrow, C. N., *23*
Darwin, C., 5, 11–12, 17–18, *22*, 35, 36, 40–*41*, 47, 66–*67*, 107–*125*, 155, 274, 279
Darwin, W. ("Doddy"), 117–118
Da Vinci, L., 35
Davis, S. N., 11, *23*
Davy, H., 93, 95–96, *103*
De Beer, M. J., 124–*125*
DeSelincourt, E., 75, 78, 84, *88*
De Waele, J.-P., *41*
Doherty, M. E., 91, *106*
Dujardin, E., 148, *168*
Dyck, J. L., 285, *287*

Koestler, A., 16, *23, 32, 42*
Kohli, M., 32, *42*
Kohn, D., *125*
Krebs, H., 48, *58–67*
Kuhn, T. S., 143, *145*
Kundera, M., 193, *206*
Kunitz, S., *168*
Kvale, S., 256, *277*

Lamarck, J. B., 113, 117, *125*
Langley, P., 44, *48*
Laplace, P. S., 51, 55, 97, 99
Lavoisier, A., 48–58, 60–61, 63–65, *68,*
   279
Lavoisier, M., 50
Lawrence, D. H., 210, 214–215
Lenoir, T., 204, *207*
Leondar, B., 142, *145*
Levinson, D. J., 20, *23*
Levinson, M. H., *23*
Lewin, K., 264, *277*
Liebert, R. S., 272, *277*
Lockhart, J. G., 30
Lorentz, H. A., 176–178, 184
Luria, A. R., 25, *43*
Luther, M., 36
Lyell, C., 109–112, 121, *125*

McKee, B., *23*
McKendrick, J. G., 34, *43*
McMaster, M. R., *287*
Mandel, B. J., *43*
Manderscheid, H., 62
Manuel, F. E., 9, *23*, 37, *43*
Margoliouth, H., 75, *89*
Martin, A., 60, *67*
Maruyama, M., 8, *23*
Maxwell, J. C., 100–101, *105*
Mendel, G., v
Merton, R. K., 9, *23*
Miller, A. I., 18, *23*, 91, *105, 187*
Miller, G. A., *23*
Miller, H., 212, 215
Milton, 11, 21
Moore, H. T., 224
Moorman, M., *89*
Morgan, L., *168*
Murray, H. A., 26, *43*
Murray, H. G., 6, *24*
Mynatt, C. R., 91, *106*

Nash, H., 129, *145*
Neisser, U., 16, *23–24*
Nersessian, N., 91, 94, *105*
Newell, A., 4, *23*
Newton, I., 5, 8–9, 37, 92–93, *105, 175–*
   177
Nickles, T., 45–46, *48*
Nin, A., 209–*224*, 280

Nin, J., 212
Nin, R. C., 212–214

Odle, A., 151–152, 165
Oersted, H. C., 96, 97, *105*
Ollis, W. D., *253*
Olney, J., 32, *43*
Ortony, A., 142, *145*
Osada, A., *287*
Osowski, J. V., *145*
Owen, W., 86, *89*

Pais, A., *43, 187*
Parrish, S., 75–76, 78–84, *89*
Pasternak, B., v
Paunonen, S. V., 6, *24*
Perkins, D. N., 16, *23*
Pestalozzi, J. H., 173
Pettavel, P., 192, *207*
Piaget, J., 8, 12, 20, *23*, 69, *89*, 171–172,
   181–185, *187*, 189–*207*, 274, 280
Picasso, P., vi, 15, 20, 29, 35–36, 38, 275,
   281
Planck, M., 177, 183
Plato, *23*, 116
Poincaré, H., 18, *24*, 36, 47, 155
Polanyi, M., 163, *168*
Powell, A. L., 157, *169, 287*
Pribram, K. H., *23*
Prickett, S., *24*, 71, *89*
Proust, M., 148, *169*

Rank, O., 210–212, 216, 221, 224–*225*
Rapaport, D., 6
Raphael, R. A., 240, *253*
Read, H., 86–87, *89*
Reynolds, R. E., 142, *145*
Richards, F. A., *186*
Richards, I. A., 129, *145*
Richards, R., 119–120
Richardson, C., 149–150
Richardson, D. M., 35, 147–*169*, 221, 279
Ricoeur, P., 257, *277*
Rodin, A., vi
Rogers, N., 283, *287*
Rosenberg, J., 148, *169*
Rosenzweig, S., *24*
Rothenberg, A., 19, *24*
Rowbotham, S., 152, *169*
Rowlands, M. J., 124–*125*
Rubin, D., 163, *169*
Rudwick, M. J. S., 143, *145*
Runyon, W. McK., 36–37, *43*
Rushton, J. P., 5–6, *23–24*
Russell, B., 35, 38, *43*, 173, *187*

Sachs, A., 282
Sacks, O., 28, *43*
Sarbin, T. R., 257, *277*
Scheinbaum, M. L., *253*

Subject Index

Abstraction, and use of metaphor, 141–142
Action-at-a-distance theory, 93, 95, 99, 102
Addition law for velocities, 184
Adolescence
  of Anaïs Nin, 212–214
  formation of purpose and, 39
  as part of creative life, 15, 38, 39
  Piaget's developmental theory of, 197–199
  Woodward's work during, 228, 232, 243, 244–245
  Zink and, 258
Aesthetics, in Woodward's work, 229–230, 232–238, 242, 247–248, 250
Affect. *See also* Emotion
  insight and, 18–19
  Piaget and, 202
  Woodward's work and, 241, 246
Age of discovery. *See* under Zink
Altruism, 284–285
Anschauung, 172, 173, 181. *See also* Intuition
Apprenticeship, 15
  of Faraday, 93–94
  Nin and, 214–217
  Darwin and, 110
Art
  forms of, in Nin's work, 220
  purpose and, 15
  in work of Woodward, 227, 229–230, 232–235, 250
Artistic medium
  versus material, 268
  as personal idiom, 266–268
  role of, 272–275
Artists, 215. *See also* Zink
Assimilation/accommodation process, in Einstein's thinking, 182–185
Atmosphere, composition of, 52, 53–55
Author-reader relationship, 159–160
Autobiographical novel, 166. *See also* Richardson
Autobiographical poem. *See* Wordsworth
Autobiography
  changing perception of past and, 32
  "decontextualizing" function of, 189–190

Einstein and, 180
versus fiction, and truth, 157
investigator-subject relationship and, 32
omissions from, 189–190, 204
Piaget and, 189–190, 204
Richardson and, 149, 150–151, 166

Balance sheet method, 51, 56, 57–58
Behaviorism, 11
Biography. *See also* Autobiography
  investigator-subject relationship and, 30–31
  place of childhood in, 37–39
  problems of, and network of enterprise concept, 204–205
  public versus private in, 34–35
  theoretical commitments in, 39–41
  work-life dichotomy in, 33–37
Brain-mind relation, and James's current metaphor, 133–135

Calcination, 53–54, 67*n*6
Calorimetric method, 51
Carbon dioxide. *See* "Fixed air"
Case study method
  availability of information and, 33–34
  contextual frames in, 36–37
  focus on development in, 33–36
  historical tradition and, 25–26, 27
  investigator roles in, 31–32
  investigator-subject relationship and, 30–32
  place of childhood in, 37–39
  private-public distinction and, 34–36
  problem of generalization and, 29–30
  psychometric variables and, 5–6
  theoretical commitments of, 39–41
Chance, 10–11, 98
Change. *See also* Stream of thought metaphor; Transformation
  in behavior, and Darwin, 112–113
  human history as, 193
  in James's theory of mind, 130, 132, 133, 136, 140
  metaphors for, 140
  in work of artists, 272–275